The Making of the Irish Constitution 1937

'It should be borne in mind that there is nothing more difficult to arrange, more doubtful of success, and more dangerous to carry through than initiating changes in a state's constitution!'

Niccoló Machiavelli
The Prince

This book is dedicated to the team of senior civil servants who drafted the 1937 constitution, including John J. Hearne, Maurice Moynihan, Patrick Lynch, Philip O'Donoghue, Stephen Anselm Roche and the many others who contributed to the drafting process.

THE MAKING OF THE IRISH CONSTITUTION 1937

Bunreacht na hÉireann

DERMOT KEOGH & ANDREW J. McCARTHY

MERCIER PRESS
WHAT YOU NEED TO READ

MERCIER PRESS
Douglas Village, Cork
www. mercierpress. ie

Trade enquiries to CMD Distribution
55A Spruce Avenue, Stillorgan Industrial Park,
Blackrock, County Dublin

ISBN: 978 1 85635 561 2

10 9 8 7 6 5 4 3 2 1

A CIP record for this title is available from the British Library

Mercier Press receives financial assistance from the Arts Council
/An Chomhairle Ealaíon

Printed and bound by J.H. Haynes & Co. Ltd, Sparkford.

CONTENTS

ACKNOWLEDGEMENTS

The Making of the Irish Constitution was brought to completion in 2005–7. That necessitated checking and re-checking the original files in Dublin. Despite the disaster of the total loss of the most recent edition of the book, caused by a calamitous computer crash in 2006, the book was reconstructed and brought to final form. Although I had the original idea to write a monograph of this kind, my colleagues' efforts have ensured it has come to fruition in 2007. In the final stages, Andrew McCarthy was very ably assisted by Ms Máirín MacCarron and Paul Loftus who undertook the reading and checking of the complete manuscript.

My thanks to my departmental colleagues who formed part of the PRTLI 1 team since 2000: Dr Mervyn O'Driscoll, Dr Andrew McCarthy, Mr Gabriel Doherty and Dr Diarmuid Scully helped edit the volumes listed in the footnotes in my preface. Mr Finbarr O'Shea sub-edited those volumes with great expertise and also helped prepare *The Making of the Irish Constitution* for publication in its final stages. Our thanks also to Charlotte Holland, Sheila Cuneen, Déirdre O'Sullivan, Geraldine McAllister, Norma Buckley and Veronica Fraser.

Ms Mary Feehan of Mercier Press never lost faith in the project and drove all of us on to completion with timely reminders of deadlines and of deadlines missed. We are also grateful to the entire production team at Mercier Press, especially Brian Ronan and Catherine Twibill.

The research team participating in the project were as follows: Dr Carmel Quinlan, based at UCC, and Dr Robert McNamara in Dublin. The latter worked in the National Archives, the University College Dublin Archives and in the archives of the Dublin archdiocese, and other archives. His prodigious work helped press this project forward and his contribution is acknowledged in different parts of a text that is the result of extensive scholarly cooperation. This built on my research at those archives, and elsewhere, since the late 1970s, when I was the first historian given access to the files in the Taoiseach's office on the constitution. For assistance in arranging this access, my thanks to the former government press officer, Frank Dunlop.

Ms Eileen Compagno worked diligently for some time on the project and helped lift morale. She was joined at different stages by Drs Emma Cunningham, Diarmuid Scully, Mark Hull, Timothy J. Guerin, Tracey Connolly, and Messrs Eoin Hartnett, John Paul McCarthy and Finbarr O'Shea. They all contributed valuably to this project over time.

Thanks is due to numerous staff at a variety of institutions over the years for facilitating access to records and copying of material. To Fr Ignatius and the staff of the Franciscan Archives, Dun Mhuire, Killiney; the National Archives, Dublin, particularly Caitriona Crowe, Aideen Ireland, Gregory O'Connor and Tom Quinlan; the Dublin Diocesan Archives, and in particular to David Sheehy; the Irish College, Rome; the Vatican Archives; the Archdioceses of Armagh Archive; the Jesuit Archives, Leeson Street, particularly Fr Ferghus O'Donoghue, SJ. I was treated with great courtesy from the first day I visited the Jesuit Archive as a doctoral student. Fr Fergal McGrath, a distinguished historian and expert on Cardinal Newman and Irish education, located in the late 1970s, the archives I requested. He also followed up my query regarding the minutes of the Jesuit Committee on the Constitution, 1936, about which he had no personal knowledge. But his investigations yielded results and the relevant material was located for me.

Thanks also to the late Fr Paddy O'Donoghue of the Vincentian Fathers (son of Philip O'Donoghue), who provided comprehensive answers to a number of questions relating to the work of his father, and his reminiscences of the various visits by John Hearne and others to the family home when the constitution was being drafted. Professor Irene Lynch of the law Department in UCC provided important biographical and legal notes on the former Attorney General, Paddy Lynch, who was an uncle to her grandfather. Our thanks also to Maeve McDonagh and Professor David Gwynn Morgan of UCC for their help and encouragement. Roy Irwin, son of Dr James Alexander Hamilton Irwin, provided invaluable background information on the former Presbyterian moderator at the time the constitution was being drafted.

Thanks and gratitude is due to Dr Gerard Hogan of the Law School, Trinity College Dublin, for his invaluable comments on the text, and for the addition of a most insightful foreword to this volume.

Thanks to the following individual and institutions for permission to reproduce documents and photographs: Fr Fergus O'Donoghue, Jesuit Archive; Seamus Helferty, UCD Archives; Dr David Craig and Aideen Ireland, National Archives; the Central Bank of Ireland; the Office of the Attorney General; the Department of Justice; and Angela Cahill.

Thanks to the Arts Faculty of University College Cork for financial assistance with the publication of this work. Thanks is also due to the Michael O'Sullivan, UCC Vice President for Planning, Communications and Development.

PREFACE

In the latter part of the 1980s a decision was made to open a section of the Éamon de Valera papers which were then housed in the Franciscan House of Studies, Killiney, County Dublin. That was before the entire de Valera archive was moved to the Department of History Archives at University College Dublin. The decision by the trustees to open a section of the papers in the late 1980s was a source of great importance for the writing of the history of the Irish state.

Éamon de Valera had been much written about but most of the biographies were based on secondary sources.[1] The 'official' biography by Dr Tom O'Neill and Lord Longford had provided an important foretaste of what might be contained in what was known to be an extensive personal collection of private and official papers.[2] The collection did not disappoint. It was a cornucopia of files, official for the most part, and personal minutes and correspondence, chronicling the drafting of the Irish constitution. It provided a framework on which a detailed study could be based.

Taken in conjunction with the extensive files of the Department of the Taoiseach, it was possible to consider seriously the writing of a history of the drafting of the 1937 constitution.

I had been fortunate to gain access to official files on the constitution while writing my doctoral thesis at the European University Institute, Florence, in 1978/9. At the time, I had also consulted relevant papers belonging to Fr Edward Cahill in the Jesuit Archives, Leeson Street, Dublin. I had also found material in the archives of the archdioceses of Dublin and Armagh in the Edward Byrne and Joseph MacRory papers respectively.

Unfortunately, I did not then have access to the Archbishop John Charles McQuaid papers until they were opened by Cardinal Desmond Connell – a courageous and progressive act. I did not have much success in the late 1970s tracking down personal papers for many of the civil servants who had played such an important role in the drafting of the constitution. In particular, I was thinking of John J. Hearne, Department of External Affairs, Stephen Roche, Department of Justice, Maurice Moynihan and Michael McDunphy, Department of the President (later Taoiseach), J. J. MacElligott, Department of Finance, and Philip O'Donoghue, Department of Justice, and indeed many more public servants of this era. But it was very obvious that a systematic study of the drafting of the constitution was a desirable academic project.

The scholarly field was opened up by the enlightened decision of the de Valera trustees – the Franciscans, an order noted for its scholarship and intellectual commitment to the writing of Irish history – to open that section of the de Valera papers dealing with the writing of the constitution, and for which I was particularly grateful.

At the same time, I was given access by the then secretary of the Department of Foreign Affairs, Seán Donlon, to a file in the secretaries files series that recorded the history of a visit by the secretary of the Department of External Affairs, Joseph Walshe, to Rome in April 1937 to discuss with the Vatican secretary of state, Cardinal Eugenio Pacelli, the content of the draft Article 44. This research resulted in my publishing two articles and a book, the last chapter of which contained some material on the drafting of the constitution.[3]

My exposure to the archives in the late 1970s on this subject, and again a decade later, reinforced my views that there was a need to produce a volume which explained the ethos of the 1930s and the historical context in which the document was crafted and put together. This is all the more timely in view of the persistently mistaken descriptions of the constitution which have appeared in recently published history surveys and monographs. My task in addressing this issue has been simplified completely by the appearance of Dr Gerard Hogan's article in the *Irish Jurist* entitled 'De Valera, the Constitution and the Historians'.[4] Reading contemporary Irish historians on the origins and making of the Irish constitution, Dr Hogan says the following in his opening paragraph:

> It is sometimes said that Wagner was unlucky with his kings. But whatever the limitations of Amfortas in *Parsifal* or King Marke in *Tristan and Isolde*, they were at least Wagner's own artistic creation. Mr de Valera, on the other hand, has definitely been unlucky with his historians so far as their treatment – continuing for a moment with this Wagnerian *motif* – of his own Holy Grail, namely, the enactment and impact of the Constitution of Ireland, is concerned.[5]

The writer kindly describes my article, 'The Irish Constitutional Revolution', as 'the classic account'.[6] He also singles out Michael Gallagher for his chapter on 'The Constitution and the Judiciary'.[7] Dr Hogan correctly argues that historians have:

> over-emphasised the Catholic influences on the Constitution. They have also failed to take account of the extent to which that document was an improvement on its predecessor and how it has made a notable and significant contribution to the protection of individual rights. In general, it may be said that the sophistication of the constitutional model prepared by John Hearne and his drafting team has not been widely appreciated or understood by historical commentators.[8]

Amen to that.

This book is born out of a desire to go beyond the confines of the essay I wrote in 1988 and explain in direct terms the drafting of the 1937 constitution. It is further stimulated by the need to respond, as Dr Hogan has, to the lack of empirical research on the topic, the consequence of which he has analysed in his article cited above. I have long wished to take the small but highly significant team involved in the drafting beyond the profiles in caricature which pass for serious intellectual biography. At least, J. J. MacElligott is the subject of an extensive study in Ronan Fanning's history of the Department of Finance.[9] John J. Hearne has come to life in the series *Documents on Irish Foreign Policy*.[10] His later career as the first Irish ambassador to Canada is the subject of an excellent doctoral thesis by Emma Cunningham: 'Irish-Canadian Diplomatic Relations, 1939–1950' (NUI, UCC, 2001.) But there is much more to learn about this outstanding civil servant, constitutional lawyer and diplomat.

Maurice Moynihan was another extraordinary figure of that generation, and certainly one of the main architects of the constitution. A significant section of his professional career was covered in John Paul McCarthy's MPhil, 'Portrait of a Mind: Maurice Moynihan and the Irish State, 1925–1960' (UCC, 2004). Moynihan is also the subject of Deirdre McMahon's sensitively edited *The Moynihan Brothers in Peace and War*.[11] She has also contributed an appreciation in *Studies*.[12] The secretary of the Department of Justice, Stephen A. Roche, has been profiled in Seosamh Ó Longaigh's doctoral thesis, 'Emergency Legislation in the Irish Free State, 1922–1948: An analysis of its evolution and use' (NUI, UCC, 1998). This has been published as a monograph, entitled *Emergency Law in Independent Ireland, 1922–1948* (Four Courts Press, Dublin, 2006). Although Roche did not play as important a part in the drafting process as might have been expected, Dr Ó Longaigh's work brings this relatively hidden figure to the fore.

My own work on Irish foreign policy has featured the professional life of the secretary of the Department of External Affairs, Joseph Walshe.[13] Various volumes cover aspects of his career.[14] My study of the making of the constitution also features the intervention of this important figure.[15]

Therefore, the new scholarship of a new generation of young historians has helped bring many of the civil servants who helped draft the constitution out of the shadows and out of the wings of history. They figure more and more in the new writing on Irish history. The work of other historians has helped to establish the social and intellectual context in which that generation worked. Scholars such as Don O'Leary, Maurice Craig and Finín O'Driscoll have added to our understanding of the complexities of the Catholic world of the 1930s.[16] In 2000, the History department at UCC was awarded a sum of money from the Irish government-funded PRTLI 1 programme to complete a project entitled 'Culture contact – Nation and State'. The industrious team who worked on this project produced a number of edited volumes and monographs.[17] This also led to the publication of chapters in books and articles in journals.[18]

However, central to that PRTLI 1 programme was a proposal to write a history of the making of the Irish constitution. It was hoped to provide a very full and well-documented history of the drafting process, a description of the central figures involved, and a profile of the times in which the document came into being.

Moreover, there was also a great need to assess the role of the Catholic Church in an empirical light. Hypotheses about the all-powerful Catholic hierarchy had to be addressed and answers found in the archives. The role of Fr Edward Cahill and the Irish Jesuits had to be demythologised.[19] It was necessary to find a balanced appraisal of the place of the future archbishop of Dublin, Dr John Charles McQuaid, in the process. What part did the Holy See play at a critical phase in the drafting process? Why did de Valera seek the opinion of Pope Pius XI on the framing of the article on religion?

The end product is the realisation of a personal professional desire to take the history of the constitution out of the realm of ideology which so often passes for scholarship. There is a great advantage in working as the director of a research team. There is energy, originality, dynamism and hard work. But it requires a new approach to doing empirical research. After a professional lifetime in archives, flying solo, it is hard to teach this old dog new tricks.

This monograph reproduces a number of key documents as appendices at the end of the book. The following website will provide the reader with the full text of the constitution, together with the wording amendments.

www.constitution.ie

FOREWORD

I

Few things have shaped and controlled Irish political and legal culture as decisively as the Constitution of Ireland. The system of elections and government, the office of President, judicial review of legislation, the fundamental rights provisions, popular sovereignty and the provision for the referendum are all critical and essential features of the State which are determined and mandated by the Constitution itself. It has led – to admittedly varying degrees – to a form of dialogue between the judiciary and the other branches of government, with the former sometimes requiring or prompting the legislative and executive branches to effect political and social change.[1] Professor Kelly noted this trend over twenty five years ago when he observed that:

> If the judgment of the average liberal observer were asked for, he would probably say the overall impact of the courts on modern Irish life, in their handling of constitutional issues, has been beneficial, rational, progressive and fair.[2]

More recently, Colm Ó Cinnéide spoke in the same vein when he favourably compared the Constitution with the European Convention of Human Rights:

> In general, there is no doubt that the ECHR is a much more limited system of rights protection than that provided for in the *Bunreacht*. The rights protected in Irish law are more extensive and further reaching than those embedded in the ECHR text. The Irish Constitution is deeply rooted in popular affections, with an essentially untouchable political status which encompasses the constitutional case-law. The ECHR in contrast is an international and cosmopolitan court, which is less rooted in national contexts, and is, in any case, a partial and limited international instrument. In any case, there is considerable overlap when it comes to the norms and values that underpin both the Irish constitutional system and the ECHR.[3]

And yet for much of the seventy years of the Constitution's existence, the circumstances in which it came about and the general drafting process has remained a mystery. With the publication of this ground-breaking and excellent book, Professor Keogh and Dr McCarthy have therefore done us all an invaluable service in laying bare much of the complex drafting processes which led to the enactment of the Constitution.

Why the drafting of the Constitution has remained heretofore largely unexplored remains something of a mystery. The absence up to now of a full-length text dealing with these issues has, however, contributed to the emergence of conventional wisdom concerning the Constitution itself. This may be the place to scrutinise further some of this conventional wisdom.

II

Perhaps the most common refrain about the Constitution is that it was unduly influenced by Catholic social teaching.[4] Of course, no one seriously disputes that the Constitution was influenced by Catholic thinking and social values. But with honourable and notable exceptions, most of the historians have overemphasised the Catholic influences on the Constitution.[5] Most non-legal commentators have likewise focused on the Constitution as enacted and have failed to recognise that even if specific provisions were influenced by Catholic social teaching, 'the case law has long since broken loose of that particular inspirational source'.[6] They have also failed to take account of the extent to which that document was an improvement on its predecessor and how it has made a notable and significant contribution to the protection of individual rights. In general, it may be said that the sophistication of the constitutional model prepared by John Hearne and his drafting team has not been widely appreciated or understood by historical commentators. *The Making of the Irish Constitution* may indeed go some way towards ensuring the posthumous recognition of Hearne's immense contribution, as he – along with figures such as Chief Justice Kennedy, Mr Justice Gavan Duffy and Mr Justice Kingsmill Moore – must rank as among the foremost jurists who graced the first forty years or so of an independent Irish State.

Up until relatively recently Mr de Valera was considered to be the principal drafter of the Constitution, albeit perhaps assisted by some clerical friends,[7] and the role of Hearne, Moynihan, O'Donoghue and McDunphy was either unknown or under-played.[8] Moreover, much of the political commentary on the Constitution focused on its controversial features, such as Articles 2 and 3, the ban on divorce in Article 41 and the special position of the Catholic Church. In addition, much of this commentary was written in the 1970s and 1980s when, as a result of the civil conflict in Northern Ireland, many commentators were keen to eradicate those features of Irish society which were seen as confessional or offensive to the minority religious and political traditions. Viewed from that perspective, it was easy to criticise those features of the Constitution as originally enacted and the easy assumption, that the 1937 document compared unfavourably with its 1922 predecessor, was frequently made. Thus, writing in 1972 in his seminal book, *States of Ireland*, O'Brien said of Articles 2 and 3 and the special position of the Catholic Church in Article 44 that it would be hard to think of 'a combination of propositions more likely to sustain and stiffen the siege-mentality of Protestant Ulster.'[9] Speaking of the conditions prevailing in 1937, O'Brien added that:

> The main opposition party, Fine Gael, was not at this time complaining – as some of its spokesmen were to do later – about Mr de Valera's abandonment of the relative liberalism of the first Constitution.[10]

The same easy assumption permeates Whyte's analysis of the two Constitutions:

> There was, however, one other important difference between the Constitutions, apart from the elimination of the Crown. This was in the treatment of fundamental rights. The 1922 constitution had been a typical liberal-democratic document which would have suited a country of any religious complexion. The only article on religion was one which briefly guaranteed religious freedom and equality. The other personal rights guaranteed were what might be described as a stock list – freedom from arbitrary arrest, inviolability of the home, freedom of speech and of association and the right to free elementary education.[11]

The clear impression created by these two highly influential commentators was that the 1922 Constitution was a far superior document. Such criticism could only fairly be described as unbalanced. There is no mention of the fact that the 1922 Constitution had ended 'in almost total failure'[12] or that it had proved wholly ineffective as a means of protecting individual rights. In addition, neither of them made any effort to analyse those provisions of the 1937 Constitution which had, for example, strengthened fundamental rights (such as, e.g., Article 40.3.2 with the entirely new guarantees of the right to life, person, good name and property rights) or which had enhanced the system of judicial review (such as, e.g., Article 15.4 and Article 26).

The assessment of the Constitution by Professor Lee in his seminal work, *Ireland 1912–1985, Politics and Society* is in this respect more balanced and fair-minded.[13] But even he seemed sceptical of the value of certain fundamental rights guarantees:

> When the [ban on divorce is] considered in conjunction with section 17 of the Criminal Law (Amendment) Act 1935, which prohibited the sale and importation of contraceptives, it was difficult to avoid the impression that the State considered it a duty to impose specifically Catholic doctrine on all citizens, irrespective of their personal convictions. Critics might be excused for dismissing as hypocrisy in these circumstances the appar-

ently comprehensive guarantee in Article 44.2.3 that 'the State shall not impose any disabilities or make any discrimination on the ground of religious profession, belief or status.'[14]

Yet, quite apart from the fact that the legislation in question did not *as such* seek to discriminate against non-Catholics, the fact remains – which Professor Lee does not mention in this context[15] – that when the matter was actually put to the test in *McGee v. Attorney General*[16], the Supreme Court did hold that section 17 of the 1935 Act was unconstitutional on the ground that it violated the personal rights of privacy and family autonomy protected by Articles 40 and 41 of the Constitution.

In this context, we may examine two central criticisms which are leveled by historians, namely, the extent to which the Constitution was influenced by Catholic social teaching and the extent to which it discriminated against women.

III

As we have already observed, no one denies that the Constitution was influenced to some extent by Catholic teaching and doctrine. There are still express traces of this, most noticeably in the Preamble which:

> still conveys a very nationalist view of history in which unionists could not recognise themselves and along many other areas of the Constitution, has a broadly Christian, often specifically Catholic, tone that does not match the political culture of the State as well as it did.[17]

In other cases:

> there is nothing visibly Catholic about the phraseology to the uninformed eye – only those familiar with Catholic social thought would be able to identify the origins of the expression used.[18]

That, however, the Constitution was influenced by Catholic social teaching is surely unremarkable given the historical context of 1937. What is more remarkable, however, is the extent to which that document also reflected secular – one might almost say 'Protestant' values – values of liberal democracy, respect for individual rights and the separation of the Church and State and the extent to which *it does not* reflect Catholic teaching. This analysis, however, is but rarely reflected in non-legal commentaries. Take, for example, the comments of Foster in *Modern Ireland: 1600–1972*:

> But the democratic, popular-sovereignty approach [of the Constitution] was combined with an assumption that the nature and identity of the Irish polity was Catholic, reflected

in five articles defining 'rights'. These were much influenced by papal encyclicals and current Catholic social teaching. Divorce was prohibited; the idea of working mothers denounced; the Roman Catholic Church was granted a 'special position … as the guardian of the faith professed by the great majority of the citizens', though the rights of minority Churches were defined.[19]

This passage merits some extended analysis.

Exhibit A in the Foster analysis is the provisions of the (now repealed) Article 44.1.2 and Article 44.1.3 dealing with the special position of the Catholic Church.

2. The State recognises the special position of the Holy Catholic Apostolic and Roman Church as the guardian of the Faith professed by the great majority of the citizens.
3. The State also recognises the Church of Ireland, the Presbyterian Church in Ireland, the Methodist Church in Ireland, the Religious Society of Friends in Ireland, as well as the Jewish Congregations and the other religious denominations existing in Ireland at the date of the coming into operation of this Constitution.

In many ways, however, it is very difficult to see why these provisions gave rise to so much fuss. It must be recalled that the express recognition of the minority religions gave rise to some controversy at the time.[20] Moreover, insofar as these provisions gave rise to any legal effects, these were slight and affected marginal aspects of what might be termed lawyers' law, such as discreet aspects of the law relating to charities.[21] But this was as nothing compared to the situation in most other European countries in 1937 (France here being the notable exception), many of whom provided for some form of an established religion in one shape or another.

In the United Kingdom, for example, section 2 of the Act of Settlement 1701 provided that the monarch and his or her spouse were all required by law to be members of the Established Church. The monarch was further required to take an oath of office to uphold the supremacy of Protestantism; bishops from the Established Church sat in the House of Lords and up to 1975 both the equivalent of the Chief Justice and the Minister for Justice were required to be members of the Church of England.[22] One can imagine the capital which Professor Foster would have made had, for example, the Constitution required the President to be Roman Catholic and subscribe to an oath upholding Catholicism; if Catholic bishops sat in the Senate and if for good measure the Chief Justice was required to be a Catholic!

Nor was this approach confined to the United Kingdom. Thus, for example, Articles 2 and 4 of the Norwegian Constitution provide:

Article 2

All inhabitants of the Realm shall have the right to free exercise of their religion.

The Evangelical-Lutheran religion shall remain the official religion of the State. The inhabitants professing it are bound to bring up their children in the same.

[Jesuits are not tolerated].[23]

Article 4

The King shall at all times profess the Evangelical-Lutheran religion, and uphold and protect the same.

There was, moreover, a close similarity between the then Article 44.2.2 and Article 114 of the 1921 Polish Constitution:

Article 114

The Roman Catholic religion, being the religion of the preponderant majority of the nation, occupies in the state the chief position among enfranchised religions. The Roman Catholic Church governs itself under its own laws. The relation of the state to the church will be determined on the basis of an agreement with the Apostolic See, which is subject to ratification by the Sejm.

Article 115

The churches of the religious minorities and other legally organised religious communities govern themselves by their own laws, which the state may not refuse to recognise unless they contain rules contrary to law.

The relation of the state to such churches and religions will be determined from time to time by legislation after an understanding with their legal representatives.

Article 116

The recognition of a new, or hitherto not legally recognised religion, may not be refused to religious communities whose institutions' teachings and organisation are not contrary to public order or public morality.[24]

Nor is this approach confined to pre-war constitutions. Thus, for example, Articles 7 and 8 of the Italian Constitution of 1948 provide:

Article 7

1. State and Catholic Church are, each within their own reign, independent and sovereign.
2. Their relationship is regulated by the Lateran pacts. Amendments to these pacts which are accepted by both parties do not require the procedure of constitutional amendments.

Article 8

1. Religious denominations are equally free before the law.
2. Denominations other than Catholicism have the right to organise themselves according to their own by-laws, provided they do not conflict with the Italian legal system.

3. Their relationship with the state is regulated by law, based on agreements with their representatives.'

A similar approach is to be found in the 2001 Greek Constitution, Article 3 of which provides:

Article 3

1. The prevailing religion in Greece is that of the Eastern Orthodox Church of Christ. The Orthodox Church of Greece, acknowledging our Lord Jesus Christ as its head, is inseparably united in doctrine with the Great Church of Christ in Constantinople and with every other Church of Christ of the same doctrine, observing unwaveringly, as they do, the holy apostolic and synodal canons and sacred traditions. It is autocephalous and is administered by the Holy Synod of serving Bishops and the Permanent Holy Synod originating thereof and assembled as specified by the Statutory Charter of the Church in compliance with the provisions of the Patriarchal Tome of June 29, 1850 and the Synodal Act of September 4, 1928.
2. The ecclesiastical regime existing in certain districts of the State shall not be deemed contrary to the provisions of the preceding paragraph.
3. The text of the Holy Scripture shall be maintained unaltered. Official translation of the text into any other form of language, without prior sanction by the Autocephalous Church of Greece and the Great Church of Christ in Constantinople, is prohibited.'

Finally, we may note that Article 9 of the Spanish Constitution of 1978 provides:

1. Freedom of ideology, religion, and cult of individuals and communities is guaranteed without any limitation in their demonstrations other than that which is necessary for the maintenance of public order protected by law.
2. No one may be obliged to make a declaration on his ideology, religion, or beliefs.
3. No religion shall have a state character. The public powers shall take into account the religious beliefs of Spanish society and maintain the appropriate relations of cooperation, with the Catholic Church and other denominations.'

From this (necessarily incomplete) survey, we can see a broad pattern emerging which was true both in 1937 and (only to a slightly lesser extent) today: the Protestant states of northern Europe normally provided for an established Church. The Catholic countries accorded a variant of the 'special position' status to the Catholic Church, while also often expressly providing for a concordat of some kind. The Orthodox countries also provided either a form of establishment or 'special position' status.[25]

Of course, in one sense, Whyte was quite correct to say that the religious freedom provisions of Article 9 of the 1922 Constitution 'would have suited a country of any religious complexion'. It must be recalled, however, that these provisions more or less replicated the provisions of Article 16 of the 1921 Treaty and the religious provisions of the 1922 Constitution had to be drafted against that background, if only to ensure compliance with the Treaty.[26] Those provision of Article 9 were, however, so secular in character that they would, for example, have readily suited the countries with a very strong tradition of the separation of Church and State such as France and the United States. It was, however, unrealistic to expect such entirely secular provisions to be adopted in a country such as Ireland in 1937 with a very different historical tradition in circumstances where the new Constitution was being drafted free from those particular constraints of the Treaty, especially where establishment or 'special provision'-type clauses were the norm throughout Europe.[27]

None of this is to suggest for a moment that the 'special position' clause ought to have been retained. It is, however, to suggest, contrary to the implicit assumptions of commentators such as Foster and Whyte, that judged by the contemporary European standards of 1937 – and even judged by the standards of today – there was nothing particularly exceptional about Article 44.1.2. If anything, the only surprise was that the reference to Catholicism simply reflected the historical facts and that Mr de Valera did not go further. Again, not surprisingly, the Catholic Church was ultimately disappointed with the contents of Article 44.[28]

Of course, once the 'special position' provisions were deleted following the 1972 referendum, the underlying secular nature of the rest of Article 44 fully shone through.[29] Freedom of conscience and free profession and practice of religion, subject to public order and morality, is guaranteed.[30] The State is precluded from endowing any religion and Article 44.2.3 provides that the State shall not:[31]

> impose any disabilities or make any discrimination on the grounds of religious profession, belief or status.

The Supreme Court has, moreover, held in *Campaign to Separate Church and State Ltd. v. Minister for Education*[32] that any UK-style establishment of a Church would of necessity 'be impossible to reconcile with the prohibition of religious discrimination in Article 44.2.3'.[33]

The exception here, perhaps, is the *Tilson* case where the Supreme Court held that the doctrine of paternal supremacy had not survived the enactment of the Constitution and proceeded to uphold as against a Protestant father a pre-nuptial agreement which governed the religious education of the children.[34] Here, perhaps, is not the place to argue that the Supreme Court decision has been widely mis-understood or that case was *not* based on the 'special protection' provisions of Article 44,[35] since the pain which that decision caused (and still causes) the minority religious community is still evident.[36] But it is nevertheless fair to say that, but for the unfair impact which this decision had on the minority religions, nobody would defend the constitutionality of a common law rule which gave *fathers* alone the right to decide on the religious and educational upbringing of children or give a moment's thought to a Supreme Court decision which (correctly) held that such a common law rule was inconsistent with Article 42 of the Constitution, given that this provision expressly gave these rights to *parents* and not simply to *fathers.* It is likewise easy to overlook the fact that the courts were giving effect to a pre-nuptial agreement between the parents, even if, judged by contemporary standards, that promise was extracted from the father under a form of duress. The unfairness of *Tilson* (and all that followed from the decision) was that the Catholic Church had exploited its dominant position in Irish society at the time by insisting that Protestant partners submit to the *Ne Temere* decree. But the blame here lies with the Catholic Church and not with Article 44 of the Constitution.[37]

The second contention made by Professor Foster was that the Constitution assumed that the 'nature and identity of the Irish polity was Catholic, reflected in five articles [Articles 40 to 45] defining 'rights'.[38] These were much influenced by papal encyclicals and current Catholic social teaching.'

Of the five articles dealing with fundamental rights, Article 40 is by far the most important, guaranteeing equality before the law; the protection of life, person, good name and property; personal liberty; habeas corpus and habeas corpus procedure; the inviolability of the dwelling and the rights to free speech, assembly and association. In addition, Article 40.3.1 – which roughly corresponds in this regard to the hugely important 14th Amendment of the US Constitution – imposes the general obligation on the State by its laws 'so far as practicable' to defend and vindicate the 'personal rights of the citizens'. Just as with the 14th Amendment, Article 40.3.1 has been the vehicle whereby the courts have subsequently held that a number of fundamental rights – not otherwise expressly enumerated elsewhere in the Constitution – are implicitly protected. Article 40.3.2 likewise protects the right to 'life, person, good name and property rights of every citizen', while the 14th Amendment provides that 'nor shall any State deprive any person of life, liberty or property without due process of law.'

But, one might ask, what is so specifically Catholic about these provisions of Article 40? Writing over fifty years ago, Declan Costello (then a Dáil deputy, but subsequently Attorney General from 1973 to 1977 and a judge of the High Court from 1977 until 1999) argued that, in contrast to Article 41, Article 42 and Article 43, Article 40 derived from 'secular and rationalist theory'.[39] Indeed, one would be hard put to find *any* Catholic influences whatever in Article 40, unless it be the anti-abortion provisions of Article 40.3.3 inserted by referendum in 1983. Indeed, another distinguished historian, F. S. L. Lyons, writing some twenty years previously, had described Article 40 as being 'very much in the liberal, almost one might say, the egalitarian, tradition'.[40] O'Donnell has recently echoed these view with regard to the property guarantees in Article 40.3.2:

> However, the Constitution did not simply repeat the teaching of *Quadragesimo Anno*. Instead, in guaranteeing the protection of individual property rights in Article 40.3 in exactly the same terms as all other fundamental personal rights, it seemed to lean towards the classic, liberal, Blackstone, common law theory of the importance of property rights – not enough perhaps for commentators such as Wheare, but more than enough to alarm the Catholic Church.[41]

It is true that some contend that Article 40.3 was influenced by the wording of *Rerum Novarum* – which contains a broad general injunction that public authorities must 'prevent and punish violations of rights' – but even if this is so, the structure and wording of Article 40.3 bears too much of a resemblance to that of the 14th Amendment to avoid the conclusion that it was directly influenced by this cornerstone provision of US constitutional law.

The provisions dealing with the family and education in Article 41 and Article 42 fall into another category and it is generally acknowledged that these provisions were influenced by contemporary Catholic social teaching. Taken in isolation, however, this statement might serve to create the misleading impression that these provisions were exceptional in themselves. Most continental constitutions contain similar provisions dealing with the protection of the family, as does Article 8 of the European Convention of Human Rights. A good example here is provided by Article 6 of the German Basic Law (1949):

1. Marriage and family enjoy the special protection of the state.
2. Care and upbringing of children are the natural right of the parents and a duty primarily incumbent on them. The state watches over the performance of this duty.
3. Separation of children from the family against the will of the persons entitled to bring them up may take place only pursuant to a law, if those so entitled fail in their duty or if the children are otherwise threatened with neglect.
4. Every mother is entitled to the protection and care of the community.
5. Illegitimate children shall be provided by legislation with the same opportunities for their physical and spiritual development and their position in society as are enjoyed by legitimate children.

The special case of divorce aside, is there anything so different between these provisions of the German Basic Law and Article 41 of the Constitution?[42]

1.1° The State recognises the Family as the natural primary and fundamental unit group of Society, and as a moral institution possessing inalienable and imprescriptible rights, antecedent and superior to all positive law.

2° The State, therefore, guarantees to protect the Family in its constitution and authority, as the necessary basis of social order and as indispensable to the welfare of the Nation and the State.

2.1° In particular, the State recognises that by her life within the home, woman gives to the State a support without which the common good cannot be achieved.

2° The State shall, therefore, endeavour to ensure that mothers shall not be obliged by economic necessity to engage in labour to the neglect of their duties in the home.

3.1° The State pledges itself to guard with special care the institution of Marriage, on which the Family is founded, and to protect it against attack.'

The language of Article 41.1.1 incidentally finds a remarkable parallel in Article 23.1 of the UN International Covenant on Civil and Political Rights (1966). This provides:

The family is the natural and fundamental group unit of society and is entitled to protection by society and the State.

Article 41 equally reflects the thinking of the earlier Weimar Constitution of 1919:

Article 119

Marriage, as the foundation of the family and the preservation and expansion of the nation, enjoys the special protection of the constitution. It is based on the equality of both genders.

It is the task of both the state and the communities to strengthen and socially promote the family. Large families may claim social welfare.

Motherhood is placed under state protection and welfare.

Article 120

It is the supreme obligation and natural right of the parents to raise their offspring to bodily, spiritual and social fitness; the governmental authority supervises it.

Article 121

Legislation has to create equal preconditions for children born out of wedlock, concerning their bodily, spiritual and social development, as they are given to legitimate children.

Article 122

Youth is to be protected against exploitation as well as against moral and spiritual dissipation and bodily neglect. State and communities have to take appropriate measures.

Measures which interfere by the means of force in the parents' right to raise their children may only be taken if based on a law.

Given that other provisions of the Constitution appear to have been clearly adapted from the Weimar model, it seems reasonable to assume that these provisions of Weimar were at least examined by the drafters.[43] With the exception of the special provisions of Article 121 dealing with children born out of wedlock, one could find a close fit between these provisions and Article 41 and, for that matter, much of Article 42. The reality probably is that Articles 41 and 42 reflect a diverse jumble of sources, ranging from papal encyclicals to the Weimar provisions to Article 16 of the Treaty.

It is, in any event, necessary to reflect on the scope and import of Article 41 itself. The whole object of Article 41 was to protect the autonomy and privacy of the family and to repose key decision-making with regard to the education and welfare of children in parents, subject to the right of the State – as provided for in Article 42.5 – to intervene in the case of an objective failure on the part of parents. As Hardiman J. pointed out in *North Western Health Board v. HW* this mode of thinking regarding the family is by no means confined to papal encyclicals:[44]

> Professor Goldstein [a noted US family lawyer] suggests that the common law 'reflecting Bentham's view, has a strong presumption in favour of parental authority free of coercive intrusions by agents of the State'. I would endorse this as a description of the Irish constitutional dispensation, even if any reflection of the views of Jeremy Bentham is coincidental. I do not regard the approach to the issue in the present case mandated by Articles 41 and 42 of the Constitution as reflecting uniquely any confessional view.[45]

Of course, the Foster thesis proceeds on the implicit assumption that the fact that a particular constitutional right is inspired by Catholic social teaching is a sufficient objection in itself. But what surely matters is the inherent value of the right actually protected by the Constitution as distinct from its philosophical source or inspiration.[46] If one looks at the major constitutional issues raised in the contemporary case-law – such as the right of the parents to make their own decisions about medical tests for their children,[47] or the right of parents to obtain information about medical treatment administered to their children,[48] or the right of spouses and children of Irish citizens to remain in the State,[49] or the right of divorced persons to marry their in-laws,[50] or the protection of the rights of adoptive infants[51] – I think you will find that the average litigant could not give two straws as to whether the constitutional right in question was inspired by the writings of Thomas Acquinas on the one hand or by Thomas Paine on the other. They are only concerned with whether these guarantees are likely to be of practical assistance to them.

These constitutional guarantees also plainly overlap with other legal sources and traditions. This point was graphically illustrated by the various judgments of the Supreme Court in *N v. Health Service Executive ('Baby Ann').*[52] This decision concerned the mutual rights of natural parents (who had subsequently married) and adoptive parents concerning the custody of a young infant. Reversing the decision of McMenamin J. in the High Court, the Supreme Court held that insufficient weight had been given to the fact that there was a constitutional presumption (admittedly rebuttable) that the child's interests were best served by being in the custody of its biological parents. On this point Hardiman J. observed:

> This [biological] bond is greatly valued by parents and children alike, and by natural siblings in respect of their shared parentage. It is illustrated by the frequently found phenomenon of the mature adult who, separated at birth or in infancy from his or her parents and siblings, feels a strong desire to locate them many years later. It is equally illustrated by the widespread legal recognition given to the family, even in instruments whose social and cultural context is different from, and perhaps more varied than, those of the Constitution of Ireland. I cannot escape the feeling that this factor is insufficiently emphasised in the High Court judgment here. Like Geoghegan J. and Fennelly J., I have been struck by the coincidental reporting, while the judgments in this case were being drafted, of an English case, *Re G. (Children).*[53] The context of that case is far removed from the facts of the present dispute. But it is most interesting to see that, in a jurisdiction lacking the specific social and cultural context which has led Ireland to protect the rights of the family by express constitutional provision, the interest *of a child* in being reared in his or her biological family is nonetheless fully acknowledged. I wish specifically to refer to what was said in that case by Lord Nicholls of Birkenhead:
>
>> In this case, as in all cases concerning the upbringing of children, the Court seeks to identify the course which is in the best interests of the children. Their welfare is the Court's paramount consideration. In reaching its decision the Court should always have in mind that in the ordinary way the rearing of a child by his or her biological parent can be expected to be in the child's best interests, both in the short term and also, and importantly, in the longer term. I decry any tendency to diminish the significance of this factor. A child should not be removed from the primary care of his or her biological parents without compelling reasons. Where such a reason exists the judge should spell this out explicitly.

In any event, as I have argued elsewhere with regard to the case-law on property rights under Article 43, even if it be the case that the provisions of Article 41 and Article 42 were inspired by Catholic social teaching, this is again another example of where 'the case law has long since broken loose of that particular inspirational source'.[54] The dicta in *Lord Nicholls* provide yet another example of this particular phenomenon.

IV

The other principal objection made by Foster and others is that the Constitution discriminated against women. The chief culprit here is Article 41.2, which is in the following terms:

> 2.1° In particular, the State recognises that by her life within the home, woman gives to the State a support without which the common good cannot be achieved.
> 2° The State shall, therefore, endeavour to ensure that mothers shall not be obliged by economic necessity to engage in labour to the neglect of their duties in the home.'

Almost no one today would deny that this provision is (at best) paternalistic and is wholly unsuited to modern conditions. The Constitution Review Group described it as 'a dated provision much criticised in recent years' and proposed either deleting it or replacing it with a gender-neutral provision.[55] But here again de Valera and his drafting team have been subjected to unfair and, at times, inaccurate criticism.

The case against de Valera on this point is made most eloquently by Coogan in his excellent and provocative book, *De Valera: Long Fellow, Long Shadow*. The Coogan thesis on this point is as follows: first, the 1937 Constitution 'did away with an existing guarantee' in Article 3 of the 1922 Constitution which provided that 'every person without distinction of sex ... shall ... enjoy the privileges and be subject to the obligations of such citizenship.' Second, the combination of Article 40.1 (of which more presently), Article 41.2 and certain provisions of Article 45 considerably weakened the position of women. Third, despite protestations from leading feminists such as Louie Bennett and Dorothy McArdle, de Valera refused to change position.[56]

The first thing to note is that Article 3 of the 1922 Constitution was entirely concerned with the entitlement to and the acquisition of citizenship. This is made clear by the full text of Article 3:[57]

> Every person, without distinction of sex, domiciled in the area of the jurisdiction of the Irish Free State (Saorstát Éireann) at the time of the coming into operation of this Constitution, who was born in Ireland or either of whose parents was born in Ireland or who has been ordinarily resident in the area of the jurisdiction of the Irish Free State (Saorstát Éireann) for not less than seven years, is a citizen of the Irish Free State (Saorstát Éireann) and shall within the limits of the jurisdiction of the Irish Free State (Saorstát Éireann) enjoy the privileges and be subject to the obligations of such citizenship: Provided that any such person being a citizen of another State may elect not to accept the citizenship hereby conferred; and the conditions governing the future acquisition and termination of citizenship in the Irish Free State (Saorstát Éireann) shall be determined by law.

The references to 'without distinction of sex' and 'either of whose parents was born in Ireland' in Article 3 were important because prior to that point, citizenship was generally determined by the paternal line and the extent (if at all) to which females could acquire citizenship in their own right was unclear. All that Article 3 did was to guarantee females the same right to citizenship as men, a point underscored by the references to domicile and ordinary residence.[58] This doubtless was an important advance in 1922, but – contrary to the Coogan thesis – Article 3 was not some sort of free-standing equality guarantee as between men and women.

After all, much of the discriminatory legislation – such as the Juries Act 1927 – was enacted during the period of 1922–1937 when Article 3 was in force.[59] If, as the opposition claimed during the Dáil debates in 1937, Article 3 amounted to such a guarantee, it might be asked why the Cumann na nGaedheal Government persuaded the Oireachtas to enact such legislation when they were in power and, moreover, why such legislation was not immediately challenged as being unconstitutional?[60] The reality, of course, was that the reference in Article 3 to enjoying 'the privileges' of citizenship was intended to refer to rights inherent in citizenship as such, such as the right to a passport and the right to consular assistance and this particular guarantee could not be divorced from that particular context.[61]

That Article 3 was not such a free-standing equality guarantee is, in any event, made abundantly clear by the relevant legislative history. As originally drafted, Article 3 contained an additional final sentence:

> Men and women have equal rights as citizens.

In the light of some concerns about the implications of this, that additional sentence was then amended to read as follows:

> Men and women have equal political rights.[62]

The Government then re-considered the matter and decided to drop this additional guarantee altogether for reasons then articulated by the Minister for Home Affairs (Mr Kevin O'Higgins, TD) at the Fourth Stage of the Dáil Debate on the Constitution of the Irish Free State Bill 1922:

> To trace the Government's attitude on this matter involves some little history. Article 3, as originally drafted, contains as its last sentence 'Men and women shall have equal rights as citizens.' Now we do not think that that Article or that sentence as it stood was dangerous. We do not think that it conveyed anything more than that they would have equal political rights; but presently criticism reached us on that particular clause, asking

did we propose to repeal by a couple of words in the Constitution what a very considerable body of law had recognised – a distinction between the sexes which provides for certain obvious inequalities that have always existed and, despite what anyone may say to the contrary, do still exist. Now it is understandable that, while having a very definite view in our own minds that these words would not repeal these laws, we were yet anxious to avoid raising what might bid fair to be a very angry controversy, and so we changed the Constitution slightly and inserted as a new Article. 'Men and women have equal political rights'; for we did not wish to have it in doubt for a moment that we had any intention of repealing in the Constitution such very important laws as the following existing laws – as to the guardianship of children, the existing law with reference to marital coercion and crime. That is a matter in which women have a certain privilege. They are entitled to go into Court and say they committed a crime under duress of their husbands; husbands, unfortunately, are not entitled to go into Court and say they committed a crime under the duress of their wives. The existing rule of the Civil Service under which women on marriage are required to retire on gratuity; the existing provision in regard to married women's settlements – that is a protection for women and a very valuable protection without which I venture to say many women and their children would have found themselves in a serious position, because a second husband would have otherwise disposed of the marriage settlement; the existing position under income tax laws, by which the husband makes a set of deductions for the family – children and wife – and so on. It is suggested that the wife should be able to make a like set of deductions. The existing position of the law under the Criminal Law Amendment Act, the existing difference in relation to the Divorce Laws, and so on. Now if there is a case against these laws, or any one of them, that case should be considered on its merits. It should be carefully discussed and seriously deliberated and voted on, and taken on its merits alone. It was very quickly realised that the words in the Constitution originally were taken by certain ladies in this city to mean the repeal of these enactments. It would have raised a very angry controversy hereafter when it would be discovered that that was not the intention of the Government. To avoid that bitter and angry controversy the Government inserted amendments in the Constitution emphasising that it was equal political rights were intended. Equal rights of citizenship is one thing; identical rights of citizenship is quite another thing.[63]

The second argument was that a combination of Article 40.1, Article 41.2 and Article 45.4.2 considerably weakened the position of women. We shall see presently how Article 45 was itself substantially amended in June 1937 in order to safeguard the equal right of men and women 'to an adequate means of livelihood'. But the impression created by this argument is that Article 40.1 was included in the Constitution, *precisely* so that the State could more readily discriminate against women. Article 40.1 provides:

All citizens shall, as human persons, be held equal before the law. This shall not be held to mean that the State shall not in its enactments have due regard to differences of capacity, physical and moral and of social function.

It is, however, necessary, to trace the actual origins of this provision. The idea that the fundamental rights provisions should contain a stand-alone equality guarantee originated with John Hearne, reflecting the latter's broadly egalitarian, liberal outlook. His earliest draft of the Constitution in May 1935 contained the following equality clause which seems to have been clearly inspired by the corresponding provisions of the 14th Amendment of the US Constitution:

> All citizens are equal before the law.[64]

By late February 1937, however, the equality provision had been re-drafted and the draft Article 40.1 (then numbered as Article 38.2) read as follows:

> The State acknowledges that the citizens are, as human persons, equal before the law. It shall, however, in its enactments, have due regard to individual differences of capacity, physical and moral, and of social function.

By the end of March, the proviso to Article 40.1 read thus:

> This *shall not mean, however*, that the State shall not in its *laws* have due regard to individual differences of capacity, physical and moral, and of social function.

It appears that Hearne deleted the italicised words and replaced them with 'paragraph shall not be held to mean' and 'enactments' respectively, so that by April 8 the proviso read:

> This shall not be held to mean that the State shall not in its enactments have due regard to individual differences of capacity, physical and moral, and of social function.[65]

As de Valera explained to the Dáil, he had always intended Article 40.1 to be of a 'positive character', but that the object of the proviso was to provide that:

> the first part of the section should not be stretched in a direction in which it was never meant to be stretched.[66]

De Valera admitted in the same debate that he had considered dropping the proviso altogether, but that he had changed his mind having heard the interpretation of Article 40.1 articulated by some opposition speakers:

> I was not completely and absolutely convinced of the necessity for the second part until Deputy McGilligan went on to interpret the first part in a way altogether different from the manner in which it arose originally. I think Deputy Fitzgerald-Kenney, when he was speaking on this particular matter, restricted the use of that to equal justice in the courts. I have no doubt that was the original intention, that when people came before the courts, where it was A or B, the case was investigated irrespective of who A or B was. Now,

undoubtedly, it has stretched from that meaning to mean that in all law citizens should be regarded as equal, which would make all law impossible, because we have constantly to distinguish between classes. If we want to be just we have to do it. We have to distinguish in our laws between the functions in the community. Whatever doubts I had before, I am satisfied from the way in which Deputy McGilligan has interpreted the meaning of the first part of this that it is essential that we should have the second part.[67]

It is clear, therefore, that de Valera was essentially trying to achieve what Walsh J. later said Article 40.1 had in fact achieved by importing 'the Aristotelian concept that justice demands that we treat equals equally and unequals unequally'.[68]

This is not the place to essay a full account of the effect of Article 40.1.[69] After a slow and (at times) uneven start, the case-law on Article 40.1 has nevertheless now developed to the point whereby the Supreme Court has stated that:

The forms of discrimination which are, presumptively at least, proscribed by Article 40.1 are not particularised; manifestly, they would extend to classifications based on sex, race, language, religious or political opinions.[70]

Thus, while fully recognising that there have been failures[71] as well as successes, it is important to note that among the legislation and common law rules which have been found to be unconstitutional as contrary to Article 40.1 include the effective exclusion of women from juries via the Juries Act 1927;[72] a series of common law rules which favoured husbands (but not wives)[73] or which paternalistically assumed an inferior position on the part of women[74] a provision of the Adoption Act 1974 which inhibited widowers (but not widows) from adopting;[75] gender-based statutory sentencing regimes;[76] legislation based on blood ties;[77] electoral legislation discriminating in practice against the socially disadvantaged[78] and campaign finance legislation and practices which either favoured the Government in referendum campaigns or which discriminated against new candidates as opposed to existing members of the Oireachtas in general elections.[79] In the light of this case-law, is hard to see how Article 40.1 could possibly be said to have worsened the lot of women, contrary to what Coogan argued. On the contrary and putting matters absolutely no lower, Article 40.1 may be said to have made at least a modest contribution to improving the status of women.

So far as Article 41.2 is concerned, it is, of course, objectionably paternalistic. Scannell has eloquently summarised the arguments thus:

There are two ways of looking at this Article. The first is to take de Valera at his word and to regard the first paragraph as a tribute to the work that is done by women in the home as mothers. The second paragraph, if it is to be regarded as anything other than a paternalistic declaration, can be read as a constitutional guarantee that no *mother* is to be *forced* by economic necessity to work outside the home to the neglect of her duties there. The mothers covered by this guarantee would include widows, unmarried mothers, mothers whose husbands are unable or unwilling to support their families, even relatively rich mothers with heavy expenses such as those necessitated by caring for ill or handicapped children.

The second way of looking at Article 41.2 is different. To some, it is grossly offensive to the dignity and freedoms of womanhood. It speaks of woman's *life* within the home (not just her work there), implying that the natural vocation of woman (the generic is used here, so it means *all* women) is in the home. It is the grossest form of sexual stereotyping. It can be regarded as an implicit denial of freedom of choice to women in personal matters, a freedom taken for granted by men. It speaks of *mothers* neglecting their duties, but omits to mention the duties of fathers. It fails to recognise that a woman's place is a woman's choice.[80]

But no matter how critical one can be justly of de Valera's old-fashioned paternalism as reflected in Article 41.2, it does not justify some of the more tendentious criticism which has been levelled against it.[81]

The third contention was that de Valera did not respond to the critique of the clauses dealing with women in the Constitution and refused to make any amendments in response to the criticism. Coogan cites in this regard a letter from Louie Bennett which was published in the *Irish Press* on 12 May 1937 regarding Article 45.4.2 which she described as 'the most indefensible in the Constitution'. Coogan then sets out the *present* version of Article 45.4.2:

The State shall endeavour to ensure that the strength and health of workers, men and women, and the tender age of children shall not be abused and that citizens shall not be forced by economic necessity to enter avocations unsuited to their sex, age or strength.

But this was *not* the version of the clause to which Ms Bennett had objected in her letter of 12 May 1937. The *present* version of Article 45.4.2 was only inserted by Mr de Valera at Recommital Stage on 10 June 1937 following an earlier amendment which had been moved by Deputy Rowlette.[82] The version to which Ms Bennett had objected was the *original* version of Article 45.4.2 which was in the following terms:

2°. The State shall endeavour to ensure that the inadequate strength of women and the tender age of children shall not be abused, and that women or children shall not be forced by economic necessity to enter avocations unsuited to their sex, age or strength.[83]

Whatever one thinks of the *present* Article 45.4.2, it is nonetheless clear that it represented a considerable advance over the *original* version and the reference to 'workers, men and women' went some way to contra-indicating the suggestion that women had no right to work outside the home. Another important change was that – *unlike* the original version – the *present* Article 45.4.2 is gender neutral. At Recommittal Stage Mr de Valera further amended Article 45.2.i – again in response to a promise made to Deputy Rowlette – to insert therein the words 'all of whom, men and women equally, have the right to an adequate means of livelihood'.[84] In the light of these changes, it seems somewhat unfair for Foster to claim that 'the idea of working mothers [was] denounced' by the Constitution or, indeed, for Jackson to claim that these were merely 'minor and grudging amendments'.[85]

Nor has this view been accepted by the courts. In *Murtagh Properties Ltd. v. Cleary* Kenny J. laid great emphasis on the wording of Article 45.2.i to hold that: [86]

> insofar as the right to an adequate means of livelihood was involved, men and woman were to be regarded as equal. It follows that a policy of general rule under which anyone seeks to prevent an employer from employing men or women on the ground of sex only is prohibited by the Constitution.[87]

It followed that a trade union which had picketed licensed premises because they employed women could not rely on the (then) Trade Disputes Act 1906, since that Act could not be used to confer an immunity in respect of conduct which amounted to a breach of constitutional principles.

These were by no means the only changes which de Valera made in an effort to allay the Bennett-McArdle critique. At Recommittal Stage de Valera also moved an amendment to Article 9.3 so that it now provides that:

> No person may be excluded from Irish citizenship by reason of the sex of such person.[88]

De Valera likewise moved an amendment to both Article 16.1.2 ('without distinction of sex') and Article 16.1.3 ('on grounds of sex') to eliminate any possibility whatever of gender discrimination so far as the right to vote was concerned.[89]

Mulcahy – echoing the earlier argument of Coogan – has claimed that;

> Deletion of Articles 40, 41 and 45, as demanded by women's organisations was never considered or debated by in the Dáil. These arcane articles remain today.[90]

It is, of course, strictly correct to say that the Dáil never considered deleting these provisions, but given the centrality of Article 40 in particular as the key source of fundamental rights such as life, liberty, property, good name, equality, association and assembly, the dwelling and habeas corpus, this is scarcely surprising. (How, incidentally, could any fair-minded commentator reasonably label a provision such as Article 40 as 'arcane'?) It is, however, quite incorrect to suggest – insofar as Mulcahy seems to imply – that the Dáil never debated or considered the concerns of women's organisations. Quite the contrary – these concerns were forcefully and frequently articulated by key opposition deputies. As we have seen, Article 9.1.3, Article 16.1.1, Article 16.1.2 and Article 45.4.1 and Article 45.4.2 were all amended in response to these concerns and a good deal of time on the Report and Recommittal Stages of the debate on the Constitution was taken up with these issues. It will be seen, therefore, that by these amendments – which were not merely the 'minor and grudging amendments' which Jackson has claimed them to be – Mr de Valera went at least some distance towards meeting the concerns of the women's organisations, even if, of course, he did not then go as far as either they then or we now would like.

V

Why, then, has much of this criticism from historians of de Valera and the Constitution been unbalanced and, in some instances, unfair and inaccurate? A number of reasons may be suggested.

First, much of the critical commentary of the Constitution appears, in part, at least to have been influenced by the fact that the Constitution was seen as 'de Valera's Constitution.' Many of the same commentators were bitterly hostile to de Valera on whom 'was projected our disenchantment with post-revolutionary society' and who for them had come to epitomise 'emigration, poverty and depression'.[91] In addition, such commentators tended to write from a broadly left-liberal and anti-clerical perspective who could not bring themselves to accept that de Valera's political and legal *weltanschaung* was anything other than insular and authoritarian in perspective.[92] They accordingly tended to associate the Constitution with highly contentious and reactionary measures, such as the original provisions of Article 44.1.2 (recognition of the 'special position' of the Catholic Church), the original Articles 2 and 3, and the ban on divorce and were simply unwilling or unable to look beyond these provisions and analyse the Constitution on its strict legal merits.

Secondly, the absence up to now of any detailed commentary regarding the drafting of the Constitution itself has handicapped fair historical evaluation.[93] This in turn has meant that historians have focused on the easy targets of Articles 2 and 3, the ban on divorce and the 'special position' and 'women in the home' clauses. Far less attention was given to the conspicuous novelties of the Constitution which either strengthened the role of judicial review or which for the first time expressly enumerated new fundamental rights such as equality, life, good name or property rights. The publication of *The Making of the Constitution* will doubtless prompt a re-evaluation of much of this analysis.

Thirdly, the absence of such accounts regarding the drafting of the Constitution also perhaps has given rise to a sort of conventional wisdom whereby it is assumed that the Constitution was more or less entirely drafted by de Valera and that it 'was framed on the basis of Catholic social principles'.[94] The situation is, of course, far more complex inasmuch as:

> Constitutional lawyers have been traditionally wary of attributing such a complete and exclusive influence to de Valera, mainly because the sophistication, style and general layout of the Constitution strongly suggested that its legal content and drafting must have been the work of very skilled lawyers and draftsmen.[95]

Moreover, as we have seen, the reality is that fundamental rights provisions owe more (and, certainly, judged by contemporary case-law, far more) to what Mr Justice Costello described as 'secular and rationalist theory' than to any specifically Catholic teaching.

Fourthly, the historical analysis has examined the Constitution in the abstract, divorced from contemporary practice as it existed in other European countries in 1937. If, for example, we look comparatively at the 'special position' clause, this was, as we have seen, quite unexceptionable by the European standards of 1937. Even today, many of the Protestant countries of northern Europe have clauses which go much further than the special position clause ever did. Yet the implied premise of the criticism by historians of the special position clause is that this was in some way exceptional if not, indeed, unique.

Fifthly, even if certain provisions of Article 41, Article 42 and Article 43 were influenced by Catholic social teaching, that in itself would be no more reason to reject them than it would be to reject those other provisions of the Constitution reflecting 'secular and rationalist theory' precisely because of their ultimate provenance. But even in the case of Article 41 we can find broad comparators elsewhere, most notably in the Weimar Constitution, and Article 23.1 of the (1966) UN International Covenant on Civil and Political Rights is itself virtually a verbatim copy of Article 41.1.1.[96]

Sixthly, much of the criticism assumes a static model of constitutional law and one which looks at the bare words of the Constitution, often divorced from the legal and historical context. Constitutional law, on the other hand, involves not simply the narrow words of the document – which, inevitably, is 'open textured' ('trial in due course of law', 'defend as far as practicable the personal rights of the citizen', 'no citizen shall be deprived of personal liberty save in accordance with law') – but legal tradition and reason. Perhaps many non-lawyers do not appreciate:

> the extent to which constitutional law is capable of organic evolution through the growth of case-law and the emergence of an *acquis constitutionnel*.[97]

At this stage, any fair-minded critique of the Constitution must also have regard to the vast corpus of case-law which has been generated since 1937. If, for example, Article 40.1 and Article 41 were one of a number of constitutional provisions which 'to some read like a feminist's nightmare',[98] how can this assessment be reconciled with cases such as *CM v. TM (No.2)99* which held that the rule of dependent domicile of married woman was 'a relic of matrimonial female bondage which was swept away by principles of equality before the law and equal rights in marriage as between men and woman which were enshrined in the Constitution'?[100] Likewise, even though in the second edition of his magisterial book, Whyte fairly chronicled much of the ground-making case-law of the 1970s, he wondered how decisions such as *McGee* had been 'wrung out of a Constitution so specifically Catholic as the 1937 document had been?'[101] The obvious answer, of course, is that the Constitution was not, in fact, as specifically Catholic as he had claimed and that he (in common with many others) had failed, for example, to give sufficient weight to the 'secular and rationalist' theory sub-tending Article 40 on which many of the Supreme Court judgments in that case were based.[102]

There was undoubtedly much to be critical of in the Constitution as originally enacted. The well-worn criticisms of the historians and others of provisions such as Articles 2 and 3, the ban on divorce, the 'special position' and 'women in the home' clauses are telling and entirely well-taken. Nor can it be realistically denied that these clauses often sent the wrong message about the fundamentals of the Constitution and were liable to cause offence to the majority population in Northern Ireland. But, as I have sought to argue in this Foreword, there is another side to this Constitution as well – its clear articulation of the separation of powers; the enhancement of the democratic process through special protections for electoral fairness and the referendum; the recognition of general principles of international law; the improvement in the system of constitutional protection and judicial review of legislation and the articulation of important new rights such as equality, life, the person, good name and property rights. Symbolism aside, in practice this side of the Constitution is vastly more important than the original clauses (such as the old Article 2 and Article 3 and the divorce ban) to which objection was readily taken. The fact, however, that the historians have tended up to now to focus on one side to the (almost) complete exclusion of the other has meant that such criticism has been unbalanced and at times even unfair.

This is not to suggest that the Constitution could not be further improved. In this respect, it scarcely necessary to go further than the *Report of the Constitution Review Group* (1996) to consider the extensive changes recommended therein. But even if all of these changes were recommended, the fundamental structure established in 1937 would still remain, which is its own tribute to the fact that the Constitution 'as a whole possesses the kind of widespread acceptance and legitimacy that the Irish Free State Constitution never attracted'.[103]

VI

It remains only to thank Professor Keogh and Dr McCarthy for their tireless and indefatigable efforts. They have given us a splendid book on the drafting of the Constitution which should prove to be a revelation to both the historian and the lawyer alike and will certain prompt a re-evaluation of much of the conventional wisdom regarding the drafters, the drafting process and, of course, the Constitution itself. *The Making of the Irish Constitution* demonstrates many things, not least the fact that Hearne was the principal drafter and that most of the legal and constitutional innovations brought about by the Constitution may fairly be attributed to him. Of course, de Valera had the foresight to choose a talented drafting team composed of individuals such as Hearne and Maurice Moynihan who:

> transcended the limitations of their own times. Both helped to infuse the document with a balance and basic humanism which stood in marked contrast to the legal positivism of the decade in continental Europe ... The broad-based culture of these men prevented the triumph of extremism.[104]

As Professor Keogh has previously argued, if others less skilled and far-sighted had been chosen as drafters, it is more likely that the content and design of the Constitution would have suffered accordingly. Indeed, in the hands of others, it is likely that the Constitution would have proved a far more ephemeral document, fatally damaged (in the long term) through the influence of the confessional, reactionary and authoritarian thinking which was fashionable in certain influential circles in the Ireland of the 1930s.

De Valera's own personal achievements were nevertheless considerable. *The Making of the Constitution* provides further evidence that he had the clarity of thought to sketch out the constitutional model he wanted, while at the same time allowing innovation on the part of the drafting team; he resisted Church pressure to have an established Church; he demonstrated a consummate understanding of the legal issues during the course of the Dáil debates and he also took on board many (admittedly not all) of the useful suggestions made by those opposition deputies such as Rowlette and McDermott who had constructively engaged with him and, finally, he had the courage to have the first ever Constitution adopted by referendum.[105]

The end product was a Constitution which brought much needed stability after the hectic constitutional changes of 1922–1937; a Constitution which, on the whole, has operated as a salutary check on the other branches of government and which has promoted the protection of individual rights and which has proved to be sufficiently durable and adaptable that it has not only survived, but which is also – if the volume of constitutional litigation is anything to go by – thriving in the every different Ireland of 2007:

> ... the 1937 Constitution succeeded against the odds in establishing a system where judicial review could flourish, even though this prospect excited considerable scepticism at the time. Moreover, compared with the constitutions of other emerging nations of Europe, the Irish Constitution succeeded where many other attempts failed.[106]

These are considerable achievements which considerably outweigh the negatives. Is it asking too much to give Mr de Valera some credit where credit is due?

VII

Much of the foregoing is, as has already been noted, adapted from an earlier article of mine. Professor Keogh and Dr McCarthy have very generously urged me to re-use this material in the present *Foreword* so that it might be laid before a wider audience. I am naturally signally honoured that such a request has been made of me in respect of such an important book as *The Making of the Irish Constitution.* Just as Professor Keogh's article in 1987 on the drafting of Article 44 proved to be a revelation in our understanding of Church/State relations, so too will *The Making of the Irish Constitution* come to be regarded as the definitive account of the enactment of our fundamental law. Both present and future generations of historians, political scientists and lawyers will be indebted to them for the production of this scholarly and erudite work.

Gerard Hogan,
Law School,
Trinity College, Dublin
10 July 2007

CHAPTER 1

The Irish Constitutional Revolution 1932–1936 – Historical and Political Overview

William T. Cosgrave, President of the Executive Council of Saorstát Éireann (Irish Free State), dissolved Dáil Éireann at the end of January 1932. The general election was fixed for 16 February. Cosgrave's Cumann na nGaedheal party had retained power since 1922, but the prevailing economic circumstances were not favourable and indeed only likely to deteriorate.[1] This uncertainty increased the chances of an electoral breakthrough for the main opposition party, Fianna Fáil, led by the enigmatic Éamon de Valera. The prospect of Fianna Fáil success alarmed both the Cosgrave and British governments. The king was deeply pessimistic, according to the Irish high commissioner in London, J. W. Dulanty. His concerns were not eased by Cosgrave's advice that the British government should not adopt too aggressive an attitude or iron hand methods since such actions 'might bring about the destruction of the constructive work that had been done by the Government in the past ten years'.[2] Fuelling fears also was the perception – or misperception! – that de Valera was an unstable character. The Dominions Office contemplated using a doctor from Leopardstown hospital as an intermediary because 'he had the medical knowledge essential for dealing with the psychological problem presented by de Valera'.[3] Dominions secretary, J. H. Thomas, warned the cabinet that should de Valera attain power, a difficult position would be produced, but no action should be taken 'which would enable Mr de Valera to say that we were forcing him out of the British Empire'.[4]

In the Free State there were additional constitutional concerns. Despite de Valera publicly eschewing physical force and embracing democratic principles, there was widespread suspicion that he intended to establish a dictatorship. Moreover, irrespective of de Valera's democratic commitment, whether democracy could survive a government with such a chequered past was questionable. Links with extreme republicans and the IRA did little to disprove the impression that Fianna Fáil was 'a slightly constitutional party', a phrase used earlier by Seán Lemass. However, Ronan Fanning illustrated that such fears were based on a misunderstanding of de Valera's attitude to violence as a means of obtaining political ends; he cited de Valera's address to the inaugural Fianna Fáil árdfheis in May 1926:

> I know that in History it is seldom that foreign tyrants have ever yielded to any other, I have believed and I still believe, that if a nation held in subjection by a foreign power were to exclude altogether the idea of using physical force to free itself, it would in effect be handing over a bound slave without hope of redemption ... but a nation within itself ought to be able to settle its polity so that all occasions of civil conflict between its members may be obviated, and no nation which even pretends to freedom will suffer a foreign power to impose conditions which make the adoption of such a polity impossible.[5]

The internal logic of his position demanded that he first strip the state of all those elements which he deemed repugnant to right-minded republicans, a process which culminated in the enactment of the 1937 constitution and the return of the ports in 1938.

Meanwhile, in 1932 it appeared that no less than the future of the Anglo-Irish Agreement of 1921 – commonly known as the Treaty – was at stake. That Agreement had given the new state the status of a self-governing dominion. The constitution of the Irish Free State, which came into force on 6 December 1922, was also a source of contention for republicans. The Treaty itself did not include a constitution but contained guidelines for that document requiring the prior approval of the British before endorsement by the Irish. Even then it was a difficult process. In May 1922, for example, the British government refused to accept that draft as a correct interpretation of the 1921 treaty, and the provisions relating to the oath of allegiance, the governor general, the Privy Council and free membership of the Commonwealth were amended.[6] The 1922 constitution provided for an oath of allegiance to the king; designated the judicial committee of the Privy Council as the final court of appeal in cases from the Free State; and appointed a governor general, as the king's representative, in whom executive authority of the Free State government was vested. Furthermore, Article 50 copper-fastened dominion status, declaring that any provision of the constitution was 'absolutely void and inoperative' if in any way repugnant to the Treaty.

Setting aside the contentious monarchical symbols, the new state was for practical purposes an independent democratic entity. The German legal scholar and acknowledged authority on the Free State constitution, Leo Kohn, outlined that autonomy as follows:

> ... full internal self-government, unrestricted fiscal autonomy, the right to maintain an Irish Police Force and an Irish Army subject only to the control of the Irish Parliament. In the sphere of external relations it involved the concession of the new international status of the British Dominions, the right to enter into agreements with foreign States,

> freedom from obligations arising from treaties not specifically approved by the Irish Parliament, full discretion in the matter of Irish participation in British wars, and, lastly, membership of the League of Nations.[7]

Kohn also pointed out that the 1922 constitution 'reduced to precise terms the conventional rules of the British constitution. Its archaic symbols had to be introduced, but their meaninglessness for Ireland was writ large in every page'.[8] The governor general, for example, despite having notional powers, including under Article 42 the right to give or withhold the royal assent to bills, or reserve them 'for the significance of the King's pleasure', exercised little power. The office was irksome more in theory than in practice. In practice, the governor general in Ireland never acted as an independent entity and signed all bills presented to him, even that abolishing the oath. Moreover, executive authority invested in him under Article 51 was effectively neutralised by the important qualification that such powers were to be used in accordance with the legal practice and constitutional usage governing the like in the dominion of Canada. It was Canadian practice for the governor general to accept the advice of his ministers on the royal assent. Again, Article 2 stated 'all powers of Government and all authority legislative, executive and judicial in Ireland, are derived from the people of Ireland and the same shall be exercised in the Irish Free State through the organisations established by or under, in accord with, this Constitution'. However, this assertion was contradicted by the existence of the oath, the vesting of executive authority in the king, the creation of a governor general, and the right of appeal to the Privy Council. Nonetheless, the import of Article 2 was that the power derived from the people was to be exercised by the crown.

Whatever the legal niceties of the 1921 treaty and subsequent constitution, de Valera and his followers repudiated that settlement. Following ignominious defeat on the Treaty split in January 1922, and further defeat at the August 1923 election, which earned him a year's imprisonment when he came out of hiding to contest it, de Valera broke with Sinn Féin in 1926. Having narrowly failed to persuade the Sinn Féin árd-fheis of March 1926 that, provided the oath was abolished, the party should enter the Dáil, he seceded and founded Fianna Fáil two months later. On their second attempt, Fianna Fáil entered the Dáil in August 1927. Dáil entry did not constitute acceptance, much less endorsement, of the Treaty settlement. On 14 March 1929, de Valera declared that the government's 'right to be regarded as the legitimate government of this country is faulty, that this House itself is faulty'.[9] Nevertheless, he accepted the *de facto* position of the Dáil as the only assembly empowered to maintain order and he later declared that anyone 'who continued on in that organisation which we have left can claim exactly the same continuity that we claimed up to 1925'.[10]

De Valera's fundamental objection remained that, however independent in practice, the new state was still for him subject in character. As Nicholas Mansergh stated: 'It was the symbols of sovereignty that signified most.' From the Irish point of view this was fundamental.[11] De Valera remained convinced when he entered the Dáil that the Treaty settlement would not end the centuries of conflict between Great Britain and Ireland. Embracing constitutional politics was a change of tactics. His long-term political strategy remained to dismantle the Treaty settlement and re-write the Free State constitution. That was how both de Valera and his party campaigned in the run-up to the 1932 election.

Almost inevitably then, a de Valera victory in the 1932 election would impact on Anglo-Irish relations. Already, Cosgrave's government had assiduously and indeed successfully pursued the constitutional path to greater independence within the imperial framework. The Irish Free State had been to the forefront in advancing dominions' independence at the imperial conferences 1926–9, culminating in the 1931 Statute of Westminster, which conceded to the dominions' constitutional legislative independence. In 1923 the Free State joined the League of Nations as a fully independent state. In 1924, under strong British protest, the Anglo-Irish Agreement of 1921 was registered with the Treaty registration bureau of the League of Nations.[12] David Harkness described the Cosgrave government's policy in the following terms: 'Their objective was full and unrestricted sovereignty: their method became the peaceful transformation of the British Empire so that the definition of dominion status might be synonymous with fullest freedom.'[13] Indeed, Cumann na nGaedheal pursued this course to the point that another commentator, Brendan Sexton, concluded that the party was only a slightly less intransigent republican party than Fianna Fáil.[14]

As impressive as the Cosgrave government's achievements were, the undeniable fact remained for de Valera that the state was still subject in character. However, advances made within the commonwealth had impressed even de Valera. 'There have been advances made,' he conceded, 'which I did not believe could be made at the time.'[15] In the interim therefore he was prepared to work within the dominion framework, to use it as a stepping stone to advance independence.[16] External association – an advanced constitutional conceptualisation capable of facilitating a sovereign republic associating voluntarily with the British government – remained de Valera's ultimate goal.[17] Yet, the British rejected outright such a formula in the lead up to the 1921 settlement and in 1932 the concept still appeared incompatible with dominion status.

However, the Fianna Fáil election manifesto of 9 February 1932 expressly indicated their intention of proceeding incrementally and constitutionally towards that goal. The abolition of the oath of allegiance was the only specific proposal for constitutional change and de Valera pledged not to 'exceed the mandate asked for without asking the people'.[18] The manifesto promised to 'remove the Article of the Constitution which makes the signing of the oath of allegiance obligatory on members entering the Dáil'. There was no mention of a republic; instead Fianna Fáil would

> strive to bring British statesmen to realise that the interests of Britain, as well as the interests of Ireland, are best secured by an understanding and settlement which will permit the people of the two islands to live side by side as independently friendly neighbours – each respecting the rights of the other and co-operating freely in matters of common concern.[19]

The manifesto also committed Fianna Fáil, if elected, to retain the land annuities 'in the State Treasury', a policy certain to appeal to those affected.[20] The electorate was given an assurance that the government would not use its majority

> to pursue a vindictive course against any minority, but to govern fairly in the interests of all sections of the community. All citizens will be treated as equal before the law, and the individual will be protected in his person and in his property with all the resources at the Government's command. Ordinarily such promises would not be necessary. Apprehensions however have been aroused, and it is necessary to allay them.

On the economic front it committed to self-sufficiency in Ireland, decentralisation of government and the 'ruralisation of industry'.

The election campaign was short and saw Cosgrave and de Valera engage in whirlwind tours of the country. The government stood on its record. On the political side it pointed to the Statute of Westminster as vindicating its external policy. It instanced the Free State's position on the council of the League of Nations as evidence that Ireland had taken its rightful place amongst the nations. However, these achievements lacked public appeal. On the economic side, the government claimed 'with considerable truth' according to the Irish correspondent of the influential commonwealth journal *Round Table*, John Horgan, that 'by its policy of scientific tariffs, improved agricultural production, conservative finance and completing land purchase that it had placed the economic life of the country on a sound basis'.[21] Law and order was a major plank in its election manifesto. In October 1931, Cumann na nGaedheal enacted the Constitution (Amendment No. 17) Act, which inserted a new Article 2A into the constitution, containing severe provisions for the control of violence in the state.[22]

However, against a background of increased unemployment, taxation, emigration and budgetary cutbacks, such claims failed to excite the electorate. The government had been forced to introduce an unpopular supplementary budget in November 1931, which simultaneously increased income tax and reduced the salaries of teachers and gardaí. Posters designed to undermine de Valera's commitment to democracy were part of the electoral strategy. One such poster entitled 'His Master's Voice' represented de Valera walking forward with an armed gunman holding a revolver to his back.[23] Yet, even *Round Table* had to admit that the government was unpopular but blamed that 'soft headed section of the community who are always prepared to condemn any strong action such as the setting up of the Military Tribunal'. It continued:

> It is quite true that any new Government, if it desired to survive, would have to adopt similar methods, but this is a simple truth, which the average Irish elector has yet to learn. It is indeed one of the strongest arguments for a change of Government, were a really strong and competent alternative Government available.[24]

Nevertheless, Fianna Fáil's economic policy was enticing. As well as pledging to restore army pensions it promised to create almost 85,000 new jobs in the manufacturing sector with a resulting reduction in emigration.[25] Various social reforms were also promised, including a maintenance scheme for the 80,000 unemployed, the building of 40,000 houses, a pension scheme for widows and orphans, the re-organisation of the transport industry and measures against profiteering in the flour-milling industry.[26] Against this, the Cumann na nGaedheal programme 'devoted one grudging paragraph out of fourteen to social and economic policy'.[27]

The election results were not entirely unexpected. With a record turnout of 75 per cent, Fianna Fáil won seventy-two seats, an increase of fifteen, increasing its share of the poll from 35.2 to 45.5 per cent. Cumann na nGaedheal lost five seats, down from the sixty-two at the dissolution, while its poll fell from almost 39 to 35.3 per cent. The Labour party's representation was almost halved, dropping from thirteen to seven seats. De Valera was five seats short of an overall majority but formed a government with the support of Labour when the seventh Dáil convened on 9 March 1932. While all the outward formalities were observed when the Fianna Fáil deputies arrived, the atmosphere was fraught with tension. Rumours of a coup by the outgoing government appeared in the Fianna Fáil organ, the *Irish Press*.[28] Frank Aiken took no chances and issued revolvers to the new ministers. The rumours proved unfounded and the Dáil firstly elected a new Ceann Comhairle (Speaker), Frank Fahy, a Fianna Fáil deputy from Galway. De Valera was then elected president of the Executive Council (he also took External Affairs) by a majority of thirteen votes. After obtaining formal sanction from the governor general he announced the new

Executive Council. Seán T. O'Kelly was appointed Minister for Local Government and Public Health and vice president of the Executive Council. Frank Aiken, a former chief-of-staff of the IRA, was made Minister for Defence, a move shrewdly designed to test the loyalty of the army to the new regime while simultaneously appealing to the diehard republican element. Seán MacEntee was appointed to Finance and Seán Lemass got the Industry and Commerce portfolio. Paddy Ruttledge was Minister for Lands and Fisheries, Thomas Derrig got Education, and Dr James Ryan was given Agriculture. All were founding members of the party with the exception of the Minister for Justice, James Geoghegan – a former Cumann na nGaedheal supporter appointed to that highly sensitive ministry precisely because he was untainted by the controversies of the previous decade.[29] Like Cosgrave's government the new administration consisted of mainly young men; it also represented a marriage of the radical and conservative elements within Fianna Fáil.

De Valera celebrated electoral victory in a radio broadcast to 'friends of Ireland' in America. He explained that the removal of the 'hateful' oath would enable all sections of 'our people' to 'send their representative to the people's assembly … without coercion of conscience or sacrifice of principle'.[30] Not surprisingly, de Valera's accession to power caused concern in Britain. J. J. Horgan opined, that 'Mr de Valera's mind has, for all practical purposes, not advanced beyond the year 1921 … he is still thinking in terms of the Treaty discussions … The position of equality which he demands has been already achieved.'[31] The London *Times* correspondent predicted that 'even within a few weeks or months a Fianna Fáil Government may do much mischief'.[32]

The difficulties facing de Valera's new government were considerable. It assumed office in circumstances without historical parallel: commanding an army it opposed during the Civil War, a police force organised by its opponents, and a civil service reshaped over the ten years of its opponents' reign. The legacy of the Civil War had left a bitter and divided society.[33] A significant minority of Sinn Féin sympathisers led by Mary MacSwiney continued to deny the legitimacy of the Irish Free State and its institutions. De Valera's hope that the abolition of the oath would entice Sinn Féin into mainstream politics proved delusional. The IRA, having supported Fianna Fáil in the election campaign, lurked ominously in the background. For them nothing less than a full declaration of a republic would suffice. And de Valera could hardly expect support from his political opponents for his constitutional campaign. In 1932, Cumann na nGaedheal was dedicated to maintaining the integrity of the Treaty for the 'treaty first perceived by its advocates merely as a means to an end became an end in itself'.[34]

Inevitably, these internal factors placed limits on de Valera's freedom of action. A declaration of a republic, while placating his more left wing supporters and the IRA, would accentuate rather than diminish divisions. Maintaining party unity – fragile though it was in 1932 – was therefore a paramount consideration which dictated both the pace and strategy of de Valera's constitutional policy, and indeed ultimately the contents of the constitution. There were also external factors to be considered. In British eyes the oath of allegiance and commonwealth membership were intrinsically intertwined. The oath symbolised the essence of the dominion settlement; but it was also the symbol that attracted most resentment in nationalist Ireland and as such had to be removed. In the words of the British government law advisers, 'The throne is the bond which knits together the Commonwealth of Nations known as the British Empire … No Constitution which is in form or substance Republican can find a place in that community.'[35] The Fianna Fáil manifesto therefore represented the first shot across the bow towards exit or expulsion from the commonwealth. The pace of events would be determined by the British reaction. As F. S. L. Lyons states:

> … it behoved the Irish Government to consider what the consequences might be. Unfortunately, this was impossible to predict. There *might* be difficulties for Irish men living in Britain … there *might* be disagreeable economic results; there *might* be all sorts of legal complications; there *might* even be, in the sphere of external relations, the unpleasant necessity to walk naked and alone in a world ill-disposed towards the sovereign independence of small, unprotected states. It was impossible to tell how things would turn out, but all these considerations counselled caution.[36]

Such fears were not without foundation. For when de Valera asked for a direct and unequivocal statement that exit from the Commonwealth would not 'expose him to war or other aggressive action' the imperial response was to reply that Ireland would become a foreign country and her citizens treated as aliens.[37]

Of immediate concern, however, was de Valera's republican flank. *Round Table* warned, in rather apocalyptic terms, that de Valera's:

> … Government will not be in power for two months before the hedgerow heroes … assert their authority by their usual methods of the threat and the gun, and Mr de Valera, as he always has done, will toe the line and do what he is told – if indeed he is not unceremoniously kicked out – and people of his Kerensky-like temperament usually are.[38]

In an effort to placate the IRA, Aiken and Geoghegan visited the political prisoners at Arbour Hill barracks within hours of the new government being elected. Aiken announced that all political prisoners would be released as soon as possible and within weeks all ninety-seven prisoners were released. On 12 March the republican organ, *An Phoblacht*, reappeared; on 18 March the Public Safety Act was suspended, dissolving the military tribunal. While these gestures comforted militant elements within Fianna Fáil, they failed to placate diehard republicans who denounced de Valera's 'external association', stating that 'the actual demand is for absolute sovereignty without equivocation'.[39] The IRA army council failed to disband; in fact, the initial response to de Valera's overtures was an increase in recruitment and public drilling. However, these gestures, coupled with his attack on the Treaty, were sufficient to maintain peace in the short term.[40]

This attack took two main forms initially: abolition of the oath and retention of the land annuities. Early attempts at negotiation failed miserably. *Round Table* correctly summarised de Valera's position:

> It is certain that he entered into negotiations just as if 10 years of negotiations and developments in relations between England and Ireland had not intervened ... what he describes as his ultimate aim is in reality the proposal put forward during the Treaty negotiations ... the famous Document No 2, for the sake of which de Valera plunged the country into Civil War.[41]

When the Dáil reconvened on 15 March, de Valera stated his intention of removing the oath. On 23 April, de Valera published the text of the Constitution (Removal of Oath) Bill. It had three clauses: the first deleted the oath itself, the second removed section 2 of the Constitution Act, the repugnancy clause, and the third removed the restriction on amendments to the constitution. The bill passed all stages in the Dáil by 19 May and was supported by Labour. Cumann na nGaedheal was only lukewarm in its opposition: General Seán MacEoin indicated that if de Valera made the same case for abolition to the British he was sure that they would agree, and in that he would have his wholehearted support. In fact, most opinion in the Free State favoured abolishing the oath: it was merely a question of method. The removal of the oath was, however, delayed when the Senate rejected the bill, making numerous amendments, the most important of which was designed to prevent the bill coming into force until agreement was reached between the Irish Free State and the British government. This action hardly endeared the upper house to de Valera and was undoubtedly one of the reasons why he abolished it in his second period of office. The Senate was dominated by members interested in preserving links with Britain and delayed passage of the bill until May 1933.[42]

De Valera's speech introducing the bill to the Senate was described as 'singularly moderate and almost persuasive'.[43] But, not unexpectedly, there was an immediate hostile reaction. Dominion secretary Thomas argued that 'The Bill is nothing more than a repudiation of the settlement of '21 as a whole'.[44] He felt that the Anglo-Irish Treaty transcended the provisions of the Statute of Westminster since it was vested with the force of fundamental law. Both the Constitution Act and the Irish Free State constitution declared that if any provision of the constitution, or any amendment thereunder, was in any respect repugnant to any provision of the Treaty, it was to the extent of such repugnancy 'absolutely void and inoperative'. Therefore the latitude allowed in the Statute of Westminster did not apply to the Irish case.

De Valera, however, based his case on indefeasible national sovereignty. Dismissing the legal arguments, he went straight to what was for him the central issue: 'Whether the Oath was or was not an integral part of the Treaty made ten years ago is now not the issue. The real issue is that the oath is an intolerable burden to the people of this state and they have declared in the most formal manner that they desire to remove it.'[45] For de Valera the crucial issue was sovereignty and he proceeded on the basis that the Treaty was not inviolable. Against this, a *Round Table* leader article took the high moral ground. Reflecting the contractual argument, it argued that 'the essence of the Treaty was that Ireland should remain in the British Commonwealth of Nations, and the oath was the earnest of her intention to do so'. The Treaty, observed for ten years, and essentially 'an agreement between two parties, had been unilaterally altered without the consent of the other party'. Therefore, *Round Table* advised, Britain should 'take a stand upon the Treaty and wait confident that the Irish nation … will return to it'.[46]

On 16 June de Valera redeemed the second of his election pledges by withholding the land annuities. Initially, he sent a note to Thomas offering to submit to arbitration provided the arbiters were not confined to commonwealth citizens. Thomas rejected the offer. The British then retaliated with duties levied on Irish imports, hitting agricultural exporters. De Valera in turn levied duties on British goods. Within a year the trade figures showed a marked deterioration. Compared to August of the previous year, imports decreased by £774,002 and exports by £1, 890,141. Cattle trade alone suffered a loss of £901,616, prompting the comment from *Round Table*:

> Unless some unforeseen intervention takes place, the two countries must now apparently face the prospect of an economic war which will finally cripple the Irish Free State.[47]

That journal had no difficulty laying responsibility with de Valera, noting in November that:

> He is a good specimen of the most dangerous phenomenon – the schoolmaster in politics. He can lecture but he cannot negotiate, and his enthusiasm for abstract propositions prevents him from facing realities. Whoever else is wrong he is always right.[48]

This Anglo-Irish 'economic war', fought against a backdrop of global economic depression, severely affected agriculture, the mainstay of the Irish economy, and the cattle trade in particular. Not surprisingly, Cosgrave tabled a motion of censure on 15 November 1932, which in turn helped precipitate the snap election two months later. On 2 January 1933 de Valera seized the initiative and dissolved the Dáil, catching his opponents completely off guard. In his dissolution statement de Valera explained that he desired a clear mandate for his campaign. According to *Round Table*, the really decisive factor was his increasing irritation with the precarious political situation. 'Pressed by Labour on the left, sniped at by the IRA in the rear, and harried by the more conservative elements in his own party on the right, his position had become intolerable for a man of his autocratic mentality.'[49]

Despite de Valera's denials, there was some truth in the *Round Table* analysis. The effects of the economic war were being felt. De Valera's allies and parliamentary prop, Labour, expressed dissatisfaction during Cosgrave's motion of censure, and relations became increasingly strained. But the decision to call an election demonstrated de Valera's keen sense of political timing. For there were rumours of a coalition between Cumann na nGaedheal and the National Centre Party – formed in November after a merging of the National Farmers and Ratepayer's League. 'These events constituted portents which Mr de Valera could no longer ignore'.[50]

During the 1933 election campaign Fianna Fáil concentrated on Anglo-Irish relations, accusing the British of undermining them on the annuities issue. It was an excellent election strategy, garnering maximum political mileage in severe economic circumstances. In contrast, Cumann na nGaedheal offered little. Already caught off guard, its political organisation was far inferior to Fianna Fáil's. In addition, the IRA decided that de Valera was the lesser of two evils and at a specially convened convention allowed its followers to work and vote against the Cosgrave candidates and 'their so called independent allies'. Accepting that the Fianna Fáil success had been an important step, it stated: 'The overthrow of the Cosgrave regime last year was carried through in the face of frightful terrorism. That great achievement removed from our land the immediate dangers of Civil War, the foulest of all the evils British rule ever forced on our people.'[51]

Much campaigning centred on the annuities question. De Valera defended the unemployment figures, asserting that 'formerly most people did not register for unemployment because it did not seem of much use to do so'. His government extended the system of registration but, he pointed out, 'there had been no increase of unemployment': 33,000 people were employed in relief schemes of national importance; 5,000 on road work; and 4,600 found work in the sheltered industries.[52] *Round Table* was, however, less sanguine about the effects of the economic war: 'It is, however, impossible to estimate accurately the losses, tangible and intangible, which both countries have suffered from this senseless dispute.'[53] On 5 January 1933, in an election speech delivered at a meeting in Dublin's O'Connell Street, de Valera announced a 50 per cent cut in the land annuities paid by farmers. He also promised that, if re-elected, the oath 'would vanish in spite of the Senate' and 'with its going will come the certainty of domestic peace'. The election manifesto was not made public until Saturday 15 January when the *Irish Press* banner headline announced: 'WE PROPOSE TO ABOLISH THE SENATE', a statement it greeted as 'an outstanding surprise'. The rest of the programme dealt with proposals for oath abolition, retention of annuities, full protection of the home market for agriculture and industry, saving the Irish language and the establishment of industries in the Gaeltacht – essentially the elements of the 1932 manifesto.[54]

The 1933 election resulted in a triumph for Fianna Fáil. The final figures saw Fianna Fáil gain five and Cumann na nGaedheal lose nine seats. De Valera, with seventy-seven seats, had a majority of one and was no longer dependent on Labour support. Fianna Fáil increased its share of the vote from 44.5 per cent to 49.6 per cent. The result was clear, the shift decisive. Cosgrave had been defeated in two successive elections, and his party vote reduced both times. The British could no longer hold out for the prospect of his return to power. It was therefore with the anti-treaty party that an agreement, if any, would have to be reached.

Fortified with election victory, de Valera proceeded with his constitutional campaign and abolished the two remaining symbols of imperial power: the Privy Council appeals and the office of governor general. Although not required by the Treaty, the British insisted on provision for the right of appeal to the Privy Council since, as a monarchy, the Free State had to accept the common law principle that justice was the prerogative of the king. It was enshrined in Article 66 of the Free State constitution. Kevin O'Higgins earlier told the Dáil that, 'inasmuch as we have accepted the King, then we have to accept the special prerogative of the King and, grant, in very special cases, right of appeal'.[55] Since the Treaty had defined the relationship of the Free State to the imperial parliament and government as being similar to that of Canada and, since Canada in 1922 did not have the right to abolish by legislation the right of appeal to the Privy Council, the presumption was that neither could the Irish Free State. The impression given to the Provisional Government at the time was that the judicial committee would 'look somewhat strictly on all applications for Leaves to appeal' and the crown dismissed the first three applications. However, in 1925 the Privy Council allowed an appeal in a civil case, which had no international implications. This was repeated in a case in 1930. The Cosgrave government then decided to act unilaterally, having failed to get agreement at imperial conferences for the proposition that each dominion should decide for itself the extent of the Privy Council's jurisdiction in domestic affairs. Using the freedom of the Statute of Westminster, it was preparing a constitutional amendment bill when it fell in 1932. De Valera completed the task: on 22 November the Constitution (Amendment No. 22) Bill removed the right to petition the king in council.[56] In a sense, de Valera's actions were the climax of a long history of Irish objections to the court.

De Valera then focused on the office of governor general – the most public manifestation of the crown in Ireland. In practice, the Irish governor general was similar to a ceremonial presidency of a republic. De Valera opposed the office in the late 1920s on three main grounds: it was too costly, at about £25,000 per annum; it was absolutely useless and filled by a rubber stamp; but the fundamental reason for his hostility was that it 'was regarded by the majority of our people as a symbol of our defeat and as a badge of our slavery'.[57] While ultimately seeking its abolition, de Valera moved with stealth, firstly stripping it of its status and prestige. In November 1933, the twentieth amendment to the constitution transferred from the governor general to the Executive Council the power of appropriation under Article 37; and the twenty-first amendment foreclosed the governor general's powers of withholding assent to bills, or reserving them to London pending the royal assent under Article 41. These powers had in fact been purely formal and they were only bringing constitutional forms into accord with reality. However, Thomas suspected that 'the real significance of the Bills ... is to make the King's Representative, so far as possible, a nonentity and to assimilate the form of Government, little by little, to a Republic'.[58] Insult was added to injury in the process as King George's private secretary, Lord Wigram, complained: 'The whole position now is ridiculous and derogatory to the King's dignity'.[59]

The king's discomfort notwithstanding, the result still fell short of de Valera's resolve to remove the 'taint', no matter how symbolic, of the crown. The real objective was of course the abolition of the office altogether. To this end, in May 1935 de Valera instructed John Hearne, legal adviser at external affairs, to draft heads of a constitution providing *inter alia* a formula recognising the king as a constitutional officer of the state in international relations, yet facilitating a popularly elected head of state executing all functions previously undertaken by the governor general.[60] He was therefore willing to leave the governor general in place, bereft of powers, until he was ready to proceed along these lines.

However, unforeseen events upset the timing of this goal.[61] James McNeill, the sitting governor general, was gradually frozen out of Irish public life. He was excluded from exercising any official role at the Eucharistic Congress in June 1932 – the greatest public occasion since the establishment of the state – and any of its major functions. The snub was worsened by the obvious use of the congress to make political capital for the government. McNeill demanded an apology, which was refused, and the published correspondence with de Valera outlined their differences.[62] De Valera, already in a trade war with Britain and perhaps slightly regretful of the incident, did not immediately dismiss McNeill, a move necessitating the distasteful invocation of king's warrant. However, on 9 September 1932 de Valera advised the king to remove McNeill from the office. George V complied having sought a fuller explanation of the reasons for terminating the appointment that would ordinarily expire in February 1933.

De Valera's intention was to have Chief Justice Hugh Kennedy undertake the functions of governor general *pro temp*. Kennedy, a firm believer in the separation of powers between the judicial and executive, declined, suggesting instead that the governor general should be stripped of virtually all his powers and merely be an agent for the king giving assent to bills. The main objection to the office, he pointed out, was the quasi-royal nature and the 'sham court' surrounding it. Since the governor general's role had been circumscribed by the Statute of Westminster, Kennedy suggested that he should be renamed attorney of the king.[63] De Valera then appointed one of his loyal supporters, Dónal Ó Buachalla, as governor general. As Kennedy suggested, Ó Buachalla resided in an ordinary dwelling house, not the sumptuous vice-regal lodge, and continued his normal duties. He dissolved and summoned the oireachtas (parliament), sent money bills, signified the king's assent to bills, appointed the president of the Executive Council, ministers of state, judges and members of the special courts under Article 2A. He also acted on behalf of the king in various diplomatic documents such as letters of credence and letters of recall, but the quasi-royal role and the 'sham court' disappeared.

Despite these measures, de Valera's problems worsened by the end of 1933. Economically, his government inherited an economy already feeling some adverse effects of the Great Depression. Emigration could no longer be relied upon to absorb the surplus of people over jobs. As the depression deepened in the USA emigration from Ireland virtually ceased – only 256 went in 1932. In Britain the national government elected in August 1931 was committed to a policy of protection in agriculture, which boded ill for Irish cattle producers. Fianna Fáil assumed power when circumstances could be said to have made a virtue of necessity. *Round Table* presented a bleak picture of the economic situation in June 1933, noting that in the last twelve months the number of people receiving poor law relief had risen by one third. Bank profits were down by 14 per cent, trade figures went down from £86m to £64m, but Lemass claimed a hundred new factories and a decrease in employment. Labour, the journal claimed, already informed de Valera that their support was conditional on implementation of their programme, involving large expenditures on unemployment grants, old age pensions, housing and social legislation.[64]

There were further difficulties for de Valera that could not be resolved through parliamentary bargaining. Sinn Féin stated immediately after the election that de Valera 'and the other prospective Ministers of His Majesty George V, may remove any oaths and test as they wish, but they will never induce Republican Ireland to accept the shameful position of surrender and subservience represented by membership of the Free State Parliament, which is not Dáil Éireann'.[65] De Valera's most immediate difficulty was the ever-growing militancy of the IRA. But acting vigorously against it would create its own problems. As Bowyer Bell outlines, de Valera had to

> tread warily between the boundless expectations of his own supporters and the sullen toleration of his political opponents, the Church, and, perhaps the professional institutions of state – after all the army ... were largely the same army he fought against only a decade before. While recognising de Valera's difficulties, the average IRA Volunteer had somehow expected a more impressive change of direction in government.[66]

However, the increased violence and activities of the organisation during 1933–4 caused a shift in the government's attitude towards them. The *Round Table* prediction that he would be a Green Kerensky proved unfounded. From early 1935 the organisation 'played a very subdued role',[67] but subsequently the IRA came into sharper focus. In May 1935 de Valera expressed his disappointment to the Dáil at the failure of the IRA to accept the principle of peaceful government by majority rule. Two ministers had been attacked by hooligan elements when participating in St Patrick's day celebrations in Dublin and Tralee just months earlier. On the night of 23 March two gardaí were shot and wounded in Dublin's Grafton Street by a group of young men on bicycles. The same evening another garda was attacked a short distance away on Burgh Quay. Earlier in February a gang disguised as gardaí murdered the son of a land agent in Edgeworthstown, County Longford. In March 1936 a member of the Somerville family was shot in Castletownshend, County Cork, for providing local young men who wished to join the royal navy with references.

Yet countering this upsurge in violence proved problematic for de Valera. So-called political murders continued to be a feature of Irish life. Nevertheless, the government acted. Military tribunals were revived and IRA members were once again in prison. Guards were placed at key installations and government ministers protected. *An Phoblacht* was suppressed although the IRA was not proclaimed. The IRA council castigated the Fianna Fáil leadership, accusing them of reverting to 'the policy of wholesale arrest of republicans' and of using Cosgrave's Coercion Act with the same intensity. And because the army had been deployed in alleviating Dubliners' transport difficulties during escalating rail and tram strikes in early 1935, the government was accused of leading the struggle against the workers.

The Catholic hierarchy became increasingly trenchant in their public criticisms. The Catholic bishop of Waterford, Dr Kinnane, held that it was a mortal sin for Catholics to be involved in that sinful and irreligious society – the IRA – which aspired to a republic on the socialist, Russian model.[68] The hierarchy's lenten pastoral in 1935 duly prohibited IRA membership. In April, it became clear that the split between the IRA and Fianna Fáil was irreconcilable. De Valera met with Seán Russell, quarter-master general of the IRA, who promised cooperation if after five years de Valera declared a republic. De Valera refused, stating 'you want it both ways'.[69] McMahon noted that the Russell meeting 'signalled the final break with the IRA'. Like Fine Gael with the Blueshirts, Fianna Fáil sloughed off its IRA skin – 'though the wounds were to suppurate slowly in the years to come … the IRA were to prove all but moribund, but they proved a singularly troublesome corpse to inter'.[70] De Valera's crackdown on the IRA slowly eroded its power, as did the programme of legislation and cabinet decrees. Several hundred men were, for example, lost to the IRA with the creation of the 'Broy Harriers', a new volunteer militia force. Bills were passed compensating republican supporters for property losses during the Civil War. Gradually, Fianna Fáil outflanked the IRA by chipping away imperial symbols and providing lucrative posts for its members. These manoeuvres drew

> the howls from the IRA-Left that de Valera was selling out to capitalism or the bitter complaints of the IRA-Right that he was not on the high road to the Republic sounded shrill and querulous to the men who read every day in the *Irish Press* of 'The Chief's' coups in the Economic War, of the dismantling of the Treaty-State, of the plain, blunt benefits of jobs and pensions and the promise of more to the loyal.[71]

The second extra-parliamentary threat to de Valera also arose shortly after he attained power, emerging in the form of the Blueshirts. On 1 May 1932, Cosgrave was prevented from speaking in Cork by IRA intimidation. Further meetings that month in Cork and Kerry were also disrupted and violence and intimidation escalated. Peadar O'Donnell, leader of Saor Éire, a radical socialist wing of the IRA, earlier stated he was 'glad the murderous government was put out of power, but these must be put finally out of public life, they must never be allowed to come on a public platform'.[72] Commenting on the violence, *Round Table*'s Horgan noted:

> We seem indeed to be rapidly moving towards that state of dual power which Trotsky, in his history of the Russian Revolution, rightly describes as a distinct condition of social crisis and a precursor of civil war. It is not to be wondered at that the *Poblacht* openly boasts that 'Cosgrave's rule is as dead as the Tsar's and Kerensky is in power.'[73]

In response to the intimidation, Dr T. F. O'Higgins, Cumann na nGaedheal TD and brother of the assassinated Minister for Justice Kevin, assumed leadership of the Army Comrades Association (ACA) in August 1932.[74] Established to protect Cumann na nGaedheal members from further attack, the trademark 'Blueshirt' uniform soon appeared, followed shortly by the sinister salute. O'Higgins committed the association to oppose communism, to protect free speech and support 'the lawfully constituted Government of the state'.[75] Despite fascist symbols, most members joined because of the IRA threat in the face of government inertia, apparent sympathy or sheer tolerance of republican activity. Under O'Higgins the association was still an anti-IRA organisation that had, he believed, since its inception saved 'property, free speech and democracy'.[76]

Its horizons widened, however, under his successor, General Eoin O'Duffy. Dismissed as garda commissioner on 22 February 1933, he became leader of the ACA by invitation on 20 July, when the organisation was renamed the National Guard.[77] His speeches expressed fascist sentiment, if in embryonic form:

> We put our trust in the rising generation of Youth. We have got to organise them but, please God, we will lead them to victory for an independent Ireland free from sea to shining sea when the time is ripe …
>
> The Blueshirt is like a flag, it is not a mere piece of cloth, it is our emblem our ideal which may be summed up in three words – service, discipline, country.[78]

O'Duffy also committed the state to law and order: 'The National Guard recognises the courts, the police, the civil service and the army as the fundamental institutions of the state. While I am in charge I will ensure that the organisation will keep within the law.'[79] Re-unification was its main aim; its constitution envisaged a corporate society in which industrial relations would be harmonised and farmers organised on a statutory basis. It proposed vocational instead of territorial representation in the Dáil – O'Duffy visualised 'no politicians and no party politics in the country'.[80] It opposed alien and untrue influence in national affairs and committed to uphold Christian influences – it was therefore *de facto* anti-semitic and could be described as 'clerico-fascist'.[81] The National Guard had all the elements – uniforms, youth and enthusiasm, anti-communism and a country in turmoil and impatience with party politics – to emerge as a fully-fledged fascist movement. However, two factors inhibited its growth: its amalgamation into the United Ireland Party and de Valera's crackdown.

Shortly after becoming leader, O'Duffy announced the revival of the annual commemoration of three Cumann na nGaedheal ministers, Arthur Griffith, Michael Collins and Kevin O'Higgins, planned for 13 August 1933. Amid rumours of a coup circulating, and heightening tension in the lead up to the parade, the government banned the march and activated the suspended Article 2A, re-activating the military tribunal. O'Duffy insisted it was nothing more than a parade but nevertheless cancelled it. The government subsequently banned the organisation, closed its offices and established military tribunals. Such action seemed to many in sharp contrast to de Valera's toleration of the IRA, and the *Irish Times* suggested his government was 'cynically inconsistent … either it is afraid to give equal status to the National Guard and the Irish Republican Army or its proclamation of the National Guard is an act of political revenge'.[82]

Banning the Blueshirts merely consolidated opposition to Fianna Fáil and on 8 September the Blueshirt treaty forces merged into the United Ireland Party, or Fine Gael, with O'Duffy at its head and Cosgrave parliamentary leader. Horgan suggested the amalgamation 'saved the various opposition parties from individual destruction' and drove de Valera to a closer alliance with Labour.[83] However, the IRA also became invigorated by these new developments: 'Nothing could have done more to unite the IRA and give it a sense of mission than the amalgamation of the hated Treatyites with a movement permeated with the smell of fascism and clothed in the Blueshirts of the European right.'[84] The result was numerous violent clashes between the two forces; it was a year dominated by the 'politics of hatred'.[85]

Fine Gael comprised several contradictory elements that seemingly had only one common purpose: opposition to Fianna Fáil. Cosgrave and the centre wing of the party led by Frank MacDermott tolerated the Blueshirt symbols and organisation as necessary because of IRA intimidation, and accepted corporate elements in the party programme as a concession to fashionable Catholic social doctrine.[86] But O'Duffy later blamed this wing of the party for the failure of corporatism: 'It was like putting new wine into old bottles to entrust the corporate state to them and very annoying it proved to the bottles and dangerous to the wine.'[87] Fine Gael's manifesto looked fascist although, as Bowyer Bell points out, 'the detailed policy statement on November 11 … sounded more like Cumann na nGaedheal than Mussolini'.[88] It proposed the establishment of agricultural and industrial corporations with statutory powers; the absorption of the able-bodied unemployed in a reconstruction corps for carrying out public works on a national scale; the unconditional hostility of the party to nationalism; the abolition of class consciousness and of narrow and intolerant conceptions of patriotism; and the creation of a national spirit based on cordial and constructive cooperation between all sections of the community. *Round Table* noted 'the proposal to abolish proportional representation and the suggestion that "disciplined service" is to be inculcated through the Blueshirt organisation would seem to suggest that the new organisation intends to take a fascist direction'.[89] James Hogan, the young professor of history in Cork and leading Fine Gael intellectual, and Michael Tierney, who dominated the policy committee that drafted the 1933 constitution of Fine Gael, were convinced corporatists. As John Regan points out, Tierney and Hogan in their own minds 'were not so much drawing up the constitution for a political party as drafting a blueprint for the reorganisation of Irish society'.[90] Both attempted to direct Fine Gael to their view that democracy could not meet the crisis – but dictatorship was rejected: Catholic corporatist organisation was superior, and the state should be diminished. Hogan wanted 'a practical alternative which is based on the principles of Christianity ... in the sense that it is a civil equivalent of a Christian theology'.[91] The corporatist philosophy of vocationalism rapidly became an indispensable element in the Fine Gael assault on de Valera's economic policy.

The party's new newspaper, *United Ireland*, began to stress familiar words of the European right: authority, efficiency, order and discipline, while criticising communism, liberalism and individualism. However, by 1934, the party began to disintegrate. Cosgrave and the more experienced members became alarmed at O'Duffy's speeches and increased militarism. The cleavage between the Blueshirts and their political wing came to a head after the first annual Blueshirt congress on 19 August 1934. It passed a resolution calling on the farmers to withhold their annuities from the government, itself an affront to the cherished Fine Gael values of law and order. Worse still, O'Duffy indicated his readiness to take up arms against Britain – sentiments Fine Gael undoubtedly felt more appropriate to the IRA. Internal relations became increasingly strained. Professor Hogan resigned from the party on 30 August, deprecating O'Duffy's annuities stance and attempt to organise the Blueshirts in the north. Hogan stated that his resignation was the strongest possible personal protest he could make against the destructive leadership of O'Duffy, who controversially resigned on 22 September.[92] *Round Table* surmised that

> The gallant General had ... not only no political experience ... but little discretion ... He is one of those people, possessing boundless energy but ill directed enthusiasm, who so often come to the top in a revolutionary struggle, but who are unable to adjust themselves

to the more prosaic requirements of ordinary political life.

... Both the professional politicians and the General had been persuaded by clever university professors among their advisers to adopt in haste a rather amphorous political programme which aimed eventually at creating here a corporative State on Italian lines, the implications of which were neither fully considered nor completely understood ... a policy of this nature ... was not likely to appeal to our easy-going people, whose political movements have always proceeded on the principle of *solvitur ambulando* ... All this leaves the Opposition in a pretty hopeless position. Mr Cosgrave remains Parliamentary Leader, but has lost prestige ... Mr de Valera remains the undisputed master of the political scene ...[93]

Cosgrave emerged at the head of Fine Gael and corporate doctrines were dropped from the party's programme. Fine Gael appointed Edmund Cronin as leader of the Blueshirts in response to O'Duffy's nebulous resignation, a move contested by the latter, resulting in two competing movements each losing membership in the ensuing internecine struggle. The government crackdown on the IRA also led to its demise; Fine Gael members felt that the Blueshirts were no longer necessary. In October 1936, Fine Gael voted to eliminate the autonomous executive of the Blueshirts and replace it with a standing committee of the Fine Gael executive. This decision 'marked the end – the very definite end – of the Blueshirt movement'.[94] The implications of the O'Duffy–Fine Gael debacle were aptly summed up in *Round Table*: 'For the present Mr de Valera remains the undisputed master of the political scene, and his opponents cannot hope to make any impression on him by the method of head on collision, which seems to be their only idea of political tactics.'[95] Another consequence was that the prospect of vocationalism exerting a major impact on Irish politics faded as it was identified with O'Duffy's tenure as leader.[96] It should be noted, however, that the corporate concept did not begin or end with O'Duffy. It was to influence de Valera in framing his constitution. In the Ireland of the mid 1930s, corporatism, diluted by Catholic social thought and known as vocationalism, had a fashionable following among members of the clergy and laity.

Before 1931, corporatism made little impact on Irish politics despite the pervasive Catholic ethos. In contrast, the philosophy of vocationalism was influential on continental Europe. Its principal concepts were enshrined in numerous papal encyclicals. Supporters revered a bygone age when medieval guilds dominated a social system that supposedly secured peace, stability and justice.[97] The publication of *Quadragesimo Anno* in 1931 did, however, increase interest in Ireland. This encyclical provided the crucial impetus for the permeation of vocationalist thought into the Irish political establishment. Furthermore, following the immensely successful Eucharistic Congress the government was bound – if not obliged – to note any social propositions emanating from the Vatican. During this period of triumphant Catholic celebration, vocationalism became a serious political force in Ireland. *Quadragesimo Anno* 'provided social Catholicism with a document of vital importance that was to serve as the ideological basis for a programme of socio-economic reconstruction'.[98] Vocationalism and vocationalists received increasing publicity in the national broadsheets, and especially from Catholic religious publications, in particular *The Standard.*

The influence of the clergy in promoting the corporatist ideal in Ireland was crucial. Chief among these promoters was Fr Edward J. Coyne, who later contributed to the drafting of the constitution and largely wrote the massive 1943 report on vocationalism in Ireland. Coyne's deep mistrust of enlightenment philosophy and its attendant secularisation of society was one of the chief motivations behind his involvement in the vocationalist lobby. His rejection of post-Reformation philosophy and the parallel development of western parliamentary democracy characterised the outlook of the Irish vocationalist movement. More than anything else, the vocationalist mentality struggled to overcome this foreign influence, which threatened the intrinsic nature of Irish Catholicism. Coyne believed that Ireland was in dire need of change because Irish society owed 'little or nothing to distinctively Irish thought and not very much to distinctively catholic thought'. But most Irish Catholics were unaware of their erroneous ways. He felt that the economic and political aspects of Irish national life were not just a legacy of English rule but had developed also under 'the false principles of European philosophy'.[99]

Therefore, in terms of Irish corporatism or vocationalism, the national was elevated above the international, with Catholicism representing the core value of the movement. Another integral feature of Irish vocationalism was the promotion of rural living over urban life. Because urbanisation was allegedly linked with individualism and decadence, vocationalism exalted the rural idyll, a phenomenon which later commentators deemed 'rural fundamentalism'. The vocational ideal favoured the landed labourer in the countryside or small town over the industrial worker. Moderate proponents of vocationalism campaigned for reform in Irish politics. To depoliticise the movement or at least remove it from the clutches of any single political party, vocationalists called for independent vocational councils representing diverse interest groups such as education, agriculture and trade unionism. Their principal function would be to recommend policies, reform existing legislation and formulate alternative approaches along Catholic social guidelines. De Valera was clearly not indifferent to certain elements of the vocational ideal. He told the 1936 Fianna Fáil árd-fheis that he:

> ... would like personally to see such an [vocationalist] organisation developed, but I would like to see it developed voluntarily – I don't believe in State imposed organisations of that kind. I believe they only last for a while. The regime may support them with its

power, but once the regime breaks they break. There is nothing permanent about them, and they are not natural. I hope, therefore, to see developed gradually here a functional organisation of our society by voluntary action.[100]

But de Valera sensed the potential for vocational councils to usurp privileges and authority that were the preserve of the executive. Thus he shied away from granting vocational councils statutory rights, merely approving of voluntary bodies, active at local level, acting as a support network. But de Valera need not have worried, as an increasingly lukewarm response from the Irish bishops to proposals for a vocational council in education eased the pressure. Following representations from educationalists such as University College Cork's registrar, Professor Alfred O'Rahilly, the hierarchy feared such a concession would undermine their considerable influence over education. Yet, in public, the hierarchy unreservedly eulogised *Quadragesimo Anno*: in practice, they either opposed or failed to support.

However, as seen already, O'Duffy's interpretation of vocationalism did not correspond with that of its main proponents in the Catholic clergy and laity. O'Duffy professed his support for a vocational state modelled on Mussolini's Italy. His adherence to this example and the fascist paraphernalia accompanying his political bid to oust de Valera only strengthened Fianna Fáil and simultaneously distanced would-be moderate supporters of vocationalism. As a result, the hierarchy distanced itself from O'Duffy's militant brand of corporatism as support for the vocationalist campaign ebbed away in favour of de Valera's moderate politics. O'Duffy's failure to distinguish between the fascism of the corporate state in Italy and the societal corporatism preached by the Roman Catholic Church contributed substantially to public apathy towards vocationalism.

De Valera's constitutional campaign was further strengthened in April 1935 by the judgement of the judicial committee of the Privy Council – delivered on 5 June – in the case of *Moore et al versus the Attorney General*. Ironically, it was a case designed to establish whether the Irish legislation abolishing appeals was void. The judgement effectively declared the repugnancy clause defunct: the oireachtas now was free to pass legislation repugnant to imperial legislation. De Valera did not hesitate in taking the initiative and in April two bills were passed – the Citizenship Act and the Aliens Act – edging him closer to his aim of external association.[101] These acts not only defined Irish nationality and provided for reciprocal citizenship between the Free State and other countries, but defined 'alien' as anyone not a citizen of the Free State, including British citizens.

There was legislation in other areas also, though Anglo-Irish relations absorbed de Valera during this period. Economic considerations were not high on his agenda: he once told the Dáil that he was prepared to see the extinction of the cattle industry if necessary, and he was fond of referring to the need to make the people face up to economic hardship for the national good.[102] Although Fianna Fáil TDs were 'outraged by the sight of children with bare feet in winter living in tenements', their radical social policies were hindered somewhat by economic realities. Nonetheless, there was some reforming legislation by Fianna Fáil governments in the 1930s, including The Unemployment Assistance Act, 1933, which widened eligibility for unemployment benefits. The National Health Insurance Act, 1933, ensured that wider categories were entitled to receive sickness benefit. In 1935 the Fianna Fáil government enacted The Widows' and Orphans' Pension Act, which made provisions for payments to dependants of workers irrespective of whether the deceased had been a contributor under the Social Welfare Acts.

Government sponsored bodies mushroomed in this period, including in 1933 Comhlucht Siúicre Éireann and The Industrial Credit Company. The Turf Development Board (later Bord na Móna) and Ceimicí Teoranta followed in 1934, and Aer Lingus was established in 1936. The legislative record of the Fianna Fáil government was impressive. In addition to social welfare reforms, housing legislation was amended to improve financial assistance to local authorities' building programmes, and ensure the supply of building material at reasonable prices. The Labourers' Act, 1936 provided legislation whereby tenants of labourers' cottages were enabled to buy out their houses. There was a marked increase in the number of local authority houses constructed in the Free State in the 1930s, and an impressive increase in the number of houses built 'under state-aided schemes' in the same period, as indicated in table below.

TABLE 1: NUMBER OF HOUSES BUILT UNDER STATE-AIDED SCHEMES, 1931–7

Year	1931–32	1932–33	1933–34	1934–35	1935–36	1936–37
Local Authority	1,732	1,117	3,552	6,734	6,245	6,094
Private-Public	3,489	1,004	3,138	6,519	8,039	8,270
Total Houses Built	5,221	2,181	6,960	13,253	14,284	14,364

Source: Statistical Abstract of Ireland 1938. Section V. p. 108

The party's conservatism in sociosexual matters manifested itself in the Criminal Law Amendment Act, 1935, designed to 'make further and better provision for the protection of young girls and the suppression of brothels and prostitution'. Significantly, this act also made it unlawful 'for any person to sell, or expose, offer, advertise, or keep for sale or to import or attempt to import into Saorstát Éireann for sale, any contraceptive'.[103] The oireachtas debates on this bill are an interesting illustration of contemporary mainstream opinion on the questions of sexual morality. Fianna Fáil also manifested its policy towards religion in a more direct way. In June 1932 the fifteenth centenary of the arrival of St Patrick to Ireland was celebrated by the Eucharistic Congress. Dublin city was awash with flags and thronged with crowds. Pius XI sent his papal legate, Cardinal Lorenzo Lauri, to Ireland. De Valera, together with members of his Executive Council, held a reception in Dublin Castle at which he formally addressed Cardinal Lauri in Irish and in Latin. Lauri was told of the steadfast faith of the Irish people. The rhetoric of de Valera suggested that the legacy of St Patrick was exclusively Roman Catholic: 'Who can fail on this day to recall to mind the utterances of our apostle, recorded of old in the *Book of Armagh*: 'Even as you are children of Christ, be you also children of Rome.' The congress confirmed and celebrated the powerful Roman Catholic ethos that now personified the Irish state.

The abdication crisis in December 1936 that is examined in detail in Chapter 4 gave de Valera the opportunity to make his external relations concept even more explicit. The crisis only precipitated what had already been in train, for it had been known for some time that de Valera was at work on a new constitution. Edward VIII having removed himself from the throne before de Valera had the opportunity of removing him from the constitution, de Valera faced the situation with the introduction of two new bills.

The first removed all reference to the king and the governor general from the law of the Irish Free State. De Valera stated that the 'effect of the Bill was to eliminate the King from all Articles in the Constitution … in the case of the Governor General the appointment and executive functions are being deleted'. One of the deleted references was Article 60, which required the governor general to be appointed 'in like manner as the Governor-General of Canada'.[104] The External Relations Bill allotted the crown a defined place with limited functions in the external field. Diplomatic and consular representatives were to be appointed and every international agreement to be concluded on the authority of the Executive Council. Thus the act acknowledged the role of the crown in the commonwealth without explicit or implicit recognition of Irish allegiance; relations with the crown and the commonwealth had been taken out of the constitution and had become matters of external policy for the government of the day.

In January 1937 de Valera placed what had been done in perspective. He told Sir Henry Battersby, the permanent under-secretary at the Dominions

Office, that he regarded the recent legislation as 'the end of the story'.[105] By this he meant the end of the status story. The 1921 settlement had been undone.

The fact that de Valera felt it still necessary to proceed with the drafting and enactment of an entirely new constitution after the abdication crisis was significant. Historians might ponder why de Valera felt the need to go any further than the Executive Authority (External Relations) Act of 1936, which after all achieved his main policy goal of external association, involving an affirmation of Irish sovereignty and the voluntary as distinct from obligatory association of the Free State with the British commonwealth. De Valera might easily have called matters to a halt having reached this stage by Christmas 1936. His expressed determination to continue with the work on the new constitution is illustrative of his nationalistic equation of legitimacy with origin. The Saorstát constitution had been stripped of all symbols and procedures identified by de Valera as repugnant to Irish nationalist aspirations. Yet it retained one fundamental flaw that convinced de Valera to replace it *in toto*. He 'had almost reached the limits of reasonable amendment of the existing Constitution'[106] and 'No matter how republican the Free State Constitution was made by amendment, it could never escape its basis in British law'.[107] Its origins lay in the Treaty of 1921 and the repeated British threats of war 'immediate and terrible' if the Irish did not accept both the articles of agreement and the constitution drawn up under the auspices of the then secretary of state for the dominions, Winston Spencer Churchill. Having been conceived under duress and enacted through a series of threats, de Valera considered the Free State constitution an imposition rather than a document worthy of a free and proud people. Consequently, even though by 1936 he had arguably succeeded in destroying the dominion settlement of 1921, complete with its oath of allegiance to the crown, its facility for appeals to the Privy Council in London and its office of governor general, he still remained adamant that if the Irish people wanted a truly legitimate basic law then it would have to come ultimately from themselves. His concern at this stage was as much with the circumstances in which a constitution was drafted and enacted as it was with its basic contents. The Constitution (Amendment No. 27) Act and the Executive Authority (External Relations) Act of 1936 left the question as to the head of state unanswered. Similarly they contained sentiments which jarred with a constitution that had its origin in a British act of parliament and a treaty that de Valera never recognised as legitimate.

A constitutional amendment abolished the Senate in May 1936. In the course of a long Dáil debate at the end of which the motion to abolish the Senate was passed, de Valera stated that the second chamber, as at present constituted, appeared to him to be an absolute menace to the country. It had hampered the government from taking measures they considered necessary to maintenance of order: accordingly he concluded it had to be abolished. He then announced that he hoped that in the autumn they would have 'a measure here outlining a new Constitution. Whether that Constitution is to be based on the principle of a Single Chamber or two will depend upon whether it is possible to devise a Second Chamber which can be of value and not a danger.' He claimed that the electorate knew of his plans to abolish the Senate before the last election and consequently that the electoral victory of Fianna Fáil was an endorsement of that policy.[108] He ended the debate by calling for all interested parties to get involved in the drafting of the new constitution: 'I assure everybody, both here and those outside who may read the report of this debate, that the one desire of the Government is to get for our State a Constitution which will deserve respect and that will get respect. We want the help of everybody who has views on the matter.'[109] De Valera had formed a constitutional committee in 1934, the function and findings of which are discussed in the next chapter.

On Friday 29 May 1936, in an elegiac speech on the last day the Seanad met, the cathaoirleach gracefully bowed to the inevitable:

> We have finished our labours, and nothing remains to be done but to ring down the curtain … On the 11th December, nearly 14 years ago, we met here in bleak December. We met in darkness. We emerge in light, conscious that we did our duty, and conscious that, in our every act, we tried to build and strengthen this infant State … So far as God gave us light we fulfilled our duty, and we leave the stage conscious of our own rectitude. I thank you all, and I declare the Seanad adjourned *sine die*.[110]

Theoretically, the abolition of the Senate meant that the last line of defence against a government with a simple majority abolishing any clause in the 1922 constitution was removed. The impulse to abolish the Senate was the catalyst that set in train the processes that led ultimately to the constitutional settlement of 1937. As Brian Farrell notes, de Valera could have set up a dictatorship perfectly legally such was the lack of constitutional safeguards left after the abolition of the Senate.[111] Instead, he created a new constitution.

CHAPTER 2

The Constitutional Options, 1934–1936

The previous chapter has provided the general historical and political context in which de Valera and his government worked, at the less than ideal time politically, when the perhaps surprising decision was taken to embark upon the writing of an entirely new constitution. Quite at what point de Valera's personal deep dissatisfaction crystallised into a decision to jettison the 1922 constitution is not clear. There is simply no archival material to hand which points to a precise date on which the decision was taken to write a new constitution. Neither is it very clear whether or not de Valera sought the advice of the Executive Council in helping him reach such a decision. The role played by his cabinet colleagues, even those who were very close to him politically, in the making of such a singularly important decision is less than transparent. What follows below is a systematic attempt – based on extensive use of all relevant archives – to provide a close narrative account of the drafting of *Bunreacht na hÉireann*. The constitution of 1922 was vulnerable to change as it could be altered by the passing of ordinary legislation in the Dáil. In the course of the debate on the Constitution (Amendment No. 24) Bill – Report on 17 May 1934, the Fine Gael deputy and former Attorney General, John A. Costello, moved an amendment requiring that articles in the existing constitution which contained democratic safeguards should be immune from amendment by ordinary legislation.[1] The intervention took place in the context of a heated debate on the highly controversial bill to abolish the Senate. In the course of a long speech, Costello declared it was obvious:

> … that if these fundamental rights are to be continued in any way that will give any safeguard to the citizens there must be some check, after the passing of this Bill abolishing the Seanad, against depriving the citizens of this State of these fundamental rights by the passage of a mere Act of the Oireachtas which could be done in the course of a few hours in the Dáil.[2]

He warned that under the system of unicameral legislation which would obtain, were the Bill to become law and if Article 50 were allowed to stand as it was at the moment, 'there will be no effective guarantee for the Constitutional rights, which, for the moment, are set forth in the Constitution.'[3] In his reply, de Valera distinguished between two types of articles – those that were in the constitution because they were forced on the country by 'threat of war and outside pressure' and those that might be in the constitution of any democratic state. He did not accept Costello's amendment but proposed:

> … to have carefully examined these fundamental Articles dealing with the democratic foundations of the State. I do not mind if these are fixed so that they cannot be changed by ordinary legislation without some such provision as a Referendum to the people, but I do not want that done by way of an amendment.[4]

Later in the debate de Valera stated:

> This Constitution was framed originally under exceptional circumstances. There were certain Articles in the Constitution which were forced upon the people of this country. There are certain Articles which represent democratic ideals. Those that represent these ideals, in so far as a thorough examination by people who have had experience of administration goes, are consistent with practical government. These Articles ought, with all possible speed, be examined, and be made as lasting as it is possible for anything to be made lasting, in a Constitutional way, without the danger of a cast-iron Constitution which, as I said, is always a temptation to revolution.[5]

His proposal 'to have these fundamental Articles carefully examined' was realised by the setting up of a constitution committee.

The constitution committee was never intended to be a bipartisan body drawing membership from the opposition. Neither did de Valera intend that members of the Executive Council would play a daily role in the review process. In keeping with his philosophy of closed government, he hand-picked the following civil servants to work as a closely-knit group: Stephen Roche, secretary of the Department of Justice; Michael McDunphy, assistant secretary, Department of the President; John Hearne, legal adviser, Department of External Affairs; and Philip O'Donoghue, legal assistant to the Attorney General. All were noted for their legal and constitutional expertise and would be joined later in the process by other civil servants. As the above personalities play an important part in the process that moved from making certain specific recommendations to the drafting of a new constitution, it is important, yet difficult, to provide a detailed intellectual and professional biographical sketch of those involved.

John Hearne (1893–1969) was the person who played the most consistent and central part in the drafting process. He could with justification be called the 'author' of the new constitution. Born in Waterford, he was the son of Richard Hearne, one of Ireland's first boot manufacturers who also served as mayor of Waterford. Hearne, the future legal officer of the Department of External Affairs, attended Waterpark Christian Brothers School in Waterford City and later obtained a BA and an LLB the National University of Ireland in Dublin. He spent some years in St Patrick's College, Maynooth, training for the priesthood before leaving to study for the bar at King's Inns and barrister-at-law. Having been called to the bar in 1919, he served as assistant parliamentary draughtsman from 1923 to 1929, a position that would equip him well for his later work as drafter of the constitution. In 1926, he was technical adviser to the Irish delegation at the imperial conference in London. He also took part in subsequent conferences and was recognised as an expert on constitutional law. Hearne served as legal adviser to the Department of External Affairs from 1929 to 1939. He was a delegate to many international legal seminars in the 1930s including the International Labour Conference, the Hague Conference on International Law, the 1932 Disarmament Conference, as well as several sessions of the League of Nations.

When Éamon de Valera led Fianna Fáil to victory in the 1932 election, he became president of the Executive Council and was his own Minister for External Affairs. He soon recognised the calibre of Hearne, to whom he gave responsibility for the drafting of a number of bills of constitutional significance including the bill to abolish the oath of allegiance. Maurice Moynihan wrote that when Hearne produced drafts of bills he included notes regarding the constitutional implications of their introduction. His thesis, according to that authoritative source, was that 'he was pointing out the need for a new Constitution if these Bills were introduced'.[6] Hearne had the advantage of having both a solid legal education which equipped him to be a constitutional lawyer and a theological education from his time at Maynooth, which gave him a grounding in canon law. Hearne, it would appear, retained an interest in philosophy and theology throughout his life. He continued his practice of dating his personal correspondence liturgically (e.g., first Sunday of Advent), which pointed to a man for whom the spiritual life and the life of the Catholic Church was important. He was known to his contemporaries as a devout but independent-minded and scholarly Roman Catholic and a daily communicant.

His contemporaries varied in their opinions as to the extent of his contribution to the drafting of the 1937 constitution. C. S. (Todd) Andrews wrote that he had heard 'Dev' say that it was 'entirely the work of John Hearn (*sic*) and that his own contribution amounted only to dotting the "i's" and crossing the "t's".'[7] Maurice Moynihan took quite the opposite view however, and was unequivocal in ascribing the constitution to de Valera:

> [De Valera] conceived it. Hearne did the drafting and dotted the 'i's' and crossed the 't's'. De Valera was the main architect who inspired, dictated and supervised at every stage. Hearne was more his amanuensis than his architect ... They were a team in creating the Constitution.[8]

In his diary entry for 15 January 1935, Nicholas Mansergh recorded a visit to Hearne at the Ministry of External Affairs where he described him as being in 'his best form and widely discursive'. The impression given in this brief entry is of the writer's pleasure in his visit to an interesting man whose conversation was worth reporting. Hearne is described in a footnote as '"architect in chief" and draftsman of the Constitution of Ireland 1937'.[9] In later life Hearne was a distinguished diplomat who served in Ottawa and Washington until his retirement in the 1960s.

Philip O'Donoghue, a friend and contemporary of Hearne, was born in Macroom in 1896. He, too, came from a middle-class background, his father being the local dispensary doctor. He was educated in Castleknock College and afterwards went to University College Cork where he was awarded a first class honours degree in legal and political science. He attended King's Inns from 1917 to 1919 where he was a brilliant student and a noted orator and debater. He was the recipient of many prizes including the Fitzgibbon medal for legal practice in the 1917–18 session. He also won the O'Hagan prize for oratory in each of the two years he read for the bar.

While at King's Inns, he met and became a lifelong friend of John Hearne. They shared 'digs' during their student days and both men were called to the bar together in 1919. Philip O'Donoghue commenced his legal career on the Munster circuit in 1919. In 1922 his 'talent and integrity' were put to the service of the newly formed state when 'armed with his textbooks and a revolver' he was appointed district justice in Limerick. His ability was again recognised in 1929 when he was appointed legal assistant to the then Attorney General, John A Costello. He served twelve attorneys general until his retirement in 1959. In 1965 he was appointed to the European Commission of Human Rights and became judge of the Court of Human Rights in Strasbourg in 1971. He retired having brought 'his great qualities of justice and, the rarer gift, common sense to the international stage'.[10] As well as possessing a keen intellect, O'Donoghue was gifted with charm, courtesy and a sense of humour and was a man of 'rock-like religious faith'. His obituarist wrote of him in the *Irish Times*: 'He had the barrister's fondness for a good anecdote, but he never spoke ill of people or showed impatience at the failings of others.'[11]

Hearne and O'Donoghue remained in close contact throughout their lives, corresponding regularly when Hearne served in Ottawa and Washington. Their friendship only ended upon Hearne's death in 1969. In the words of O'Donoghue's son, Fr Patrick O'Donoghue (a Vincentian Father), his father 'greatly admired Hearne's ability to draft difficult legal concepts and constitutional relationships'. Although not immediate neighbours, they lived within easy walking distance of each other in what is now Dublin 6. Hearne lived in Temple Road and O'Donoghue in Merton Road and much of their discussions on the drafting of the constitution took place in walks around the district when the weather was good. Otherwise, they met in Hearne's house. The area in which both men lived, then as now a desirable leafy suburb, was popular with senior civil servants, which facilitated such unofficial meetings. Both Hearne and O'Donoghue were called to the inner bar in 1939 in recognition of their part in the drafting of the 1937 constitution.

Michael McDunphy, born in 1890, was educated in North Richmond Street Christian Brothers school, Dublin. A barrister, he entered the public service in August 1912 but was dismissed in 1918 for refusing to take the oath of allegiance imposed on civil servants at that time. Re-instated in 1922, he served as assistant secretary and, for two periods, secretary to the government. When the constitution came into operation in 1937, he was appointed secretary to the President and clerk to the council of state, the first holder of such an appointment. He retired in September 1954 at the age of sixty-three and was immediately appointed to the board of the Irish Assurance Company Ltd. He was director of the Bureau of Military History from its inception in 1946.[12]

Stephen Anselm Roche was born in County Kerry in the early 1890s and was educated in Blackrock College, Dublin. He distinguished himself as a schoolboy by winning medals for English at every grade, a feat never before accomplished. He obtained a BA and LLB from Trinity College Dublin, and entered the civil service in 1909. He served for a short time in Edinburgh and was then transferred to the estate duty office in Dublin. On the change of government, in 1922, he was one of a small group of administrative officers who were chosen to staff the newly created Ministry of Home Affairs under Kevin O'Higgins. He became successively assistant secretary and then secretary of the Department of Justice in 1934. In Justice, he was responsible not only for every single one of the courts of justice acts – with the exception of the act of 1924 – but also for the Juries Act, a lengthy and extremely intricate piece of legislation. During the Blueshirt and IRA campaigns of the post-1932 period, he worked behind the scenes on legislation to ensure the preservation of law and order. For years he played a major part in all the public services, notable in the preparation of legislation affecting the courts of justice and the administration of justice.[13]

Patrick Gregory Lynch, although not a member of the committee, deserves to be included because, as Attorney General during the relevant period, he played an important advisory role in the drafting of the new constitution.[14] Born on 10 February 1866 at Latoon House, Newmarket-on-Fergus, County Clare, he received his early education at Killaloe Diocesan College at Springfield, Ennis, and subsequently studied at the Royal University of Ireland. He was admitted to the bar in the trinity term of 1888 and was called to the inner bar on 30 June 1906. He was a member of the Munster circuit and was appointed senior crown prosecutor for Kerry in 1908, thereby benefiting as all local prosecution briefs were sent to that particular counsel. This role was clearly used against Lynch's later election attempt in 1917 in East Clare, but given that his electoral opponent was Éamon de Valera it can hardly be described as the most significant factor in his defeat. Paddy Lynch died on 8 December 1947 in Blarney. His wife, Rita, predeceased him, having died on 1 August 1943, and he is buried along with her in Deansgrange cemetery, Dun Laoghaire.

From descriptions of his life, Lynch's work as a lawyer was completely intertwined with his political views. He was elected and re-elected as a nationalist candidate in the Millstreet ward in 1890, 1893 and 1896. In January 1887 he was elected to the Ballyvaughan Poor Law Union and in 1890 was elected solicitor to the Kildysart and Ennis Poor Law Unions. He was one of a deputation of Clare nationalists who in January 1891 met with and invited Parnell to speak in Ennis, which he did in February 1891. One of the more formative events in Lynch's life must have been his involvement with his eldest brother in a case involving the East Clare by-election of 1893. In the general election of 1892, Willie Redmond had been defeated in Cork and subsequently campaigned for the seat in East Clare which he won in January 1893. Another candidate, J. R. Cox, petitioned on the grounds that the election was tainted with evidence of 'bribery, corruption, undue influence, personation, illegal expenditure, and the procuring of minors to vote'. Redmond's election was successfully defended by Paddy Lynch, who was briefed by his own brother, Thomas, as solicitor.

After the split in the Irish Parliamentary Party, Lynch sided with Parnell. He became the Irish Party candidate in the East Clare by-election of 1917. Éamon de Valera was his opponent and, as was expected, Paddy Lynch was defeated decisively.[15] He was later invited by de Valera to serve as Attorney General, which he did from 22 December 1936 to 1 March 1940. After his defeat in East Clare, Lynch remained active as a lawyer. During the War of Independence he defended many republicans and in many cases he did not receive payment. He was very active in relation to the activities of the military courts, which had been declared immune from control by the ordinary courts in the decision of *R v. Allen* because a state of war existed.[16]

Amongst the many legal trials in which Lynch was involved at that time, one of the most notable concerned the conviction of Erskine Childers in 1922 for possession of firearms. Whilst waiting for the case to go on, they were approached by a Free State army officer and informed that Childers had been executed. This experience, particularly the interface between the operation of military courts and the ordinary court structure in the criminal field, resonates with his later role as Attorney General during 1939–40.

Once the Irish Free State was established, Lynch became one of the government-appointed commissioners to hear circuit court appeals. He became a bencher to the King's Inn in 1925 and was a senator from 1934–6. He was appointed Attorney General in 1936 – the first appointee serving under the present 1937 constitution. Significantly, Paddy Lynch served as Attorney General during the constitutional transitional period in 1937. Article 59 of *Bunreacht na hÉireann* – one of thirteen transitional articles – provides that 'On the coming into operation of this Constitution, the person who is the Attorney General of Saorstát Éireann immediately before the coming into operation of this Constitution shall, without any appointment under Article 30 of this Constitution, become and be the Attorney General as if he had been appointed to that office under the said Article 30.'[17]

Given the calibre and professionalism of the men described above, de Valera's worries on taking power in 1932 that the civil service might be disloyal were groundless. Since the birth of the state, the civil service had been characterised by the highest standard of integrity, professionalism, devotion to the public good, and loyalty to the elected government; virtues epitomised by the members of the 1934 constitution committee.

The terms of reference of this committee were;

> … to examine the Constitution with a view to ascertaining what Articles should be regarded as fundamental, on the ground that they safeguard democratic rights, and to make recommendations as to steps which should be taken to secure that such Articles should not be capable of being altered by the ordinary process of legislation.[18]

De Valera's statement in the Dáil – that it was 'necessary to ensure, in cases of real urgency and real public emergency, that an executive would not be prevented from taking the action that might be considered necessary to safeguard public interests'[19] – was given 'special consideration' by the constitution committee.[20] Article 2A of the Free State constitution, which dealt with special powers in times of national emergency, was not originally there, but was inserted by the

Constitution (Amendment No. 17) Act of 1931 on 17 October of that year. The act allowed for an insertion 'immediately after Article 2' in the constitution, known as Article 2A. Its stated purpose was 'making better provision for safeguarding the rights of the people and containing provisions for meeting a prevalence of disorder'. The article was to come into force 'whenever the Executive Council was of the opinion that circumstances exist which render it expedient', and then only by special order of the Executive Council. Article 2A allowed for the setting up of a tribunal, consisting of five members of the defence forces not below the rank of commandant, which was removable at the will of the government. This tribunal had considerable powers, including the convicting and sentencing of those charged with named offences. Offences specified included any offence declared 'to be treason, or a felony or a misdemeanour' by the Treasonable Offence Act, 1925. Offences under the Juries (Protection) Act, 1929 and Firearms Act, 1925 were also included, as were offences stipulated in the Appendix to the Constitution (Amendment no. 17) Act. Those so convicted had no right of appeal. The tribunal had power to declare 'any book, issue of a periodical, pamphlet, poster, or other document to be seditious'.[21] Significantly, Article 2A held that:

> Article 3 and every subsequent Article of this Constitution shall be read and construed subject to the provisions of this Article, and in the case of any inconsistency between this Article and the said Article 3 or any subsequent Article, this Article shall prevail.[22]

The constitution committee went about its task speedily, holding ten meetings between 28 May 1934 and the production of its report on 3 July 1934.[23] The minutes of its second meeting on 29 May recorded that the constitution had been examined 'Article by Article', and that the committee concluded that its final report 'should take the form of a new Constitution'. It was not proposed that the committee should present a finished draft, 'that being considered a matter for the Parliamentary Draftsman'.[24] The minutes of the third meeting, however, make it clear that de Valera did not want the committee to draft a new constitution. Hearne and O'Donoghue were absent from this meeting but it was agreed, Mr Hearne's concurrence being secured by telephone, that it was now clear that what the President wanted was not a new constitution, but

> (a) a selection within the framework of the present constitution of those articles which should be regarded as fundamental;
> (b) a recommendation as to how these should be rendered immune from alteration by ordinary legislation.

The report is reproduced as Appendix 1. A summary table is below and commentary follows.

Table 2: Comparison of the 1934 Constitution Committee Recommendations with *Bunreacht na hÉireann, 1937*

Articles recommended for special immunity from change by 1934 Committee.	**Corresponding Articles in 1937 Constitution**
Article 6. The liberty of the person/habeas corpus. Article 7. The inviolability of the dwelling. Article 8. Freedom of conscience and religion. Article 9. The right of free expression, peaceable assembly and to form unions.	Article 40. Personal rights
Article 18. The privilege of members going to and from the Dáil. Article 19. The privilege of utterances and publications of members. Article 43. The oireachtas shall have no power to declare acts to be infringements of the law which were not so at the date of their commission.	Article 15 The National Parliament
Article 61. All revenues of the state should form one central fund.	Article 11 The state
Article 62 and 63. The comptroller and auditor- general.	Article 33 Comptroller and auditor general
Article 64. Judicial powers. Article 65. The powers of the high court. Article 66. The powers of the supreme court. Article 68. The removal and remuneration of the judiciary. Article 69. The independence of the judiciary. Article 70. The jurisdiction of military courts.	Articles 34–36 The courts
Articles RECOMMENDED for protection which required amendment to remove references to the British crown	
Article 24. **The oireachtas shall hold at least one session each year.**	
Article 28. **The rules of general election and the date of reassembly of the Dáil.**	

Article 41.	**The prevention of the executive from delaying a bill which had passed all stages of the parliamentary process.**
Article 46.	**The exclusive right of raising armed forces vested in the oireachtas.**
Article 50.	**War can only be declared by the oireachtas.**

Article 51 (amendments to the constitution) was left for Part II of the report which was to consider *how* to provide articles with immunity from change. However, in the event the committee was overtaken by events and did not submit the second part of its report.[25] Nonetheless, the committee's work was of considerable importance in that it identified the key elements of the constitution necessary for the preservation of democracy.

The committee noted difficulties with some of the articles: Article 9 (which outlined the rights to free expression and peaceful assembly without arms, the right to free association and to form unions), for instance, was felt to limit the powers of the government and police to control public meetings even if they caused public nuisance or danger. In 1934, legislation for just such a purpose was in abeyance because it was felt to be unconstitutional. The committee therefore recommended that additional powers to control meetings were needed. Article 49 stated that: 'Save in the case of actual invasion, the Irish Free State shall not be committed to active participation in any war without the assent of the Oireachtas.' The committee was anxious to remove the word 'active' as this had been included at the behest of the British in 1921; it held that as long as Britain – and therefore the king – was at war so also were the rest of the dominions. Article 65, which provided that the high court's judicial power should extend to the question of the validity of any law having regard to the provisions of the constitution, also gave concern. The committee observed that the 'principle that some court should have power to decide on the validity of laws having regard to the provisions of the Constitution is in our opinion fundamental'. The committee was unable to reach a unanimous verdict on whether this power should be vested in the supreme court alone, or in a special 'constitution' court appointed or designated for that purpose, e.g. a combination of the supreme and high court, or to continue the present system of high court with right of appeal to the supreme court. The committee was further unable to decide whether there should be a fixed time limit for the testing of the validity of any law by the courts.[26]

Stephen Roche was the most sceptical member of the committee about the value of written constitutions, believing that in 'a unitary State with full adult suffrage the idea of a written Constitution, not capable of alteration by a majority of the elected representatives of the people, is unsound in theory and dangerous in practice'. It was unsound because no parliament and no generation 'has any right to bind future parliaments or future generations'. The country, he believed, wanted 'a strong Executive' that would not be 'hampered and humiliated at every step by long arguments in the Courts, or by propaganda of a threatening and seditious type'. He continued:

> Further, I believe that the doctrines of 'judicial independence' and the 'separation of the functions' are being overdone and that the Courts have been given or have assumed a position in our civic life to which they are not entitled. There was a time in England when the Judges' job was to save the people from an irresponsible Executive: it may be necessary, in turn, for a responsible Executive to save the people from irresponsible judges.[27]

Michael McDunphy was alive to the danger of an unchecked government as he annotated the above with the comment: 'Strong executive could conceivably be a real danger instead of a blessing. Something more than "strength" is essential.' Roche proved to be the most consistent critic of the 'human rights' allowed under the 1937 constitution and firmly believed that document granted too much power to the courts and to criminals and subversives.

Roche saw the existing Article 2A as 'grotesque as an Article of the Constitution'. He recommended in its stead a two part strategy: (a) 'the declaration of an "emergency period", and (b) 'The measures which may be taken by the Executive once an "emergency period" has been declared'. On 28 June, the committee considered Roche's revised proposals for dealing with Article 2A, and agreed to discuss it the following day. Roche's proposals were largely accepted – or 'the principle was agreed on but it was decided to set it out in different form'. McDunphy was assigned this task and Stephen Roche's plans for schemes A and B were given substance. Scheme A recommended that special courts and the machinery drawn up around them should be retained. Hogan states that this suggestion was 'the clear outline of what eventually became Article 38.3 of the Constitution which permitted the establishment by law of special courts quite independently of any declaration of emergency under Article 28.3,3.' Scheme B proposed replacing Article 2A with a new article authorising the oireachtas to provide by ordinary legislation such powers as it might consider necessary. Powers included the suspension of any article of the constitution, to meet the requirements of any period during which the ordinary laws were not adequate for the preservation of public order. This could only be done after the Executive Council had requested that the president of the high court (or the next senior judge if he or she was not available) summon all the judges exercising criminal jurisdiction in the lower courts to meet and advise the Executive Council whether the ordinary laws were not adequate for the preservation of public order. The judges should have the power to decide whether or not there was a state of emergency. In the event of a state of emergency thus identified, the Executive Council should be enabled to activate the emergency powers legislation. The powers would lapse after six months unless the Executive Council went through the defined process of getting the judges to meet again.[28]

Despite Roche's energetic participation in the work of the committee, he was dropped from the small team which ultimately took responsibility for the drafting of the new constitution. However, he was in no sense marginalised and made important suggestions at the revision stage in April 1937.

In the event, de Valera did not act on the committee's report. Why? Perhaps the reason was contained at the end of the report, which noted that the articles selected by the committee included all those proposed for special treatment by opposition members John A. Costello, Patrick McGilligan and William T Cosgrave.[29]

No documentation has been found to determine the sequence of events between 3 July 1934, when the report was submitted, and mid 1935. De Valera appears to have paused for breath in his consideration of a new constitutional settlement and it was April 1935 before work resumed in earnest. The only other significant constitutional change that reached the statute book from the middle of 1934 until the December 1936 abdication crisis was the Constitution (Amendment No. 26) Act, 1935, enacted on 5 April of that year. It amended Article 3 on citizenship, dispensing with a provision restricting enjoyment of the privileges and liability to the obligations of citizenship to 'the limits of the jurisdiction of the Irish Free State (Saorstát Éireann)'. The amendment substituted the expression 'citizenship of' with 'citizenship in the Irish Free State'. This amendment was closely connected with the Irish Nationality and Citizenship Act, 1935, which was enacted on 10 April of that year.[30]

In the intervening period, de Valera reached the conclusion that it was better to jettison the old constitution and begin the necessary task of drafting a new one. In a more conventional administration, he might have been expected to give the task to the Attorney General's office. Instead, he chose a civil servant in whom he appears to have developed a great personal confidence. During 30 April and 2 May 1935, de Valera instructed John Hearne, the legal officer in the Department of External Affairs, to draw up the preliminary draft heads for a significant constitutional change. Hearne's Draft Heads are reproduced as Appendix 2.

Hearne wrote that his 'Preliminary Draft Heads' were 'based upon verbal instructions given by the President on Wednesday 30 April and Friday 2 May'.[31] In his explanatory memorandum submitted with the draft heads on 18 May, Hearne, reflecting the intentions of de Valera, discussed amending the 1922 constitution 'rather than an effort to construct – at this stage – a completely new Constitution'. This, according to Hearne, had the advantage of effecting 'a far reaching Constitutional reform within the framework, as far as possible, of the existing State rather than to establish a new state with a constitutional system fundamentally different from that now obtaining'.[32]

The state was to retain its title of Irish Free State, which was in line with de Valera's instruction to the 1934 committee. However, in the interim, de Valera appears to have changed his mind and wrote on the Hearne draft that 'The name of the state shall be Éire.'[33] Because of its importance to subsequent developments the Hearne document is reproduced in full as an appendix. Hearne's draft, as can be seen from the appendix, contained fifty-three articles. Articles 48–52 were concerned with fundamental rights (equality before law for all citizens, freedom of conscience, expression, assembly, association, inviolability of the person and the dwelling) and could be amended only after a referendum. The remaining articles could be amended by an act of the oireachtas. However, the emergency powers provisions allowed the government to suspend these provisions and set up special courts.[34]

On 29 May 1935, de Valera told the Dáil: 'It is true that we are operating a Constitution which has not been wholly ours. I hope before our term expires that we will be able to bring in a Constitution which, so far as internal affairs at any rate are concerned, will be absolutely ours.'[35] On that occasion, de Valera also emphasised the continuing need for emergency powers:

> If the ordinary operations of law cannot be relied upon to maintain order and secure justice, then if there is to be government at all the Government have to seek and use the powers which will make law operate. They have to do it; there is no way out for them. I will frankly say that I dislike it intensely, I dislike it to-day as much as I did when we opposed it from the opposition benches. I would like to say that the best alternative of all would be to see the ordinary law operating freely throughout the country. But if people will go into courts, local courts, and try to make an absolute mockery of them, if there is to be intimidation of jurors, if there is to be the possibility of citizens losing their lives as a result of an organisation of a kind in which guns are used, then it is clear the ordinary operation of law cannot be effective and if there is need, and I am sorry to think that there is possibly going to be need here, we must use those extraordinary measures.[36]

De Valera's hand was further strengthened when the judicial committee of the Privy Council agreed that the government had the right to change any aspect of the Free State constitution it pleased. It declared that the Statute of Westminster had removed 'the fetter that lay upon the Irish Free State legislature' by reason of the Colonial Laws Validity Act.[37]

Lemass announced in Dublin on 12 December 1935 that the constitution would soon be further revised. A republican constitution would result from the legislation to be shortly introduced.[38] However, there was no visible movement on the drafting of a new constitution until the middle of 1936. Perhaps de Valera was uncertain over the path to future constitutional change?

As the previous chapter has demonstrated, the early months of 1936 were particularly difficult for the Fianna Fáil government, faced as it was by a deteriorating economic situation, a recrudescence of IRA violence and the continued, but now more muted, extra-constitutional activity of Eoin O'Duffy and his remnant of Fine Gael supporters. The outbreak of the Spanish Civil War on 18 July 1936 created further difficulties for the head of government. That foreign policy issue became the subject of popular debate and public demonstrations.

It is very likely also that personal reasons prevented him from applying himself to the constitutional question. His son Brian was killed in a riding accident on Sunday, 9 February 1936; he was twenty years old and understandably his death was 'shattering to the family'. Terry de Valera recalled: 'The effect upon my parents was immense.'[39] This tragedy was followed by severe eye trouble which necessitated an operation and a prolonged stay in Zurich where he was accompanied by his son Éamon, a final year medical student. He returned to Ireland in early May. Whatever his reasons were, de Valera waited until the middle of 1936 before proceeding further with definite plans to draw up a new constitution.

Presumably, and here may reside the major reason to explain the issue of timing, de Valera felt it necessary to await the passing of legislation abolishing the Senate before proceeding with his plans. The anti-Fianna Fáil majority in the Senate could easily stymie the passage of a constitution bill.

King George V died on 20 January 1936 and was succeeded by Edward VIII less than a week later. The Irish high commissioner in London, John Dulanty, did not sign the proclamation of accession or attend the accession council. On 5 June, de Valera was authorised by the Executive Council to prepare a draft constitution and inform King Edward that the Irish government planned to introduce a bill for the purpose of setting up a new constitution at the beginning of the autumn session. That memorandum is reproduced below. This constitution, the king was told, 'will deal with the internal affairs of Saorstát Éireann, leaving unaffected the constitutional usages relating to external affairs. Amongst the provisions of the new Constitution will be the creation of the office of a President elected by the people and the abolition of the office of Governor-General.'[40]

It is difficult to trace in detail the calendar of events in mid 1936. There is a rough draft of the constitution in de Valera's own handwriting on a maths copybook. While this is certainly an early draft it is very difficult to date it. It could have been written at any time after May 1935 but it is most likely to have been written sometime between August and October 1936 as it is more developed than the fundamental plan of constitutional law drawn up by Hearne in August but less comprehensive than the draft which was shown to the Executive Council in October.

The de Valera draft contains an early version of the preamble, (reproduced below) which was to prove one of the most difficult aspects of the constitution to draft. This original 'Squared Paper' draft is reproduced as Appendix 3, and is transcribed below as the original is difficult to read:[41]

MEMORANDUM
Sent to Ed. VIII 8th June.

The Government of Saorstát Eireann, in pursuance of their policy of establishing conditions for permanent peace and harmony amongst the Irish people and providing a more secure basis for friendship and co-operation with the people of Great Britain, intend, at the beginning of the Autumn session of Parliament, to introduce a Bill for the purpose of setting up a new Constitution. This Constitution will deal with the internal affairs of Saorstát Eireann, leaving unaffected the constitutional usages relating to external affairs.

Amongst the provisions of the new Constitution will be the creation of the office of a President elected by the people and the abolition of the office of Governor-General.

Source: UCDA P150/2372

> [Page 1]
> Preamble – The I[rish] people acknow[ledging] their depend[ence] on Almighty God, thanks Him for the preservation of their nation & dedicating Themselves to his Service, accept the ten comdts [commandments] as final law give themselves this constitution ^ fundamental org[anic] law[?] so as to
> 1) [Blank] 2) [Blank] 3) [Blank] [42]

Underneath the preamble the words 'See Proc[lamation]1916, Doc[ument] of In[tent] 1919[?] and Dem[ocratic] prgm' are written, which perhaps reveal de Valera's continuing dedication to the sentiments expressed in that document.

The affirmation of the ten commandments as final law confirms that the Christian ethos was central to the proposed document. This very rough draft continues with the following references to the portions of the constitution, which were titled the Nation and the State.

The document continues:

p. (2)
The name of the State shall be ~~Éire.~~

1. Éire is a sov(reign) indep.(ent) Democ. State.
2. The Territory of the Éire Shall be such as from time to time may come within the Jurisdiction of Éire.
3. In Éire the ultimate Sov. Power shall rest with the people who shall be the ultimate court for deciding national and political questions.
4. From the people under God all Governmental authority

p. 3. (5) Cont[inue]d.
Shall be exercised by the organs of Gov.[ernment] set forth in this Constitution.

6. This Constitution shall be changed or amended only by a referendum.

– Vote of the people – citizens over 21 years taken.

p. (4)
6a. The Body of citizens shall be —

7. The legislature shall consist of Dáil Éireann selected – proportional representation and Seanad (?) Éireann.

Immunities [written in middle of page]

p. (5)
Notes on Constitution
Flags, Language, religion
Coat of arms
Regency: Constitutional Court.
[Council of State]
X Regional and Subordinate Parliaments
Page 187 – German Pres TFA
After a 2/3 vote of Dáil the P. may be invoked to assume office may be (invoked) (proposed) to assume office
– a further (words obscure)
[Phrase about President's death and subsequent election impossible to decipher with certainty]
Deputies etc to abide by Constitution Declaration

p. (6)
If Éire is assoc with any league or group of States it shall be lawful to make the necessary.
Every ten years such assessment Shall be reviewed – or at any time.

p. (7)
Organic laws cover

1. – Election of President
2. – Election of Dáil + constituencies
3. Election of Senate and Composition
4. Plebiscite – assign rules
5. Law setting up judiciary.
6. Length of Office of Parl[iamen]t
7. Secretary + Min Acts
8. Constitution 2^A law
9. Treason

p. (8)

Transitional

1. The next parliament shall be at liberty to pass organic laws to have immediate effect – but must be ratified by referendum at time of next general election.
2. Existing laws carried

Over (1) Electoral boundaries

2. Dáil Clerk
3. Judiciary
4. Ministries + Secretaries

p. (10)

Éire may associate itself with any other state or group of States or become a member of any League of States or nations. Organic laws may specify the [ends suddenly]

p. (11)

[Much of what is written on this page is difficult to read]

1. S.W F note as legislation [???]+ shows no^ real apprec[iation] of the fundamentals in the problem.
2. As many time pointed out the I[rish] people have no imperial interests or aspirations. They want to keep out of war.
1. The one right they concede is that I[rish] soil should not be used as basis of attack on Britain
2. When common threat Invasion of the two islands – co-operation w[oul]d come.

The State guarantees to all its citizens

To the family it guarantees etc

p. (12).

1. Secret Voting –
2. Powers + duties in addition to those prescribed in Const[itutio]n by law
3. Number present when law – organic is being discussed
4. Presid[en]t's residence within State + VP
5. Laws of treason

Constit[utio]n Court determines such not to taken into account p.53 S McN

p. 13.

Referendum –	1.	Am[en]d[me]nts of Constitution.
	2.	Organic Laws at discretion of P[arliament].
	3.	Major legislation at request of may [??] of 2nd H[ouse]

Recall

Tribunal

Amend[men]t [May sum[mon] constit[utional] assembly with notice of the referendum]

Phrasing, order,
Tribunal,
K send me draft   Transitional– at end and to disappear

Some of the phrases used here, many of which were to appear in the constitution itself in a similar form, describe the primary point of the whole constitutional exercise – that is to renew the declaration of independence.[43]

This draft shown to the Executive Council on 20 October 1936 survives as a fragment only a few pages long and is reproduced in Appendix 4. This extract is annotated in de Valera's hand and is what remains of de Valera's working copy of the draft first shown to the cabinet on 20 October and discussed on that day and the two days following. We can date another longer, more substantial draft, which is from around the same time, as it has the same provision about the President and other similarities and is reproduced also as Appendix 5.

The second draft contains provisions which were not included in later drafts. Article 34 included the provision: '(3) Contraception and advocacy of the practice of contraception are prohibited and the possession, use, sale, and distribution of contraceptives shall be punishable.' The following subheads of Article 34 were also excluded from later drafts:

5. The State shall encourage early marriage and foster the production of large families by appropriate grants of remission of taxation in respect of children, by the promotion of saving and thrift schemes and by facilitating the provision of housing accommodation on reasonable terms.
6. Maternity is under the special protection of the State. Provision may be made by law for the supervision and inspection of lying in hospitals and maternity nursing homes.

Likewise, in draft article 37 there were numerous clauses not reproduced later:

1. The State undertakes to take measures to prevent the corruption of public morals.
2. The State will in particular maintain, duly administer, and, as the Oireachtas may determine, improve laws regulating the following matters, that is to say,

(a) the protection of young girls, the suppression of brothels and prostitution and the punishment of sexual crimes,
(b) the conditions of employment of women and young persons in industrial works,
(c) a censorship of publications,
(d) a censorship of cinematograph performances, stage plays and other entertainments,
(e) the sale of noxious drugs and intoxicating liquors, and

(f) the licensing and supervision of clubs and public dance halls.[44]

These specific references to acts of the oireachtas were presumably inserted to protect against constitutional challenge to the validity of the Conditions of Employment Act, 1935, the Criminal Law Amendment Act, 1935 and the Censorship of Publications Act, 1929. It is clear that de Valera included the provisions on marriage before he received the contributions of Dr John Charles McQuaid. This provision on marriage is very similar to that in the O'Rahilly draft constitution of 1922.

Article 40 may well have been inspired by a combination of influences as varied as the Democratic Programme, Alfred O'Rahilly's draft constitution of 1922, and Fianna Fáil's party objectives. It declared:

1. The ownership, distribution and use of the land are under the special control of the State, and such control and supervision shall be exercised so as to promote the maximum number of economic holdings privately owned, the relief of congestion, and the establishment of working farmers on the land.
2. It is hereby declared to the duty of landowners to work their holdings in accordance with proper methods of husbandry so as to maintain and develop the productivity of the soil to their own advantage and for the benefit of the community.[45]

Articles 42 and 43 are verbatim copies of Articles 66 and 67 of the O'Rahilly/ Murnaghan Draft C, while Article 40 is closely based on Article 62 of that draft. They read:

Article 42

The transport system of Ireland – including railways, waterways for general traffic, roads and air-service – must be administered, worked, co-ordinated and developed so as to facilitate the agricultural and industrial needs of the community in time of peace and the defence of the country in time of war.

Article 43

It shall be the aim of social legislation to promote the association of employees with employers in the management and control of industry, to favour the diffusion of property, to encourage cooperative ownership and organisation and to facilitate the formation and function of professional gilds.[46]

The material in this draft relating to these social policy aspects of the constitution is also in the McQuaid papers and was presumably given to him as a guide. What is notable about these articles is that they lack the elegance of the finished draft. They are very much a work in progress.

This draft reveals that what eventually became Articles 2 and 3 were in the process of evolution. De Valera pledged to Éamon Donnelly, the Fianna Fáil

TD most concerned about partition, that there would be no boundary placed on the nation in the constitution. De Valera annotated the word 'territory' on the plan of fundamental constitutional law from August 1936 next to Article 2.[47] By October the formula considered acceptable was as follows.

Article 2

Declarations

(a) that the national territory consists of the whole of Ireland and its territorial seas;

(b) that the right of the Nation to the whole of the national territory is absolute and indefeasible;

(c) that without prejudice to the right referred to provision may be made for the application of the laws of E___ to such portion of the national territory as is for the time being under the jurisdiction of the Parliament and Government of E____.[48]

An earlier draft of this suggested for (b) that 'The right of the sovereign Irish people to the whole or any part of the nation can never be renounced.' Someone (possibly de Valera) in this early version had written 'Pending the Vol. Union' next to (c).[49] That phrase, which possibly might have avoided a lot of future controversy, did not make it into the final version.

There is a substantial summary of the draft constitution dated 5 November 1936 in the de Valera papers. This shows that the document was far advanced at this stage. Furthermore, it had received the approval of two important bodies – the Executive Council and Fianna Fáil's national executive. It is important to note also that, at this stage, although the Jesuit contribution had been received by de Valera on or around 22 October 1936, it would appear that McQuaid had not yet had any input.

SUMMARY OF MAIN PROVISIONS OF THE CONSTITUTION[50]

Date 5.XI.36.

The general scheme of the Constitution will be as follows.

- First there will be a Preamble acknowledging that all lawful authority comes from God and setting forth the ideals of the Nation and the purposes of the people in establishing this new Constitution.
- The Articles will be grouped in a number of Sections or Parts. The First Part will contain declarations relating to the Nation, the national territory, the national language and the sovereignty of the Irish people.
- The National territory will be declared to be the whole of Ireland and the territorial seas of Ireland, and the right of the Nation to the whole of the national territory will be declared to be absolute and indefeasible.
- The declarations relating to sovereignty will be to the effect that sovereignty resides

in the people, that the people have the right to determine the form of government and of the institutions of government under which they desire to live, and also the right to determine the extent of the co-operation of the State with any other State or any league or group of States. The people will be declared to be the ultimate arbiters on all disputed issues of national or public policy.

THE STATE

- The State will be declared to be a sovereign, independent, democratic State. The powers of government will be exercisable only through the organs established by the Constitution.
- The flag will be the tricolour of green, white and orange.
- The official language of the State will be the Irish language. The English language will be recognised as a second official language.
- Irish nationality and citizenship will be defined in relation to the Nation and the State.

THE PRESIDENT

There will be a President of the State who will be elected by direct vote of the people, and he will hold office for seven years. The powers and functions of the President will in general be as follows: to summon and dissolve the National Parliament, to promulgate laws, to appoint and terminate the appointment of Ministers, Judges, etc., to hold the supreme command of the Defence Forces, to exercise the right of pardon, and to exercise any additional powers and functions conferred on the President by law.

- Save where otherwise provided by the Constitution, the powers and functions of the President will be exercisable by him only on the advice of the Government.
- There will be a Council of State consisting primarily of certain officers of State whom the President must consult before exercising those of his functions which he exercises on his own responsibility. The President will e.g. have the right after consultation with the Council of State to communicate by message or address with Parliament or with the Nation on matters of national or public importance.
- Three members of the Council of State will exercise the functions of the President in the event of his death, resignation, etc. until a new President takes office.

THE NATIONAL PARLIAMENT

The National Parliament (the "Oireachtas") shall consist of the President and two Houses, a Primary House or Chamber of Deputies (Dáil Éireann) and a Second House (Seanad).

- The Oireachtas shall be the supreme legislative authority of the State, and no other legislative authority shall have the power to make laws for the State. The Oireachtas shall have the exclusive right to raise and maintain armed forces and no armed forces other than those so raised and maintained shall be raised in the State for any purpose whatsoever. The State shall not declare or participate in any war except with the consent of the Oireachtas. The Oireachtas shall hold at least one session in each year.

- Each House of the Oireachtas shall elect its own Chairman and control its own procedure. Official reports and publications of the Oireachtas shall be privileged.

DÁIL ÉIREANN

Dáil Éireann shall be constituted as heretofore.

THE GOVERNMENT

The Government of the State shall consist of a Council to be called the Council of Ministers. The President of the Council of Ministers shall be called the Prime Minister and the Vice-President will be called Deputy Prime Minister. All members of the Council of Ministers must be members of the Oireachtas, two may be members of the Second House.

- The Council of Ministers will act as a collective authority and will be collectively responsible to Dáil Éireann concerning any Department of State administered by the members of the Council.
- The Prime Minister and the other members of the Council of Ministers will retire from office in the event of the Prime Minister ceasing to retain the support of a majority in Dáil Éireann.

THE COURTS

Justice will be administered in public courts by judges appointed in the manner provided by the Constitution. The judges will be independent in the exercise of their functions, subject only to the Constitution and the law. The jurisdiction and organisation of the Courts and the tenure of office of the judges thereof will generally be the same as heretofore.

THE COMPTROLLER AND AUDITOR GENERAL

There will be a Comptroller and Auditor-General with a tenure of office and functions as heretofore.

CONSTITUTIONAL GUARANTEES

The following fundamental constitutional rights shall be guaranteed to all citizens: equality before the law, freedom of conscience and freedom of expression and practice of religion, subject to public order and morality, the right to free expression of opinion, subject to public order and morality, the right to assemble peaceably and without arms, the right to form associations and unions, liberty of the person, and the inviolability of the dwelling. Power will be taken in the Constitution to enact laws for the purpose of preventing or controlling meetings which are calculated to cause a breach of the peace or to be a menace or a nuisance to the public. Religious associations will be guaranteed the right of assembly for the conduct of religious services in public and in private, subject to public order and morality. No religion shall be endowed by law. Legislations providing for State aid to schools will contain no discrimination against the schools under the management of a particular religious denomination. The property of any religious denomination will not be diverted save for the purpose of works of public utility and on payment of compensation.

- Special recognitions will be given to the family in the State as the basis of social discipline and ordered society. The right to private ownership of property will be affirmed as a natural human right and the protection of private ownership of property will be guaranteed, subject to the law.
- All citizens will be guaranteed the right to free elementary education.

POWER TO SUSPEND CERTAIN PROVISIONS OF THE CONSTITUTION

Provision will be made for the suspension during a grave state of public disorder or threatened public disorder of certain of the constitutional guarantees just mentioned, for example that relating to the liberty of the person and inviolability of the dwelling.

AMENDMENT OF THE CONSTITUTION

Certain provisions of the Constitution will be declared to be fundamental and changes in those Articles will not be made unless the amendment is approved by the people in a Referendum held for that purpose. The Referendum will be regulated by law.

MISCELLANEOUS

There will be a part containing miscellaneous provisions, provision e.g. for trial by jury (except in certain cases) and the repeal of the Constitution of 1922.

TRANSITORY PROVISIONS

There will be a number of transitory provisions. These provisions are necessary to provide for the continuance of certain laws of an administrative character pending the full working of the new Constitution. There will, of course, be a provision containing laws generally subject to the new Constitution.[51]

This summary is an important progress report on the evolving constitution. While it is a highly developed submission – the constitution ends up following this scheme to a significant extent – it is notable for a number of omissions. Apart from the reference to the special position of the family and the ban on divorce, it is a document reflecting the ideas of Hearne and O'Donoghue. Both men preferred a short concise document; their legal training and tradition favoured brevity. But they were to witness the inclusion of other forces in the drafting process and they were, much to their deep regret, unable to control or contain that change.[52]

De Valera also received, at the beginning of October, material from the 'second house commission', a group set up in June 1936 to consider the powers and composition of any new house. In June 1936, after informing the British of his intention to introduce a new constitution, de Valera agreed to set up a commission under Chief Justice Hugh Kennedy on whether to reconstitute a second house of the oireachtas in the forthcoming constitution. He did this in spite of his often self-confessed dislike of second chambers. At a meeting of the Fianna Fáil parliamentary party on 12 March 1936, questions were raised regarding a second house. De Valera made a lengthy statement covering the whole position with regard to the Seanad, to its abolition and to the abolition of university representation. He asked the deputies to consider carefully what the attitude of the country was towards a single chamber government or the establishment of some form of second chamber.[53] It would appear that there was enough concern expressed to make de Valera look at a proposal for a second house, though there is no evidence as to what finally made him decide to do so.

Significantly, John Hearne was among those appointed to the commission, which sat twenty-seven times and reported on 30 September 1936. It produced a majority report and two minority reports on the subject.[54] The majority report recommended the second house should be reconstituted with a power of delay of only ninety days and no power to delay money bills. The removal of judges would have to be approved by the second house. It also called for the second house to have the power to refer bills to change the constitution to the people. The majority report also called for the Dáil to have the ability to push through emergency legislation without delay from the second house. Other important recommendations called for those nominated to the body to be persons with a competent knowledge of public affairs, of the national language, be over thirty-five years of age and that some should be women. The greatest division in the commission was over the method of election. Some felt that it should be elected by direct vote of the people, others on the basis of provinces, and others on the basis of nomination. The majority of the commission favoured that one-third should be nominated by the president of the Executive Council and the rest should be elected by Dáil Éireann voting on a proportional basis of first preferences in the previous election. The nominees, it was felt, should be drawn from a variety of cultural, economic and educational panels.[55]

Hugh Kennedy disagreed with the minority report, considering that a House that was not directly elected would be better not set up at all. Since he could see no possibility of elections being made on a functional basis, he suggested a 'council of Ireland' with forty members. Half would be elected – five from each province – and twenty would be nominated by a committee made up of the ceann comhairle, the president of the Executive Council, the leader of the opposition, and leaders of all parties with more than five members and a representative of the independent members. He suggested that the work of the council should involve revising legislation in committees by making reports on bills to the Dáil.[56] (This would appear to be strongly influenced by the provisions in the Portuguese constitution.) The most radical proposals were contained in the second minority report.[57] They viewed the primary function of the second house as the safeguarding of fundamental human rights, as well as the continued existence and peaceful development of democratic institutions against encroachments of the executive and the majority of the Dáil. Therefore they recommended that the chamber should have the power to refer to a referendum of the people any Dáil bill which raised some vital national issue that had not yet been pronounced upon by the people. There was to be no other power of delay. It would have the right, however, to amend and improve legislation. The method of election called for the formation of functional and vocational panels nominated by representative bodies who would then be elected by the Dáil.

De Valera was inclined to accept the need for a second chamber purely on the grounds that it was supported by a considerable body of opinion. However, he wished it to be curtailed by making sure the Taoiseach was free to nominate enough members so that there would be a permanent government majority in the second chamber. The scheme that was arrived at took ideas from all three reports. The Senate's power to veto a bill was now confined to just three months. It was given a right in concert with four-ninths of the Dáil to petition the President to force a referendum on contentious legislation. De Valera, though, seemed to draw greatest inspiration from the vocational ideas contained in the minority report. The problem of electing the body proved to be the hardest part of the drafting clause. Certain principles guided it. One was that a substantial number of members would be nominated by the prime minister. De Valera also wished there to be representation from the universities. The remainder were to be elected from panels containing candidates with a) knowledge of public administration, b) persons engaged in agriculture, c) persons engaged in industry and commerce, d) labour and e) education. The candidates were then to be elected from a 'college of electors' made up of candidates from the Dáil Éireann election who could cast one vote for every one thousand first preferences they received in the election.[58] Seán MacEntee was the minister most interested in the problem of getting a Seanad that would reflect the Dáil's general makeup to a considerable degree but would not be a complete creature of the body. He suggested that the Seanad should be elected by members of the local authorities with votes weighted according to the number of first preferences they received; otherwise the whole second house would be a creature of the Dáil and of no use beyond patronage.[59] The potential for cronyism of the Senate became a long-standing subject of tension between de Valera and MacEntee.[60] Towards the end of 1936, de Valera and the Irish government were given an unexpected gift and an opportunity to change even more profoundly the basis of Anglo-Irish relations. This proved to be a major step on the road to constitutional revolution. King Edward VIII's public declaration of intent to marry Mrs Simpson as soon as she could secure a divorce from her husband created a deep constitutional crisis in Britain. The government of the United Kingdom led by prime minister Stanley Baldwin was obliged to consult the governments of the dominions, including the Irish Free State, all of whose basic laws contained references to the British sovereign. Abdication would require an amendment to British law to attempt to regularise the situation created by the king's marriage. This required the consent of the dominions, whose position as co-equal members of the commonwealth had been guaranteed by the Statute of Westminster in 1931.

Baldwin set down an account of the events leading up to Sunday, 6 December 1936 in a minute prepared for the president of the Executive Council, Éamon de Valera. The Department of External Affairs' summary of events, including the Baldwin correspondence, is reproduced as Appendix 6.

At the time of the completion of the above minute, the situation was still far from clear. The British prime minister was due to make a statement in the House of Commons on the afternoon of Monday, 7 December. The minute described opinion amongst large sections of the British public as being against abdication, while it detected a weakening in the resolution of his majesty's government to force a voluntary abdication.

On 10 December 1936, the day of the abdication of Edward VIII, de Valera summoned a special meeting of Dáil Éireann for the following morning, 'for the purpose of considering, in connection with the proposed abdication of His Majesty King Edward VIII, proposals for the amendment of the Constitution and other legislation'.[61] In this regard the government introduced the Constitution (Amendment No. 27) Bill, which removed all references to the king from the basic law of the Irish Free State. In proposing the bill for a second reading, de Valera explained that:

> The effect [of the bill] simply is to eliminate the King from all those articles of the Constitution which seem to give him function here in our internal affairs. We are taking these out. The whole purpose is to do that. In the case of the Governor General, the appointment and executive powers provisions are being deleted.[62]

Amongst the changes consequent to the amending act was the deletion from Article 41 of a requirement that a bill, when passed by parliament, should be presented to the governor general for signification of the king's assent, and the substitution of one whereby the chairman (ceann comhairle) of Dáil Éireann should sign such a bill, which would thereupon become law.[63]

Although the first bill sought to remove all references to the king from the constitution, the Executive Authority (External Relations) Bill, with which it was explicitly linked by de Valera, sought to redefine the position of the king with regard to the executive powers in the Irish Free State.[64] Where the first bill undermined the position of the king, the second bill sought to retain him for use in certain circumstances. The cumulative effect of both bills was described by de Valera in the following terms:

> What is happening, then is that from the King are being taken away any functions internal, either direct or indirect, in the Administration of the Government and in the internal Executive of the country, and we are retaining the King for those purposes for which he was used hitherto. He is being retained for these purposes because he is recognised as the symbol of this particular co-operation in the States of the Commonwealth. If the Irish people do not wish to continue him for these purposes they can end that by legislation. They can end the whole situation by law or limit the exercise of these powers by law.[65]

The External Relations Bill sought to define the source of ultimate political authority in the Irish Free State. Except in specific circumstances, the ultimate authority derived from the Executive Council or cabinet. The king was authorised to act on behalf of Saorstát Éireann 'for the like purposes as and when advised by the Executive Council' only:

> … so long as Saorstát Éireann is associated with the following nations, that is to say, Australia, Canada, Great Britain, New Zealand and South Africa, and so long as the King recognised by those nations as the symbol of their co-operation continues to act on behalf of each of those nations (on the advice of the several governments thereof) for the purposes of the appointment of diplomatic and consular representatives and the conclusion of international agreements.[66]

The bills were passed by Dáil Éireann on 11 (Constitution Amendment) and 12 (External Relations) December.

De Valera's approach to the question of the abdication of the king seems to have been decided upon within the context of his intent to clarify Ireland's constitutional relationship with the United Kingdom and the wider commonwealth and his ongoing commitment to the drafting of a new constitution for the Irish state. Concluding the debate on the External Relations Bill, the President argued that as a result of the twin measures envisaged by his government:

> Quite clearly, what we have got to do now is either to regularise the position or declare a republic. We came into office with a certain policy. We have pursued that policy honestly the whole time we have been here. I am anxious to see a condition established here in which the people of this country can be on friendly terms with the people across the

> water. But I know it cannot be done without satisfying the aspirations of our people. I believe that the existing situation does not satisfy their aspirations and what I am trying to do in this, and will propose to do in the coming Constitution, is to get nearer to a position which will satisfy their aspirations.[67]

Responding to certain critics who remained unconvinced by de Valera's assurances regarding the authority of the king in the proposed bills, he stated:

> Certain doubts were raised last night. One of these was that somehow, if we did pass the Bill, it would give certain external functions to the successor of King Edward VIII; that King Edward VIII himself seemed to hover around looking for some corner in which he would have authority to act in virtue of the fact that he was previously King. It is to cover that situation that these words 'all other (if any) purposes' are inserted … If there is any hole or corner in which the disembodied spirit was hovering or trying to get into, then, if that does exist, it will be filled already by this country. We do not see any at the moment. I do not know of any functions internally that are left for the King, whether it be the King we were supposed last night to be completely removed from or his successor. I see no internal functions left for him. Some sort of vague title or something of that sort is probably there, but there are no internal functions left as far as I know. The purpose of this Bill was to remove the King from the exercise of any functions whatever internally.[68]

Considering the implications of the two acts, Michael McDunphy, assistant secretary in the president's department, noted that the:

> … President was advised by the Department of External Affairs that the amendment to that act, by deleting Article 60 of the Constitution, had abolished the office of the Governor General.[69]

Consequently, the creation of a new office of head of state, Uachtarán na h-Éireann, under the new constitution, assumed more urgency as a result of the events of December 1936.

It must be noted however that, while the abdication crisis was the catalyst for the enactment of the External Relations Act, the principles contained in the legislation were under discussion as early as August 1936. The idea of a sovereign republic associating voluntarily with the British commonwealth and accepting the crown as the symbol of that association went back to the Treaty negotiations of 1921. Christened 'external association' by de Valera then, he viewed this scheme as the best way in which to satisfy Irish nationalist aspirations with the reality of British imperial power and its sensibilities.

John Hearne was already working on a draft bill to reflect the principle of external association with a view to incorporating it into the new constitution then under consideration in August 1936, a full four months prior to the abdication crisis.[70] The bill set out the fundamental declarations, aimed at proclaiming the full sovereignty of the Irish people in matters both external and internal.

Hearne also noted that 'the new Constitution would contain an enactment to the effect that the manner and form in which all or any of the prerogatives referred to shall be exercised or exercisable may be determined by law'.[71] The ultimate effect of the three declarations was to allow the Irish Free State to authorise the king to act on behalf of the people in circumstances that would be carefully outlined according to the oireachtas and which would not prejudice the right of the people to determine their own affairs in all matters, a right proclaimed in the first two declarations mentioned by Hearne. Hearne argued that his draft bill would 'throw the whole question of the use of the Kingship for purposes of external relations only into its proper context, namely, the context of the sovereignty of the State'.[72] In line with de Valera's wishes as expressed in all of his speeches on the constitutional position of the Irish State *vis-à-vis* the British commonwealth, Hearne argued that the proposed bill 'places a ringing emphasis upon the authority and control of the people in every aspect of the external relations of the State'.[73]

The abdication crisis compelled de Valera to rearrange his preferred timetable for constitutional change. It did not alter the conceptual nature of his constitutional project but affected the sequence of its execution. Hearne's minute to Seán Moynihan explaining the thinking behind the External Relations Bill shows that de Valera had intended first to bring in the new constitution, complete with its affirmation of complete sovereignty over internal and external affairs, and then to subsequently determine Irish relations with the crown and commonwealth by an act of the oireachtas. Nicholas Mansergh points out that:

> It would clearly have been at once more convenient and more logical to determine future relations with the Commonwealth after, and not before, the new Constitution was approved. But the Irish convenience and logic were minor casualties of royal impetuosity. The determination of external relations accordingly had to come before the Constitution.[74]

On 11 January 1937, Hearne produced what is described as the 'third draft' of the new constitution. The first section was a preamble (which was not included), followed by fundamental declarations. Some of the divisions following the preamble were as follows:

Part I – the State (Articles 1–6),
Part II – The President of Éire (Articles 7–8),
Part IV – The Government (Article 23),
Part V – The Council of State (Articles 24–27),

Part VI – The Courts (Articles 28–30),
Part VII – The Comptroller and Auditor General (Articles 31–32),
Part VIII – The Referendum (Article 33),
Part IX – Constitutional Guarantees (Articles 34–38),
Part XI – Amendment of the Constitution (Article 39),
Part XII – General (Articles 40–44).[75]

Although the drafting of the new constitution had been kept a closely-guarded secret, and remained the work of a very small number of civil servants hand-chosen by de Valera, news of the process had leaked. The following two chapters will examine the contributions of Fr Edward Cahill and the Jesuit province and that of a future archbishop of Dublin, John Charles McQuaid. The former was a personal but not a very close friend of the president of the Executive Council. The latter was a close friend of the de Valera family and had taught a number of the president's children in Blackrock College where he had been president. By confiding in McQuaid, de Valera may, unwittingly, have opened the floodgates to a deluge of drafts, comments and correspondence from a source with a very strong ideological point of view. While de Valera's inner thoughts were never revealed on this point, Hearne and his small drafting team did not welcome the paper avalanche which followed in the late autumn of early 1936 and the early months of 1937.

CHAPTER 3

Fr Edward Cahill, the Irish Jesuit province and the order's submission on the Constitution[1]

The historian, David Fitzpatrick, has put forward an arresting thesis regarding the influences on the writing of the new Irish constitution, suggesting that much of this 'had been drafted by Jesuits and other clerical advisers'.[2] This view, however appealing, has little foundation in fact. The following attempts to describe in detail the role of the 'Jesuits' in the crafting of *Bunreacht na hÉireann.*

Fr Edward Cahill SJ was de Valera's main link with the Jesuit order. He was a cultural nationalist, a strong critic of Freemasonry, a pioneer and founder of Catholic Action in the country, and a polemicist of great energy and determination. He was also a correspondent of de Valera's for some years before the drafting of a new constitution was ever mooted. Cahill wrote to de Valera after his victory in the 1932 election and thanked God that 'the ten year "nightmare"' was over and that de Valera was in 'charge of the helm again'.[3] Cahill again wrote to de Valera after the 1933 election, congratulating him 'very sincerely on the splendid endorsement' he had received and wishing him God's assistance in the 'arduous task' that was before him.[4] De Valera replied to Cahill's letters in a polite but formal manner. Although, in response to a gift of a copy of his *The Framework of a Christian State* he wrote warmly: 'Is fiú é'léigheamh agus a aith léigheamh agus is minic d'ar liom, a raghfar chuige chun comhairle agus treórú 'fhagháil.'[5]

However despite de Valera's appreciation of the gift he did not use Cahill's work as his political *vademecum* or source of primary inspiration. The president of the Executive Council knew ecclesiastical politics so well by the time he came to office in 1932 that there was little danger of his confusing mainstream Catholic thought with views from the periphery of the Irish ecclesiastical world. Apart from their strong commitment to the revival of the Irish language, Cahill was friendly with, but not an intimate of, de Valera. Both men were from County Limerick, but they did not have much in common intellectually apart from a shared commitment to the radical tenets of cultural nationalism. Nevertheless, de Valera appreciated also the political support that he received from the outspoken and highly energetic Jesuit.[6]

Cahill lobbied de Valera in 1934 seeking amendments to the proposed Criminal Law Amendment Act. He asked that the age of consent be raised from fifteen years to '18 or even 19 years' and he also wanted more draconian penalties imposed 'in connection with contraceptives'. He believed that there was a growing traffic in contraceptives almost certainly conducted 'wholly by non-Catholics' and felt that 'the Nation in which it [contraception] takes root is doomed'.[7] De Valera assured him that he realised the importance of the matters raised.[8]

In September 1936 Cahill again wrote to de Valera from the Imperial Hotel, Lisdoonvarna, where he had been 'sent unexpectedly' by his superior. He enclosed 'papers' on the constitution that he considered 'far from satisfactory' as they were in their present form little more than a 'rough draft'. He intended, on returning to Dublin, to 'get the opinions of some others of our fathers who are interested in the matter and revise the present draft'. De Valera returned his manuscript together with a typed copy of it and while he found 'some of the principles might be set forth in a preamble' he feared that there was not 'much that could be incorporated into the body of the Constitution'. However, he suggested that Cahill should 'put into the form of draft Articles, with perhaps a draft preamble' what he thought 'should be formally written into the Constitution'.[9] Cahill responded that he would like to 'secure the advice of some others'.[10] A committee of members of Jesuits was in place three days later. The minutes of their meetings are reproduced as Appendix 7.

Whether this was the result of Cahill's seeking the advice of his *confreres* or of the Jesuits' concern at the prospect of Cahill making individual submissions to the President we do not know. The second possibility is the more likely, however, as Fr Patrick Bartley (the committee's president) wrote to the order's provincial concerning his disquiet at the possibility of Cahill adding his own recommendations to the committee's findings: 'These recommendations … by their singular character are likely to bring discredit on the very solid findings of the Committee.'[11]

The committee's brief was to 'advise on certain matters connected with Constitution'. The report was to be in 'a formal submission which would be sent to de Valera as an official presentation from the Irish Province of the Jesuits'. Patrick Bartley was to act as president; John McErlean was appointed secretary; and Joseph Canavan and Edward Coyne were also appointed.[12] These Jesuit priests who formed the committee which advised on the drafting were described in a letter by the order's provincial as 'the best heads we have in matters of this kind'. This was not an idle boast. The collective intellectual power of the small group is impressive. In age they ranged from forty (Fr Coyne) to sixty-eight years (Fr

Cahill). The following profiles, which are compiled from their obituary notices, give a flavour of the attributes these men brought to the task. It must be stressed that these sources, while listing their considerable achievements, are not eulogistic but candidly discuss their subjects, warts and all.

De Valera's communications were with Fr Cahill who (from the available correspondence at least) appears to have passed on the committee's suggestions as his own. Whether or not de Valera realised it, a group of remarkable men with fine minds had applied themselves to the task of assisting him in the drafting of his constitution.

Fr Patrick Bartley, born in 1879 in Boher, County Limerick, was educated at Crescent College in Limerick city but entered the Jesuit novitiate at Tullabeg at the age of fifteen. He was a brilliant student at the Royal University of Ireland, obtaining an MA (classical) at twenty-two. His scholarly pursuits included the study of oriental languages in Université St Joseph in Beirut. He was, at different times, professor of church history and Hebrew, of philosophy and of scripture in Milltown Park. However, he never paraded his learning; only 'those who had the privilege of living in intimate daily intercourse with him could fully appreciate either his encyclopaedic knowledge … or that gentleness of disposition' which endeared him to others. His kindness of character can be seen in his treatment of Fr Cahill.[13]

Edward Cahill was born in 1868 in Callow, County Limerick and was educated in Mungret. He entered the Jesuit order in 1891 having spent a number of years in Maynooth. After ordination he spent time in Mungret successively as master, rector and superior and, after a year as spiritual director in Clongowes, he went to Milltown Park where he was professor of church history and lecturer in sociology. In 1926, the year the feast of Christ the King was inaugurated, he founded An Rioghacht ('The League of the Kingship of Christ') with the aim of promoting Catholic social policy. This organisation published pamphlets, ran study-circles and held public meetings and unsuccessfully attempted to publish a weekly newspaper. However, Fr Cahill succeeded in broadcasting his ideas through other means; he was a prolific contributor to *The Irish Ecclesiastical Record* and wrote a regular column, 'Notes on Sociology', for *The Irish Monthly* from 1923 to 1929. Perhaps significantly his work was not published in the scholarly Jesuit periodical, *Studies.* His published works include a play, books and pamphlets and his major work, *The Framework of the Christian State.* His work shows that he entertained a somewhat unhealthy obsession with the machinations of international Freemasonry, linking it 'closely' with 'modern Judaism (including the Rationalistic Jews, as well as those of the Talmud and the Cabala) and [freemasonry] is largely under Jewish influence and guidance'.[14] In Ireland, he believed that Freemasonry was practically identifiable with the imperialist and non-Catholic portion of the population. The programme of Freemasonry included, in his opinion, the banishment of religion from government, the secularisation of institutions such as marriage, the introduction of divorce, state education, freedom for all religions 'except the true one', unrestrained freedom of the press and 'the promotion of radical feminism'.[15] All factors of this programme were anathema to him. On the positive side he was deeply committed to the retention of the Irish language as he believed that if it died 'the intensity and vigour of national life, never surpassed and rarely equalled' would die with it.[16] In this he had common cause with de Valera. He was very interested in the concept of Ireland's 'golden age', which he identified as happening from the sixth to the ninth centuries.[17] He credited the Irish with spreading enlightenment all over Europe: 'The Irishmen's inborn sympathy with the national sentiments and traditions of the peoples whom they taught was rooted mainly in their own national literary training and their love and appreciation of their own national language.'[18] He implicitly and explicitly linked his idealised version of the medieval Irish past with 1930s Ireland in terms of political freedom and devotion to the Catholic Church. His idealised (and anachronistic) picture of ancient and medieval Ireland's social system was what he, perhaps unrealistically, wished to recreate through a new constitution. He attached great significance to the Eucharistic Congress of 1932, seeing it as a 'magnificent display' that 'heralded the glimmering of a new dawn'.

His obituary spoke of his 'enthusiastic' teaching methods and the writer added that his students 'might, on occasion, smile at his homely illustrations or novel remedies for very complex social ills'.[19] While 'his achievements show Fr Cahill to have been a man of more than ordinary mental ability … it was his qualities of character which most influenced people rather than his intellectual gifts'.[20]

Fr Joseph Canavan was born in Khandalla, India in 1886. He was educated at St Mary's College, Bombay but came at fifteen years old to Clongowes Wood. He regarded his time there as significant; he said that he was taught to accept both victory and defeat with equanimity and also learned the traits of 'truth, chivalry and manliness'. He was a scholar of distinction; having entered the Jesuit novitiate in 1904, he was awarded a BA in philosophy in 1911 and later 'the coveted degree of Magister Aggregatus of the Gregorian University' of Rome. He devoted the remainder of his life to teaching and was professor of philosophy and of theology in Milltown Park. He was a gifted teacher who loved metaphysics and who had the capacity to forge interconnections between disciplines. Fr Canavan appears to have been a polymath who lectured on a variety of subjects as well as philosophy and theology, and was deeply interested, both theoretically and practically, in social science. His obituarist wrote of him: 'He had a masterly grasp of business and a fund of tact and patience which made him an excellent committee-man.' His ability was also recognised by those outside his order. He was chairman of the citizens' housing council and a member of the governmental commission on the civil service.[21]

Fr Edward Coyne, born in Dublin in 1896 of an academic father who as well as being professor of political economy at the Royal University was a founder of the Department of Agriculture and Technical Instruction. He was educated in Clongowes where he excelled, not only at academic subjects but also at sport. He was a member of the college social study club and in 1914 won the union prize for his essay on 'The Necessity of Social Education for Irishmen'. He entered the novitiate in Tullabeg in 1914. He read history and economics in UCD and achieved first place in both subjects. While studying philosophy in Milltown, he achieved an MA (first class), the subject of which was Ireland's internal transport system. He subsequently studied theology in Innsbruck and was later a student in Westphalia, and continued his studies at the Gregorian, the Sorbonne and at the Action Populaire. He spent three months in the International Labour office in Geneva. His teaching career, at which he excelled, did not prevent him from serving on the commission on vocational organisation and on the commission on population. He was deeply interested in industrial and labour problems and 'placed his knowledge of the social sciences at the disposal of countless individuals, clerical and lay, Government commissions, public boards, trade unions, industrial committees and Co-Operative societies'. He was president of the Irish agricultural organisation society and served for many years on joint industrial councils and was a wise and sympathetic friend to both businessmen and trade union officials. With Fr Canavan he founded the Catholic workers' college and participated in the Jesuit summer school in 1936 which had as its subject 'The Constitutional problem from the Catholic point of view'.[22]

Fr John McErlean was born in Belfast in 1870 and was educated there at St Malachy's College. While a Jesuit novice at Tullybeg, he completed his degree in the Royal University of Ireland (RUI) in 1892. His further education took place in Holland, Spain, Italy and Portugal. He was primarily a scholar of early Irish texts which he edited in scholarly editions for the Irish texts society. He was an admirable Latin and Greek scholar. He knew Sanskrit and Hebrew and was practised in modern European languages including Spanish, German and French. His mind was acutely critical not only in matters of scholarship but in the discussion of current topics. He had remarkable dialectical skill and could defend his views with great ingenuity.

The theme of the Jesuits' 1936 summer school, 'The Constitutional problem from the Catholic point of view', reflects the order's interest in the constitutional question. Government officials including Seán Moynihan and his brother, Maurice, attended and, according to his biographers, de Valera took great interest in the papers of Michael Browne, the professor of theology at Maynooth and Cornelius Lucey, also of Maynooth.[23] Browne's paper pointed out that it was contrary to the teaching of Leo XIII and Pius X to imagine that in democratic systems the people retain authority and govern by mandate. The people, the popes insisted, merely designate the ruler 'who thereupon has the authority of natural law'. Lucey's paper discussed Catholic political thought which held that the 'government of civil society is the supreme guardian of the natural law, that it is bound to respect the rights of inferior society such as the family and the personal rights of individual citizens, but that it may, and must interfere with them in order to preserve and promote the observance of the Natural Law'. He described 'the modern prejudice in favour of democracy as only a prejudice'.[24] Fr Coyne declared that a constitution 'should define … the rights of the individual … which he could not surrender to any Government'.

This committee of well-educated and talented, if not remarkable men met for the first time on 24 September 1936. Fr Bartley presided and Fathers Cahill, Canavan and Coyne were present; the secretary, Fr McErlean, was absent on retreat. A decision was taken to draft a preamble on the model of the preamble in the Polish constitution. Articles were to be prepared on the following subjects:

(a) The rights of the family, particularly with regard to the education of children.
(b) Religion to be taught in all schools, which were to be denominational whenever there was no 'insuperable obstacle'.
(c) The state could not dissolve a valid marriage.
(d) The relations between the Catholic Church and the State were to be defined by a Concordat.
(e) Freedom of religious worship.
(f) Ecclesiastical property.
(g) Private property.
(h) Freedom of speech and of the press, and the limitations of that freedom.
(i) Any other matters that might be suggested by a study of concordats and existing constitutions.[25]

On 1 October the next meeting of the committee discussed three drafts of the preamble submitted by Cahill, Canavan and Coyne. Certain changes were approved and the matter was scheduled for further consideration 'in its new form at the next meeting'. The meeting also approved 'with slight modifications' an article 'on relations between the Catholic Church and the State submitted by P. Bartley'. But the article 'declaring that the State cannot dissolve a valid marriage was found hard to draft'. The committee was unsuccessful in finding 'a satisfactory wording that would embrace all possible cases' and it was resolved to discuss it further at the next meeting when drafts on private property, liberty of conscience, press and meetings would be examined.

At the meeting of the committee on 8 October 1936, 'many drafts were considered and approved with slight modification'. Bartley's article on Church–state relations was passed with an addition proposed by Canavan. All members, with the exception of Canavan, approved Bartley's draft on Catholic marriage and the state. It was decided to include Canavan's draft as an alternative. Bartley also drew up the articles on freedom of worship and freedom of the press, which were approved. Canavan suggested an article stating that 'the same control should also be exercised by law over cinema, radio, theatre and suchlike', and it was decided to include it. A draft by Coyne on the family was approved as was the article drafted by Coyne and Bartley on parents and education of children in schools. The article on religion in schools was to be taken, with slight changes, from the Polish constitution.

There was also progress on the articles on private property, religious property, family and a living wage. Coyne was the main drafter of articles in these areas while Canavan also had suggestions for discussion. This responsibility was perhaps an acknowledgement of the two men's interest in social matters. In drafting these articles the committee drew heavily on the Polish constitution. On 15 October it was agreed to include the proviso that 'the State should aim at a wide distribution of private productive property especially in land'. While this last suggestion could be seen to be radical, the committee was naturally dedicated to the Jesuit order's *raison d'être* as educators of a Catholic elite in its suggestion of an article on private education. The meeting of 18 October suggested some slight changes, including a suggestion that 'boys and girls of adolescent age shall be educated separately'.

The committee's deliberations were complete at the end of five sessions on 18 October 1936. Bartley sent the provincial a progress report on 11 October, in which he announced that the work of the committee would be concluded within a week. He proposed to hand over 'our suggestions to Fr Cahill, who will deliver them in the proper quarter. It is of the utmost importance that no time should be lost if our recommendations are to be in before the official draft is completed.' Bartley told his superior that the 'work has been very harmonious so far. Fr Cahill is in full agreement with it, and has shown no desire to veto anything.' The tone of the letter suggests that this harmony was contrary to expectations. However in the event of difficulties, he thought they would have to be 'met by diplomacy: and I think it can be so met'. He thought it likely that:

> Fr Cahill will almost certainly want to add recommendations of his own to those approved by the committee. Now these recommendations, partly by their sheer bulk and partly by their singular character, are likely to bring discredit on the very solid findings of the committee, especially if they are delivered at the same time as the committee's findings.[26]

Bartley advised the provincial that Cahill should be asked to add nothing when he delivered the committee's findings. If he wished to send additional recommendations, he could do so at a later date, provided that these were approved by any two of those who had served on the committee with him. By that time, the committee would have ceased to exist. Bartley considered it justified to so censor Cahill for the good of the Jesuit reputation:

> The source of Fr Cahill's recommendations will be quite well known to a small number of very important people. The reputation of the Society will be involved; and the Provincial has the right to watch over that reputation.[27]

Bartley's laconic summing-up of the difficulties relating to Cahill reveal his abilities as a skilful draftsman with a masterly use of understatement: 'I know for certain that he is preparing voluminous recommendations and that some of them at least are rather singular.'[28] As president of the Jesuit committee it was his responsibility to prevent Cahill from making inappropriate 'singular' recommendations that would threaten the reputation of the order. His actions reveal him as a clever manager of a difficult situation; he also appears to have been sensitive to Cahill's feelings. Ironically the report and correspondence reveal that Cahill played a rather passive role on the committee. The reports show that while he produced a draft preamble, he did not make a substantial contribution to the drafting of any of the articles. Perhaps he knew that his contributions would not be acceptable to the committee and decided to submit his ideas independently of it. However, it is obvious that he had revealed to Bartley the fact that he was preparing 'voluminous recommendations' for de Valera.

After the meeting of 11 October, Bartley informed the provincial that 'our committee finished its collective labours today'. Harmony had been maintained 'to the end' despite his fears of 'some dissension in the last session'. Bartley was preparing the final report and Cahill was going to type it. A meeting had been arranged for Sunday, 18 October, to 'give this report a final look over'. Bartley explained how he had told Cahill that the committee was 'authorised by Your Reverence to deliver this report through him in the proper quarter' and also that the provincial had instructions to give him regarding the report. 'I did not profess to know,' Bartley wrote, 'the nature of these instructions.' Bartley advised that the provincial's instructions should be sent to Cahill at once: 'I am now more convinced than I was before that they are necessary. They should reach him on Saturday at latest.'[29]

On 16 October, two days before the committee met for the last time, the provincial wrote to Cahill. Having dispensed with the niceties in his opening sentences, his letter continued:

> Now as that document will be the product of the best heads we have in matters of this kind I think it would be well if it were presented as it stands by your Reverence to Mr de Valera. It may be that you would like to add to some of the matters dealt with in this report, or possibly to suggest alternative recommendations. I have no objection to your doing this, but think 1) that this second document ought not be handed in with the first or at least not as forming part of the first: and 2) that since what you recommend will be regarded as emanating from the Society ... I would ask you to submit for censorship to any two you may select of the committee members the document you proose (sic) [propose] to hand Mr De Valera.[30]

These were the instructions advised by Bartley, with one exception. He had suggested that the provincial forbid Cahill to add anything of his own when he presented the committee's findings; in the event he wrote that there was 'no objection' to Cahill's submitting his own suggestions provided that they were not presented as part of the report.

At the final meeting of the committee on 18 October, at which all members were present, the preamble was changed slightly and now read:

> In the Name of the Most Holy Trinity and of our Lord Jesus Christ, the Universal King, we the people of Ireland [so] full of gratitude to God who has so mercifully preserved us from innumerable dangers in the past; hereby, as an united independent Christian Nation, establish this Sovereign Society of the Irish people ... and so in accordance with the principles laid down we freely and deliberately to the glory of God and honour of Ireland, sanction this constitution and decree and enact as follows.[31]

The committee agreed that references to the constitutions and concordats of Catholic states should be added to the various 'assertions' made in the document so 'that those who have the task of drawing up the constitution may come to know what the Catholics of other European States have already secured'. The report of the Jesuit Committee is included as Appendix 7. Cahill was to type the document and submit it. It is difficult to understand why he was allowed do this as it surely is at odds with the curb that the provincial, albeit at Bartley's instigation, wished to place upon him. We are left with the dichotomy of Cahill presenting the committee's findings as his own together with the distinct possibility of his later producing 'singular' and 'voluminous' additions, which presumably would comply, neither in style nor content, with the committee's draft articles. Perhaps it did not strike the provincial or Bartley that Cahill would pass off the collective work as his own – maybe the content of the report was their only concern. If this were so, the dilemma, and potential embarrassment, of Cahill's further submissions still remained.

On 21 October 1936, Cahill wrote to de Valera enclosing the committee's preamble and articles. This letter and accompanying submission is reproduced as Appendix 8.

The letter accompanying the submission was unambiguous in its claim that Cahill was responsible for the work: 'I have, in drawing them up, confined myself to the minimum that I would consider necessary to realise a Christian Constitution, as I feared to outstep the limits of what you asked me to do.' His declaration that he had 'availed' himself of the advice 'of three or four others, some of whom have made a special study of these matters' is disingenuous in the extreme and does not suggest at all that an efficient committee, to which he was but a minor contributor, had laboured to produce draft articles. It is, of course, a clever letter as, technically, he informed de Valera that others worked with him but his admission that he 'availed' of 'some advice' is, as has been seen, far from the full story. We cannot know if the Cahill submission would have carried more weight with de Valera had he known that it was the work of a distinguished committee.

The letter to de Valera provides some evidence for Cahill's own personal position, which he obviously had not expressed very strongly at committee meetings. He referred to the fact that there were a number of omissions in the articles. These were to be settled by concordat. He itemised civil observance of Sundays and holy days, and the juridical personality of religious congregations and communities in regard to property. Influenced by the Portuguese constitution, Cahill advanced the idea of forming parochial councils in rural areas. He wanted recognition of this in the constitution. If the councils were elected by heads of families, this would 'serve to give a statutory recognition to the Christian family, such as is given in the Portuguese Constitution, making a definite departure from the Liberal, unchristian ideal and a return to the solid Christian tradition'.[32]

The submission itself was made up of a preamble and six draft articles on religion, marriage, the family, education, private property and liberty of the press. The preamble was much longer than that eventually adopted but it began similarly to the final wording: 'In the Name of the Most Holy Trinity …'

IN THE NAME OF THE HOLY TRINITY AND OF OUR LORD JESUS CHRIST THE UNIVERSAL KING,

We, the people of Ireland, being the parent nation of the Irish race, mindful of the long centuries of persecution we have had to endure, and full of gratitude to God who has so mercifully preserved us from innumerable dangers in the past; hereby as an independent Christian nation establish this sovereign Civil Society of the Irish people.

This Jesuit version continues at considerable length and includes commitments to equality of citizenship. It also declares authority and powers exercised under the subject to divine law, natural and positive, which were not adopted. The Polish preamble, on which this is significantly based, also has an evocation of past oppressions – in their case Russia. This evocation was a strong influence on the final draft of the preamble to the constitution. The article on religion was also to prove of considerable importance. The religious article read:

(a) Freedom of Religious worship (in public and private) is guaranteed to all within the limits of *public order and morality.*
(b) The Catholic Faith, which is the faith of *the vast majority* of the nation, and which is inseparably bound up with the nation's history, traditions and culture, occupies among religions in our country a unique and preponderant position.[33]

The second clause in the article on marraige required that the conditions required for the civil validity of the betrothals and marriages of Catholics shall be identical with those laid down in the code of canon law of the Catholic Church. It also decreed that the Catholic Church would be the 'competent authority' in deciding the existence or non-existence of the marriage bond when one of its members was involved. The article on education with its emphasis on the rights of parents as primary educators and with free choice in schools was to be a significant element in the education article. However, a constitutional provision to make the teaching of religion within schools maintained or subsidised by the state obligatory was never really considered acceptable.

De Valera rejected a number of the specific ideas in the Jesuit draft. In particular, he did not warm to the suggestion of regulating Church–state relations through a concordat. The titles of the articles and the structure of the Jesuit submission may have influenced de Valera.

When de Valera later admitted that Cahill may have been influential in specific areas, he was almost certainly referring to the Jesuit submission, which he had been deliberately misled into believing was virtually all Cahill's work. Cahill wrote again to de Valera on 13 November 1936 with a submission of his own. He stated that he had been 'delayed unavoidably much longer than' he foresaw.[34] This may have been a reference to the fact that he had been obliged to submit his work to two censors of his choice from the disbanded committee. The material given to de Valera on that occasion was based, as Cahill had indicated, on the Portuguese constitution. He again proposed parish committees in the countryside, set up on the basis of the family. In the final analysis, Cahill was not influential in the drafting of the constitution except for the fact that de Valera's request to him was the catalyst for the formation of the 'Jesuit committee', some of whose suggestions were ultimately adopted. De Valera may have considered that he owed Cahill more than was actually the case because of the deliberate confusion over the authorship of the Jesuit submission. However, neither Cahill as an individual nor the Jesuits as an order had nearly as much influence on de Valera as the small core of civil servants who bore the brunt of the drafting process. Irish Jesuits had emphatically not drafted the 1937 constitution.

CHAPTER 4

Fr John Charles McQuaid and the Draft Constitution, autumn 1936 to March 1937

The mystique and mythology surrounding the name of the Holy Ghost Father, John Charles McQuaid, has grown in the latter part of the twentieth century. As archbishop of Dublin between 1940 and 1972, he has been ascribed very great power – in one case making him more powerful than the Taoiseach. But setting such discourse and polemics aside, at the time of the drafting of the constitution, McQuaid had not been elevated to high office. He was a distinguished member of a major teaching order in Ireland which ran, among other schools, Blackrock College. He was a friend of de Valera and of his wife Sinéad. As president of Blackrock and a noted English teacher, he had the de Valera boys in his class. He was, moreover, a neighbour, living very close to the de Valera household.

In order to gain some understanding of this complex and highly influential person, it would be worthwhile to provide a short biography based on his obituary as it appeared in a publication of the order.[1] John Charles McQuaid was born on 28 July 1895, in Cootehill, County Cavan. From an early age he displayed that he was academically gifted, completing the six year course in Cootehill boys' national school four years after enrolling. From there he went, first to the nearby St Patrick's College, and then at fifteen to Blackrock College where, under the care of the Holy Ghost Fathers, he took first place in Ireland in Latin in his intermediate certificate. Transferring to the Jesuit-run Clongowes Wood, he was awarded the gold medal in English and first place in religious knowledge. On leaving school he entered the noviciate of the Holy Ghost Fathers with the intention of spending his life on the 'foreign missions'. While a clerical student he attended UCD where again he excelled academically, receiving first class honours in his BA degree and was awarded an MA with first class honours for a dissertation on the life and philosophy of Seneca.

McQuaid was sent to Rome to study for a doctorate in theology. However, his studies were cut short when he was recalled in 1925 to take up the position of dean of studies at Blackrock College; the previous year he had been ordained in St Mary's College, Rathmines. He did not get the opportunity to return to complete his postgraduate theological studies. Dr McQuaid was destined to spend fifteen years at Blackrock, becoming its president in 1931 where he proved himself to be an excellent administrator and a teacher with progressive ideas, fostering interest in art and sport. In relation to discipline, he pleaded that it should not be severe and allowed the pupils much more freedom than was usual in Ireland at the time. On 11 November 1940, he succeeded the late Dr Edward Byrne as archbishop of Dublin, an appointment which met with some surprise since traditionally bishops were drawn from the secular clergy. Within a brief period, through his enormous energy and administrative ability, the diocese was placed on a sound economic footing.

In view of de Valera's concern to keep the drafting process secret and the work confined to a few trusted civil servants, how did McQuaid become so involved? The answer may be similar to that provided in the case of the Jesuits: Fr Edward Cahill and Fr John Charles McQuaid were both friends of de Valera, but the nature of these friendships differed greatly. McQuaid was within de Valera's inner family circle in a way that Cahill had never been. The future archbishop of Dublin was indeed a family friend. He was a great source of comfort when the de Valeras lost a son in a riding accident in 1936. McQuaid was a very well-known figure in Catholic education circles. But that itself would not have brought McQuaid into the confined circles responsible for bringing the first draft of the constitution together.

No evidence has been found of an invitation being issued to McQuaid to get him involved in the process of drafting a new constitution. The matter may have arisen casually in conversation between the two men in the autumn of 1936 when the first tentative steps were being made to put a new constitution together. But what may have started off as a casual and unofficial engagement grew and grew. The small drafting team, led by John Hearne, were almost certainly not very welcoming of the material that began to cascade onto their desks, through de Valera, from that source. In July 1960 Éamon de Valera, at a celebration marking the centenary of Blackrock College (his *alma mater*), said of McQuaid's involvement: 'The parts he approved of then have never been questioned, the parts he disapproved of have been criticised.'[2]

The documentary evidence suggests that McQuaid did not become actively involved in the drafting process until November 1936, but it may have been earlier. He had written notes on the back of an envelope sent by de Valera and dated 11 November 1936:[3]

> Preamble=paragraph, 1916 proc, 1919,
> Nation. Territory. Indefeasible Language, Sovereignty resides in people
> State, Guarantees, Citizen, Status of Rel Assoc, Education, Family

Unfortunately, much of the correspondence from McQuaid to de Valera is undated. In the earliest dated letter, written on 16 February 1937, McQuaid expressed his appreciation for being afforded the opportunity to participate in the project. It is clear from the text of this letter, however, that matters were well advanced by that stage. In addition to a mention of a work of criticism of the French constitution of 1814, the letter stated:

> I also send three new paragraphs for private property section. I hope they are according to the idea you had in mind. At least they are accurate for I spent the day on an analysis of *Quadragesimo Anno* and *Rerum Novarum* – which proved extraordinarily helpful to me, in my understanding of the Pope.[4]

By the time that letter was written, a pattern had developed. From early 1937, de Valera received frequent correspondence, sometimes twice a day, from McQuaid. The letters contained suggestions, ideas, documents and references on nearly every aspect of what was to become *Bunreacht na hÉireann*. As well as copies of papal encyclicals, notes and supporting documentation, de Valera was given two books, both in French, *Manuel Sociale* by the Belgian Jesuit, Fr Vermeersch, and *Code of Social Principles*, published at Malines by the International Union of Social Studies. Two copies of the 1918 *Codex Iuris Canonicis* were also given and a concise edition of McQuaid's on Rousseau's theory of civil authority.[5]

McQuaid's general approach to the constitution was set out in an undated document entitled *Directive Principles*, which declared that a constitution was 'a thesis of philosophy and theology'. The document, he thought, should 'be guided and delimited by the teachings of Catholic philosophy and theology. It should enshrine and set forth what ought to be our Christian endeavour in social policy.' The document continued: 'We desire – within the vast freedom of the social encyclicals to achieve common good of the nation on Christian lines and by Christian methods.'[6]

In a letter dated 10 March, McQuaid is concerned with punctuation. He asked de Valera if there was any objection to the document 'having a few more commas', while he also informed him that there was a 'bracket missing before final semi-colon'. This letter also suggests that de Valera was appreciative of the meticulous care that McQuaid brought to the task as he had presented the latter with 'the very thoughtful present of Miss [Dorothy] Macardle's book'. McQuaid's letter continued: 'When I next see you, you will perhaps autograph it. I need not say that I have put it on one side as instructed!'[7] This would suggest that all of his spare time was devoted to his work on the constitution.

At this point McQuaid may have already received two versions for consideration: the third complete draft of the new constitution (November–December

1936)[8] and Alfred O'Rahilly's 1922 Draft C. McQuaid found the latter unsatisfactory. He wrote to de Valera: 'With O'Rahilly's draft I feel very disappointed, but I suppose it was hasty and was all that could be done at the time.'[9]

Although it is clear that McQuaid had a not insignificant role in the drafting process, any definitive assessment as to the nature and degree of his influence is problematic. Very few of the draft documents have dates. Drafts have cryptic titles such as X, Y and Q. Although Q was de Valera's occasional shorthand for McQuaid, it does not necessarily mean that any document with Q on it was written by McQuaid.

The probable methodology of the drafting process was that McQuaid assembled the relevant excerpts from the papal encyclicals which were passed on; de Valera, John Hearne, and Arthur Matheson used some of his ideas to guide them in the drafting process. On a private and informal basis, de Valera returned the draft articles to McQuaid, who annotated them and in some cases redrafted them. Alternatively, it is possible that McQuaid was given *carte blanche* by de Valera to draft the relevant articles himself, provided they conformed to the instructions that he had been given; however, this seems improbable.

Further difficulties confront the historian. McQuaid wrote much of his material in longhand, including extracts from encyclicals, redrafts of articles produced by Hearne, or even drafts of new articles that he had created himself. These longhand drafts were then reproduced in a typed copy with a blue type.

There is also a difficulty contextualising the letters McQuaid wrote to de Valera. These were enclosed with material from encyclicals. However, the letters were separated from their enclosures, thus rendering them difficult to interpret. The different typefaces used in the McQuaid dossiers also suggest that some of this material may not have emanated from him. There appears to have been a division of labour in the process after November 1936, as Hearne's drafts omit fundamental guarantees, property, family and social provisions. There is a note written on one draft from October–November 1936 which states that Part IX was given to Dr McQuaid (Part IX dealt with material that became Article 40–45). However, it is apparent that McQuaid was also involved in commenting on the drafting of other provisions. But a definitive assessment of the extent of that involvement is problematic.

One piece of material, however, provides possible clarification of the method of the drafting process that involved McQuaid. In a letter to Seán Lemass, written at the height of the difficult negotiations with the Irish hierarchy concerning the Health Bill of 1953, de Valera explained:

> Were I at home, and able to consult with the minister, I would suggest that each particular proposal of ours to which objection was made be taken up with the Archbishop, and

> that he be asked to make a draft with the qualifications that would satisfy him. This draft could then be examined from our point of view and amended if necessary, until an agreed text was arrived at. That is more or less what happened in regard to the corresponding articles of the Constitution.[10]

In a letter dated 16 February 1937, McQuaid enclosed three paragraphs on private property which he hoped were 'according to the idea' that de Valera 'had in mind'. He knew what was in de Valera's mind, or he was confident enough – after discussion – to bring his grasp of the central ideas to fruition in a draft; but how influential was the future archbishop of Dublin?

On 16 February 1937, McQuaid wrote that if de Valera wanted him 'for discussion' he was at his service.[11] In another letter, McQuaid wrote that they could discuss a suggestion of his 'when next we meet'.[12] He reiterated this point later in the letter when he assured de Valera that 'any time' the latter wanted him for discussion, he would 'be delighted to go over'.[13] On March 16 1937, he wrote: 'It is such a joy to see it in print now it remains to see it enacted. It reads very well. I think I note the few changes made.'[14] In a letter on 25 March 1937, McQuaid stated: 'Herewith I send with great pleasure the remaining dossier, point by point, for the Family, Education and Private Property. By tonight I hope to have Church and State all typed. These are auspicious days for the work.'[15] However, it should be noted that although there are discernible differences between these articles and the corresponding articles of the 1936 drafts, McQuaid was generally responsible for a change in emphasis rather than in the direction of the original drafts.

On 29 December 1937, the day the constitution came into effect, McQuaid wrote as follows: 'Many have desired to see what we see and have not seen.' That adaptation of a biblical text is a sign of the intimacy of the communications which had emerged between the two men during the process of the drafting which lasted from autumn 1936 until late April 1937.

Professor T. P. O'Neill and the Earl of Longford, in their biography of de Valera, state that McQuaid was very influential in the drafting of certain articles, particularly those dealing with fundamental rights which were to become Articles 40 to 45. These consisted of personal rights; the family; education; private property; religion, and directive principles of social policy. It is not possible here to track all of McQuaid's contributions to the drafting process. A few areas have been chosen as an example.

Personal rights were dealt with in what eventually became Article 40 of the constitution and were influenced by various factors, including the 1922 constitution and papal encyclicals. Article 40.1 in the final version stated:

> All citizens shall, as human persons, be held equal before the law. This shall not be held to mean that the State shall not in its enactments have due regards to differences of capacity, physical and moral, and of social functions.

This had been amended only slightly from the 'X' draft which stated: 'The State acknowledges that all citizens shall, as human persons, be held equal before the law.' This clause was broadly in line with the teaching of Leo XIII in *Humanum Genus* where the pope argued that while all persons are equal as far as their origins and ends are concerned, in terms of their abilities, their powers of mind and body, disposition and character 'it is most repugnant to reason to endeavour to confine all within the same measure, and to extend complete equality to the institutions of civil life'. This point was reiterated in *Rerum Novarum* where it was stated that it was 'impossible to reduce civil society to one dead level'.[16]

McQuaid wrote to de Valera, defending the wording and the principle underpinning the article, claiming that it was wrong 'to read into it an attack on women, or any special class, or a threat of a future attack. It is a graver error still, to see in it any tincture of modern fascism.' The article merely acknowledged that 'distributive justice – which has regard to inequalities, natural and acquired, and to diversity of social function – will be observed in the enactments of law'.[17]

Article 40.3 would appear to have been influenced by the encyclical *Rerum Novarum*, an extract from which had been sent from McQuaid to de Valera. This stated:

> Rights must be religiously respected wherever they exist, and it is the duty of the public Authority to prevent and to punish violation of rights, and to protect every one in the possession of his own … wherever the general interest or any particular class suffers or is threatened with mischief which can in no other way be met or prevented, the public Authority must step in to deal with it.'[18]

A rejected earlier draft of this article had stated:

> The State guarantees to respect and defend the personal rights of each citizen, those that are inalienable, indefeasible and antecedent to positive law, as well as those that have by law been granted and defined. Accordingly the State shall take all necessary measures to prevent abuses, enforce respect for social order and punish offenders against its laws.[19]

The version of 16 March in the first printed draft was virtually identical with the final form. It read:

> 40.3.1. The State guarantees in its laws to respect and, as far as practicable, by its laws defend and vindicate the personal rights of the citizens.
>
> 40.3.2. The State shall, in particular, by its laws protect as best it may from unjust attack and in the case of injustice done, vindicate the life, person, good name, and property rights of every citizen.[20]

The Family

The Alfred O'Rahilly draft constitution, dating from 1922, had the following article:

> **Article 53.**
>
> 1. Marriage, as the basis of family life and national well-being, is under the special protection of the State: and all attacks on the purity, health and sacredness of family life shall be forbidden.
> 2. The Irish State shall recognise, as heretofore, the inviolable sanctity of the marital bond.
> 3. The civil validity of religiously solemnised marriages shall be recognised, provided that the details of registration prescribed by legislation are duly complied with.[21]

In their initial October draft, de Valera and Hearne drew on O'Rahilly's work. Article 34 stated:

> 1. The State guarantees the constitution and protection of the family as the basis of moral education and social discipline and harmony, and the sure foundation of ordered society.
> 2. (1) The constitution of the family depends upon valid marriage.
>
>   (2) Marriage, as the basis of family life, is under the special protection of the State; attacks on the sanctity of marriage or of family life are prohibited.
>
>   (3) Contraception and advocacy of the practice of contraception are prohibited and the possession, use, sale, and distribution of contraceptives shall be punishable.
>
>   (4) No law shall be enacted authorising the dissolution of a valid consummated marriage of baptised persons. No law shall be enacted authorising the annulment of marriage save on the following grounds, namely, that either or both of the parties did not agree to enter into the marriage contract, or was or were not free to enter, or did not freely enter into the marriage contract, or that the marriage was under the law for the time being in force invalid in form. Subject to the foregoing, the contract of marriage shall be regulated by law.
>
>   (5) The State shall encourage early marriage and foster the production of large families by appropriate grants of remission of taxation in respect of children, by the

promotion of saving and thrift schemes and by facilitating the provision of housing accommodation on reasonable terms.[22]

The Jesuit submission and Fr Cahill's own submission made similar provisions:

> The Civil Powers cannot dissolve a marriage validly contracted and betrothals and marriages of Catholics shall be identical with those laid down in the Code of Canon Law of the Catholic Church.[23]

As with all other official drafts, the McQuaid article (Q is written at the top of the page) attributed a central position to the family. By the end of February 1937, the X (Q) formula on the family was as follows:

1. The State recognises the Family as the natural primary and fundamental unit of society, and as a moral and juridical institution possessing inalienable and imprescriptible rights, antecedent and superior to all positive laws.
2. The State therefore guarantees to protect the family in its Constitution, Authority and Government, as the necessary basis of order as indispensable to the welfare of the Nation.
3. In particular the State recognises that by her life within the home, woman gives to the State support with which the common good can be achieved. The State shall therefore make it an aim to see that women, especially mothers and young girls, shall not be obliged *to enter avocations unsuited to their sex and strength.*[24]
4. The State pledges itself to guard with special care the institution of marriage, on which the Family is founded, and to protect it against attack.
5. No law shall be passed which shall impair its essential properties of unity and indissolubility. No person whose marriage has been dissolved under the Civil Law of any other State shall be capable of contracting a valid marriage in Éire during the lifetime of the other party to the marriage so dissolved.[25]

The protection and reverence accorded to the family, and the treatment accorded to women in this article, was strongly influenced by Leo XIII's Encyclical, *Rerum Novarum*. The pope argued against the contention that the state had the option to intrude into and exercise intimate control over the family and the household; he called this 'a great and pernicious error'. Only in the cases of extreme necessity was it right that the state should interfere in the family.

The clause on mothers was also influenced by *Rerum Novarum,* which stated that 'a woman is by nature fitted for homework, and is that which is best adapted at once to preserve her modesty and promote the good bring up (*sic*) of children and the well being of the family'.[26] The family, according to McQuaid, was 'an institution of nature, a moral institution in the sense that, on the analogy of the human person, it possesses rights and is bound by obligations'.[27] Five pages of the McQuaid dossier on the family were dedicated to answering the question: 'What is a natural right, antecedent and superior to all positive law?' McQuaid gave his own definition of natural law: 'God's design evident in his words and in nature and in hist[ory] of man'. In the final two pages, McQuaid examined the issue in some detail, relying heavily on the works of Thomas Aquinas.

McQuaid's proposal that 'no law shall be enacted authorising the dissolution of a valid consummated marriage of baptised persons' was accepted. This was echoed in Article 41.2 in the final draft which read: 'No law shall be enacted providing for a grant or a dissolution of marriage.' McQuaid stated that it was

> ... hardly possible to describe how great are the evils that flow from divorce. Matrimonial contracts are by it made variable, mutual kindness is weakened, deplorable inducements to unfaithfulness are supplied, harm is done in the education and training of children, occasion is afforded to the breaking up of homes, the seeds are sown of dissension among families, the dignity of womanhood is lessened and brought low, and women run the risk of being deserted after having ministered to the pleasure of men.[28]

He informed de Valera that the radical women's criticisms were very 'confused. Both *Casti Connubii* and *Quadragesimo Anno* answer them'. McQuaid referred him to Pius XI's statement that 'mothers will above all devote their work to the home and things connected with it'.[29]

McQuaid emphasised that, to recognise the special importance of women's role in the home, women's work elsewhere could not be denigrated:

> Nothing will change the law and fact of nature that woman's natural sphere is the home. She is perfectly free not to marry or to marry: to choose this or that career. No Article in the Draft Constitution even attempts to deny woman's fundamental rights as a human being.
>
> Article 41.2,1 merely acknowledges a fact: the dignity and indispensable role of those women who choose to get married.
>
> Art. 41.2,2 having acknowledged that fact, guarantees that it will endeavour to see, not that women will be prevented from engaging in this or that career, but a certain class of woman, namely Mothers, will not be forced, by pressure of need, so to engage in work as to neglect their proper home-duties.[30]

Within the Dáil, de Valera ably defended the article and, objecting to an opposition amendment to replace work 'in the Home' for 'work for the Home'. He declared, echoing McQuaid's sentiments: 'We state here that mothers in their homes give to the State a support which is essential. Is there anybody who denies it? Is it not a tribute to the work that is done by women in the homes as mothers.'[31] Indeed de Valera described the word 'home' as 'sacred'.[32]

Echoing McQuaid's attitude in his defence of the article, de Valera used the word 'woman' and 'mother' interchangeably. When James Dillon of Fine Gael suggested that the word 'mother' should be used instead of 'woman', de Valera refused, stating: 'There are mothers and wives too, and not all wives happen to be mothers … I have made up my mind that this is accurate and I am not going to put in anything else.'[33]

Education

The article of the 1937 constitution dealing with education also appears to have been directly influenced by McQuaid. The teaching in the encyclical *Divini Illius Magistri* of Pope Pius XI would appear to have been paraphrased in the final version of Article 42.3 of the constitution. The limited role of the state in family life and in the socialisation of children was continued in Articles 41–42 which embodied the doctrine of subsidiarity by recognising the family as the 'natural, primary and fundamental group in society' and as the primary and natural educator of society. Pius XI's encyclical emphasised the role of the family as the primary educator.[34]

However it is clear that in all these ways of promoting education and instruction, both public and private, the State should respect the inherent rights of the Church and of the family concerning Christian education, and moreover have regard for distributive justice. Accordingly, unjust and unlawful is any monopoly, educational or scholastic, which, physically or morally, forces families to make use of government schools, contrary to the dictates of their Christian conscience, or contrary even to their legitimate preferences.[35]

The above extract from *Divini Illius Magistri* is mirrored in Article 42.3,1 of the constitution which reads as follows:

> 42.3,1° The State shall not oblige parents in violation of their conscience and lawful preference to send their children to schools established by the State, or to any particular type of school designated by the State.

The next clause which guarantees a basic education to children of the state reads:

> 42.3,2° The State shall, however, as guardian of the common good, require in view of actual conditions that the children receive a certain minimum education, moral, intellectual and social.

This had echoes of the same papal encyclical:

> The State can exact, and take measures to secure that all its citizens have the necessary knowledge of their civic and political duties, and a certain degree of physical, intellectual

and moral culture, which, considering the conditions of our time, is really necessary for the common good.[36]

In *Divini Illius Magistri*, Pius XI made it clear that it was the duty of the state to protect the rights of the child when inadequate parenting meant that the child was not receiving proper physical or moral care whether by default, incapacity or misconduct. This papal teaching was included in Article 42.5 of the constitution, which states:

> In exceptional cases, where the parents for physical or moral reasons fail in their duty towards their children, the State as guardian of the common good, by appropriate means shall endeavour to supply the place of the parents, but always with due regard for the natural and imprescriptible rights of the child.

Of note is the fact that the article omitted reference to denominational education or separate education for boys and girls, both of which had been included in the Jesuit submission:

> Schools, maintained or subsidised by the State shall be in principle denominational; and, except in special circumstances to be defined by law, boys and girls of adolescent age shall be educated separately.[37]

The Jesuits had emphasised the rights of parents as primary educators entitled to a free choice of schools. This was to be a significant element in the final education article:

> It is the natural right as well as the duty of parents to provide, as far as in them lies, for the education religious, moral, physical and intellectual of their children. Parents may freely choose teachers for their children, and freely select the schools to which their children's education is to be entrusted.[38]

Usefully, the Jesuit report included references to the Catholic teaching which underlay each suggested article. The reference given for the above is Pius XI's *Divini Illius Magistri*. Article 42.1 and 42.2 of the constitution would both appear to have been influenced to some extent by the Jesuit clause reproduced above.

> 1.1 The State acknowledges that the primary and natural educator of the child is the Family and guarantees to respect the inalienable right and duty of parents to provide according to their means, for the religious and moral, intellectual, physical and social education of their children.
>
> 1.2 Parents shall be free to provide this education in their homes or private schools or in schools recognised or established by the State.

It is fair to say that McQuaid and, to a lesser extent, the Jesuits, to whose report he had access, were important influences in the drafting of education Article 42.

Personal Property and Directive of Social Policy

From the available evidence it would appear that John Charles McQuaid had a considerable influence on the articles that eventually became Articles 43 and 45, i.e. those dealing with personal property and social principles respectively. In earlier drafts, including the first printed draft of 16 March 1937, the personal property article and what eventually became directives of social policy (finally Article 45) together made up Article 41. McQuaid wrote to de Valera on 16 February enclosing 'three new paragraphs for the private property section'. He hoped they were 'according to the idea' that de Valera had in mind. McQuaid stated that they were accurate as he had 'spent the day on an analysis of *Quadragesimo Anno* and *Rerum Novarum*'.[39] These two encyclicals were closely connected; *Quadragesimo Anno* was issued by Pius XI on the fortieth anniversary of Leo XIII's *Rerum Novarum* as a tribute to, and a reiteration of, the message contained therein. Leo XIII had stated that private property was in accordance with natural law but both he and Pius XI had stressed that the state had the right to delimit this power on the grounds of the common good.

The table below, prepared by Dr Robert McNamara, and amended by Andrew McCarthy, outlines the influence of the encyclicals, and by definition of McQuaid, on the personal property Article 41 of the first printed draft of 16 March 1937.

Table 3: Comparison of the Papal Encyclicals with the First Printed Draft of the Constitution

Extracts from Encyclicals	First Printed Draft. Article 41.
The right to possess private property is derived from nature, not from man; and the State has the right to control its use in the interests of the public good alone, but by no means to absorb it altogether. (*Rerum Novarum* 47)	1. The State acknowledges that man, in virtue of his rational being, has the natural right, antecedent to positive law, to the private ownership of external goods.
	2. The State recognises that the exercise

Therefore, the riches that economic-social developments constantly increase ought to be so distributed among individual persons and classes that the common advantage of all, which Leo XIII had praised, will be safeguarded; in other words, that the common good of all society will be kept inviolate. (*Quadragesimo Anno* 57)

Hence, the institutions themselves of peoples and, particularly those of all social life, ought to be penetrated with this justice, and it is most necessary that it be truly effective, that is, establish a juridical and social order which will, as it were, give form and shape to all economic life. Social charity, moreover, ought to be as the soul of this order, an order which public authority ought to be ever ready effectively to protect and defend.
(*Quadragesimo Anno 88*)

But to abuse the years of childhood and the limited strength of women is grossly wrong. Mothers, concentrating on household duties, should work primarily in the home or in its immediate vicinity. It is an intolerable abuse, and to be abolished at all cost, for mothers on account of the father's low wage to be forced to engage in gainful occupations outside the home to the neglect of their proper cares and duties, especially the training of children. (*Quadragesimo Anno 71*)

of this natural right is not only allowable, but is, for social needs, absolutely necessary, and therefore guarantees to pass no law attempting to abolish the right of private ownership.

3. Since the use by individuals of private property ought, in civil society, be regulated by the principles of social justice, the State may lawfully delimit this use when the need arises with a view to reconciling it to the common good.

4. The State shall use its best endeavour to provide that the material resources of the nation may be so distributed among private individuals and the various classes of the population as adequately to procure the common good of the community as a whole.

5. The State shall strive to promote the economic welfare of the whole people, by securing, protecting and defending, as effectively as it may, an economic order in which social justice and social charity shall imbue all the institutions of public life, and in particular:
i. Endeavour to ensure that the adult working man, especially the fathers of families, shall receive a wage sufficient to meet adequately their domestic needs, present and future.

ii. By providing, as best it can, opportunities for work for those who are willing and able to work.

iii. By attempting to regulate, according

Every effort must therefore be made that fathers of families receive a wage large enough to meet ordinary family needs adequately. But if this cannot always be done under existing circumstances, social justice demands that changes be introduced as soon as possible whereby such a wage will be assured to every adult workingman. (*Quadragesimo Anno 71*)

In the first place, it is obvious that not only is wealth concentrated in our times but an immense power and despotic economic dictatorship is consolidated in the hands of a few …

This dictatorship is being most forcibly exercised by those who, since they hold the money and completely control it, control credit also and rule the lending of money. Hence they regulate the flow, so to speak, of the life-blood whereby the entire economic system lives, and have so firmly in their grasp the soul, as it were, of economic life that no one can breathe against their will. (*Quadragesimo Anno 105-106*)

But free competition, while justified and certainly useful provided it is kept within certain limits, clearly cannot direct economic life … Therefore, it is most necessary that economic life be again subjected to and governed by a true and effective directing principle.

to social justice, with the cooperation of vocational groups and associations, such a scale of wages as shall offer to the greatest number opportunities of adequate means of livelihood.

iv. By ensuring that the tender age of children or the adequate strength of women shall not be abused nor mothers forced to engage in labour to the neglect of their own proper duties.

6.1. The State shall make it a duty so to restrain free competition, within just limits, that no combination shall be formed whereby the undue monopoly of the resources of the State or of a particular class of goods may pass into the ownership and control of one or of a few individuals.

6.2. In particular the State shall see to it that the economic domination of the few, in what pertains to the control of credit, shall not endanger the common good of the community as a whole.

7.1. The State pledges itself to safeguard with special care the economic rights of the less favoured classes of Society, to contribute to the support of the infirm, the widow, the orphan, and the aged poor who are past their labour.

7.1. In particular, with a view to obtaining a more just balance between wealth and poverty, to securing a more abundant yield of the produce of the

(*Quadragesimo Anno* 48)

If working people can be encouraged to look forward to obtaining a share in the land, the consequence will be that the gulf between vast wealth and sheer poverty will be bridged over, and the respective classes will be brought nearer to one another. (*Rerum Novarum* 47)

earth, and to attaching its citizens more closely to their native country, the State shall endeavour to give to as many families as practicable a share in the land.

8. The State shall have regard for such distribution of the centres of industry, that, while an opportunity is given for necessary development, the traditional preference of our people for rural life may be duly fostered and maintained.

9. The State shall favour and where necessary supplement private economic initiative.

10. With a view to procuring the common good of the Nation as a whole, and to securing a more equitable social balance, the State shall favour the due constitution of vocational groupings, on the basis of the various forms of social activities.

A letter to de Valera serves to illustrate how McQuaid constantly amended, honed and polished the articles on which he worked, frequently in consultation with de Valera:

> I beg to enclose a draft of the paragraphs on free competition etc., which, after much, I feel to be more logical and compact. I hope the correction will not prove inconvenient. In the paragraph on 'share in the land', I have recast the third reason, making it more accurately represent the famous passages in Quadreggisimo Anno and also Rerum Novarum. With O'Rahilly's draft, I feel very disappointed: but, I suppose it was hasty and was all that could be done at the time.[40]

The final sentence reveals that he had studied O'Rahilly's 1922 draft and was politely dismissive of it. It is clear from a letter of 8 March 1937 that McQuaid also drafted the clauses on widows and orphans when he points out that he had retained the word 'support' to counter any claims from people of complete dependence on the state.[41]

The limits of his influence are also clear from this letter when he talks about dealing with the question of unsettled strikes:

> Further, we have, at no point, met the most potent form of social agitation: the unsettled strike. A great deal of the venom of Communism could be neutralised, if where strikes do occur, a mode of settlement, fair to both sides, could be found. I venture, therefore, to suggest a small paragraph – which is both correct in social doctrine and capable of averting immense evils.[42]

There is a draft containing such a clause in the McQuaid papers calling for the 'setting up in cases of dispute between employers and employed when the parties themselves shall have failed to find a satisfactory solution, an Arbitration Board, whose verdict shall, if either or both parties refuse to yield, be compulsorily enforced'.[43] This proposal was not accepted by de Valera however, and the clause did not appear in subsequent drafts.

This chapter provides a snapshot of McQuaid's interaction with de Valera. It shows the intensity of the exchanges between the two men and of the richness of their intellectual exchanges. But what it does not show is the interaction between McQuaid's voluminous submissions and the drafting team of John Hearne, Maurice Moynihan and the others leading civil servants who brought the different drafts to finality. There is likely to have been a real tension between those like Hearne who wanted a relatively short document and McQuaid who wished to convert the constitution into a Catholic document rooted in the Papal encyclicals and in Thomistic philosophy. The future archbishop of Dublin was determined to make Ireland a model Catholic state with a model constitution which would condition the development of the country. However, there is another discourse. That is the determination of the drafting team to rise to the task of writing a new constitution which would be based on universal principles and on the constitutional tradition as reflected in the 1922 document and the documents of Dáil Éireann, 1919. Moynihan, Hearne and other drafters represented a wider nationalist tradition than that championed by John Charles McQuaid. They wanted a constitution for all citizens. As this chapter has shown, even if the case is overstated, McQuaid did exercise a strong influence over de Valera. His interventions were more problematical for the drafting team. But it did not matter to the drafting team if a clause was inspired by Catholic principles based on encyclicals. What concerned civil servants involved in the drafting process was that a citizen's right was enshrined in, and protected by, the new constitution. There is at least one area where both de Valera and the civil service drafters drew a line in outright defiance of the Holy Ghost father. That related to the contents of the religious clause – Article 44. This showed de Valera's determination, and that of the drafting group, to withstand all pressure to frame an article which would be offensive to the other churches in Ireland. The line was held – but with great difficulty. This process will be examined in chapter six.

Professor Enda McDonagh described the Irish constitution in 1961 as 'by no means perfect – either in its democratic aspirations or in its adaptation of Catholic teaching'. Despite his reservations, he was convinced that it was 'a fairly successful union of democracy and Catholic teaching'. By and large it 'is a splendid achievement and its general solution of the Church–State problem has much to offer to modern politicians and theologians in their search for a satisfactory formula'.[44] But de Valera had a long road to travel between mid-March and late April 1937 before the 'one true Church' formula was jettisoned and the final wording agreed. The reasons for this are examined in detail in Chapter 6.

CHAPTER 5

RESPONSES TO THE FIRST PRINTED DRAFT OF CONSTITUTION

The cabinet minutes of 12 March 1937 approved 'general procedure' in regard to the enactment of a new constitution. These consisted of arrangements for the submission to the Dáil for approval of the necessary legislation for a plebiscite. The minutes also mentioned 'the Chamber of Deputies elected at the general election, the polling day for which shall have taken place on the same day as the plebiscite'.[1] On 16 March 1937, the Executive Council, secretaries of government departments and other senior officials received the first official printed draft of the constitution. Conor Maguire, president of the high court, George Gavan Duffy, judge of the high court and James Geoghegan, judge of the supreme court, also received numbered copies.[2]

On 10 March, de Valera had circulated a copy of the constitution to a very small group of trusted and intimate advisers. The copy on the file is that of the secretary of the Department of External Affairs, Joseph P. Walshe. It contained a draft article on religion (then Article 42 – eventually Article 44). Reaction to that article was extremely negative as it was left blank in the draft constitution circulated on 16 March 1937. The full text of the earliest draft is included as Appendix 9.

Before proceeding with the reconstruction, the table below provides a timeline for the passage of the constitution.

TABLE 4: CHRONOLOGY OF EVENTS, 1937

Introduced in Dáil	10 March
Provisional draft (limited circulation by de Valera)	10 – 15 March
First draft circulated	16 March
First Revise circulated	1 April
Second Revise circulated	10 April
Third Revise	23 April
Published and circulated	1 May
Second Reading	11–13 May (69 to 43)

Third Reading (committee stage)		25 May–3 June
Fourth Reading (report stage)		9–14 June
Approved by Dáil, and recommended for adoption		14 June (62 to 48)
Enacted by the people		1 July
For	686,105	
Against	526,945	
Majority	159,160	
Date of coming into operation		29 December
1938		
Senate met		27 April
President elected		4 May
President entered office		25 June

Observations of the Department of Finance

The President 'on receipt of Ministerial, Departmental and other comments officially appointed this Committee'.[3] This was much more than an editorial committee. It had the responsibility to integrate all relevant suggestions into the draft document and cope with queries and criticisms. Again, de Valera did not depend upon hierarchy. He picked the new secretary of the Department of the President since 1 March 1937, Maurice Moynihan, the brother of Seán who had worked in the same office before being transferred, to take the chair. He had first served as de Valera's private secretary in 1932 before moving to the Department of Finance.[4] Between 11 March 1936 and 28 February 1937 he was 'on loan' to the Department of the President where he helped in the early stages of the drafting of the new constitution.

Maurice Moynihan, described in his obituary as 'one of the greatest civil servants in the history of the State', was born in Tralee in December 1902 and educated by the local Christian Brothers. He achieved a first class honours degree in commerce from University College Cork, and became a civil servant in 1925 when he entered the Department of Finance. He became secretary to the government on 1 March 1937, at the age of thirty-four, a post he held until 1960 when he was appointed governor of the Central Bank.[5]

His role in 1937 as permanent head of the chief executive's office and as head of the cabinet secretariat automatically included responsibilities as de Valera's principal private secretary. Given de Valera's commitment to the new constitution it was natural that Moynihan too had a critical influence on the drafting process. His 'ability to virtually anticipate de Valera's response to any particular issue was widely acknowledged'.[6] He attended a conference on Catholic social and political thought in Clongowes Wood College in summer 1936 which outlined the Catholic interpretation of key political concepts, the nature of society, individual rights and responsibilities. These concepts would have been central to the underlying ideology. He was kept closely informed by de Valera on all draft documents and had been the recipient of the fourth copy of the secretly drafted copy of the new constitution of 4 March 1937. He was one of only two civil servants sent to communicate with senior members of religious organisations during the period of consultation concerning the religious article. He visited Archbishop Gregg to discuss the planned wording of what eventually became Article 44. He also worked on the Irish language version of the documents. Patrick Lynch has written that Moynihan had a:

> unique acquaintance with de Valera's mode of thought and way with words. It was a rare gift and a gift that de Valera was known to appreciate. Maurice's exquisite mastery of language in Irish and English was reflected in the simplicity and clarity of style and facilitated his remarkable skill as a draftsman.[7]

He was described as 'one of the few who founded the public service and helped to build it'. Joe Lee said of him that he was 'a man in whom the institution of the State found an absolutely trustworthy protector'. His role was 'one of the classic anonymity of the civil service' and his personal hallmarks were 'modesty and lack of pretension'. All accounts of him highlight his great personal charm and his ability to reconcile opposing views – traits that must have been an asset in committee meetings.[8]

De Valera retained control of the drafting process as the constitution evolved through further revisions, before the final version was made available to the public, press and the opposition and was printed in the newspapers on the first day of May 1937. Hearne, O'Donoghue and McDunphy continued to play a central role in the final stages of the drafting process under the watchful eye of Moynihan.

Of the departments only Finance and Justice sent in significant contributions on receipt of the first printed draft. Another Kerry man, James J. MacElligott, the secretary of the Department of Finance, was the most active in his criticism of the draft. The secretary of the Department of Justice, Stephen Roche, also made an important submission on behalf of his department. The response was varied from other heads of government departments and selected senior judges. As mentioned earlier, some departments obviously felt that they only needed to comment on matters pertaining to their own areas of responsibility.

Finance was the exception. Its response, dated 23 March 1937, consisted of a three-page opening statement divided into six numbered paragraphs and a thirty-nine-page commentary on individual articles of the constitution.[9] MacElligott, who had been secretary of the department since 1927, wrote it. Seán MacEntee, who was the Minister for Finance, may not have discouraged his senior civil servant from making swingeing criticisms of the document.

James MacElligott was born in Tralee in 1890 and came from a family of high achievers; of his four brothers three were civil servants and the fourth a doctor. James joined the civil service in 1913 as a first division clerk. He was a graduate entrant holding a BA in classics. On Easter Monday 1916 he heard of the Rising while at Fairyhouse races and joined in on his way home. He had the distinction of being the most 'senior civil servant of the Insurrection'.[10] He fought in the GPO and was taken prisoner and spent time in Stafford jail. He was, of course, dismissed from the service. On his return from imprisonment, he enrolled as a medical student and worked in financial journalism, which seemed to take precedence over his medical aspirations, as in March 1919 he was appointed by *The Statist* as a contributor. By 1920 he was acting editor of the journal and became managing editor in March 1922. He completed his MA dissertation in economic history in 1920 with a thesis entitled 'Manufacturing Industries in Ireland 1760 to 1820'. His reputation as an economic commentator and his impeccable Irish revolutionary credentials made him an obvious choice for recruitment to the finance department of the new civil service, where he was appointed assistant secretary in 1923. He was promoted to secretary in 1927, which post he held at the time of the drafting of the new constitution. He subsequently became governor of the Central Bank. He seems to have been far removed from the image of the stereotypical civil servant; he was known in London as 'a bit of a dandy' who used a pince-nez, 'with elegant attachments'. He was remembered in *The Statist* as 'an open handed toff', a generous man who tipped the office boy a £5 note when he was leaving for Ireland.[11]

MacElligott's response to the draft constitution emphasised that the department 'was not called upon to praise but rather to point out possible defects and difficulties, so what follows is conceived in that spirit'.[12] He pointed out that there were 'questions of complexity and expence' involved in the constitution. The document dealt most extensively with Articles 1–3, which the draft constitution entitled 'The Nation'. The section dealing with Articles 1–3 and Articles 38–41 (ultimately Articles 40–45) – which dealt with social policy and personal rights – contained the most outspoken criticism in the entire document. The observation that Articles 1–3 dealt with the 'Nation as distinct from the State (a distinction which many political scientists would not admit)' set the tone of the comments. It continued with the opinion that Articles 1–3 seemed to 'vitiate the Constitution, by stating at the outset what will be described, and with some justice, as a fiction'. These articles imported 'an even greater fiction' into the draft constitution than the 'fictions' contained in the existing constitution, which the state has been 'at such pains to omit'.

MacElligott argued that it was 'not usual in a Constitution to define the national boundaries' and warned that 'from the point of view of international law, it is not clear whether we are on safe ground in claiming sovereignty and jurisdiction over land recognised internationally, *de jure* and *de facto*, as belonging to another country.' These claims would 'give offence to neighbouring countries with whom we are constantly protesting our desire to live on terms of friendship'. Those countries might use the doctrine of repugnance – present in the constitution – to bring a case against the state to the League of Nations or the Hague court, potentially winning a rebuff against the state that would set back 'the cause we wish to advance'. Articles 1–3 would not 'contribute anything to effecting the unity of Ireland, but rather the reverse' and would 'impose an additional and more severe strain on our relations with the members of the British Commonwealth of Nations, relations which are already difficult enough, and which coming events, apart from the Constitution, will make even more difficult'.

The Finance document next posed the question whether 'The Irish Nation' included 'all Irishmen whether living in or outside Ireland'. Commenting on Article 9.3, Finance assumed that 'Love of the Motherland and loyalty to the State' (as the constitution expressed) to be 'fundamental and inherent in nationality'. Concern was expressed that any successful international legal challenge to Articles 1–3 'would be rather wounding to the national pride'. In its comments on Article 41.8, constitutional assumptions concerning the Irish people's national traditions were challenged. The article sought to foster and maintain 'the traditional preference of our people for rural life', and the Finance document rather sharply responded that 'traditional preference is open to doubt' since 'Irish emigrants to the U.S.A., for instance, have shunned rural life'.

The document challenged the constitution's choice of name for the state. Commenting on Article 4, it called the use of the name Éire a mistake 'from a realistic point of view', even if justifiable from 'the traditional and scholarly point of view'; this was because 'The land is generally known internationally as Ireland or one of the derivatives of that name'; the proposed name in the draft would result in a 'long period of confusion and uncertainty before the unaccustomed name conveys a definite meaning to educated people throughout the world'.

The extent to which recognition was given to the doctrine of repugnance introduced 'a degree of uncertainty' to the constitution. The Finance report pointed to Articles 22 and 23 (which allowed bills passed by both houses of the oireachtas to be referred to the president) and Articles 38–41 (on personal rights and social policy) as examples. Retention of Articles 38–41 raised the possibility that 'many efforts will be made to upset bills properly passed and this would be undesirable'.[13]

Finance warned that 'an enormous mass of consequential legislation' would follow the adoption of the constitution and occupy the parliamentary draftsman's office and government departments 'to the almost total exclusion of other business and certainly to the detriment of their daily administration'. The document emphasised the need to preserve 'those parts of the existing Government machine which have worked efficiently … and with them the laws under which they operate'.[14] The question was raised whether Article 49, 'dealing with the continuance of laws to the extent to which they are inconsistent with the Constitution, provides the means of enabling the administration to be carried on and the various powers under existing laws to be exercised in all their fullness'.[15]

In Paragraph 6 caution was expressed that consideration had not been given to the 'possibility of reprisals of an economic or other character following the enactment of the Constitution' and a suggestion that its adoption might 'be held to deprive us automatically of any preferences we enjoy in British and Dominion markets'.[16] As a result the state might have 'to undertake the entire cost of our own defences by sea, on the coast and otherwise', adding to 'a heavier bill presented by the new Constitution to the taxpayer'. Finance's response then dealt with articles of the draft constitution seriatim. There were no page or paragraph numbers to use as references.

The Department of Finance response further objected to the reference in Article 11.7 to 'public personages', suggesting that the word 'citizens' be employed instead and drawing attention to Article 38.1,1: 'The State acknowledges that all citizens are as human persons equal before the law.' It argued for the omission of Article 9.3: 'Love of the Motherland and loyalty to the State are fundamental political duties of all citizens of Éire.' This statement does not require inclusion since such matters are 'so fundamental and inherent in nationality'

Although it objected to Article 4's designation of Éire as the name of the state on the grounds that it would cause confusion, the department response suggested that 'for the sake of consistency, and for the purpose of encouraging the use of Irish "forms", the titles of Officers of State should be provided in Irish only, even in the English translation of the Constitution.' (Article 27.2): 'The use of the forms "Chairman of Dáil Éireann" and "Chairman of Seanad

Éireann" seems unnecessary as the public is already familiar with the Irish forms of those titles.' Finance argued for a change to Article 21.4,5, which required the clerk of the Dáil or another officer to issue 'an authoritative text in the Irish language of every law enacted by the Oireachtas'. An authoritative English text of every law would be needed 'for many years to come … if hopeless confusion is to be avoided' and noted that the limitation of authoritative texts to Irish alone is at variance with Article 8.2, which recognises English as the state's second official language.

The Finance document discussed Articles 38–41 at length. Its approach to these articles is somewhat similar to its response to Articles 1–3. In both cases, Finance uses blunt language and rejects what it describes as 'fictions' (commentary on Articles 1–3) and 'declaratory phrases' (commentary on Articles 38–41). While Finance's review of Articles 1–3 states that it is not usual for a constitution to define the national boundaries, its commentary on Articles 38–41 states that these articles 'are not of a kind usually enshrined in a Constitution'. They were criticised because they contained 'a number of mandatory provisions making it compulsory on the State to do a number of vague and undefined things, e.g., "to have due regard to individual differences of capacity, physical and moral, and of social function" (Article 38.1,2), and to imbue "all the institutions of public life" with social justice and 'social charity' [Article 41.5], etc.'

Finance then described Articles 38.1,2–3 as two 'declaratory subsections … obscure in their object and meaning … [and] it is difficult to see how practical effect can be given to them by legislation'.[17] If the latter provision had for its object the restriction of the low-paid employment of women and children (but not necessarily overtaxing their sex and strength), it would be welcome to many interested in contemporary social problems. This particular problem was further dealt with in Article 41.5, ii, IV and I. Practically every one of these declaratory passages was capable of different interpretations and being utilised for different objectives by different individuals, e.g. fixing of minimum wages, of appropriate scales of wages, the control or decontrol of industry and manufacture, etc.

The argument was advanced that Articles 38–41's 'various declaratory phrases are of an idealistic tendency which, while individually unobjectionable as a statement of social policy, may, if launched out into the void in the draft Constitution, recoil like a boomerang on the Government of some future day in circumstances not anticipated by the originators'. As an example, the response suggests that if Article 38.2,2 had been included in the existing constitution, it would have greatly increased the government's difficulty in dealing with the compensation claim lodged against it by Mr More O'Ferral, 'whose son was murdered and whose family have been forced to emigrate'.[18]

For similar reasons, Finance took issue with sections 4, 5 and 6 of Article 40. It recommended that 40.4 and 40.6 should use the word 'may' and not 'shall'. The articles' use of the word 'shall', it argued, would commit the state to the provision of 'a certain minimum education, intellectual and moral, physical and social' for all citizens and to 'supply the place of parents' to children whose parents 'for physical or moral reasons fail in their duty'. The existing constitution's Article 10 recognised the right of all citizens to free elementary education. It commented that there was 'some doubt whether it does not commit the State to the provision of school books and other school requisites free to pupils of public primary schools. Section 5 of Article 40 of the Draft Constitution seems to be capable of a similar interpretation and perhaps an amendment is necessary.'

It was also feared that the provisions of Articles 38–41 would 'provide a breeding ground for discontent, and so create instability and insecurity. They are consequently objectionable and even dangerous. Their provisions … afford grounds for disaffection to sections of the community, who might claim that the Government were not living up to the Constitution.' Constitutional recognition of the doctrine of repugnance makes these provisions 'the more objectionable'. The document identified a number of the articles' provisions or 'declaratory subsections' as 'highly dangerous'. Article 41.6,2 pledged that 'the State shall see to it that the economic domination of the few, in what pertains to the control of credit, shall not endanger the common good of the community as a whole'. This reference to 'the economic domination of the few in what pertains to credit' was 'not understood. Insofar as one can attach any meaning to it, it is untrue, but it could easily be worked up by agitators as a weapon of attack on the Banks, the Agricultural Credit Corporation, the Industrial Credit Co., or against any large joint-stock concern.' The phrase could be 'interpreted by everyone according to his individual outlook on life and could be easily worked up to lead people astray'.

Article 41.6 which was defined as dangerous if used in conjunction with Article 41.9, 'by critics as a condemnation per the Constitution of the action of the present Government in establishing practical monopolies in the manufacture of tyres, sugar, industrial alcohol, cotton yarn, the refinement of crude oil, certain forms of transport, and retention of a monopoly of electricity and the carriage of postal material'.[19] Since the state had established 'monopolies in important articles such as sugar, electricity, cement, tyres, oil, etc', the articles' provisions were contradictory. Article 41.8 was also problematical to the Department of Finance. It could be used to agitate for the extension of the scope of land division 'when the present amount of land available for distribution is exhausted and when the only means of extension of this process would be by compulsory subdivision of the holdings already distributed'.[20] Furthermore, Finance argued that Articles 38–41 contained provisions that were also 'mostly unnecessary'. It was felt that: 'Distinct advance along the lines of the social and economic policy outlined have already been made without the aid of these declaratory provisions, some of which are themselves, it should be noted, repugnant to Government policy, e.g. we do not settle "as many families as practicable" on the land. "Five acres and a cow" would suffice if that were the policy. We create economic holdings of twenty-five acres.' This is a reference to Article 41.7,2, which stated that 'the State shall endeavour to give as many families as practicable a share in the land'.

The opinion that the state had already enacted legislation giving effect to 'the ideals expressed in these declaratory passages without being bound to do so by the express terms of the Constitution' was put forward in the response. Without any commitment to the pledge affirmed in Article 41.7,1 the state had already in numerous acts like the old age pensions acts, the army pensions acts, the blind pensions acts, the widows and orphans, 'given effect to the ideals underlying the provisions of this subsection, and there was nothing to stop further legislative progress in the same direction without putting in the hands of enthusiasts for any particular cause an unnecessarily powerful instrument of agitation which it is feared might be freely used in support of all sorts of unreasonable and impracticable proposals for further social legislation'.

The response of Finance was both practical and far seeing. It commented on Article 39.2,2 concerning the indissolubility of marriage, which stated: 'No law shall be passed which shall impair its essential properties of unity and indissolubility.' If this prohibition carried 'with it the corollary of abrogating any existing law of the same tendency, it would be necessary to repeal existing law in the Saorstát which provides for judicial separation'.

True to the department's ethos the opening statement of its response stressed the 'expense involved in the Constitution'. Concern regarding the increase in expenditure caused by the adoption of the new constitution is a theme that runs throughout Finance's response to the draft.

Article 60.1 of the draft constitution stated that the constitution shall come into operation 'on the day following the expiration of a period of six months after its approval'. In its commentary on the article, Finance suggested a delay because of the preparations needed and 'the effect the Constitution will have in increasing expenditure'. It suggested that the constitution should start to operate as from the beginning of a financial year. The necessary budgetary provision, etc. could then be made. In its commentary on Article 4, it urged that even if the constitution should come into force after six months, the state should continue to use existing coinage and banknotes (minimum stock: two years) in order to limit expenditure. Finance stated that the constitution's adoption of a new name for the state – Éire – would entail the alteration of currency, bank notes, coinage, seals of state and government departments, 'and all kinds of Government stationery'. It emphasised the expense that these changes would cause and urged the continued use and exhaustion of existing stocks after the adoption of the constitution.

The commentary on Article 13.16 warned that the extension of facilities provided free of charge to public representatives might 'involve additional expenditure'. Its commentary on Article 24.1 observed that the lack of a fixed upper limit to the number of members constituting the government appeared 'undesirable on financial grounds'. It was an 'unnecessarily expensive' provision that circuit judges and district justices should attend the appointment of judges as they would have to travel to Dublin 'from all over the country'. Defence was another area where the new constitution could cause increased expenditure. The possibility was raised that the state would have to assume sole responsibility for the defence of its coasts. This would 'add considerably to what will, in any case, be a heavier bill presented by the new constitution to the taxpayer'. As previously noted, Finance warned of the possible economic consequences of the new constitution's Articles 1–3; their claims could provoke British economic reprisals or deprive the state of any preferences it enjoyed in British and dominion markets.

The review, featured above, of Finance's response to Articles 38–41 on social policy and personal rights further indicates the department's financial and economic policy concerns. Its comments on the ensuing expense caused by the possible constitutional commitment to the provision of free schoolbooks and other requisites to primary schoolchildren (commentary on Article 40) indicated a determination to limit state expenditure. Finance further identified some of the articles' 'declaratory phrases' as open to an interpretation that would oppose government economic policy and practice including the establishment of practical state monopolies (commentary on 41.6,1 in conjunction with 41.9) and land distribution (commentary on 41.8).

Commenting on Article 12.6, Finance raised no objection to the vesting of supreme command of the defence forces in the president. It cited the examples of republics, the USA, France, Germany and Poland, and monarchies, Italy and Britain, where the head of state held this position. Finance noted that the existing constitution makes the Executive Council head of the defence forces, exercising its power through the Minister for Defence. The Department of Finance was of the opinion that the president's 'unfettered power to appoint judges and to exercise the right of pardon and remission in respect of sentences imposed by the Courts' was problematic and at variance with other sections of the same articles, 'which are careful to indicate by whose advice or whose nomination the President must act. Presumably, however, the exercise of the President's functions under Sections 8 and 11 are governed by the provisions of Section 14 of the same Article.'

Finance commented on Articles 15.2,2 and 3 (money bills) as follows: 'The introduction of the President, with a possible veto, is an innovation, the necessity for which is not apparent. The matter of procedure regarding the question whether a Bill is or is not a Money Bill might well be left to the two Houses of the Oireachtas.'

Finance's comments on Article 11.10,1 concerning the impeachment of the President provide an insight into its understanding of the oireachtas and the role of the Dáil and Seanad. Article 11.10,1 states: 'The President may be impeached at the instance of Seanad Éireann for treason as defined in this Constitution or other high crimes and misdemeanours.' The Finance response declared: 'It is open to doubt whether the impeachment should not be taken on the initiative of Dáil Éireann and the tribunal should be the Seanad. Presumably impeachment will be in the nature of a safety valve at some time of popular excitement so that the drive for impeachment would more naturally be expressed through the popular assembly; whilst the calm and judicial atmosphere necessary for a tribunal' would be more likely to be found in the Seanad than in the Dáil.

Finance expressed concern for the maintenance of public confidence in the political system and for the political composition of the Seanad. Article 20.7, which provides for the curtailment of the Seanad's normal time for consideration when a bill is certified as urgent, would be improved if the certificate of urgency were made subject to the assent of the President. As the section stands, it is open to abuse, and any abuse of it would adversely affect public confidence.

Commenting on Article 16, which concerned the election of members of the Seanad, Finance stated that subsection 1 of section 7:

> Does not state who will actually draw up the list of names on each of the five panels, presumably the Government, with or without some outside assistance. To preserve the non-party character of the Second Chamber some outside assistance would seem to be necessary.

It was the opinion of the Department of Finance that the oireachtas would be the forum for 'acutely controversial discussion' following the implementation of the legislation that would 'almost certainly' follow from Article 43, 'which provides the Constitutional foundation of an emergency Court'.

Article 24.6,1 stated: 'The Taoiseach, the Tánaiste and the member of the Government who is in charge of the Department of Finance shall be members of Dáil Éireann.' The Department of Finance response to this article could be said to be an affirmation of the importance of the ministry itself – MacElligott obviously saw his ministry as the most senior one:

> It is urged that the Minister for Finance should, in all cases, hold the office of Tánaiste, in which event he would be *ex-officio* a member of the Council of State. Alternatively, the Minister for Finance should in his own right be a member of the Council of State in view of the importance of his special functions and of his general supervisory powers over State expenditure of all kinds.

The subject of the role of the Minister for Finance was mentioned again in the commentary on Article 27.2,i. There, it was argued that the Minister for Finance should take the place of the comptroller or auditor general as an *ex-officio* member of the council of state, unless the Minister for Finance always held the post of Tánaiste. The writer pragmatically outlined the reason for the inclusion:

> [It] would increase his prestige and his effectiveness as Minister and it would bring to the Council a fuller and more general knowledge of the work of administration and of the financial and economic affairs of the State than any of the ex-officio members named in the Article, with the exception of the Taoiseach, could possess. His special experience of the conduct of Parliamentary business and especially Money Bills make him a more suitable ex-officio member of the Council of State than the Comptroller and Auditor-General.

As stated earlier, paragraph 6 of Finance's opening statement on the draft constitution warned of economic and other possible reprisals by Britain or the British commonwealth against the state following the adoption of the constitution. Its commentary on Articles 1–3 likewise emphasised Britain's potentially hostile response to the adoption of those articles and raised the possibility that Britain might take an action against the state's claims concerning the national territory to the League of Nations or the Hague court. The articles would 'impose an additional and more severe strain on our relations with members of the British Commonwealth of Nations, relations which are already difficult enough, and which coming events, apart from the Constitution, will make even more difficult'. It was noted that the state was 'constantly protesting our desire to live on terms of friendship with neighbouring countries to which its claims will give offence'.

Commenting on Articles 47 and 48, which concerned the repeal of the Free State constitution and the continuance of laws, MacElligott's document was anxious to protect the rights of transferred officers, 'able and willing officers of the State' who transferred from British to Irish administration and whose interests were guarded by Article 78 of the Free State constitution and Article X of the 1921 treaty. Commenting on Article 48.1, the Finance response called for the preservation of Department of Finance rights derived from British treasury practice via the 1922 Transfer of Functions order.

As noted earlier, Finance's commentary on Articles 1–3 doubted if the state was 'on safe ground in claiming sovereignty and jurisdiction over land recognised internationally, *de jure* and *de facto*, as belonging to another country'. It envisaged a situation where Britain might challenge the articles' claims and so 'expose us to the risk of adverse judgement from international bodies such as the League of Nations or the Hague Court'.

Article 25 of the draft constitution was entitled 'International Relations'. The document commented on the article generally: 'In the absence of an explanatory Memorandum the various reactions and repercussions of this change are difficult to understand.' Finance called for clarification from External Affairs. It warned: 'In certain eventualities, serious economic and financial consequences may follow, and even if the latter could be averted no preparation to avert them can be made unless the precise intention of this Article as regards our international position is known.' The commentary on sections 6 and 7 of Article 25 stated: 'Every international agreement to which the State becomes a party shall be laid before Dáil Éireann: this provision shall not, however, apply to international conventions of a purely technical and administrative character' and 'The State shall not be bound by any international agreement involving a charge upon public funds unless the terms of the agreement shall have been approved by Dáil Éireann.'

It was further stated that 'the State subscribes to quite a number of international institutions and organisations under agreements, the terms of which are never laid out before and formally approved by Dáil Éireann. It is questionable also whether the need for compliance with the sections might not cramp the style of Departments in the matter of negotiation for International Agreements.'

The Department of Finance document insisted on clarity of expression throughout the constitution. It objected to the formulation of some articles on stylistic grounds and to others because obscurity of language would make their interpretation and application difficult or troublesome. For example, it objected to the formulation of Article 41.5, i–iv on grounds of syntax: 'the plural and singular are mixed up at times, the verbal construction is faulty'. Concerning 41.8, it stated: 'Generally the wording seems vague, colloquial and lacking in precision.' Finance connected imprecision of language with muddled, or at least, imprecise thinking. This was particularly evident in the department's treatment of Articles 1–3 on the nation and Articles 38–41 on social policy and personal rights, as noted earlier. For instance, concerning Article 1, which proclaimed the right of 'the Irish nation' to choose its own form of government, etc, it asked: 'Does the expression "The Irish Nation" not include all Irishmen living in or outside Ireland?' The document further stated that Articles 38–41 contained 'declaratory subsections … obscure in their object and meaning', so that 'it is difficult to see how practical effect can be given to them'. Their 'provisions are too vague to be of positive assistance to any Government and are yet sufficiently definite to afford grounds for disaffection to sections of the community, who might claim that the Government was not living up to the Constitution'. Occasionally a change in the wording of an article was recommended in order to neutralise any possible misinterpretation or difficulty. Concerning the government's powers, Article 6 stated: 'These powers are exercisable by or on the authority of the Organs of State established by this Constitution.' Finance's response to this stated:

> No subsequent Article formally establishes Organs of State. It is presumed that the reference is to legislative, executive and judicial organs though not so stated. Possibly there would be less apparent need for defining Sections if the word organs were printed without a capital letter, or a colourless phrase, such as bodies, institutions, or authorities, introduced.

There were also instances of requests for clarification of particular Articles' provisions in the response document. Concerning time of war, Article 13.7,2 stated: 'In the case of actual invasion, however, the Government may take whatever steps they consider necessary for the protection of the State' which in turn provoked the question: 'Would attack from the sea or from the air, without any landing force, constitute 'actual invasion' within the meaning of the subsection?'

Observations of the Attorney General on the first Draft of the Constitution[21]

These observations of the Attorney General were outlined in a document of ten numbered sections. The document was accompanied by a covering letter from the Attorney General, Patrick Lynch, stating that: 'Time available does not enable a complete analysis of the document to be made and there are probably points which have been overlooked.'[22] The Attorney General exhibited the caution of the lawyer from the outset. The following are the most significant points raised by him:

It will be appreciated that the ideal of a sovereign national parliament can only be approached by reducing to the narrowest limits any constitutional restrictions. It follows from this that the greater the number of matters expressly covered in the constitution, the greater will be the consequent limitation on the powers of the legislature under that constitution. This is merely mentioned because of the probability of acute criticism in the Dáil, which renders it more necessary to be guarded in one's criticism of the draft constitution.

The Attorney General stated that Article 22 'provides for obtaining the authoritative opinion of the majority of the Supreme Court on the possible repugnancy of a Bill'. He commented that: 'It is wisely provided that minority opinions will not be stated on these occasions.' He urged that:

... encouragement should not be given to persons or organisations to raise questions of constitutionality when they may be disposed to do so in order to cause embarrassment or delay ... One can visualise wealthy federations or robust trade unions thinking it profitable to speculate on the chance of obtaining a minority judgement in their favour or even delay by assailing legislation on the ground, for example, that it infringed the respective provisions of Article 41.

When discussing Article 43 the Attorney General observed:

The suspension of constitutional guarantees in a time of grave emergency may not be lightly undertaken but when such procedure is invoked it should not fail to achieve its purpose because of regard for any constitutional niceties. Therefore it is suggested that the Habeas Corpus provision should also be suspended as well as the setting up of Military Courts.

When discussing Article 44.1,1 the Attorney General suggested inserting a clause denying the proposed tribunals the power to inflict the death penalty.

Observations of the Department of Local Government and Public Health

These observations were preceded by a covering letter from the minister, Seán T. O'Kelly, and were contained in a ten-page document.[23] When discussing Article 14.4, the department urged that section 4 of the article:

... must not invalidate a General Election if owing to an emergency, such as a storm, the polling at a particular place was not held on that day. This has happened at a General Election and provision was made for the holding of the Poll at a later day under a special provision of the Electoral Act dealing with emergencies and difficulties.

The Department of Local Government and Public Health agreed with the Department of Finance's comments on Article 40.5. It too observed that the words 'particularly by providing free primary education' might imply the provision by the state of the full cost of such education, including free books and the full cost of erection of schools, etc. In relation to Article 41, concerning private property, the document stated that it was 'important that the existing powers of Local Bodies to acquire private rights to property for public purposes should not be weakened'. With regard to social policy, 'it is thought that a statement of leading principles would tend to greater elasticity and provide sufficient guide for subsequent legislation on social matters.' It called the subsections of 41.5 on social policy 'somewhat vague'. It saw problems with constitutional pledges on a sufficient wage. Article 41.5's 'underlying principles would not be susceptible of easy application' (41.5,iii dealt with the state regulating wage scales with the cooperation of vocational groups and associations). It understandably displayed interest in how proposed social welfare suggestions were to be funded. The department recommended that sections 4, 5, and 6 of Article 41 should be combined into one section 'setting out the leading principles which should guide the State in promoting the economic welfare of the people and in establishing an economic order regulated according to social justice'. It asked if section 7's pledge to support the infirm, the widow, the orphan, and the aged poor who are past their labour would be met by the assistance 'given by Local bodies out of local funds, or would it involve direct provision by the State out of State funds?' It asked if a means test was envisaged in relation to applications for help by those applying for state aid. It also cautioned that: 'It would appear to be inadvisable to include a rigid provision on the lines of Section 10 of this Article without a full examination of the method of forming vocational groupings and some experience of the working of such a system.'

When discussing Article 46 the Department of Local Government and Public Health usefully provided a catalogue of corrupt practices at Dáil elections: 'bribery, personating, treating, undue influence, aiding and abetting, counselling or procuring the commission of the offence of personating, and knowingly publishing a false statement of the withdrawal of a candidate at an election'.

Observations of the Department of Defence

In its response, which consisted of nine pages,[24] the Department of Defence suggested in relation to Article 12 'that a provision be inserted in Section 6 to the effect that the command of the forces in time of war should be delegated to a military officer'. Section 11 of Article 12 suggested that 'as a matter of military necessity, the power of remitting, commuting, or suspending sentences of military tribunals for the enforcement of military discipline must be vested in the authorities more immediately concerned with military discipline.'

Amendments were suggested to Articles 13.6, 1 and 2, so that it read as follows: 'The right to authorise and regulate the raising and maintenance of military or armed forces is vested exclusively in the Oireachtas' and 'No military or armed force other than a military or armed force the raising and maintenance of which is authorised and regulated by the Oireachtas shall be raised or maintained for any purpose whatsoever.' In relation to Article 36.1,2, the Department of Defence urged the extension of the jurisdiction of courts martial to 'persons who at the time of trial have civilian status'. Those persons were (1) persons who committed offences against the article while subject to it and then ceased to be subject to it, and (2) members of voluntary aid societies including the Red Cross working under 'military law and regulations' on active service. The department further suggested the deletion of 36.1,2's last line and the substitution of the following words: 'of offences against military law alleged to have been committed by persons while subject to military law'. In the case of Article 38.5 the following addendum was suggested: 'In the interests of discipline, military law may restrict for members of the Defence Forces the rights conferred by this section.'

Observations of the Department of Agriculture

The document is only four pages long,[25] which perhaps explains the alacrity with which it was returned (18 March 1937). The Minister, Dr Jim Ryan, provided a covering letter, which stated: 'I have purposely refrained from comments on Articles 38 to 41 inclusive because I have a great deal to say about these Articles and I expect to have very much more when I have studied them more closely.' His comment on Article 8 – concerning the constitution's statements on the state's two official languages, conveys the impression that Ryan was interested in official business being carried out in Irish whenever possible. He feared that:

> ... a person convicted at a court held in Galway at the moment could appeal on the grounds that he did not get a fair trial as Irish is not the only language in general use in the district. If we could achieve the position in which Irish is permissible to anybody while English is only permissible in certain districts, we would reach the ideal. This might be done by deleting Section 3 and by adding to the end of Section 2 'in districts in which Irish is not in general use'.

It was noted that this Article 11.2 provided for the election of the President by direct vote of the people and the following comment was added: 'I would like to be sure under this Article that a candidate returned unopposed would be validly elected'. In the proposed Article 24.4,2 the constitution stated:

> The Taoiseach shall keep the President generally informed on matters of domestic and international policy and of the decisions taken thereon by the Government, and shall duly report to the President on all such matters as and when desired by the President to do so.

Ryan noted: 'This throws a very heavy burden on the Taoiseach. If we have a conscientious or pernickety President the position of the Taoiseach will become almost impossible.'

Observations of the Parliamentary Draftsman, Mr Arthur V. Matheson

In a two-page document submission to the Attorney General,[26] Matheson pointed out a few sections where there were ambiguities or where all possibilities had not been catered for. The most notable suggestions were in relation to Article 13, and the draftsman noted that:

> ... the effect of paragraph 3 is to prevent legal proceedings against the President only during his term of office; that paragraph does not prevent legal proceedings being brought against the President *after* the expiration of his term of office in respect of things done by him during his term of office.

In relation to Article 24, he suggested that:

> In Section 6 provision should be made for members of the Government retaining office during a dissolution of Dáil Éireann; a member of the Government could not comply with this section as it stands because, during a dissolution, there would be no Dáil Éireann. I would also suggest that it should be made clear whether, when the same Government returns to power after a dissolution, the Taoiseach and the other members of the Government require re-appointment.

Observations by the Ceann Comhairle[27]

This document is twenty pages long and provided a five-page commentary on Article 11, the provisions for the President's impeachment. The ceann comhairle, Frank Fahy, suggested that a 'supplementary law working out the form and process of impeachment' would be necessary, and put forward France, Poland and Czechoslovakia as examples of countries which employed separate enactments to govern procedures for a presidential impeachment. He further argued: 'If removal from office is to be the only punishment, it is feared that the proposal will provoke considerable criticism as being totally inadequate for the crime of treason as defined in the Draft Constitution.' He noted the United States' constitution's provisions for the indictment, trial, judgement and punishment according to law of an impeached President. His concern with the presidency was central to his submission. He noted the proposed Article 12.12,3, which provided that: 'No action at law or in equity or other legal proceeding, civil or criminal, shall lie against the President during his tenure of office.' Fahy felt that:

> This is another sub-section, which, it is surmised, will provoke unfavourable criticism, when read in conjunction with the impeachment provision. Furthermore, it seems to embody a change in policy in regard to road traffic cases. After considerable pressure in the Dáil, the Minister for Local Government and Public Health put forward, and had accepted, a section in the Road Traffic Bill of 1933, making liable the Minister for Finance for accidents caused by cars used by officers of State ... A personal view-point on the sub-section, as a whole, is that it is anachronistic.

On a different note, he also argued that 'the term "Taoiseach" has acquired a military significance, which might be considered objectionable. Would not "Príomh-Aire" be a better term?' The ceann comhairle also felt that in relation to Article 16.4, the

> ... extraneous consideration probably makes it advisable to grant equal representation to both Universities [in the Seanad]. Could the question be considered in the abstract, it would seem reasonable to assign greater representation to the National University which has three constituent colleges and which enters more largely into the life of the nation.

Fahy also queried the constitutional requirement in Article 21.4,5, that the clerk of the Dáil should cause to be issued an 'authoritative text' in the Irish language of every law passed. He asked:

> What would be the authority – since presumably the Irish text will not have been the version before the Oireachtas? The clerk can cause to be issued an authorised translation – which he has done up to the present – the authority being the standing orders.

He suggested the inclusion of the following sentence:

> The Clerk of Dáil Éireann or such officer as aforesaid shall cause a translation to be made of each such law into that official language other than that in which the said Bill was signed.

Observations by the Department of Lands

This is a one-page document, which addressed only Article 41.7,2, an article which would have been of great relevance to the work of this department.[28] This draft article stated: 'The State shall endeavour to give as many families as practicable a share in the land.' The Department of Lands was unhappy with this phrase and advised that it 'should not be allowed to stand as drafted'. The department argued with conviction:

> ... there can be few more dangerous suggestions ... than that it should be made the object of the State to give as many people as possible a share in the land. There is no easier way of distributing land than to give all comers a share; *but there is no more certain method of wasting and misusing a national asset.* There is no advantage to the community unless the land distributed is to be worked on by competent agriculturalists who will live on it without further assistance from the State and who will produce from it more than it has been producing and will maintain on it and out of it a greater number of human beings than have been maintained in the past ... It is most strongly suggested that the subsection should be amended in such manner as the following: 'the State shall endeavour to place as many families as practicable in a position of economic security on the land.' This would give the approval of the Constitution to the ideal of raising the many poor, uneconomic holdings to an economic level and placing as many families as possible on smallholdings capable of maintaining them in reasonable comfort.

Observations of the Department of the President on the Constitution[29]

This document is extremely useful as it did not merely contain comments on the draft constitution but also lists de Valera's instructions on whether or not he required amendments as a result of points raised. The covering page of this document was signed by Michael McDunphy. The document contained eighty-three unnumbered pages. It follows the following format: in its treatment of individual articles of the draft constitution, the relevant article or its relevant section and/or subsection was first quoted and was followed with comments entitled 'Observations'. Many observations are in turn followed by a statement of decisions reached and/or the President's opinion in smaller print (these statements will here be noted under the title 'Response').

Article 1. Under **Observations**, McDunphy, on behalf of the Department of the President asked: 'Do the words "within the national territory" restrict us in any way from passing laws with extra-territorial effect?' **Response**: 'President agrees to deletion.' There was no response to the question regarding the omission of the word 'cultural' from the article's statement on the Irish nation's right to develop its own life, 'economic, social and political', free from external interference.

Article 8. In its **Observations**, the document stated: 'The President, after consultation with the Executive Council, wants this Article further considered with the greatest care. The exact relative positions of the two languages in the State as a whole and in any particular area affected by legislation under Section 3, e.g. the six counties or the Gaeltacht, requires special attention.' **Response**: 'Article to be completely rewritten.'

Article 9. Under **Observations,** it was noted that 'The exact relation between the expressions "Irish nationality", "Irish citizenship", "Citizens of Éire" is not clear.' It called for an examination of the article's provisions 'in the light of the existing law dealing with nationality and citizenship' and calls for 'special consideration' of their implications 'in relation to other Articles of the Constitution dealing with the rights, etc. of citizens, e.g. Article 38 (2)'. **Response**: 'Article to be amended.'

Article 11.7. Under **Observations,** a request was made for a definition of 'public persons'. **Response**: 'Leave as it is.'

Article 12.2,1. Under **Observations,** it was stated: 'The President should be required to consult the Council of State before refusing to dissolve Dáil Éireann under this sub-section.' **Response**: 'No. Absolute discretion.'

Article 12.11. Under **Observations,** McDunphy wrote: 'The use of the word "exercised" suggests that the right of pardon vests with some authority other than the President. The President is satisfied that the words "vested in" should be inserted before the word "exercised".' The following statement then appears in smaller print:

> I. Mr Kinnane of Justice is very worried about this Article. If the President *alone* can pardon or remit, and there is no power of delegation, the position will be *impossible*. At least 20 minor cases, now dealt with by the M/Justice at his own discretion, pass through Justice each day. If all these things have to go to the President, through the Govt., the position can be imagined.
>
> II. What about rights of third parties. Can these be cancelled by the President? Why not omit this Article altogether. Article 48 (2) is adequate and much more practical.

Response: 'Redrafted and approved in its final form by the President. 26-03-37.'

Article 12.14. Under **Observations** it was advised that: 'This sub-section should be extended by words to the following effect, "or at any time in respect of any action or function performed by him in his official capacity during his term of office", reserving, of course, the right of impeachment under Article 11, Section 10 of the Constitution'. **Response**: 'Leave as it is, but change the expression "tenure of office" to "term of office"'.

Article 12.15. Under **Observations,** 'it is regarded as undesirable that additional powers should be conferred on the President by ordinary law. The matter is of sufficient importance to justify amendments of the Constitution for this purpose.' **Response**: 'No, to be by law.'

Article 13.6,2. Under **Observations**, the Department of the President advised: 'The effect of this section when enacted will be such that the presence of British Forces at present at our ports will be a breach of the Constitution. The position, perhaps, might be met by amending the subsection so as to read "maintained by or with the permission of the Oireachtas".' There was no response.

Article 13.7,1 and 2. Under **Observations**, it was advised that:

> The powers conferred on the Government under sub-section 2 should be rigidly limited to those necessary to deal with an actual invasion and to provide against the recurrence. It should not be possible for a Government to take advantage of such an action to commit the State, without the consent of the Dáil, to participation in a war which might conceivably involve the country to an extent and for a period far beyond that necessary to deal with the invasion. Sub-section 1 should, therefore, be made absolute, and subsection 2 be made definitively subordinate to it.

Response: 'To be amended. Dáil to be summoned forthwith.' McDunphy observed further:

> In my opinion sub-section 2 is dangerous. As it stands it would permit a Government to avail of the mere fact of invasion to declare war and so commit the State to an extent far beyond that necessary. I think it should be made definitely subject to sub-section 1, and that the prohibition of declaring war without the consent of the Oireachtas should be made absolute and should extend to all occasions whatsoever.

Response: 'We discussed this matter at length with the President. He thinks that it will be sufficient to provide in sub-section 2 that the Dáil shall be summoned forthwith.'

Article 14.2,1. Under **Observations:** 'The Presidents [sic] wants it made clear that members of Dáil Éireann shall be representatives and not delegates and that they should be representative of the country as a whole and not merely of constituencies.'

Article 17.3 [regarding the dissolution of Dáil Éireann]. Under **Observations,** McDunphy wrote that the 'section is not clear and the President considers that it might be deleted'. **Response**: (dated 26 March 1937) 'Deleted, but consult Matheson.'

Article 21.4,5. Under **Observations**, it was written that: 'Provision in respect to legislation in English should be made for Bills in Irish.' **Response**: 'Text has been amended.'

Article 22.1,2, and 3 and 22.2,1 and 2. The department's **Observations** specified:

> Note 1. The court should be the whole of the Supreme Court, any absentee therefrom being replaced by a Judge of the High Court nominated for that purpose by the Chief Justice.
> [Note] 2. The President is of opinion that where possible a definite question should be referred to the Court in each case, that is to say, that the Court should not be asked whether a Bill as a whole is unconstitutional but whether a specific provision to be specified by the President is or is not unconstitutional. I understand that this is the view of the President of the High Court.
> Note 3. Where a Court decides that a provision in a Bill is repugnant to the Constitution they should be required to state the respect or respects in which it is so repugnant and their reason for so deciding.

Response: Notes 2 and 3. 'Leave to practice.'

Article 24.1. Under **Observations,** it was asked: 'Should there be a maximum number of Ministers?' **Response**: 'Maximum to be 15.'

Article 24.4,2 [regarding the Taoiseach keeping the President informed on domestic and international policy]. **Observations**:

1. What machinery is contemplated to give effect to this dection [(sic) should it read section?]. Is it intended that written reports will pass between the Taoiseach and the President.
2. In the event of conflict between the President and the Taoiseach, it would be open to the President to create a very difficult situation by insistence upon frequent reports, particularly if they had to be in writing.
3. If the President is to be kept informed of decisions taken on matters of domestic and international policy by the Government, that means in essence that the President will be entitled, and can claim to see all Cabinet minutes. The practical objections to this are serious.
4. It would of course be possible to send to the President a copy after every meeting, but this is most undesirable. Unless the staff of the President and of the Taoiseach are identical in personnel, and this does not seem to be contemplated, such a position would create a position in which the custody of confidential cabinet records would pass out of the control of the Government.
5. I suggest that this subsection should be worded much more generally, and that the use of the word 'reports' should be avoided. All words after the word 'policy' in the second line might well be deleted.

Response: 'Executive Council on 24–3–37 agreed to deletion of all words after "policy". Mr Hearne has amended the subsection accordingly.' It is interesting to note that Hearne rather than Matheson was the person inserting amendments at this time; he was, of course a member of the committee now engaged in examining and drafting.

Article 22.10. **Observations** stated that this section was unclear as it seemed to state 'that a Government which secures a majority in the Dáil can remain in office without any time limit … the text of the subsection, owing to the succession of conditions, is somewhat difficult to follow'. **Response**: 'To be left as it is.'

Article 25.4. **Observations** asked:

> (a) Does this section cover our association with members of the British Commonwealth? It seems to be straining the ordinary interpretation of international if this is the case. An association of the Scandinavian or Baltic or the South American states would scarcely be described as an association for the purpose of international cooperation, and our position vis-à-vis Great Britain and the Dominions appears to be somewhat on the par.
>
> (b) A second point arises. Would it be possible for a pro-British Government in Éire to invoke this section so as to revert to Dominion status?

Response: 'The Article was subsequently amended and this section omitted.'

Article 26.1. Under **Observations,** McDunphy asked: 'Is it necessary that the Attorney General should be in the Constitution?' **Response**: 'To be left in.'

Article 27.2. Under **Observations,** McDunphy suggested omission of comptroller and Attorney General – as ex-officio members – from council of state.

Response: 'To be deleted.' Regarding presidential appointments to council of state in Article 27.2, **Observations** of department noted that it might be charged in the Dáil that it would be possible in certain circumstances for the President by exercising the power under this section to overload the Council of State in a particular direction. It warned against introducing 'a new element of conflict within the State'.

Response: 'The President thinks that there is no danger of the type mentioned. The maximum number to be so appointed is five.'

> General notes on Articles 38–41 held that: 'These sections deal with Social and Personal rights. It is clear that as they stand many of them could be invoked so as to create very difficult situations.' Article 38.1, 'unnumbered subsection' regarding titles of nobility and orders of merit. **Observations**:
>
> (a) If the King, on the advice of the British Government, confers a title on one of our citizens, as frequently happens, does this constitute a breach of the Constitution, and, if so, what remedy is there?

(b) Mexican Constitution, Article 12. No titles of nobility, prerogatives of hereditary honours shall be granted in the United States of Mexico, nor shall effect be given to those granted by other countries.

Response: 'This whole Article is being revised.'

Article 43.4. Under **Observations,** the wording of 43.4 was repeated:

The State shall use its best endeavour to provide that the material resources of the Nation may be so distributed among private individuals and the various classes of the population as adequately to procure the common good of the community as a whole.

Response: The President's intention [then typed above: 'opinion'] is that a number of these sections are merely statements of moral principles and should not be created positive rights. I have accordingly suggested the following formula which should be inserted at the beginning of this portion of the Constitution – 'the State shall be guided in its general policy by the principles embodied in this Article, but the said Article shall not of itself operate to confer rights.'

Article 49. **Observations**:

Add the following clause as suggested by Mr Matheson: 'Laws enacted before, but expressed to come into force after, the coming into operation of this Constitution shall, unless otherwise enacted by the Oireachtas, come into force in accordance with the terms thereof.'

As revisions were introduced and the revised drafts introduced, further reactions were elicited from departments of state. Obviously these were not as detailed as the reactions discussed above but they are a useful illustration of the extent to which the respondents felt their concerns were dealt with.

Observations of the Department of Justice

Stephen Roche, the Justice Secretary, worked through St. Patrick's Day and prepared a lengthy and wide-ranging memorandum which he submitted on 22 March.[30] Roche expressed his antipathy to judicial review of legislation and raised concerns about the potential for judicial activism under the draft constitution. However, his concerns were not taken on board as on 13 April he prefaced the department's critique of the second revise with a plea to McDunphy, arguing:

As you know, I dislike the whole idea of tying up the Dáil and Government with all sorts

> of restrictions and putting the Supreme Court like a watch-dog over them for fear that they may run wild and do all sorts of indefensible things ...I think that there is a serious inconsistency in the present Draft ....[31]

The nub of the problem was outlined further in the Justice Department submission:

> Generally the Department felt that the draft Constitution went into too much detail whereas the Department's feeling is that the shorter and more general the Constitution is the less likely it is that the maintenance of law and order will be impeded by limitations on the power of the Dáil and by conflicts between the judiciary and the executive. The Departmental view on these particular matters and on the general policy remains unchanged but presumably a decision has been taken in favour of the opposite point of view and there is nothing to be gained by re-opening the matter.[32]

As Dr Hogan argued from these comments, Roche evidently considered that the drafting committee was so determined to enshrine the system of judicial review of legislation coupled with fundamental rights guarantees that further resistance was futile. If, therefore, de Valera had not intended to give such a prominent role to the courts in relation to these matters, it cannot be said that he had not received adequate advance warning about the direction which the draft constitution might have been taking.[33]

Although described on its title page as an 'authoritative translation' the original of this draft was, of course, written in English. It was ultimately translated into Irish. That the opposite was suggested reveals the dedication of de Valera to the concept of Irish as the first official language. Although the Irish version of the constitution was to be the 'authoritative text',[34] its drafting post-dated the English drafts. De Valera outlined the method that would be adopted: the English text would be taken first. The Irish text would then be examined to see whether it 'produces faithfully the intentions of the Dáil as expressed in the English text'.[35] Any amendments he hoped would be of a grammatical or literal nature. The drafting process was conducted through English. However, Maurice Móynihan acted as a bridge between his committee and the parallel process that brought into being the Irish version of the document – which would become the text that would take precedence in the event of a dispute over meaning.

Mícheál Ó Gríobhtha, who was assistant to the chairman of the terminology committee in the Department of Education, and Risteárd Ó Foghludha, editor of publications also in the Department of Education, did the bulk of the work. Ó Foghludha had been a classmate of de Valera's in Blackrock College. Again, the President used his personal knowledge of civil servants to influence his judgment in the selection of a small team for such a difficult, delicate and demanding task.

In October–November 1936 they were seconded to the Department of the President. Their terms of reference were to translate the English drafts into Irish; the translation was not to be literal but had to convey the general sense of the English text. According to Maurice Moynihan it was Mícheál Ó Gríobhtha who was 'responsible for the initial spadework'.[36] Breandán Mac Giolla Choille outlines their *modus operandi* as follows:

> Micheál first writing the Irish Text as a precise and exact translation of the legal wording of the English version: Risteárd editing Micheál's work, section by section and word by word, to make it more legible as Irish prose, or to bring it closer to ordinary speech as far as possible, without diminishing the meaning of the original version as regards law … After the editing on the first version … the alterations were so numerous that Micheál had to sit down and write out a clear copy with Risteárd's corrections inserted in it, before they could start on the second drafting. From then on draft followed on draft…[37]

It is estimated by Mac Giolla Choille that Risteárd and Mícheál worked on six drafts between November 1936 and 30 April 1937.

By April 1937 a number of other people were selected to join an expanded Irish drafting committee under the chairmanship of Maurice Moynihan: Tomás Page and Liam Ó Rinn joined Ó Gríobhtha and Ó Foghludha. The new appointees were joined by the oireachtas translation staff.[38] Professor Tomás Ó Máille made contributions of a 'specially valuable nature'.[39] Tomás Ó Rathaille, a former professor of Irish at Blackrock College, 'revise(d) generally the entire text and also contributed a certain amount of original translation'.[40] The committee worked at high pressure, at weekends and bank holidays often past midnight.[41]

The first, second and third revises of the draft constitution were circulated to the departments and government ministers on 1, 10 and 23 April respectively. All was moving to finality. But the entire process was in danger of foundering over the failure to reach agreement on the wording of the religious clause which was ultimately Article 44 when the draft constitution was finally published in both Irish and English on 1 May 1937. This diplomacy and politics of consensus-building is worthy of a chapter to itself.

CHAPTER 6

THE DRAFTING OF THE RELIGIOUS ARTICLE – ARTICLE 44[1]

The month of April 1937 was a time of concentrated activity during which there were four revisions of the draft constitution, culminating in the publication on 1 May 1937. The constitution committee was 'in constant touch with the President'. They met and revised 'without a break, up to the end of April, some of the sittings lasting until midnight or later'.[2]

The first revise of 1 April was circulated to selected persons and the process of re-examination commenced. This version was not sent to the departments. The second revise, produced on April 10, was circulated to the department secretaries and the subsequent responses were considered as part of the procedure of redrafting. McQuaid received the drafts and continued to correspond with de Valera on the contents. The responses to this document from the government department secretaries were much briefer and more limited than those elicited by the 16 March draft. The secretary of the Department of Justice, Stephen Roche, wrote to Michael McDunphy on 13 April 1937, in response to the 10 April revise. He pointed out that there was nothing in the proposed constitution to prevent an unscrupulous government in power passing legislation to institute detention without trial. The legal guarantees offered to citizens in the document would be then worth nothing, 'the victim would be detained in accordance with law'. *Habeas Corpus* would be of no use to him and since he would not be tried at all, the provisions of trial by jury would not apply.[3] Roche also sent a copy of 'Departmental Observations for the consideration of the Minister for Justice' dated 13 April 1937 to McDunphy. Presumably this was Roche's analysis of the version circulated on 10 April prepared for his minister.

In a covering note to McDunphy, Roche said: 'Attached copies may be used by you, as you think proper, or not at all!'[4] Roche's document complained that many points raised in the March submission of the Department of Justice had not been dealt with in the revised draft. Roche, on behalf of Justice, had argued for a much more succinct document. He now recognised that this was a lost cause.

Generally the Department felt that the Draft Constitution went into too much detail, whereas the Department's feeling is that the shorter and more general the Constitution is the less likely it is that the maintenance of law and order will be impeded by limitations on the power of the Dáil ... but presumably a decision has been taken in favour of the opposite point of view and there is nothing to be gained by reopening this matter.[5]

The document proceeded in numerical sequence to comment on 'particular articles'. In Article 2 it was asserted that there was confusion between the concept of citizen and people 'belonging to the nation'. Roche asked, referring to Article 10, did all citizens of Saorstát Éireann automatically become citizens of Éire? He suggested that Article 14, section 9 be amended to allow the minister to remit or reduce prison sentence without referring to government or the President which would also avoid unnecessary multiplication of papers and formalities. He felt that clarification was requested regarding special powers of police (Article 41), the committal of children to reformatories (Article 43) and Article 58 concerning the obligation of judges to make the 'new declaration' laid down in the draft.[6]

A long letter from the Department of Education to the President concentrated on its own area of responsibility. The first point concerned the committal of children to industrial schools. The problem was whether the Children's Act of 1929 was rendered unconstitutional by the fact that 'poverty' was one of the reasons specified in the act which allowed the state to place children in industrial schools. Education realised the point was a small one but legal advisers might consider looking into it.[7] The main point raised in the letter, however, was a request that the concept of 'state schools' should be retained in the new constitution. This point had been mentioned in the March submission of the department. The letter reiterated that 'in this country' the practice of state schools was definitely opposed:

> In this respect the attitude of the Church in this country, and the practice that has arisen as a result of this attitude, has been narrower than the official Catholic position as defined in the 1929 Encyclical [*Divini Illius Magistri*] ... This definite statement of the official position of the Church should be a sufficient defence of the inclusion in the Bunreacht of the phrase 'established by the State' as applied to schools ...[8]

The secretary of the Department of Finance, J. J. MacElligott, who had been responsible for the lengthiest response to the first draft, again submitted a document in reply to the revise of 10 April. He found Articles 1 to 4 less emphatic and more aggressive. He was particularly critical of the claim to territory 'which does not belong to us'. This, he said, gave a 'permanent place to a claim to "*Hibernia Irredenta*".'[9] McDunphy's comment appended to this criticism said simply, and with an air of finality: 'This is a matter of policy'. MacElligott was the only respondent to refer to the absence of the religious article. He pointed out that: 'It is most important that as much time as possible is available for consideration of its terms'.[10] As the month progressed, the work of the committee became more and more intense. The document took final shape. It was much longer than Hearne and his original group would have wanted. But they had little choice in the end but to incorporate some of the ideas and areas covered by Fr John Charles McQuaid. However, it was on the question of the religious article that the President and McQuaid most significantly parted company.

It is necessary here to retrace our steps slightly. On 9 March 1937, twelve galley proofs of the draft constitution were pulled. This draft contained Article 42, known as the 'one true Church' formula,[11] which was circulated at the time to a limited number of people – the members of de Valera's inner circle. However, apart from Joseph Walshe, the secretary of External Affairs, whose name appears on one of the copies, the identities of those who received the 'one true Church' formula are not known. There is no list on the file of those to whom the draft was sent in confidence. No doubt Michael McDunphy, Patrick Lynch (the Attorney General) and Arthur Matheson (the parliamentary draftsman) would have received copies. Fr John Charles McQuaid may also have been given one, for he wrote to de Valera on 10 March informing him that he 'read the text very carefully' and appended a few points for his consideration.[12]

One week later, on 16 March, a new draft appeared entitled the 'Authoritative Translation', from which the 'one true Church' formula had been expunged.[13] It was quite apparent to de Valera from the reaction to the limited circulation that the wording was not in accord with the fundamental principles of a government that sought to preserve equality before law for religious minorities and to protect those rights in the new constitution. The formula had to be replaced by a less confessional article and provide for parity. As noted earlier, the article on religion was removed before the first circulation in mid-April to members of the Executive Council, secretaries of government departments, and various members of the judiciary and the drafting committee. It was 'in blank' and was to stay that way until the last week in April.

It is not known what happened at the Executive Council meeting when the text was discussed. It is unlikely that the 'one true Church' formula was mentioned, for Seán MacEntee, though not present, stated later in interview that the document was warmly received, and de Valera was given a mandate to negotiate on the basis that the outcome would not establish any single Church.[14] That interview with MacEntee implied that the religious article was an issue of contention at the Executive Council table. But that surmise is based on a reminiscence of over forty years after the event.

Fr John Charles McQuaid, on receiving the draft of 16 March, did not make reference to the omission, simply noting: 'It is such a joy to see it in print; now it remains to see it enacted. It reads very well. I think I note a few changes made.'[15] On 21 March McQuaid sent a few emendations. His letter is of interest, although it is not clear to which section of the constitution he is referring:

> (a) That the natural sense of the words will be maintained.
> (b) That the mind of the legislator will be duly regarded.
> (c) That moral – not mathematical – possibility will be envisaged.
> Otherwise, any private citizen – or indeed, jurist – could drive any law or any interpretation of law to an impossible conclusion concerning the obligations of the State.[16]

On 22 March 1937, McQuaid wrote again about 'the case we discussed'. The statement that he was sending was 'a combination of two more Papal pronouncements! So we are in good company.' He asked de Valera to note that they had 'put in the rational and Christian concept of work'. He sent two letters on Holy Thursday, 25 March 1937. He apologised for being 'somewhat late' with his submission: 'I enclose the more useful excerpts connected with Religion. There are a few more valuable ones, but they can follow.' Later that day, he sent 'with great pleasure the remaining dossier, point by point, for the Family, Education and Private Property'. He added that: 'By tonight I hope to have Church and State all typed.' On Good Friday, 26 March 1937, he sent 'the last of my dossier: with the sincere hope that it will prove of some avail. What of the Secret Societies clause? I hope you are not too tired after the nights of labour; and that all goes well.' On 27 March, McQuaid wrote: 'This letter is unusual for me: it is only one of good wishes for a peaceful Easter. I hope you will soon draw breath – whatever breath my friends, the jurists, will have left you.' On 31 March, McQuaid made another submission: 'I think the enclosed is safe and sure.' In a postscript, he asked: 'Perhaps you will have the sheet of suggestions on Art. 41 by this evening. I can work on them too.'[17]

During the second week in March, de Valera's point of departure had been the following:

Article 42

1. The State acknowledges the right of Almighty God to public worship in that way which He has shown to be His Will.
2. Accordingly, the State shall hold in honour the Name of God and shall consider it a duty to favour and protect religion and shall not enact any measure that may impair its credit.
3. The State acknowledges that the true religion is that established by our Divine Lord, Jesus Christ Himself, which He committed to His Church to protect and propagate,

as the Guardian and interpreter of true morality. It acknowledges, moreover, that the Church of Christ is the Catholic Church.

4. The State recognised the Church of Christ as a perfect society, having within itself full Competence and sovereign authority, in respect of the spiritual good of men.
5. (1) Whatever may be ranked under the civil and political order is rightly subject to the supreme authority of the perfect society, the State, whose function it is to procure the temporal well-being, moral and material, of Society.
   (2) The State pledges itself, therefore, in virtue of this sovereign authority conferred on it by God within its temporal sphere to enforce respect, by its just laws, for the inalienable rights of the citizen and the family, and to preserve, as best it can, conditions of right social and moral well-being.
   (3) In cases where the jurisdiction of Church and State requires to be harmoniously co-ordinated, the State may come to a special agreement with the Church and other Religious Bodies, upon particular matters, civil, political and religious.
6. The State guarantees to its citizens freedom of religious conviction and liberty to practise their religion, in private and in public, having due regard however to social order and right morality.
7. The State pledges itself not to impose any disabilities on the ground of religious conviction that would be contrary to natural rights and social justice.
8. Every religious association recognised by the State shall have the right to manage its own affairs, own, acquire and administer property, movable and immovable, and maintain institutions for religious and charitable purposes.
9. The property of a religious denomination shall not be diverted save for necessary works of public utility and on payment of just compensation.
10. Legislation providing State Aid for schools shall contain no discrimination against schools under the management of a particular religious denomination.

The article on religion remained the major stumbling block. In an effort to find an acceptable formula, de Valera decided to engage in ecclesiastical 'shuttle' diplomacy with the leaders of the main Churches. Just how busy this schedule was can be seen by the following copy of de Valera's own record of his talks:

Table 5: De Valera's Negotiations with the Churches, 1937

April 3	Called on the Nuncio (*Saturday*)
April 5	Saw the Cardinal at the Nunciature (*Monday*)
April 5	Called on Archbishop Byrne (*Monday*)
April 10	Saw the Nuncio, who promised to see Cardinal (*Saturday*)
April 10	Saw Archbishop Byrne (*Saturday*)
April 10	Saw Dr Irwin (*Saturday*)
April 11	Saw the Nuncio at Seán T's (*Sunday*)

April 12	Called on Archbishop Gregg [Church of Ireland] (*Monday*)
April 12	Called on the Nuncio (*Monday*)
April 12	Saw Dr Irwin (*Monday*)
April 13	Phoned the Nuncio (*Tuesday*)
April 13	Saw the Rev. W.H. Massey, head of the Methodist Church in Ireland (*Tuesday*)
April 14	Saw Dr Irwin (*Wednesday*)
April 16	Saw Dr Irwin, the Moderator, and the Moderator Designate, who travelled from Belfast (*Friday*)
April 16	Saw the Nuncio at Seán T's (*Friday*)
April 16	J.P.W. [Walshe] went to Rome (*Friday* evening)
April 22	Called on the Nuncio (*Thursday*)
April 23	Nuncio phoned to say Cardinal approved Christian Churches (*Friday*)
April 24	Saw Nuncio and Cardinal (*Saturday*)
April 26	M. Moynihan saw Arch. Gregg and D. Robinson got letter from Gregg to D'Arcy (*Monday*)
April 27	Robinson goes to see D'Arcy (*Tuesday*)[18]

Between the negative reaction of his most trusted advisers by mid-March and his round of talks which lasted through the first three weeks of April, de Valera had made visible progress and had come up with a number of new ideas.

Starting on 3 April, de Valera approached the papal nuncio, Paschal Robinson, to garner support and advice for his change of direction on the religious article. The nuncio may have visited Cardinal MacRory in Drogheda on 3 April. This was the first of numerous contacts with the nuncio between then and 27 April. Robinson, having arranged for de Valera to meet MacRory on 5 April in the nunciature, proved to be most helpful to the president of the Executive Council throughout that difficult month. De Valera explained to the nuncio that the 'one true Church' formula would have to be changed, although he 'wished to go as far as was practicable but he could only go so far'.[19] De Valera brought three documents with him to the nunciature, marked A (original religious clause), B9 (revised version of this) and C (the preamble).[20] The nuncio was shown both versions of the religious article. The difference between draft A and B was that section 2 had been reduced to: 'Accordingly, the state shall hold in honour the name of God and shall consider it duty to favour and protect religion.'

Sections 4 and 5 were deleted. The old section 6 became the new section 4, and the last line was changed to read: 'having due regard however to public order and morality'. There was an interesting change in the old section 7 (now 5):

> The State guarantees not to impose any disabilities on the ground of religious conviction that would be contrary to natural rights and social justice, nor shall the State place any barrier to employment in the public service on such a ground.

The old section 10 became the new section 6 and remained unchanged. What is of particular interest about these changes is that they are made in de Valera's handwriting. The nuncio was shown both versions of the religious article.

These changes were a radical departure from the 'one true Church' formula. De Valera did not leave the original version with the nuncio for he had obviously decided that McQuaid's article was no longer feasible.[21] He informed the nuncio that the original clause 3 'was impossible'; while he was prepared to leave it in for the moment he 'would inevitably be pushed either backward or forward'. He was personally in favour of leaving the revised clause 3 out. 'The Nuncio agreed.'[22]

Originally, de Valera intended to see Archbishop Byrne of Dublin the following day but 'agreed' to meet with Cardinal MacRory of Armagh instead on being informed that he would be in the city on Monday. The president of the Executive Council must have suspected that the archbishop would not be agreeable to such proposals.[23] The nuncio saved de Valera from making a bad mistake of protocol, as Armagh was the head of the Catholic Church in Ireland.[24] Beginning at six o' clock in the evening on 5 April, the meeting went relatively well but a strong difference of opinion emerged. MacRory, as suspected, adopted a less than helpful attitude towards the ideas behind the draft religious article. The following formula, which is to be found amongst his papers typed on nunciature notepaper, reflected his position at that moment:

> The state reflecting the religious convictions of 93 pc of its citizens acknowledges the Catholic religion to be the religion established by Our Divine Lord Jesus Christ; while guaranteeing at the same time to all its citizens the fullest liberty to practise their religion in public and in private, with due regard however for public order and morality.[25]

On the same piece of headed nunciature notepaper MacRory minuted some weeks later: 'De Valera would not accept this and the question went to Rome. The Holy Father at first agreed with me but eventually in view of the six counties etc., allowed the form that stands in the F.S. [sic] constitution.'[26] But that anticipated what happened in the last week in April. De Valera minuted after the meeting on 5 April: 'He [The Cardinal] felt the omission of any mention of the Holy Catholic Church would cause considerable difficulty and cause me to be attacked. He would himself not attack, as he understood the difficulties.'[27]

In contrast, Archbishop Edward Byrne, whom de Valera met the same day, 5 April, was far more positive in his reaction to the drafts of an amended preamble as well as Article B minus clause 3 which had been merely crossed out in the draft shown to the nuncio.[28] The fact that de Valera brought with him the draft article on the family and education no doubt helped Byrne in his positive response. De Valera minuted: '(He) liked the Preamble immensely and with the Preamble was prepared to see if I thought it necessary, the omission of the Catholic Church as such.'[29]

Paradoxically, Byrne was considered to be as strongly pro-Fine Gael as MacRory was deemed to be a republican sympathiser. But those positions were reversed on the religious article of the constitution. The archbishop of Dublin was persuaded by the totality of the document. MacRory, as leader of the Catholic Church in Ireland, was concerned about its alleged 'down-grading'. Regardless of Byrne's support, the leader of the government faced the substantive problem of having to find a formula acceptable to both Dublin and Armagh and, at the same time, bring the other Churches in the country along with him.

On 6 April, the day after his round of discussions with the nuncio, Armagh and Dublin, de Valera thought over his problem. It occurred to him and to his advisers that: 'We might put in a clause recognising the fact that the Catholic Church was the Guardian of Faith of the majority of the citizens.'[30] Working along those lines, a new formula emerged by 10 April. A comparison between this and the Jesuit submission indicates that the new article reflected part of the approach in that submission.[31] The new draft article read as follows:

Religion

1 The State acknowledges that the homage of public worship is due to Almighty God. It shall hold His name in reverence and respect and honour religion.
2 The State recognises the special position of The Holy Catholic and Apostolic Church as the guardian of the Faith professed by the great majority of the citizens.
3 The State also recognises the Church of Ireland, the Presbyterian Church, The Methodist Church, the Hebrew Congregation and the other religious denominations existing at the date of the coming into operation of this Constitution as guardians of the Faith of their respective communities.
4 Freedom of conscience and the free profession and practice of religion are, subject to public order and morality, guaranteed to every citizen.
5 The State guarantees not to endow any Religion. And shall not impose any disabilities or make any discrimination on the ground of religious profession, belief or status.
6 Legislation providing State aid for schools shall not discriminate between schools under the management of different religious denominations, nor be such to affect prejudicially the right of any child to attend a school receiving public money without attending religious instruction at the school.
7 Every religious denomination shall have the right to manage its own affairs, own, acquire, and administer property, movable and immovable, and maintain institutions for religious and charitable purposes.
8 The property of any religious denomination or any educational institution shall not

be diverted save for necessary works of public utility and on payment of compensation.[32]

De Valera may have been strengthened in his resolve by visits to the leaders of one of the minority Churches. On 10 April, he arranged to meet a close friend, the Presbyterian moderator, Dr James Irwin.[33] A member of the Fianna Fáil executive from 1945–54, he was intent on being as helpful as possible to the president of the Executive Council. An arrangement was made to meet later the following week with another prominent Presbyterian leader. De Valera also saw Archbishop Byrne on 10 April; the meeting was satisfactory.

But the question remained: could Cardinal MacRory be won over? De Valera met the nuncio later that evening. Concerned about the attitude of the cardinal, Robinson agreed to go see him in Drogheda the following day, Sunday, 11 April 1937. By that date, the cardinal had already put pen to paper. Dated 9 April, MacRory wrote to the nuncio:

> I feel that I acted right in not agreeing with the President. Though very unworthy, I am the head of the Irish Church; and as such I think I couldn't do less than insist that not only the Preamble but the constitution itself should show some special recognition of our religion. As it is, the Constitution makes us no better than the Quakers. But I can see the President's point of view.[34]

In an earlier contact with MacRory, Robinson may have suggested that the cardinal might like to write to the relevant section of the curia on the matter, for MacRory continued, in the same letter:

> It never occurred to me to write to His Eminence Card. Fumasoni Biondi.As he wrote to your Excellency, it is better for you to reply to him. Of course if you wished me to do so I would do so, and I hope you will do it yourself.[35]

MacRory took it for granted that the nuncio would do so 'unless I hear to the contrary'. He concluded that he was not going to attend the coronation in London of George VI, adding: 'It is a pity I can't. It would be interesting to see the Orange reaction to my presence.'[36] There is no reason to conclude that a letter, dated 9 April, would not have been with the nuncio the following day.

Robinson, before he set out to see the cardinal on 11 April, was fully aware of the depths of his objections to the draft constitution. The nuncio brought with him the new documentation supplied by de Valera. Meanwhile, on Sunday, 11 April, Robinson received a letter from the vice president, Seán T. O'Kelly. Internal evidence in the letter suggests that it was probably received after the nuncio's return from meeting the cardinal. It read:

Your excellency,

I have been speaking to the President about a rendez-vous for tonight and he tells me he has an engagement that will occupy him from about 7.30 to 9.30 or so tonight. He has asked me to be with him so I will be occupied at the same time.

The President would of course be anxious to hear the result of your visit and he requested me to enquire if Your Excellency would think it possible to come here a little after 9.30 pm …

The President is really worried at the idea of suggesting such a late hour, knowing that Your Excellency will have such a fatiguing day and that you are also such an early riser and he would gladly go out to see you at the nunciature but he hesitates to go again to the Park on account of all the gossip going round about his recent visits.

If your Excellency will be so kind as to ring up Phyllis [O'Kelly's wife] tonight (I will be home till about 7.45) and say if it will be convenient for you to come here tonight I will be most grateful. She will send me word.

With many apologies for troubling you so,

Most respectfully yours, Seán T Ó Ceallaigh.[37]

There is no minute of what transpired in O'Kelly's home that evening. But evidently some progress had been made.

On Monday, 12 April 1937, de Valera was confronted by what is termed in more contemporary parlance a 'worst-case scenario'. With the exception of the Presbyterians, he had not yet begun to consult the leaders of the other Churches. That day, de Valera held another round of meetings. He met the Church of Ireland archbishop of Dublin, Dr John Gregg, who resembled the president of the Executive Council in appearance. He was mistaken for de Valera on more than one occasion during the civil war years. De Valera quickly discovered that Gregg was quite happy with the drafts presented to him.[38] Gregg wrote in his diary: 'Mr De V calls and speaks three quarters of an hr. in regard to religious clauses of the new Constitution.'[39] He proved to be very helpful and made a number of suggestions which helped to resolve the president's difficulties over terminology. Gregg reinforced de Valera's judgment that the article on religion should be descriptive, and provided him with the help he needed:

> Our Constitution should win the respect of all sections of the Community, and the members of all Churches should, if possible be satisfied. But here was my difficulty. I knew that some members of our Church objected to being called Roman Catholics, whilst many in your Church objected to being called non-Catholics or Protestants.[40]

Gregg suggested de Valera adopt the simple device of using the term by which each Church described itself. Consulting a volume of the Decrees of the Council of Trent Gregg read out the title, 'The Holy Catholic and Apostolic and Roman Church'. Gregg told de Valera that the correct title for his church was the Church of Ireland; although the use of that was to cause difficulties later, de Valera refused to be moved by his Catholic friends on the radical right. By 14 April, Gregg's recommendations were in the new draft, which now read:

> The state recognises the special position of the *Holy* Catholic and *Apostolic and Roman Church* as the guardian of the Faith professed by the great majority of the citizens.
> The State also recognises the Church of Ireland, the Presbyterian Church *in Ireland*, and the Methodist Church in Ireland, the *Jewish* Congregations, and the other Religious denominations existing in *Éire* at the date of the coming into operation of this Constitution.[41]

Meanwhile, de Valera had also met the leader of the Presbyterians, Dr Irwin, on the same day as his meeting with Gregg. He called, too, to the nunciature to meet Robinson and spoke with him on the phone the following day.

On 13 April, de Valera also met the president of the Methodist Church, W.H. Massey,[42] who later advised that: 'We find nothing either in the substance or wording of the section submitted to which we could fairly take exception.' As regards the special position of the Catholic Church it was pointed out the Methodists were

> … quite satisfied that it should be used as the official title of the Church of the great majority in this country, so long as it is not used in any deliberately exclusive sense. The succeeding paragraph in the draft copy in which the other 'Churches' in this country are recognised as such removes any doubt on this point.[43]

On 12 and 14 April, de Valera had met with Irwin. Two days later, 16 April, he again met Irwin, who was accompanied by F. W. S. O'Neill, the outgoing moderator, and the moderator designate, R. Hanna. They took away with them the preamble and the article on religion. On reflection, the Presbyterians had a problem with the description 'Catholic Church', and, like Gregg, suggested an enlarged description to include Apostolic and Roman. However, the most significant suggestion was the phrase 'the other Christian Churches' in place of the phrasing 'other Religious denominations'.[44] The matter remained unresolved.

There is no evidence that de Valera met with the leaders of the Jewish congregation. This may have been due to the fact that the chief rabbi of the Irish Free State, Isaac Herzog, had departed for his new position in Palestine. However, there was a close personal friendship between de Valera and Herzog which went back to the days of the War of Independence. That personal relationship was sustained through the 1920s when de Valera was in the political wilderness. Following the founding of Fianna Fáil in 1926, de Valera kept up contact with Herzog. When he came to power in 1932, de Valera remained on very friendly terms with the leaders of the Jewish community in Dublin. The president of the Executive Council held Herzog's views and counsel in high esteem. His departure meant that de Valera had to rely on the former chief rabbi's views on the subject of Church and state learned during their years of friendship. When the constitution was enacted de Valera received a letter from the Jewish rabbinate committee, which 'noted with great satisfaction and due appreciation that the Jewish Congregations are included in the clause giving equal recognition to the Religious bodies in Éire'.[45]

De Valera had not yet broken the logjam with the cardinal. Another problem arose of a serious kind as it emerged that opposition within clerical circles to the new religious article might be more widespread than anticipated. Fr Seán Farragher, who is an historian of the Holy Ghost order in Ireland, has written that one rather heated discussion on the wording of the religious article took place between John Charles McQuaid and the President in Bellvue, de Valera's home, on 14 April.[46] The future archbishop of Dublin, uncharacteristically, lost his temper and harsh words ensued over the redrafted religious article. Two letters of apology from McQuaid also supports the contention that a bitter dispute arose between the two friends. 'I may have so shown my disappointment as to be wanting in courtesy, if I did in the least way I am very sorry for it,' McQuaid wrote.[47] The argument between the two men appears to have been precipitated by the inclusion of the phrase 'the other Christian Churches' and the phrase 'Church of Ireland'. McQuaid would have found these inclusions totally unacceptable from a theological standpoint. A letter supports the contention that the nub of the argument was related to the designation of 'Christian' to the other minority Churches rather than outright objection to the broader article.

> I have been thinking very much about it, of course they claim the title but as very many in all these churches deny the divinity of Christ unlike their ancestors they have truly ceased to be Christians. Very often they are only ethical.[48]

He had been prepared to accept compromises up to a point and had gone so far as to interpret the encyclical *Immortale Dei* in a manner which would have been comforting to de Valera:

> Hence the society and the Government ought per se to profess the true faith and legislate in accord with it, per accidens it may not be prudently possible to have that public admission. This seems to me to be the meaning of Leo XIII. Of course once the state acknowledges God's right to public worship, it cannot be secular even if it be not Catholic. And when the state legislates according to natural law, of necessity, it legislates according to Catholicity, because the latter is guardian of natural law.[49]

But those phrases regarding the Protestant churches were, for McQuaid, taking matters too far.

Confronted by the impasse over the wording of the religious article, de Valera decided on 15 April to send the secretary of the Department of External Affairs, Joseph Walshe, to Rome to secure the advice of the Holy See. In normal circumstances, the President would have used the good offices of the Irish envoy to the Holy See, W. J. B. Macaulay, to resolve matters. But the gravity of the situation was underlined by the decision to send Walshe. Before setting out on the evening of 16 April, Walshe had a meeting with the nuncio. Later that evening, de Valera again met the nuncio at O'Kelly's house. In order to prepare the Holy See for Walshe's arrival, Robinson sent an extensive report to the cardinal secretary of state, Eugenio Pacelli, the future Pope Pius XII. Dated 17 April, he informed Pacelli that de Valera had come to the nunciature to confide in him in a 'secret and confidential' way about the article on religion in the new constitution which would be put before the Irish people in the near future, probably on the same day as a general election. He reported that de Valera had also confided in Cardinal MacRory and Archbishop Byrne. De Valera, he wrote, wanted to follow all the norms outlined in the papal encyclicals and in the public pronouncements of the Church but he had encountered a number of difficulties.[50]

Robinson outlined the first of those as being that the new constitution was for the Irish Free State but in another sense it was a document to be applied to the whole of Ireland. It was the ardent desire of all the leaders of the Free State to form one day a state embracing the whole of the island. But in Northern Ireland, the majority was notably Protestant, he wrote, and very pugnacious. De Valera wanted to show to the Protestants of Ulster [NI] in the new constitution 'the tolerance and the good will of Catholics'. De Valera wanted to avoid any recrimination on the part of the Protestants on the island.[51]

Robinson noted that the preceding constitution of 1922 did not name the Catholic Church and limited itself to proclaim liberty of conscience for all. De Valera did not feel that he could change that approach to the religious article because it would result in a grave reaction, he wrote. In those circumstances, Robinson urged his superiors at the Holy See to respond with a favourable consideration of de Valera's position. In the nuncio's opinion, it truly appeared that, in the present circumstances, it would be difficult to obtain more than what had been formulated in the draft articles.[52]

De Valera's decision to send a special envoy to Rome was not an act of piety or political weakness. It was rather a measure of last resort, underlining the dilemma in which he found himself. The historical experience of republican and

Fianna Fáil leadership with the Holy See had cautioned minimal contact in the past as far as domestic Irish politics had been concerned. Pius XI had not shown himself to be particularly friendly towards Irish nationalism. The memory of the would-be peacemaker, Monsignor Salvatore Luzio, sent by the pope in 1923 to try and end the Civil War, still rankled with certain members of Fianna Fáil.[53] There were residual suspicions that the Vatican was pro-British. Therefore, de Valera had no reason to feel confident about the Vatican's political judgment as far as Ireland was concerned.

Since coming to power in 1932, de Valera's name undoubtedly evoked connotations of 'republicanism' at the Vatican. The Eucharistic Congress, which was held in Dublin in 1932, helped change de Valera's international profile in a positive way.[54] This was followed by an official visit to the Vatican during the Holy Year of 1933 when it was evident that the Irish President had not yet won fully the confidence of senior officials of the papacy. Further efforts were made to counteract a negative outlook by a succession of ministerial pilgrimages. The vice-president, Seán T. O'Kelly, was generally entrusted by de Valera with the task of establishing better relations in that area.

Between 1933 and 1937 Irish interests were protected in Rome and government policy helped slowly reassure the doubters at the Vatican regarding Fianna Fáil's religious orthodoxy. Between 1934 and 1940, Irish diplomacy at the Vatican was in the able hands of W. J. B. Macaulay (not to be confused with the other Irish diplomat, Leo T. McCauley). Against this historical background, it could only have been with the greatest reluctance that de Valera decided to send Walshe to Rome on 16 April 1937. But the conflicting positions within the Catholic Church, in that small circle taken into de Valera's confidence, had potentially dangerous political consequences. Were the substantial differences over the wording of the religious article to become public, the chances of having the constitution passed in a plebiscite appeared remote. It was a calculated risk, quite how calculated de Valera would never really know.

Undoubtedly, de Valera was advised by the nuncio on possible options facing the Vatican. Joseph Walshe does not appear to have played a central role in the drafting of the constitution and he may have been anxious to go to the Vatican anyway. The Irish envoy could have handled the matter, but the sending of the secretary of the Department of External Affairs emphasised the delicacy and importance of the undertaking.[55]

Walshe took four documents to Rome: a draft of the proposed preamble, the revised article on religion, a set of instructions and a *pro memoria*. The instructions were clear and unambiguous:

1. General approval for religious part.
2. To get the official name of the Catholic Church.
3. To get permission to phrase ARTICLE 3 so as to include the phrase 'The State also recognises the other Christian Churches, namely, Church of Ireland, etc., as well as the Jewish Congregations and the other religious bodies existing in Éire at the time of the coming into operation of this Constitution.[56]

The *pro memoria* outlined de Valera's dilemma and provided an insight into the mind of the President as a working politician. The document was not a philosophical tract stating objectively the tenets of de Valera's world view. It was a diplomatic document designed to furnish Walshe with the arguments necessary for the Vatican to understand the particular political difficulties of a state with diverse religious groups in its jurisdiction. It was to serve Walshe as a 'reminder'.[57] Therefore, it was not to be presented to the cardinal secretary of state, Eugenio Pacelli. The objective was to publish the constitution on 24 April 1937.[58] Walshe was instructed to argue that 'the Articles concerning religion are not the Catholic ideal as regards the relationship between Church and State'.

PRO MEMORIA

1. The accompanying documents and drafts of proposed Articles in the new Constitution which it is hoped to publish on April 24th.
2. The lawyers may desire some changes in form or phrasing, but the substance is likely to remain unchanged, except in the case of document which presents the difficulty of reducing Catholic theory to a practical form.
3. The Articles concerning religion are not the Catholic ideal as regards the relationship between Church and State. In the actual conditions, however, it is not deemed possible to go farther than is provided.
4. About one-fourth of the population of Ireland is Protestant. Until recently, in all State relations the Protestant churches were the dominating influence.
5. The Church of Ireland was until 1869 the State Church here, and the Protestant religion the State religion.
6. The Protestant Churches in this country are closely associated with the corresponding churches in Great Britain, in which there are over 40,000,000 Protestants. With this strength so close to hand, and with the recollections of their past supremacy, the Protestant members of our population find it hard to accept a second and subordinate place.
7. If the attempt were to be made to embody in the new Constitution the full Catholic ideal there would be an immediate outcry from the Protestant section of the population, and a bitter religious controversy might easily ensue.
8. In the present circumstances, such a controversy would in every way be disastrous. The Government would be charged by a large section even of its own supporters with having needlessly caused this controversy and with having wilfully disturbed the present religious calm in this part of Ireland.

9. The Government would likewise be charged with having provided the occasion for a renewal of the bitter attacks on our fellow-countrymen in Belfast and in the rest of that part of Ireland in which Catholics are a minority.
10. The Government would further be charged with having raised a new barrier to the reunion of our country, and with having recklessly caused offence to a section of our countrymen whose ancestors produced many patriots whose names are revered in many a Catholic home. Wolfe Tone, Robert Emmet, Parnell, etc.
11. On the other hand the recognition of the Protestant Churches, even though they are put in a subordinate place, will produce considerable appeasement, will lead to better feeling and understanding between the different religious bodies here and may also lead to the desired political reunion of our country.
12. The effect of the recognition given will, I am convinced, secure the united influence of all the Christian bodies against Atheism which present world conditions seem to indicate to be the enemy now most dangerous.
13. The premier and special position accorded to the Catholic Church as 'guardian of the Faith of the great majority of the citizens' will mean in practice that the Catholic Church will be the Church associated with the State on all public occasions.
14. Under our democratic Constitution the vast majority of the Ministers of State are certain to be Catholic, who will profess their religion openly and will attend religious functions in a Catholic Church on all occasion in which a manifestation of religious belief is called for.
15. In the past Ministers in a body have annually attended Mass on St Patrick's Day at the Catholic Pro Cathedral; the Government and Members of Parliament have attended a special Mass on each occasion in which a new Parliament meets after the dissolution; At the Eucharistic Congress the State was officially represented by all the Ministers.
16. The proposed draft will have the tacit, if not the expressed and explicit, approval of the religious bodies mentioned in paragraph 3.
17. His Eminence, the Cardinal, and His Grace, the Archbishop of Dublin, as well as His Excellency, the Apostolic Nuncio, having regard to all the conditions, see no cause to disapprove.
18. It is requested that the above considerations be placed before the Holy Father with a view to obtaining his approval and blessing before publication.

The typed draft [of the article on religion] in Joseph Walshe's possession was that dated 14 April, which excluded the phrase 'the other Christian Churches', yet his instructions said specifically that he was to seek approval of this. This lends further credence to the suggestion that the argument between McQuaid and de Valera was about this phrase in particular rather than specifically the description of the Catholic Church. Matters had become so critical and urgent that there had not been sufficient time to type a new draft.

De Valera waited anxiously for the outcome of the Walshe mission. Both men were in daily contact between 19 and 23 April 1937. Ably assisted by

W.J.B. Macaulay, Walshe, who had arrived on 17 April, began a round of protracted discussions with officials of the Secretariat of State. A series of coded telegrams kept de Valera informed. For example, on 19 April Walshe sent a coded message:

> Saw Assistant Secretary of State [Monsignore Pizzardo] yesterday. Gave him message. Secretary of State sees us tomorrow having informed Pope. Hope send telegram announcing complete approval tomorrow afternoon. Do not foresee any difficulty.

Walshe produced a long handwritten report on 22 April after the completion of his round of discussions with senior Vatican officials. It is worth looking at the content of this document because it throws light on the subtleties of high diplomacy. The contrast in diplomatic styles between Pacelli and Walshe is quite striking. The exchanges demonstrate the determination of the Vatican not to allow itself to become involved in the internal politics of a Catholic state. Pacelli had no desire to allow the Vatican to become co-opted by any group in Ireland.

Walshe, who ought to have known better because of his experience during the nuncio negotiations in 1929, had been told by Pizzardo that he 'saw no difficulty in getting the desired approval'. It was on that basis that Walshe had sent a telegram to Dublin promising an announcement of 'complete approval'. However, as things happened, that 'proved to be excessive optimism'.

The first three sections of Article 45 (which became Article 44 in the final draft) were left with Pizzardo for Pacelli. What Walshe did not know was what Pacelli had written on the file of the secretariat of state concerning the documentation supplied by Dublin. The cardinal secretary of state was responsible for a number of minutes which said that Article 45 [became Article 44] 'suoni un po' male; perche il parlare soltanto di adorazione di Dio ha sapore di Teismo'. But Pacelli was prepared to accept that it was better than Article 8 in the constitution of 1922. There was an understanding of the difficulties in de Valera's position. But a number of the draft answers were far from encouraging: 'The Holy Father does not approve. Since He could not but disapprove, He prefers to refrain from expressing his judgment … If He had to express a judgment, it could not be other than unfavourable (disapproval). The Holy Father does not oppose; He could not but disapprove if He were to express a judgment.'[59] Fortunately for de Valera, the final answer was very much more encouraging than Pacelli's minutes quoted above.

Walshe and Macaulay saw the secretary of state the following day, 20 April. According to the Walshe report, 'the cardinal was most amicable'. He kept them for over an hour which was well into lunchtime, as he did also on the two following days. Walshe explained de Valera's policy, emphasising 'particularly the aspect of the "apeasement" [*sic*] which you desire to bring about not only amongst our own people of all religions and political beliefs but also between our people and the British people'. Pacelli appeared very interested and asked endless questions:

> I thought it well to say at a very early stage that you fully realised that the sections of the Constitution under discussion did not correspond with the complete Catholic ideal. You would like to have the approval of the Vatican in so far as it could be given. At any rate you wished to have the satisfaction of having let the Card. Secy. and the Holy Father see the sections relating to the Church before putting them before parliament.

Pacelli expressed his great joy that de Valera had done so and suggested that the President should understand that whatever he and the holy father might say they were in the fullest sympathy with de Valera and his government in his difficulties. They appreciated how great a task it was to achieve anything like the Catholic ideal in the special circumstances.

But Pacelli was determined to speak with complete frankness. He had discussed the matter briefly with the pope and would do so again the following day:

> He felt however that the 'special position' given to the Catholic Church had no real value so long as there was not a formal acknowledgement of the R.C. Church as the Church founded by Christ. Moreover its importance was based on numbers only (as far as the test was concerned) and the recognition given to the other Churches nullified any advantage which might have been derived from exclusive recognition. He thought we should use the word 'tolerates' in regard to them. He could see no juridical consequences flowing from the text used which could confer advantages on the Catholic Church not equally conferred on the other bodies. Ireland was *the* Catholic country of the world, and he thought we should have made a very special effort to give to the world a completely Catholic constitution.

Walshe made a passionate defence of the official position, trying to keep to the 'realities' of Irish politics. Pacelli, who was very friendly throughout, said that he was talking as a churchman must talk. Walshe ascertained very early on in the conversation that he would never succeed in getting approval of the text from the Vatican: 'From the nature of things they have to stake their full claim, and formal or indeed informal approval was not to be given to a text which did not come down completely on the side of strict Catholic doctrine.' Pacelli told Walshe with a smile 'but quite truthfully that according to the strict teaching of the church we were heretics to recognise any church but the one true church of Christ'. Walshe immediately countered, only to be told by Pacelli that 'the church would not take our heresy too seriously'. Pacelli was telling the Irishman politely that the Vatican had no intention of becoming involved in domestic Irish politics. The secretary of state had pointed out that if the Vatican were to do so it would have to seek the 'one true Church' formula. In his report, Walshe expressed the view that he was disappointed when the cardinal returned the following day, having seen the pope, with the words '*Ni approvo ni non disapprovo; taceremo.*' Pacelli did not leave Walshe in any doubt as to the meaning; the answer: 'I do not approve, neither do I not disapprove; we shall maintain silence.' Walshe tried to translate the 'evil out of this double negative but the cardinal held me to the sense'. Pacelli went on to say that the pope was doing 'quite a lot in saying that he would maintain silence'. Pacelli, according to Walshe, saw the pope's position in a positive light from the Irish standpoint:

> It was an attitude of complete neutrality. He might have taken the text without bearing in mind all the implications of the explanations I had given, because the text after all was what counted, but he refrained from disapproving. He would not say 'I approve' and while he would not say 'I do not disapprove' he took the middle position of keeping silence. So argued the Cardinal and while he clearly wanted to give us a crumb of consolation he had to maintain that the Pope went to the extreme limit to which his position allowed him to go.

Walshe also had an exchange with Pacelli on the question of marriage. He claimed that there the Irish state was 'also heretical'. He argued in favour of giving legal recognition to a specifically Catholic position. Walshe countered by saying how difficult it was to adopt such a position in a country of mixed religions where divorce was forbidden to all. Pacelli pushed the point and Walshe:

> ... insisted again and again that we regarded the fundamentally sound position of the church in the hearts of the people as an infinitely greater safeguard for Catholic doctrine than forms in any document whether Constitutions or concordats – and that that conviction was never absent from your mind when drawing up the Constitution. The Holy Father and he, the Cardinal, would realise – as our state evolved – that we had acted in the best interests of the Church as well as of the people.

There was further discussion of a somewhat light-hearted nature about attendance at the coronation ceremony of George VI in London, an event Cardinal MacRory had not attended.

On his final meeting with Pacelli, Walshe learned how pleased the cardinal was to know that de Valera intended to use the full official title of the Church in the constitution. He compared the wording carefully with the text of the Lateran Treaty. Pacelli was not prepared to approve formally the phrase 'other Christian Churches'. He preferred 'bodies' but 'let it go without taking any responsibility for it'. Walshe concluded his long report, which does not appear to have been put on file in the Department of External Affairs, thus:

> ... I want to express my great regret at not having been able to do what I was sent out to do. But I have learned a great deal about the attitude of the Holy See to such matters – and I can assure you, most confidently, that at the back of their adherence to rigid forms and dogmas there is very sincere respect, and even gratitude for the extent to which you have been able to go in making our const. Catholic; notwithstanding the very great difficulties which they understood better than they pretend to understand them. I will of course amplify this report viva voce on my return.[60]

The question is whether MacRory actually went to Rome himself to press his case or whether he had it done on his behalf. There is no reference in the de Valera papers, or in the state archives, to prove that he did the former. But the Irish envoy, Macaulay, was to recall many years later to a relative how he had softened up the cardinal with whiskey and got him to intervene with the Vatican to drop its insistence on giving canon law some express recognition in the constitution.[61] I have found no evidence to confirm that MacRory went to Rome at that time. Neither have I been able to find any evidence that the cardinal exercised any influence on the Holy See by letter to show that he was in favour of, or rather not opposed to, the new draft religious article. It is certainly the case that he did not attempt to try to campaign against the final article other than to speak directly with the nuncio. It is probable, although not recorded, that the cardinal and the archbishop of Dublin were in contact with each other during the critical period in April when the text of Article 44 was being finalised. But MacRory conveyed his ideas to Rome through the nuncio.

Because of the news from Rome sent by Walshe, de Valera's position was growing in strength. While Robinson would have got news from Rome by phone and by telegram between 18 and 23 April, he did not receive official word until Pacelli wrote to him on 10 May giving the formal decision of the pope:

> The Holy Father has asked me [Card. Pacelli] to respond to Mr Walsh, secretary to the department of foreign affairs, in the following way regarding article 44 of the new Irish Constitution.
>
> In regard to the article proposed for the new Constitution, the Holy Father has responded: We do not approve nor do We not disapprove: We shall remain silent in the matter, but his silence does not signify consent: We shall learn of it from the newspapers. And if the proposers are, as they affirm, unable to do more, they will do what they can.[62]

What Walshe did not know was what Pacelli had written on the file of the secretariat of state concerning the documentation supplied by Dublin. It is probable that the cardinal secretary of state was responsible for a number of minutes which said that Article 45 [became Article 44] 'suoni un po' male; perche il parlare soltanto di adorazione di Dio ha sapore di Teismo (doesn't sound well, because even in speaking of the adoration of God gives it a flavour of theism)'.[63] But the writer was prepared to accept that it was better than Article 8 in the constitution of 1922.

Robinson would only have had verbal confirmation of the decision when he met de Valera on 22 April at the nunciature to discuss the final wording of the article on religion.[64] They discussed the draft, based on the previous day's work (with only minor changes).

On 23 April, MacRory was in Lucan. He phoned the nuncio. Seán T. O'Kelly may have had a part in the exchanges that followed. In the end, the nuncio phoned de Valera to say that the 'Cardinal approved "Christian Churches"'.[65] However, de Valera may have already decided what he was going to do before the telephone call: a draft, dated that same day, 23 April, had restored the original section 1.2, and the phrase 'the other Christian Churches, including … etc.' in section 1.3 had been removed.

On 24 April, de Valera met the cardinal and the nuncio. Presumably, the President had undertaken to brief MacRory on the outcome of Walshe's visit. Whether the cardinal was in full agreement or not, de Valera had decided to proceed with the formula as drafted on 14 April 1937. While there was no mention of 'the other Christian Churches', neither was there anything left of the 'one true Church' formula.

If de Valera had suffered a temporary loss of nerve, he had completely regained his political composure by 24 April. The decision to drop the phrase 'other Christian Churches' was not a capitulation to bigotry. It was superfluous to the meaning of the section and could have been dropped with justification on stylistic grounds. It was much more important for de Valera to hold his ground against the lobby to include a 'one true Church' formula in section 1.2. He succeeded. On 26 April, Maurice Moynihan was sent by de Valera to see Gregg. Moynihan was asked by Gregg what legal basis should be attached to 'recognise', used in the religious article. The matter was referred back to de Valera who phoned Gregg. De Valera noted that Gregg was 'satisfied' with whatever answer he gave him.[66]

However, the use of the phrase 'Church of Ireland' continued to cause problems. It was not accepted by Cardinal MacRory, who wrote to de Valera in May to change the wording. Fr Edward Cahill and Fr P. J. Gannon[67] also took exception to the phrase. The former described it as nothing less than 'authoritative approval of a piece of lying propaganda'.[68]

The Presbyterians did not now express any difficulties with the omission of the phrase 'Christian Churches'. O'Neill, the outgoing moderator who had accompanied Dr Irwin at their meeting with the head of the Executive Council, wrote to de Valera expressing his 'best thanks for the very cordial reception of our delegation, and for your very sympathetic attitude to our observations. All three of us were impressed and pleased.'[69]

The complete text was available to the Executive Council on 27 April. On Good Friday, 26 April, de Valera, anticipating opposition from Gerry Boland, Minister for Lands in 1937, took a long walk up the Dublin mountains to persuade him to accept the new article. A later interview given by Boland suggests that the new article still caused concern:

> It would be equivalent to the expulsion from our History of great Irishmen like Tone, Russell, McCracken and even Parnell, Childers and many more. None of these men would live in Ireland under a sectarian Constitution, and I would not live under it either. I would take my wife and children and put myself out of it. It seems to me that it is bowing down before all of those who were against republicans all the time and still are.[70]

De Valera succeeded in his task, but it was a close-run thing. Did the president of the Executive Council have an equally difficult time at the Executive Council? That would seem most unlikely. There were those in the cabinet who would have considered the writing of a new constitution a distraction from the main task of transforming the economy and bringing about greater and more rapid industrialisation. There was a fear of providing a range of issues on which to attack the Fianna Fáil government. Seán Lemass, who succeeded de Valera as Taoiseach in 1959, was much more pragmatic in his approach to constitutional reform. He had been one of the least enthusiastic about the drafting of a new constitution in the 1930s. On one occasion, a senior civil servant passed an open door in Merrion Street where de Valera and Lemass were in discussion about the constitution: 'But you can't put the Papal Encyclicals into the Constitution.'[71]

But once de Valera had finally decided to embark upon such a venture, he was powerless to stop the process. He could only try to ensure that no hostages were given unnecessarily to fortune or to the opposition. What had emerged in the final document was less than ideal. It had to be passed by the popular will of the people. That thought alone tempered any residual hostility in the cabinet. Moreover, de Valera had sufficient support among his ministerial colleagues to be sure that there would not be a public division on the constitution. A show of unity was considered absolutely necessary.

Seán MacEntee summed up the position of the Fianna Fáil front bench when confronted by the draft constitution:

> Now, look, here is what has to be remembered in relation to the Constitution. The purpose of the Constitution was to get rid of the oath, and the Irish Free State Constitution. And we had to go a long way … I mean how many people, including Dev, had to subordinate any private views they may have had in relation to these questions, particularly the question of the Church, to the fact that we had to get a majority of the people. And we felt and it was true, that we wouldn't get it if we gave the Bishops any chance to attack us.[72]

On 28 April, the final revise was sent to McDunphy, and the final text sent for printing that same day. The article which remained unchanged until amended in 1972 read as follows:

Article 44

1.1 The State acknowledges that the homage of public worship is due to Almighty God. It shall hold His name in reverence and respect and honour religion.

1.2 The State recognises the special position of The Holy Catholic and Apostolic Church as the guardian of the Faith professed by the great majority of the citizens.

1.3 The State also recognises the Church of Ireland, the Presbyterian Church in Ireland, the Methodist Church in Ireland, the Religious Society of Friends in Ireland, as well as the Jewish Congregations and the other religious denominations existing in Ireland at the date of the coming into operation of this Constitution.

2.1 Freedom of conscience and the free profession and practice of religion are, subject to public order and morality, guaranteed to every citizen.

2.2 The State guarantees not to endow any Religion.

2.3 The State shall not impose any disabilities or make any discrimination on the ground of religious profession, belief or status.

4. Legislation providing State aid for schools shall not discriminate between schools under the management of different religious denominations, nor be such to affect prejudicially the right of any child to attend a school receiving public money without attending religious instruction at the school.

5. Every religious denomination shall have the right to manage its own affairs, own, acquire, and administer property, movable and immovable, and maintain institutions for religious and charitable purposes.

6. The property of any religious denomination or any educational institution shall not be diverted save for necessary works of public utility and on payment of compensation.

Article 44 produced only two dissenting voices when the draft constitution was debated in Dáil Éireann in May–June 1937. Frank MacDermott (Independent) stated the 'special recognition' 'would be better absent as far as Partition is concerned'.[73] He had no problem with its inclusion *per se* since it 'appears to me to be entirely without meaning'. De Valera asserted in the Dáil that he was merely recognising sociological fact.[74]

In the end, the Vatican was pleased with the result: 'It is a Constitution which embodies the Catholic principles of the Irish nation – a Constitution which found its inspiration in the Papal encyclicals.'[75]

CHAPTER 7

The Passing of *Bunreacht na hÉireann*: Debate and Reaction

Bunreacht na hÉireann was duly placed before Dáil Éireann for its second reading on 11 May 1937. De Valera's speech introducing his draft was largely explanatory and delivered initially in Irish.[1] However, because of the controversy surrounding the presidency, he spent considerable time dismissing allegations that the new President would possess dictatorial powers. But de Valera was in complete charge of the process. Although willing to consider amendments, he told the Dáil on 25 May that 'I cannot, obviously, meet the Opposition on matters of principle which we shall have to settle by division. On matters of detail, to get the widest possible acceptance of this Constitution, I am anxious to go as far as I can.'[2] De Valera was emphatic also that *Bunreacht na hÉireann* would not be a mere amendment to the 1922 constitution. The Dáil, he emphasised, would not be the enacting authority but would merely act as a consultative committee: '... it is not this Parliament that is to enact it. On the last stage here the motion will be, not "that this measure do now pass" ... the proposal will be "that this Draft Constitution as amended ... shall go to the people for them to enact it".'[3]

In addition, practically single-handedly de Valera guided and defended the constitution through all stages. Seán MacEntee and Frank Aiken were among the few ministers offering significant contributions. On the opposition side, William Cosgrave played little part. It was left to the two lawyers, Patrick McGilligan, law professor at UCD and former Minister for External Affairs and future Minister for Finance and Attorney General, and John A. Costello, former Attorney General and future Taoiseach, to take up the fight. Labour leader William Norton made some significant contributions, tabling nine amendments. However, it was the independent deputy, Frank MacDermott, who was to the forefront of the debate, tabling in all some forty-two of the amendments.

Fine Gael had few objections to the fundamental principles of the constitution and focused mainly on two issues: the presidency and the position of women. Indeed, with some satisfaction, de Valera reflected in the early stages that only these two issues dominated proceedings.[4] However, Costello did complain that the constitution could not be given due consideration since 'every Article ... bristles with difficulties and possible errors'.[5] But MacEntee had earlier pointed out that there was no prior consultation with the electorate regarding the 1922 constitution. In fact, it had not been seen until the morning of the general election, a ploy MacEntee deemed 'sharp practice'.[6] De Valera made very few concessions, and certainly none in substance. The most important changes were that the President should be eligible for election only once, that the panel of candidates from which the vocational portion of the Senate were to be elected and its method should be settled by law instead of being fixed by the constitution, the free criticism of public policy was expressly permitted, that no person was excluded from Irish nationality by reason of sex. Articles relating to fundamental rights that were perceived as a covert attack on women were amended. The name of the state in English was changed from Éire to Ireland.

The debate concluded on 14 June and Cosgrave, who had taken little part, surmised that the draft constitution was the work of one man, conceived and introduced in response to no consistent demand from the people and received generally with indifference. It endangered freedom of speech, the right of public meeting, and the equality of the sexes. The people had been given neither the right nor the time to consider the document and in these circumstances he proposed to vote against it. In reply, de Valera claimed that the only limitation placed on rights were those designed to prevent those rights from conflicting with the rights of the community. The constitution would allow all parties to come together to resolve their differences without violence. They could not, he argued, go further to meet the views of those in the north without sacrificing the legitimate views of the vast majority of our people.

Bunreacht na hÉireann was passed on 1 July by a narrow majority of the voting electorate (see Appendix at end of this chapter for detailed constituency analysis), in effect marginally more than one third of the overall electorate. The plebiscite took place simultaneous with the general election, which Fianna Fáil won but on a reduced vote, its share having dropped to just over 45 per cent from over 49 per cent in 1933. All parties politicised the constitution to their advantage. De Valera painted Fine Gael as the party of the British connection and Fianna Fáil as the party of the traditional Irish nation. Fine Gael alleged that the constitution was a sinister plot by de Valera to establish himself as a dictator.

Fianna Fáil built its campaign around its leader who spoke at twenty-four rallies. The *Irish Press* wrote: 'He made triumphal entries into every town, where he was accorded magnificent receptions.'[7] At his opening election speech on 16 June, de Valera contended that Fine Gael were not true Irishmen. He emphasised that the new constitution was framed by Irishmen and was not a result of outside influence.[8] De Valera would later directly link the new constitution with the fortunes of his party: 'In order to be able to carry on our work without undue anxiety we want to have a party which will have a reasonable majority over all parties.'[9] On 25 June, de Valera hailed the constitution as 'a renewed declaration of national independence'.[10] In discussing future policy de Valera cleverly drew many parallels with the aims of the constitution, and portrayed Fianna Fáil as the party of the nation.[11] In contrast, the main opposition arguments opposed the constitution on the grounds that it was unnecessary and the presidency could lead to dictatorship. Fianna Fáil and de Valera responded by accusing Fine Gael of lying about the increased cost of living, a key election issue, and that their pronouncements on the new constitution were more of the same.[12]

Wisely, perhaps, during all this debate, there was no official British reaction. Only on 30 December 1937, the day after the constitution came into force, did the British formally comment. The government treated 'the new Constitution as not affecting a fundamental alteration in the position of the Free State, in future to be described under the new constitutions as "Éire" or "Ireland", as a member of the British Commonwealth of Nations'. However, the constitution did not give any right to 'territory or jurisdiction over territory forming part of the United Kingdom of Great Britain and Northern Ireland, or affects in any way the position of Northern Ireland as an integral part of the United Kingdom of Great Britain and Northern Ireland'.[13]

The Dáil Debate on *Bunreacht na hÉireann*

On 30 April 1937, on the eve of its publication, de Valera introduced his draft constitution to the people with a radio broadcast from Athlone. Addressing the nation – and it was relayed to America – firstly in Irish and then English, he asked that the draft be 'studied carefully and critically in every home in the country'.[14] De Valera began with a review of Irish constitutional history, stressing that the First Dáil in January 1919 adopted 'a Constitution which provided the Government to be carried on in what was fundamentally a war situation. The people were not at any time asked to sanction its provisions.' The draft constitution of 1922 was published only on the morning of the general election, without examination or discussion; and it suffered from two 'fatal defects': it was not framed altogether by Irish hands and was 'made subject to a Treaty admittedly imposed by threat of force'.[15]

Whereas the 1922 constitution had been amended twenty-seven times, de Valera claimed the new basic law would provide stability. It was designed 'to provide a firm foundation for an ordered life and peaceful political development within the community'. The draft, he emphasised, was 'not an essay in the application of the political or legal theories of any particular school', but was a document 'which should inspire as well as control, elicit loyalty as well compel it'. 'Every citizen should see in it the basic public law of his country the sure safeguard of his individual rights as a human being - God given rights which even the civil powers must not invade.'[16]

De Valera then systematically explained its provisions, stressing the increased democratic participation through the popular right to elect a president. He conceded, however, that the proposed constitution would not remove certain 'injustices' – such as partition, British occupation of the Treaty ports, and the annuities burden – but it would be flexible enough to facilitate various responses to these issues as 'all these controversies will be outside the Constitution so that the Constitution itself will not stand in the way of any remedies that may be proposed'.[17]

De Valera would emphasise many of these points again when introducing it to the Dáil for the second reading on 11 May 1937.[18] One of the recurring themes of the debates highlights the fact that de Valera's principal objection to the 1922 constitution was that it had been imposed under threat by the British. Thus, for example, in April 1937, de Valera declined requests from the British dominions secretary, Malcolm MacDonald, to see copies of the draft constitution. De Valera then insisted that 'the new Constitution should be framed by the representatives of the Irish people solely … without any consultation with any member of the British Commonwealth'.[19] Seán MacEntee pointed out in the Dáil: 'We were until 1932 living under an Irish Constitution which had been drafted for Irishmen by Englishmen. To-day the Constitution which is now before the country has been drafted by Irishmen for Irishmen.'[20] However, both Fine Gael and the Labour party attacked the presidency and concentration of power in the cabinet, especially in the office of the Taoiseach.

The direction and tone of the debates is perhaps better represented by Patrick McGilligan, when moving the first of forty-five amendments put down on the presidency:

> In analysing this Constitution, I prefer always to take this test: What could a man, ambitious of power, do, who had succeeded to this office and who, at the end of its term of years, had a subservient Government about to face the people with a certainty of being defeated? In such circumstances, what could they do to block their successors from being allowed to take over the ordinary powers of government in the country? There is no other way of getting this matter properly considered except by thinking entirely in terms of that.[21]

Interpreting outlandish powers in the office of president, Dr T. F. O'Higgins suggested the constitution was a sinister plot on the part of de Valera – 'the greatest political fanatic in the whole country' – to establish a dictatorship, or 'a throne for one individual'.[22] Costello told the Dáil: 'There is not a greater tyranny than the tyranny that masquerades under the cloak of democracy. That is the sort of tyranny that is embodied in that document before the House, a tyranny which masquerades under the cloak of democracy.'[23]

Although distaste and suspicion for de Valera was the prime factor determining the opposition's response, the wider political landscape also fuelled suspicions. O'Higgins reminded deputies that

> We have dictatorships here and there in Europe ... The Parliaments were gone or, as far as they remained, they were only just the ballet called together to applaud the *prima donna*. That, at least, is one of the possibilities and one of the things that must stare out of that document at everybody who examines it impartially.[24]

However, it was clear to Fianna Fáil that political expediency rather than genuine opposition motivated the Cumann na nGaedheal response, for as Frank Aiken pointed out: 'The principle of the Constitution as a whole has not been debated, it has not been opposed, I am glad to say, and I hope it will not be ... It is a Constitution such as the vast majority of us here in this House worked for at one time.'[25]

Press objections to Article 40 (right to free speech and association) were echoed in the Dáil. The contention of the opposition was that these were draconian measures since the exercise of these rights were subject to public order and morality, and public order and morality was that which would be dictated by Fianna Fáil. Costello argued that:

> Public opinion must be educated until it coincides with the whim, will and pleasure, the peculiar views and the constitutional pirouetting of the particular President, whether he is the framer of this Constitution, the framer of some other amendment or the exponent of some particular theory. The radio, the Press and the cinema are to be controlled so that they will not undermine public order, public order being equivalent to the ideals of the particular politician who happens to control the State at the moment.[26]

The 1937 constitution departed from its predecessor in that the Taoiseach could request a minister to resign 'at any time for reasons which to him seem sufficient' or have him dismissed by the President if he failed to comply. Costello, who would, ironically, have to exercise that power later as Taoiseach, complained of the very humiliating position of the government under this provision.[27] William Norton, the leader of the Labour party, described this as 'calculated to make "yes-men" out of the other members of the Government, calculated to make them all agree with the Taoiseach whether they like his policy or not'.[28] De Valera rejected these contentions and insisted that the responsibility of the 'Head of Government' was to assemble a team, and to do that effectively the power to dismiss those who did not fit in was necessary. He insisted that a Taoiseach would not work in an arbitrary manner:

> He is not dealing with children ... do you think it would be possible for a Taoiseach, in a purely arbitrary way, to compel the resignation of a minister unless there was concurrence on the part of the other members of the Government? Of course it would be impossible.[29]

From a historical perspective, the debates are also significant for omissions. Anti-partitionist considerations hardly figured. There was no outright opposition to the implications of Articles 2–3. During the debate, de Valera explained that his aim was to put Ireland's external relations outside the constitution and to treat them as matters of foreign policy to be determined from time to time as the people wished. The law could exactly prescribe those relations and a law had already been passed to that effect. The constitution would make no change to the existing position.

The exclusive nature of the preamble caused Frank MacDermott some concern. He wished to make it less exclusive and proposed inserting a further clause to read:

> Remembering, too, that nearly one-quarter of our people are united by ties of blood, tradition and sentiment with Great Britain; remembering the part played by our forefathers both of Gaelic and of British stock in founding and developing the British Commonwealth, and by our kith and kin to-day in guiding its destinies; remembering the security given by membership of that Commonwealth against attacks upon our independence from any quarter; remembering the long agony of Irish history due not solely to foreign oppression, but also to conflict of ideals and loyalties among Irishmen; and earnestly desiring to enable our country to grow to its full stature by conciliating our various traditions and aspirations so as to fuse them into one national consciousness and to attain that measure of unity in heart and mind which makes a nation.[30]

However, MacDermott's request came to nothing. His contribution in relation to partition was quite insightful. He pointed out that partition could only be cured when there was some unity of thought, mind and heart:

> It is not of course that any legislation here could immediately solve the problem of partition; that problem can only be solved by inducing the northern Unionists to give their first allegiance to Ireland – to put the peace, dignity and happiness of Ireland before any

> other loyalty. For this to be possible, we have got to offer them an Ireland in which a place can be found for their traditions and aspirations as well as for ours. Until we are willing to do this we are partitionists at heart, no matter how loudly we shout about unity.[31]

During the committee stage, he moved to insert a new article to the effect that the Irish nation declared its free and equal membership of the British commonwealth as a sovereign state. Cosgrave took no part in the discussion and did not vote. The amendment was defeated by fifty-six votes to three.

Article 44, concerning the 'special position' of the Catholic Church, and which caused so much difficulty for de Valera, attracted little attention. Frank MacDermott called for its removal on the basis that: 'It seems to serve no purpose except to create misunderstandings.'[32] It did 'not establish the Catholic Church in a privileged position' nor did it, according to MacDermott, 'offend in any way against the principle of equal treatment of people in different religions'.[33] But de Valera defended it in the following terms:

> The recognition of an obvious fact is there, and that fact must have considerable influence in the life of the State. It is bound to have. There are 93 per cent of the people in this part of Ireland and 75 per cent of the people of Ireland as a whole who belong to the Catholic Church, who believe in its teachings, and whose whole philosophy of life is the philosophy that comes from its teachings. Consequently it is very important that in our Constitution that fact should be recognised.[34]

He also defended section 2.3. It was important that 'notwithstanding that the vast majority of our people belong to one faith, nevertheless the State recognises the liberty of every citizen to practise his religion and to adore the Almighty in public and private'.[35] Article 41.3,2, which stated 'No act shall be enacted for the grant of dissolution of marriage' was not amended and attracted little discussion. Article 41, relating to the family, Article 42, relating to education, and Article 43, relating to private property, also attracted little attention. It is, then, worth considering in more detail the two issues that dominated the debates and public discussions: the presidency and the role of women.

The Presidency

As noted, no aspect of the draft constitution received so much time or was examined in such minute detail as those articles relating to the presidency, with three of the five days at committee stage devoted to it. Two diametrically opposed views were presented. The presidency was also discussed widely in the Irish newspapers, particularly in the *Irish Independent*. An editorial complained that: 'These powers are far in excess of those exercised by the ruler of the British Empire; they flavour more of Fascism or Hitlerism than of a "democratic state" which Éire is declared to be.'[36]

In an article by James G. Douglas, one time senator and drafter of the 1922 constitution, the danger of 'a popularly elected president' abusing his powers was highlighted:

> There is always the danger that a popularly elected President may consider himself justified in using these powers in order to obtain additional powers. This danger is increased by the questionable provision that additional powers and functions may be given to him by law. It is not a safeguard to provide that such additional powers must be exercised after consultation with the Council of State for he is not obliged to take advice given to him by the Council, and in any case, he can appoint or remove from office all but the ex-officio members of the Council.[37]

Diarmaid Ó Cruadhlaoich, BL, a judge of the supreme court set up by the First Dáil Éireann, wrote:

> There is nothing to prevent the President being, during his period of office, an active politician. He may be the leader of a political party, may control and dictate the political policy of newspapers, etc. And considering the manner in which the Senate is to be constituted, the President may consider himself safe from impeachment.[38]

The question of the presidency was also aired in the letters pages of newspapers. Alasdair McCaba suggested that a member of the royal family, such as the duke of Kent, should put their name forward to be president.[39]

De Valera promoted the new office as the bulwark which would preserve democratic representative government. The opposition, however, saw the office as a sinister ploy on his part to subvert the Dáil. In the words of Dr O'Higgins:

> ... [the] document we have here is building a throne for one individual, and that throne is to be built by materials stolen from the Parliament of the people, and the powers that are passed into the hands of that individual are powers to be filched from the Government and the Parliament of the people.[40]

In essence, the opposition suspected that office might be a vehicle for the establishment of a de Valera dictatorship, either by his becoming President and being voted considerable powers by a compliant government or by installing a 'yes man' as president. They believed that this was a power inherent in Article 13.10 which read: 'Subject to this Constitution further powers and functions may be conferred on the President by law.' This was a power which Patrick Hogan deemed 'very dangerous'.[41] Costello elaborated on this theme by asking:

> What is the justification for the election of this functionary by popular vote? Is it merely as a cloak? Is it merely for the purpose of justifying that flamboyant phrase that comes so trippingly from the President's tongue – the guardian of the people's rights? ... I tell the House there is not a greater tyranny than the tyranny which masquerades under the cloak of democracy. That is the sort of tyranny that is embodied in that document before the House, a tyranny which masquerades under the cloak of democracy.[42]

It would be unfair to characterise the opposition's approach simply as political expediency. Whereas it is true that distrust and suspicion of de Valera inhibited fair assessment of the office, suspicions and concerns were based on more tangible considerations, a fact alluded to by Professor John Marcus O' Sullivan, the former Minister for Education and Fine Gael deputy from North Kerry: 'We can expect nothing else from a man who has always shown supreme contempt, not merely for Parliamentary institutions, but for the Dáil itself.'[43]

The Carlow–Kilkenny deputy, Desmond FitzGerald, also shared these fears:

> This new functionary, the President, is given certain powers under the Constitution, and other powers may be given to him by law ... There will be a general election some time this year. If, as a result of that, his Party is returned to power, he then proceeds to enact this Constitution, and for about a period of a year he will act presumably as Taoiseach. During that period, with his Government power, he can legislate with his majority to give any additional power he likes to that functionary, then he can proceed to walk into that office to exercise those powers. He can extend those powers. He can, during that year as Government head, change the Constitution in all except two clauses. By ordinary legislation, with his majority in the Dáil, he can extend the powers of that functionary, and then having extended those powers he can step in and take them to himself.[44]

The spurious nature of the opposition's objections were well illustrated when Seán MacEntee pointed out that under the existing constitution any constitutional changes desired could be implemented. There was in fact a classic opportunity to establish a dictatorship since: 'At the present moment the position is this, that we are the most absolute Government in Europe.'[45] De Valera pointed out that:

> No people more than the Opposition were so insistent in saying that the present position leaves the Government with tremendous powers and without check, and that, in the interests of the community as a whole, it would be better not to leave them these unreasonable powers. Therefore, it is that the Constitution is necessary. It is necessary also from the point of view of bringing to completion that series of step-by-step changes which, taken as a whole, have left the old Constitution a tattered and torn affair.[46]

James Fitzgerald-Kenney, the former justice minister, raised concerns relating to control of the army, but MacEntee dismissed them as hypocrisy and asked:

> What of the position in which the Army has been placed by those who criticise us for selecting the first citizen in the land to be the supreme commander of the Army? What is the present position of the Army? If it is undesirable that the supreme command should be vested in the President, what is to be said with regard to the present position of the Army which under Section 5 of the Defence Forces (Temporary Provisions) Act of 1923 is vested in that political body known as the Executive Council, which not merely has to undergo election by the people but subsequent nomination and, in the case of the President, subsequent election and nomination by a vote of this House? Here is the present position of the Army. 'The command-in-chief of and all executive and administrative powers in relation to the forces including the power to delegate authority to such persons as may be thought fit shall be vested in the Executive Council and exercised through and in the name of the Minister for Defence.'[47]

Few aspects of the powers relating to the presidency, then, were immune from criticism or suspicion, but in the event no aspect of the office was fundamentally altered in debate either.

Women's Rights

If the controversy relating to the presidency provoked de Valera's anger, the issue of the status of women evoked genuine hurt and sadness. De Valera's dilemma was that by recognising in law the difference in capacity he could equally be deemed protectionist or oppressive. The controversy was based on the fact that unlike Article 3 in the Free State constitution, which contained a declaration of sexual equality before the law, there was no corresponding article in the 1937 draft. This omission, it was contended, could lead to a loss of the right to vote or even citizenship, especially when taken in conjunction with Article 40(1), which held that whereas all citizens were equal before the law, cognisance would be taken of the fact that there were differences in capacity, physical and social function. Could not this be used by an unscrupulous government to deprive women of their rights?

After publication of the draft on 1 May, there was widespread publicity of discussions regarding clauses relating to women. Women's organisations, the majority of which were the successors of the Irish suffrage movements that flourished from 1876 to 1918, raised objections at public meetings and in the press. However, John A. Costello was one of the first to address the issue in the context of the overall debate on the constitution. On 6 May, Costello, in a commissioned piece by the *Irish Independent* – which headlined his article 'New Constitution Curtails Women's Rights' – argued that:

> It also comes as a surprise to find the status of women in the state affected, if not expressly, certainly by implication. We read the somewhat grandiose statement that all citizens shall be held equal before the law, but we discover that the substance of that declaration is taken away by the provision that the State may, if it likes, in its legislation declare them to be unequal. The provision that the State shall not be prevented in its enactments from having due regard to differences of capacity, physical and moral and, of social functions, allows a wide latitude in the consideration of the supposed equality of citizens before the law. That provision read in conjunction with the Constitutional declaration of the 'inadequate strength of women', the omission of the significant words 'without discrimination of sex' contained in articles 3 and 14 of the existing Constitution, must appear curious in view of the substantially equal rights of voting and otherwise at present accorded to women. Under the Draft women have not, as of Constitutional right, any claim to the exercise of franchise equally with men. The draft as it stands offers its Framer as a whole burnt offering to feminists and feminist associations.[48]

The *Irish Independent* followed Costello's article with a clinical exposé by Gertrude Gaffney on the potential threat to the status of women. Far from discerning any protection for women, she warned that 'the death knell of the working woman is sounded in the new Constitution'.[49] Arguing that de Valera 'has always been a reactionary where women are concerned', she detected a pattern in his efforts to put women in their place. The constitution was merely completing the work of the Conditions of Employment Bill. Gaffney suggested that it was the combination of his 'innate prejudice against women' and the 'nightmare of unemployment' that motivated de Valera. Furthermore, she suggested that if de Valera were more attuned to reality he would realise that 'ninety per cent of the women who work ... do so because they must'. 'It is only the exceptional woman who prefers working for others to marriage, and she is found to be among the well-off classes rather than among the poor, whom this new legislation is bound most to affect.' Hanna Sheehy Skeffington, the veteran suffragette and founder of the Irishwomen's Franchise League in 1908, welcomed Gaffney's exposé, offering a personal rebuttal to the president:

> It is unfortunate, but inevitable, that the well-known reactionary views of Mr de Valera regarding women should have strongly coloured the Draft Constitution, which is his handiwork. Having been his colleague for many years on National Executives and Committees of various kinds, I can testify to this: His ideal is the strictly domestic type of woman who eschews 'politics' as male concerns, the Fascist ideal now working under Mussolini and Hitler and other dictators, by which women are deprived of free choice of avocations and opportunities as human beings.[50]

She warned that: 'It is up to women of all parties to wake up and demand the complete restoration of the clauses of the 1916 Proclamation and Clause III of the constitution, which confirms the principle of equal rights and opportunities.'

De Valera refuted Costello's arguments in a speech in Ennis, in which the *Irish Times* reported him as arguing:

> It is untrue there was a phrase in the old Constitution which is not in the new one – without distinction of sex – and I deliberately left it out, because it was a phrase applicable to a time when women were only just emerging from the position of political inferiority, and it was a badge of previous inferiority. Under the new constitution they are equal citizens, and it is to citizens that the Constitution had reference. Women were not mentioned for the purpose of depriving them of their rights, but, in my opinion, of protecting them.[51]

This merely drew further ire from advocates of women's right. On 11 May, Mary Kettle, chairperson of the joint committee of women's societies, took issue with de Valera's Ennis remarks. She warned that if the 'so-called "protection" Clauses (40, 41, 45) … become law, no women … will have any security whatever'. Instead, Kettle argued, 'The only protection women need and … ask is equality, under the Constitution, of rights and opportunities.'[52] The *Irish Press*, having published Mrs Kettle, proceeded to damn her the same day. In an editorial entitled 'A Gratuitous Libel', it suggested Kettle was too eager to follow Costello's lead, and:

> If there is equality before the law, it follows, though apparently Mrs Kettle does not realise it, that that equality applies to every sphere and relation of life. It is not a case of there being a certain point at which it ceases to operate or that it can lead to any differentiation with respect to sex, trade, occupation or profession … It is for her now to table her evidence, or to apologise to the men whom she has grossly and wantonly libelled.[53]

The same day, Kettle's organisation passed a resolution calling the attention of women voters to 'the manner in which their rights have been undermined' by the constitution. It also appointed a deputation to lobby the Dáil party leaders, and three women deputies.[54] The delegation, led by Kettle, met with Cosgrave on 13 May, and the three women Dáil deputies, Helena Concannon and Margaret Pearse of Fianna Fáil and Bridget Redmond of Fine Gael, agreed to meet a deputation the following week.[55] On 11 May, too, a 'largely attended' meeting of women graduates of the National University, chaired by Professor Mary Hayden, met to consider the 'reactionary' clauses. It instigated an emergency committee, formed a fighting fund, appointed a delegation to lobby the government and adopted proposals to cooperate with other women's organisations.[56] Hayden, a prominent historian already in full agreement with Gaffney's critique, went further, contending that: 'What is proposed by the new constitution is not a return to the Middle ages. It is something quite different and much worse.'[57] On 12

May, the *Irish Press* published the text of a letter reportedly sent by Louie Bennett, secretary of the Irish Women's Workers Union, to President de Valera. Bennett, too, took issue with de Valera's Ennis remarks, pointing out the draft constitution contained points of 'serious danger ... not so much for what they actually state as because of their ambiguity and the implications that may be given to them'. She recommended deletion of the second sentence of Article 40. 1, and suggested in relation to Article 41. 2. (1), it should be amended to read: 'In particular, the state recognises that *by her work for the home* ...', thereby acknowledging the value of work done by women in a broad field and for the common good. Article 41. 2. (2) was, she contended, 'superfluous'. However, 'Section 4 (2) of Article 45 is from the women's point of view the most indefensible in the constitution. It takes from women the right to chose their avocation in life.'[58]

The impact of these criticisms would remain to be seen. On 14 May, de Valera received deputations representing women's organisations, the joint committee of women's societies and social workers, the standing committee on legislation affecting women, and the National University Women Graduates' Association.[59] The meetings were non-committal: de Valera told the graduates' delegates he would 'give careful consideration to their desire to have a barrier set up against the possibility of the enactment of any law discriminating against women in the matters of citizenship and the franchise'.[60]

The redoubtable Alfred O'Rahilly, in a second commissioned article for the *Irish Independent*, also entered the fray, recommending that the phrase 'without distinction of sex' should be inserted in Article 16.[61] But he praised Article 41 as 'in many ways excellent and at last removes a glaring defect of the present Constitution which calmly ignores the Family.' He went on:

> The fact that this has been attacked is very surprising. I am cordially in agreement with it, but I consider it quite unnecessary in a Constitution, in which it is sufficient to place the Family and Motherhood under the special protection of the State. The rest must be left to legislation. Issues such as family wage, widows' pensions, right to a 'home' cannot in any effective sense be guaranteed in a short clause. In any case the State is only bound to 'endeavour' – a phrase which is not susceptible of precise appraisement.

O'Rahilly noted the objection raised by Louie Bennett, which appeared to him 'hypercritical if not slightly hysterical. Lady Bountiful may indeed choose her avocation; let us hope she remains within the moral laws, if not within the proprieties.'[62] The *Irish Press* discerned an 'important contribution to the controversy on woman's position' in the views of the árd comhairle of An Rioghacht ('League of Kingship of Christ') – a Catholic action association. Generally, it took the position that:

> If in the interests of women … alterations are to be made in the draft it should not be done by suppressing or toning down, on the lines of un-Christian Liberalism, provisions which are implicit in Christian teaching. Rather should the provisions for putting into operation the social teaching of the Encyclicals be strengthened and made mandatory. In this way the ideal can be more easily and quickly realised, in which it would be made possible for every young man of adult age to found a family and for every husband and father to support his family in decent comfort.[63]

Although An Rioghacht conceded 'the reality of the grievances suffered by women', nevertheless that body invoked Leo XIII's encyclical, *Rerum Novarum*, which held, inter alia, that: 'Women, again, are not suited for certain occupations.' Pius XI's encyclical, *Quadragesimo Anno*, was cited too: 'Intolerable and at all costs to be abolished, is the abuse whereby mothers of families … are forced to engage in gainful occupations outside the domestic walls, to the neglect of their own proper cares and duties.' Finally, An Rioghacht marshalled Pius XI's *Casti Connubii* recommendation that 'the man is meant to be the bread-winner, and the woman the mistress of the home'.[64]

Amidst all this public controversy the Dáil debate on the status of woman began from the outset of the second reading of the constitution on 11 May. Thus in opening the debate de Valera could argue that:

> With regard to women, they are mentioned in two Articles. But why are they mentioned? They are mentioned to give the protection which, I think, is necessary as part of our social programme, and I am prepared to go with that programme before the country. I do not care what criticism comes from anybody on the basis of it. We state here that mothers in their homes give to the State a support which is essential. Is there anybody who denies it? Is it not a tribute to the work that is done by women in the homes as mothers? Is there any woman who is a mother who will say that it is right that when her husband is idle or otherwise when she has the care of her children that she should be forced by economic necessity – she is not forced by law and is not prevented by law from doing these things – and by our social system to go and earn what is necessary to maintain the household? In regard to labour and in regard to work, our aim ought to be – we may be too slow in arriving at it, but no country has apparently done it yet – that the breadwinner, who is normally and naturally in these cases when he is alive, the father of the family, should be able by his work to bring in enough to maintain the whole household, and that women ought not to be forced by economic necessity to go out and either supplement his wages or become the breadwinners themselves.[65]

But the opposition saw the vagueness and moved to expose it. Costello challenged:

> The President is going to leave that sort of verbosity and flap-doodle behind him as a headline for his successors … I want to see these Articles in practical operation, and I will

not take account of those high-falutin', flamboyant utterances. I want the principles of social justice put in practice, and not merely set down in flamboyant terms.[66]

Helena Concannon, articulating the concerns of the graduates' association, quickly joined the debate, reading excerpts from the earlier meeting of the association on 11 May. In its statement the association expressed the fear that: 'The omission of the principle of equal rights and equal opportunities … confirmed in Article 3 of the constitution of Saorstát Éireann, was deplored as sinister and regressive ... Articles 40, 41 and 45, which leave the door open for reactionary legislation against women in every department were discussed with particular care.'[67] Although she did not believe there was any immediate danger to women's rights but rather the potential that the articles could to be misused: 'There seems to be a fear by reasons of the ambiguity of certain phrases that in future times, whatever be the intentions of the framers of the Constitution, these might lead to a lowering of the status of women.'[68]

General Richard Mulcahy saw the remedy to women's problems in the abolition of poverty rather than in any aspirational sentiments. 'I tell the President that the only thing that is wanted is to remedy the condition into which a lot of mothers and fathers in this country have got ...'[69] Concannon wondered, however, if Article 3 in the Saorstát constitution had done anything to improve women's pay. In every estimate, she pointed out, there was a difference in about £100 in the annual pay of women in the public service as compared with that of man.[70] Despite James Dillon's advice that she were 'not to be deluded by high falutin',[71] she had made a salient observation, most likely as part of Fianna Fáil strategy on the debate. For the opposition had no history in espousing women's rights in government: in fact quite the reverse, and any objections to these provisions must be seen in the context, a fact quickly emphasised by Frank Aiken:

When Deputy Costello was Attorney-General, a Bill was brought in abolishing equal treatment for women and men under the Civil Service Commissioners. In 1926 a Bill was brought in giving the Civil Service Commissioners power to exclude women from certain posts. Last night Deputy Costello pretended that this Constitution was doing away with the complete equality of men and women – that heretofore they were, not alone equal as human persons, but were taken to be of equal capacity, and that all classes in the State were taken to have similar social functions.[72]

Most of the agitation of the subject seemed to be designed at discrediting de Valera with women voters rather than to safeguard their social or political rights. De Valera's views on women's issues were not unusual and indeed were widely shared. Concannon, for instance, was broadly supportive of his vision. Despite her criticisms, she stated:

> I sincerely hope that not a comma of this noble declaration will be altered ... Do we not know that the price of each human life is some woman's agony. Do we not know that the rearing of each child is purchased at the cost of some woman's sleepless nights and hard-working days ... Why, then, should we begrudge to women that the State should honour them for their contribution to the State's support and its common good?[73]

Leaving aside her membership of the government party, she nonetheless expressed views which were then widespread. Finola Kennedy, in her seminal study *Cottage to Crèche*, has drawn on evidence from a variety of sources to argue convincingly that in 1937, as de Valera prescribed a role for women, 'a broad consensus existed at the time ... regarding women's place in the home, and it was not purely a reflection of Roman Catholic or conservative political views.'[74] Nor were such ideals peculiar to Ireland at this time. Indeed, Kennedy cited an editorial from the *Irish Times* – not an organ associated with Catholic ideas at that time – which bemoaned the 'fifty-fifty' marriage with both partners working, as it denied men and single women jobs, and hoped that

> Some day, please Heaven! The nation will be so organised that work will be available for every man, so that he may marry and assume the burdens of a home, and for every woman who embarks upon her proper profession – which is marriage.[75]

Life gets 'curiouser and curiouser'!

Press Reaction to the Constitution

Press reaction was immediate, predictably mixed given the political loyalties of the media, and sustained. On 1 May the Fianna Fáil-founded *Irish Press* published the complete Irish and English versions of the draft, and a eulogistic editorial greeted it as a 'document characterised by simplicity, concision and unambiguousness of language'.[76] The editor suggested: 'It must give a thrill to every Irish heart to know that in the forefront of the new Constitution is this appeal for Divine guidance and support and this dedication of the State to the carrying out of the works of justice and charity.' On a more analytical note, the editorial also felt the proposed constitution:

> ... confers the widest political rights on the citizen consistent with the maintenance of social order. It contains every possible safeguard against arbitrary or tyrannical action on the part of the Executive or its officials, and it guarantees to every individual and to every section of the community, the possession of their property and the full and free exercise of rights before the law. It provides for equality for all and privilege for none.

Predictably perhaps, the *Irish Independent* was critical – but aimed its criticism at Fianna Fáil, as when an editorial commented on poor attendance in the Dáil for debates on the constitution:

> There are two possible explanations. One is that the rank and file of Fianna Fáil are more in touch with the country than their leader is, and they realise the incongruity of debating high constitutional issues when the plain people are more concerned about unemployment, emigration, the increase in the cost of daily necessaries and about other more pressing problems. The other explanation is that the Fianna Fáil members have to be lashed by the Party Whip into a semblance of support for the powers which Mr de Valera is vesting in the new President, we do not know which of the two is the true explanation.[77]

De Valera was also criticised because he 'could offer no reason for transferring the command of the Army from the Executive Council to the President'.[78] Another editorial in the *Irish Independent* argued:

> In a country under normal Government a Constitution is regarded as something almost sacred, to be inspired, framed, and respected by the people as a whole. This Draft Constitution was framed by Mr de Valera, plotted by Mr de Valera without the aid of a quorum of his own followers, and passed by his Party machine as a personal and party measure. It was, as we said, capable of amendment: Fine Gael, Labour, and every Party and Group in the Dáil suggested amendments, but Mr de Valera's followers trooped in from the lawn of Leinster House to reject them because he said, 'I have made up my mind: I will not accept these amendments.' It is a dangerous instrument begotten of vanity and spleen. The existing Constitution is capable of amendment; but Mr de Valera's Draft Constitution will gag and bind the people and prevent amendments. And for these reasons the people should vote against it.[79]

On 23 June, it went further in its criticism of de Valera, accusing him of generating a red scare:

> While Mr de Valera is telling the country that this is a non party measure he is, in the same breath urging its acceptance from Fianna Fáil platforms and expressing surprise at the temerity of the opposition parties who recommend its rejection. He is now in such a panic that he has adopted the shabby trick of saying that he can understand people who 'believed in Communism' voting against it. The real truth is that he wants the people to bury their heads in this document and to forget about the cost of living, unemployment, emigration, crushing taxation, and such like questions.[80]

The question of freedom of the press was understandably of concern to members of the press. The *Irish Independent* warned: 'The freedom of the Press is definitely menaced; the Draft Constitution may place a dangerous weapon in the hands of some future Ministry, a weapon which the citizens should entrust to no party.'[81] Again the *Irish Independent* called de Valera's press acts a 'sinister proviso' and went on:

> We always understood that the right to criticise Government policy was one of the fundamental rights embraced by the terms freedom of opinion and freedom of the Press. No purpose could therefore be served by the additional words. Mr de Valera might just as well have added 'including the right to publish football results and weather forecasts'.[82]

The *Irish Times* of 9 June 1937 warned that: 'Without a free Press no nation can enjoy political liberty. In all those countries where the newspapers are muzzled the people are little better than slaves.'[83] The next day the *Irish Times* returned to the topic:

> We do not suggest that President de Valera is contemplating an onslaught on the Press, but we do suggest that the new Constitution will give the Executive powers that easily may be abused. In all conscience, the law of libel already imposes sufficiently drastic limitations upon a newspaper's freedom of speech.[84]

The *Irish Independent* commissioned articles on the constitution from some well known commentators. In a series of articles, Alfred O'Rahilly referred to his own proposals for the 1922 constitution. He had at that time suggested 'the traditional democratic doctrine of Schoolmen for inclusion in the preamble', i.e. that 'political authority comes from God to the people'. O'Rahilly continued that de Valera:

> … accepts this, and even goes further than I do. For he declared in his recent broadcast: 'By the people only, through the Referendum, can the National Constitution be amended. The sovereignty resides in them as their inalienable right … The people alone are masters.'

O'Rahilly argued that de Valera spoke in this manner 'when he is natural and uncoached'. He wrote:

> But, according to Article 6, the people merely have the right to 'designate the rulers of the State'. The language is rather stilted – Who anyway, are the rulers referred to? Mr de Valera has been led, all unwitting, by some academic theorist to adopt the subtly dangerous theory known as 'designation'. I do not propose to argue the matter here. I will refer to an article entitled 'Transfer or Designation' which I published in 1921. This is my concluding sentence: 'Unless, with the Imperialist and Protestant absolutists of a former age, we wish to confound the spiritual and the temporal, we must reject as misleading and inaccurate the recently resuscitated theory that the people do not transfer power but merely designate its recipients.'[85]

There was criticism of the fact that the 'principles of social policy' laid down in the constitution had no legal recognition in the courts. John A. Costello wrote in the *Irish Independent*:

It is peculiar to find an article in the fundamental law of a State which is expressly declared not to be a law. We find that the principles of social policy set forth in article 45 are not cognisable by the Courts. It is also somewhat astonishing to find on examination of theses principles that they are capable of any construction which any Government of any brand of political or economic outlook may wish to place upon them. They are capable of being moulded to the ideas and theories of Socialists and even of Communists.[86]

O'Rahilly raised the same point as Costello:

Why should the court be bound to take cognisance of Articles 40 and 41 and be precluded from 'cognising' Article 45? I can see no reason for this discrepant attitude towards different articles. Mr de Valera, who gives the Supreme Court power to determine the constitutionality of a law, is surely not logical in withdrawing some of the included social principles from the judges' cognisance. Personally I reiterate, I am against giving this power to the Court. My chief reason is that we do not know what principles of jurisprudence they will employ. Without being a lawyer I know enough of British jurisprudence and law-principles – in which most of our legal men are saturated – to know that on many important points they differ from the presuppositions of Catholic sociology. Hence I see no use in registering new social principles (i.e. new in relation to British legalism) in the Constitution and then allowing them to be pared down with the knife of an alien jurisprudence.[87]

O'Rahilly was also critical of the 'private property' provisions:

Article 43 enunciates the principles of private property. It is quite in accordance with the Catholic social teaching of to-day, though, not, perhaps, altogether in accordance with the mind of St Thomas Aquinas. I think there should be greater emphasis on the duties and obligations of owners and on the functional or social aspect of private property. There have already appeared some extraordinary criticisms of this Article on the part of some Catholics who do not appear to be very familiar with the Papal Encyclicals. In connection with private property there is one assertion proposed by me long ago which I should like to recall, namely, that the State has the 'right to limit the alienability of the homestead and to abolish entails and anti-social restrictions'. Of the latter you can find plenty, e.g. along the quays in Cork.'[88]

While O'Rahilly approved of the 'courageous' application of Catholic social principles, he was afraid that the document was perhaps too egalitarian and might 'render unconstitutional that necessary social control advocated by Catholic sociologists, or even that amount of control which is at present being exercised'. It is not clear whether he suggested that Freemasonry should be prohibited by the constitution when he wrote: 'Has not the time come frankly to prohibit Freemasonry as a secret society inimical to religion and State?' He argued that Article 44 did 'no good to us, and it is sure to raise prejudice in others'.

He continued: 'What about churches not mentioned or not yet in existence? Presumably the answer is that they can very well do without this "recognition" which docs not sccm to carry any implications.'[89]

In the *Irish Independent* of 2 June 1937 the republican attitude to the constitution was aired in an article by 'An Sceilg' (J. J. O'Kelly):

> Republicans urge the unqualified rejection of this projected instrument primarily because it is an open violation of the Republican Proclamation of Easter Week 1916. It seeks, moreover, to set aside the bill for the constitution of the Republic of Ireland drafted on Christian and national lines by the government of the Irish Republic, and submitted to the nation on the tenth anniversary of the proclamation of Dáil Éireann.
>
> Most of what is meritorious in the present draft constitution indeed is to be found in the republican draft; but this is vitiated through having superimposed upon it much that is out of place in a constitution and it is rendered unacceptable through its open abandonment of the Republican ambition by a party professing to be Republican.

He summed up:

> Thus it is, on its very face, a repudiation of the republic, which is not even once mentioned in its pages, and a conscious betrayal of our Republican dead. Needless to say, the Constitution does not require that the unique figure intended for the role of President be of Irish birth; and so any aspiring oversees adventurer would be eligible under this vaunted Charter of liberty for our most exalted civic office. We must only console ourselves with the reflection that a state so ancient and so insular could hardly be expected to produce such a superman. Thus, as a contribution to the better government of this island, the venture seems to have no parallel since Henry VIII endeavoured to have himself elevated from lord to king of Ireland. It remains but to add that, as it opens with the misleading statement that under it, 'Éire is a sovereign, independent, democratic state', it consistently closes with the equally unfounded pretence that 'in case of a conflict between the English and the Irish texts, the Irish text shall prevail'.

The *Irish Times* tended generally to adopt a contemptuous air about the new constitution and was invariably damning of de Valera. In an editorial on 15 May, the leader writer was unimpressed with de Valera's Dáil performance in debates on the constitution: 'His exposition of the new Constitution on Thursday was one of his feeblest efforts.' The editorial continued in the same vein: 'It is a great pity that the President had not the assistance of some trained lawyer to expound the intricacies of his Constitution for him.'[90] However, there was some support, albeit grudgingly, for the document itself: 'We do not believe that the Constitution is nearly so bad as some of its critics allege it to be.'[91] Again the *Irish Times* criticised the proposed constitution as 'a pot-pourri of vague generalisations'. It went on to criticise the make-up of the Senate:

> Is there any hope whatever that such groups, or associations or councils could be called into effective existence? Or can it be that such entirely unworkable provisions have merely been inserted to show that the creation of a 'vocational' Senate is outside the region of practical politics?[92]

In another *Irish Times* editorial the writer assumed a lack of interest in the topic which he assured readers was shared by the public:

> The fact is that the Constitution has created sadly little interest throughout the country at large. It hardly could have fared otherwise; for, when reduced to the essential terms, it contains very little that has not been part and parcel of Fianna Fáil's expressed policy for many years past. We do not know how the plebiscite for or against it will result; and we have no great concern. Far more important is the result of the general election, which will have a more decisive influence on the country's future than a dozen similar Constitutions.[93]

Again the *Irish Times* in an editorial on 9 June was at first dismissive of the constitution but went on to suggest its inherent dangers:

> As we have said on more than one occasion, we regard the new Constitution in its essentials as so much eye-wash ... There's the rub. The State will Constitute itself the supreme arbiter of what is and what is not, for the common good. The voice is Mr de Valera's voice, but the hands are the hands of Dr Joseph Goebbel's ... We believe that Mr de Valera has no conscious desire to act as a dictator, that he is convinced honestly that he is a democrat; but just as he thinks that he is the only man who can administer the Public Safety Act fairly, and in the best interests of the community, he also thinks that he is the only man who can decide whether or not the Press is undermining the authority of the State. Herr Hitler and Signor Mussolini probably are just as sincere as Mr de Valera in this respect.[94]

An earlier editorial had complained that the document: 'merely suggests that *Éire* is neither fish, flesh nor even a good red herring. It does not tell us whether we are in the commonwealth or out of it. Can it be that Mr de Valera does not really know?'[95] Within a short time it felt more certain, or at least confident enough to pronounce that Ireland would continue to be a member of the commonwealth:

> Mr de Valera has drafted his masterpiece cleverly. He will be able to tell the groundlings at the general election that he has given the final twist to the lion's tail; that the King and all his pomps have been removed from the twenty-six counties; that all that remains now is to secure the adherence of North East Ulster, and that then the Republic will be an accomplished fact.[96]

However, in the *Irish Independent* Diarmaid Ó Cruadhlaoich, BL, judge of the supreme court set up by the First Dáil Éireann, pointed out that the king maintained his role in Ireland.[97]

A letter from Maud Gonne MacBride to the editor of the *Irish Independent* had much to say, although the writer, perhaps surprisingly, made no mention of women's role in the constitution. She had criticisms of the initial articles; to her they appeared:

> ... to accord with the Proclamation of the Republic of 1916, which has been endorsed by the nation, and it is probably a wise policy to use a Constitution as a means of giving the present generation an opportunity of re-endorsing it, for every sane Irish man and woman knows that without complete independence there can be no peace or prosperity for the Irish people, and the noblest and most unselfish of our people have sacrificed everything for its attainment.

She was of the opinion however that the country was not 'free' and thought that:

> The practicality of drawing up a Constitution till freedom is attained is questionable, and was the reason the Proclamation of 1916 was terse and concise. For instance, I would endorse Sec. 6 i and ii of Article 15 on the right to raise and maintain armed force, if Éire were free, but could not till she is. Free or unfree, I would never endorse Sec. 3 i. and ii of Article 38 providing for special courts (except in time of war, when summary justice may be necessary). I consider the reason set forth immoral, when 'the ordinary courts are inadequate to secure the effective administration of justice'. Why should they be? ... Read in conjunction with Article 40, Sec. 6, i., ii, iii, on the rights of freedom of speech, of the Press, and of association, it is extremely dangerous and nullifies all idea of the even-handed justice in the same way as article 2A of the Free State Constitution does – an unholy thing in any Constitution for it is one of the worst misfortunes a nation can suffer not to be able to respect its own laws because they conflict with justice.[98]

The religious press, understandably, was most concerned with the religious clause of the constitution. The *Irish Catholic* argued that: 'Political problems are in reality of a lower order than religious ones, and the latter should, therefore, command greater attention and warrant closer examination.' The main bone of contention was the treatment of the Catholic Church:

> In the Saorstát Constitution as it stands at present [1922 Constitution] therefore, we have enshrined that hoary old heresy which many would seem to forget is a heresy at all – the false dictum that 'one religion is as good as another'. Obviously, no Catholic can subscribe to that. Yet Irish Catholics have raised no insistent voice against this article in the Constitution which tacitly and implicitly proclaims the equality of all religions. The only explanation that can be offered is, we think, a failure to realise the Article's implications. If we really aspire to the true dignity of a Catholic State; if we are not prepared to regard

> the Saorstát as merely a State of Catholics, then we should see to it that some provision is made in the new Bunreacht for an explicit reference to and an appropriate honouring of the religion which our forefathers not merely professed but died to retain.[99]

However, the adherence of the drafters to the social teaching of the Catholic Church was praised:

> Irish Catholics will rejoice in the fact that the fundamental provisions of the new Bunreacht are in close accord with Catholic social teaching. It is not merely a question of an absence of conflict between these provisions and that teaching; there is abundant evidence, too, of a sincere desire on the part of the drafter to be guided by the principles laid down in such Encyclicals as the 'Immortale Dei' and 'Rerum Novarum' of Leo XIII, and 'Quadragesimo Anno' of the present Pontiff. Mr de Valera has proved himself not merely a close student of these monumental documents, but a courageous statesman who is willing to give effect to the recommendations embodied in them.[100]

The religious invocation of the preamble pleased the *Irish Catholic* enough to suggest that the document 'is well-nigh unique in modern Constitutions – a frank and ready admission of the true source from which authority is derived, an invocation of the Most Holy Trinity, and an acknowledgement that God is the final end of man'.[101] It compared the new constitution favourably with that of 1922:

> We are especially struck by the difference between the two constitutions in the Articles dealing with religion. As had been more than once pointed out in our columns, Article 8 of the 1922 document amounted to an admission that the Catholic religion is no better than any other and thus enshrined a heresy. We expressed the hope that in the new Bunreacht there would be 'not merely an explicit reference to the religion of 90 per cent of our people, but a due honouring of it'. Our hope has been fully realised in the Draft Constitution, which only awaits the approval of our people to come into effect.[102]

While the paper conceded 'that a certain recognition is also given to other forms of religion which exist in Ireland', it pointed out that this was in accordance 'with the teachings of Leo XIII' in his *Immortale Dei*. The *Irish Catholic* was complimentary regarding the articles dealing with the family, education and with fundamental family rights and praised the inclusion of vocational groups in the Senate. An Rioghacht issued a statement:

> Especially do we rejoice at the noble Preamble ... We recognise that the articles dealing with personal rights, the family, education, private property, and religion are in general accord with the Catholic teaching, and we applaud the emphasis placed on the family as the fundamental unit in society. In addition, we note that provision is made for the Vocational Groups so insistently urged by the present Holy Father as the basis of stable order

> in society, not only in his Encyclical *Quadragesimo Anno* but also in his recent encyclical *Divini Redemptoris.*[103]

However, John A. Costello pointed out a potential flaw with the religious article in the *Irish Independent.* He suggested, however improbable it appeared at the time, that:

> ... while it is proposed that the State should recognise certain specified religious denominations and other existing ones at the date of the coming into operation of the Constitution, if members of the Greek Orthodox Church, for example, were to decide for any reason to cast in their lot with this country, their religion would have no Constitutional recognition.[104]

In general, newspaper reaction to the voting results tended to view it as a setback for de Valera. He had won the constitution vote, but the actual endorsement was lukewarm. Furthermore, Fianna Fáil's share of the vote had fallen from over 49 per cent of the vote in 1933 to just over 45 per cent. The *Irish Times* asked of the constitution: 'Who could regard such a result as a popular mandate for such an important measure, particularly as there were no fewer than 104,805 spoiled votes?' It went on to deride de Valera's claim that the constitution was an All-Ireland one. 'What would have happened if his plebiscite could have been extended to cover the thirty-two counties? Is it not perfectly obvious that it would have been rejected with ignominy?'[105] The *Irish Independent* complained that the 'net result is that a new Constitution which describes Ireland as "a democratic State" is forced upon the people by a vote which is only 38½ per cent of the electorate. In no other country could so far-reaching a change be brought about by a minority vote.'[106] The *Irish Press* conceded that the spoiled votes largely reflected hostility to the constitution.[107]

Press reaction to the constitution was not confined to the media within the Irish state; a plethora of publications in Great Britain commented on both the merits and faults of Ireland's governing charter. The earliest external reaction emanated from London, in the shape of hostile assessments by the *Daily Telegraph* and the *Morning Post.* Commenting on 1 May, the *Telegraph* deemed the new constitution the product of de Valera's insularity.[108] It denounced the provisions in the constitution designed to loosen ties between Ireland and Britain. Furthermore, since the constitution remained vague on Northern Ireland and how relations between north and south might be affected, the *Telegraph* anticipated the Northern Ireland administration remaining aloof from Dublin. Because the Northern Ireland administration would not acknowledge the new 'Irish' constitution, the *Telegraph* concluded that 'Éire cannot be sovereign'.[109]

More significantly, the *Telegraph* interpreted the constitution as a vehicle created by de Valera to consolidate a personal dictatorship in Ireland. It suspected the methods for the nomination and election of the Taoiseach and President contained inherent flaws. Central to the *Telegraph*'s interpretation was the question of authority wielded by the President over the representative assembly. As a result, the future predicted by the *Telegraph* was a dictatorship under the pretence of democracy.[110] The newspaper recalled the perceived contempt with which de Valera regarded the previous figurehead of state, the governor general, 'whom de Valera himself has reduced to insignificance'.[111] It deduced that de Valera could and would demonstrate again his disdain for constitutional office and turn the presidency into a personal dictatorship. In identifying the meaning of the Irish version of 'prime minister' (*Taoiseach*), the *Telegraph* saw more than a similarity between it and the offices of Germanic Fuehrer and the Italian Duce. However, the *Telegraph* remained adamant that the Taoiseach would fulfil a subsidiary role, behind the 'real' authority vested in the presidency and de Valera.[112]

The *Morning Post* also emphasised the ease with which de Valera seemed to remove all mention of ties to Britain in the constitution. As well as identifying that the new President of Ireland was deemed to take precedence over all other persons in the state, the *Post* was quick to point out that in effect de Valera had removed all traces of reference to the king. Such policies were not welcomed by the *Post*.[113] The *Post* reminded its readers that however much de Valera might attempt to extricate Ireland politically from Britain, economic and fiscal realities would ensure the practical link. The suspicion that de Valera renounced 'negative' links with Britain while retaining positive trade and industrial ties irked the *Post* also.[114]

In contrast, the *Observer* refrained from making any such denunciations of Free State policies, predicting only that: 'It is a constitution which will, without alteration of a comma, serve for all the purposes of an All-Ireland Republic if and when established.'[115] Like the *Telegraph*, the *Sunday Times* concentrated on the inter-relationship between the President and the Taoiseach. In theory, both functions were to remain separate, with specific duties attached to each office. However, both newspapers had difficulty in distinguishing between the two: instead of viewing both offices working independently, they foresaw them in competition. In these circumstances, the *Sunday Times* concluded that the presidency, representing the first person of the state, would assume power, and presumed that de Valera would continue to lead the government via a cosmetic transformation.[116]

The *Manchester Guardian* was less emotive and more considered in its response. Its review was a sober and ultimately prescient analysis of the constitution's details, examining its overall context. In effect, the *Guardian* differed from the other British publications in its rejection of the claim that the new constitution was a radical departure. Preferring to see its changes as cosmetic, the paper shrewdly informed its readers that much of the political apparatus existing before the introduction of the constitution remained. Far from representing the radical document intent on burning all bridges with Britain, the *Guardian*'s analysis confirmed that much remained the same: the close parallels between the governor-generalship and the presidency and the return of the Senate following its abolition in 1934. To this restoration could be added the provision for referenda and for university representation – albeit in the Senate, not the Dáil. The *Guardian's* analysis of the articles of the constitution provided a more liberal interpretation for the British readership, one which suggested that in essence it reflected the conservative sentiments of a conservative state, both spiritually and politically:

> Actually Mr de Valera's Constitution is a *conservative* rather than a radical document. It is more interesting for what it restores than for what it destroys. The Governor General has gone, but he comes back again as the President of Éire. One by one the Governor General's shadowy powers as the king's representative were stripped from him; now he is invested with not inconsiderable powers as first citizen and the chosen of the people. The Senate was abolished, but returns with all the powers of revision and delay that were the cause of its going. A curious formula had been invented for the removal of judges: the old procedure of resolution of both Houses is both restored. The old Constitution contained provision for a referendum, which was abolished, to be now restored. University representation in the Dáil was abolished: it is transferred to the Senate. The Privy Council in Ireland disappeared with the Viceroy and the rule of Dublin Castle; it comes back as the President's Council of State. There is a change of name. Instead of Saorstát Éireann we are to have Éire, although Saorstát Éireann was the Irish for 'Irish Republic', according to the republican pundits, and was euphemistically translated as Irish Free State ... Where the treaty provided for Ulster's right of choice the new Constitution contents itself with partition 'pending the reintegration of the national territory', which amounts to the same thing.[117]

The Reaction of Northern Ireland to the New Constitution[118]

This analysis is primarily based on a study of five northern Irish newspapers in the aftermath of the publication of the 1937 constitution in May of that year.[119] The papers chosen are the *Belfast Newsletter* (founded 1737) which might be described as the organ of unionism and traditional Protestantism, the *Belfast*

Telegraph (f. 1870), (*Evening Telegraph* until 1912), a staunch supporter of the union, the *Northern Whig* (f. 1824),[120] which was a liberal unionist paper and not uncritical of the Unionist Party at times, the *Irish News* (f. 1891), which under the editorship of Robert Kirkwood from 1935–68 advocated moderate nationalism and the championship of Catholic causes such as the Franco side in the Spanish Civil War,[121] and the *Derry Journal*, which was also strongly Catholic and anti-Protestant in its editorial line.

The publication of the draft constitution caused little alarm to leaders of the Unionist Party, as reflected in their public statements reported in the unionist press. In fact the evidence strongly suggests that the constitution enabled them to emphasise the separateness of the north from the south. This was further aided by the conjunction of the debate on the constitution with the coronation of George VI in May 1937. While the Dáil debated the second reading of a Constitution Bill that would effectively create a new state and copper-fasten the abolition of the crown from its internal affairs, the north, or at least the unionist part, was awash with bunting and union jacks celebrating the crowning of ironically, as his royal title stated, the last king of a 'united Ireland'. George VI's coronation oath, as the nationalist *Irish News* noted, did not recognise the separateness of 'Ulster' from the rest of Ireland and this had preceded the publication of de Valera's draft constitution by many months. De Valera, while not endorsing the coronation oath, did not condemn it even though he was given the opportunity to do so in the Dáil. He had tacitly acquiesced in the royal title of 'King of Great Britain, Ireland and the British Dominions beyond the Seas', to provide northern unionists with further evidence for their strongly held view that their loyalty, religion and culture would be under threat in a united Irish state.[122] The *Belfast Newsletter*, noting the lack of celebrations of the coronation in the south, questioned de Valera's constitutional guarantees with the claim that 'loyalists on the other side of the Border will run risks in exercising the freedom which they are promised under the new Constitution'.[123]

The reaction of the three main unionist newspapers was a combination of hostility and studied indifference. The *Belfast Telegraph* complained in its editorial on 1 May about 'a freak constitution' and that the position of a 'so called Dominion where the King's name is excluded from the Courts of Justice and from legal proceedings generally and the Governor-General is a mere figurehead, and the singing of a political ballad replaces that of the National Anthem on public occasions can only be considered anomalous'.[124] The *Northern Whig* declared that the new constitution would only serve to 'stiffen Ulster's resistance to any attempt to sever it from the British Crown or to diminish by one iota its full participation in the life of the British family of Nations'.[125] The *Belfast*

Newsletter concentrated on the claim to the north in Article 2 but noted that Article 3 avoided 'awkward complications' by stopping with just a claim. While decrying Article 2's 'audacity', the writer seemed to think that the draft constitution would 'amuse, rather than trouble, the loyal people of Ulster. The claim, after all, is ancient history, and it has no reality, whatever the Free State may call itself.'[126] To the *Newsletter* leader writers, the constitution was not so much a challenge to Northern Ireland as to the British government and the imperial conference, which was meeting in London to coincide with the coronation, on the grounds that it was both a unilateral rejection of the Treaty and a repudiation of the crown.[127] The *Northern Whig* reiterated that the claim to the north 'counts for nothing, and will not give the Government or the people of the North a single sleepless night'.[128]

Northern ministers were reluctant to criticise the provisions of a southern constitution. They instead preferred to rely on the tried and tested slogans of the past. The Minister for Commerce declared that, Article 2 or no Article 2, 'Our position is perfectly clear and safe. We in the North have a deep rooted and passionate attachment to the Crown.' He claimed, in a tone reminiscent of a scientist holding up a particularly unpleasant specimen, to look 'with curiosity on the new Free State Constitution'. Sir Basil Brooke, the Minister for Agriculture, chose to emphasise the value of free access to the English market – 'the greatest in the world'– which would be lost if the north went in with a separatist south. An Ulster [NI] Unionist MP, Sir Ronald Ross, described the constitution as 'just what one might expect. It bears no relation to reality. The whole policy of the present Government in the Free State is to get any benefits they can derive out of association with the British Empire and to refuse to undertake any of the obligations whether theoretical or actual. This Constitution is just about as likely to last as the last one, which is now entirely destroyed.'[129] Lord Craigavon, who was in London for the coronation, was of the opinion that it 'makes not a pin of difference what takes place in Southern Ireland so far as our position in the United Kingdom is concerned'. A man had not yet been born, he believed, who could govern the whole of Ireland if the north and south were to come together. In such an event, he claimed, there would be a situation comparable to that which exists in Spain, and the struggle would last for more than a hundred years. 'Isn't it far better,' he asked, 'to carry on, the North doing its best, and the South having its own way, managing affairs just as it wants.'[130] The *Irish News* was derisive of Craigavon's warnings of civil war, commenting in such an event that: 'Since his Lordship cannot hope for another Curragh Mutiny, he will be obliged to form an International Brigade of Orangemen, to guard the heights of Stormont.'[131]

The Northern Ireland parliament did not debate the constitution and its claims to be for all Ireland. A question was raised by Mr Nixon, the Independent Unionist for Woodvale, that the 'new constitution in the Free State propose[d] to wipe out this Parliament with execution deferred. What is the reason that nothing is being done about it?' The Minister for Finance, J. M. Andrews, replied that: 'Nothing further needs to be done about it, because the Free State Government have no jurisdiction over us of any kind or shape.' All further questions on the matter were ruled out of order by the speaker on the grounds that they were matters reserved for the imperial parliament.[132]

The unionist press at least was happy that de Valera's attempts to raise partition drew little or no public sympathy from either politicians or press in Britain. The *Newsletter* noted that in 'the old days the Nationalist Party's claims found ready support from the Liberal Party and Press, and those who disputed them were accused of obduracy and recalcitrance – of standing in the way of a loyal and contented Ireland within the Empire'.[133]

Nationalist opinion in the north favoured the constitution. Neither the *Irish News* nor the *Derry Journal* criticised the draft. Both ran editorials in praise. Just like the unionist press, one gets the feeling that they did not want to make any criticism of their own side that might be used by their opponents across the sectarian divide. The *Derry Journal*, which was strongly Fianna Fáil in inclination, was no exception. Its conviction was 'one of enthusiastic gratification at … the proposed new Constitution'. It saw no point in keeping the crown or the Treaty, which was what Fine Gael offered, recognising, instead, two main reasons in favour of the constitution:

> The first is that there is at least a formidable proportion of our countrymen who will never submit to such imperial absorption, and any attempt to arrange it is certain to be overthrown if not by this generation, by another. The second is that the Northern Ascendancy assert in the most unmistakable terms and temper that it would not unite with the South if the latter swallowed the British Crown whole and swathed itself in the Union Jack from head to heel into the bargain …[134]

The editorial argued that the new constitution with its concept of external association with the commonwealth offered the only realistic alternative. While admitting that there may be details of the constitution with which opinion might reasonably differ, the paper declared that these incidentals did not alter the document's achievement 'as an ideal interpretation of a truly Christian democracy'. The most important element in the constitution was 'the magnificent break it makes with the pagan conception of rule belonging to the corrupt convention of "liberalism" derived from the Grand Orient inspiration in the last century'. The paper certainly had no problem with the Catholic Church being given a special position and in fact used it to attack the unionists:

> The due and unequivocal recognition of the place of Catholicism in the heart and tradition of the nation is supplemented by the guarantee of that complete tolerance of other creeds which is so proverbially engrained in the national, as distinct from the planted, character that its insertion in any written Constitution is, in effect, a redundancy.[135]

The *Irish News*, traditionally a stalwart of the old Nationalist Party, was not particularly praiseworthy and made no great claims on the constitution's behalf. It made very little mention of the constitution in its leaders. It did, however, support the inclusion of the special position of the Catholic Church on the grounds that it was 'a plain fact'. This, the paper pointed out paradoxically, was in contrast to Craigavon's notorious description of Stormont as 'a Protestant Parliament for a Protestant People'. Nationalist politicians were reasonably impressed by the constitution's recognition of the problem of partition. Cahir Healy, the veteran nationalist MP, commented that although 'it may not mean any immediate release for Northern Nationalists, it is at least, comforting to know that they have not been forgotten.'[136]

If these reactions were both predictable and expected, there was one incident which demonstrated the explosiveness of debate in the north. De Valera's wide-ranging consultations with the leaders of the various religious denominations paid rich dividends at the Presbyterian general assembly in early June. The retiring moderator, Dr O'Neill, gave fulsome recognition to the fair treatment that he had received from both southern and northern governments. His praise of the Free State and the new constitution was effusive. He praised the goodwill of the Catholic majority, as without that 'goodwill the position would become impossible for their co-religionists'. Commenting on the religious aspect of the draft constitution, Dr O'Neill declared that it was a constitution 'unusual in modern times which, without any established Church, recognised all religious denominations existing in the country. What was still more remarkable, it is based upon a definitely Christian attitude to life.' The moderator cited the preamble and the first section of the religious article in support. He concluded by saying: 'Putting aside all other opinions about the Constitution, however important in their place, might they not be thankful to their Father for the high example set by those solemn declarations.'[137] The remarks by the moderator generated considerable public comment. The letter columns and the editorials were filled with critical comments in a debate that expanded to embrace the nature of the Northern Ireland state itself.[138]

Final Matters

Although the constitution came into operation on 29 December 1937, there were still two outstanding issues to be addressed. Firstly, the constitution, by way of transitory provision in Article 51, provided that it could be amended by ordinary legislation for up to three years after the President took office – until 24 June 1941 – subject only to the president's veto. This provision would in fact be activated with an extension of Article 28 under the First Amendment of the Constitution Act, effected on 2 September 1939. With the outbreak of war in Europe, and the state's declared neutrality, it was necessary to alter the wording, which had catered specifically for 'in time of war or armed rebellion'.

The day after the passing of the first amendment, both houses of the oireachtas passed the resolutions contemplated in the article – that a national emergency existed. The Emergency Powers Act, 1939 was passed the following day. Further acts of the same title were passed between 1940 and 1945 and the original legislation remained in force until it expired in 1946. The resolutions of the houses, that a national emergency existed, remained in force until 1976, when the houses made new resolutions in response to the security situation following the assassination of the British ambassador to Ireland.

However, this section was further amended in 1941 as part of the Second Amendment of the Constitution Act, 1941 in response to continued IRA activity. This addition meant that the provision for the oireachtas to declare a state of emergency had no limit and therefore the powers available under a state of emergency could continue indefinitely. Effectively these amendments freed the oireachtas from the limits imposed upon it by the constitution. When this provision was invoked the oireachtas became free to legislate as it willed, not merely to suspend fundamental rights but any other aspects – such as separation of powers – of the basic law as well.

The Second Amendment of the Constitution Act, 1941 was not confined to extending Article 28. It consisted of a group of some thirty amendments affecting sixteen articles. Many of these were of a stylistic nature, but there were several amendments of substance affecting the courts. Article 26.2,2 and 34.4,5 stipulated that in cases involving the constitutionality of bills under Article 26 or acts under Article 34, the supreme court had to deliver one opinion: separate concurrences as well as dissents were ruled out. Further, Article 34.3,3 provided that an act, the bill for which had been upheld by the supreme court, should thenceforth be immune from challenge. This provision compounded the difficulty created by the abstract nature of proceedings in an Article 26 referral. If later on unanticipated situations arose which showed the measure in a different light and gave grounds for doubting its validity, no relief was available. The new amendments had the effect of calcifying the law for all time. The *habeus corpus* provisions of Article 40.4 were also greatly expanded. This ensured that the person having custody of the detainee had the opportunity to justify the detention as lawful. If the high court concluded that a statute authorising the challenged detention was invalid it could state a case on the issue to the supreme court, and empowered the high court to suspend execution of a capital sentence pending a *habeus corpus* application.

The second outstanding issue was the nomination and election of the president. Article 53.3 of the constitution stipulated that the first President should enter office 180 days after the date of coming into operation of the constitution. The position of President was not filled immediately as legislation relating to electoral procedures had first to be enacted.[139] In the national newspapers there was widespread speculation about the possible identity of the new president. This speculation was reflected in a poem published in *Dublin Opinion* in December 1937:

> In this poor misty month that's gone
> They have unto the Uachtarán
> Appointed in a manner very
> Polite and Prompt, a Secretary.
> But who the Uachtarán will be
> Is still eluding you and me.

The secretary mentioned was Michael McDunphy, appointed to the newly created post of secretary to the President in November 1937.[140] However, it was not until 21 April 1938 that de Valera invited Cosgrave to a meeting to 'explore the possibilities of an agreed candidate'. The invitation, according to the *Irish Times*, was 'one of the most encouraging developments that have taken place for many a long day'. Alfie Byrne, lord mayor of Dublin, had already been nominated and appointed his election agent, Mr Lemass, a Dublin solicitor. The de Valera–Cosgrave meeting at Leinster House lasted two-and-a-half hours: P. J. Ruttledge and Gerry Boland attended for Fianna Fáil; James Dillon and T. F. O'Higgins sat in for the opposition. It is not known exactly what happened at that meeting but Dr Douglas Hyde emerged as the unanimous choice of both parties.

Reaction in Ireland was overwhelmingly favourable. His name had been suggested earlier when, on the occasion of his receiving the first Gregory Medal from the Irish Academy of Letters, the *Irish Times* advocated his appointment on 27 May 1937 in the following terms:

Douglas Hyde has been one of the great formative influences of the Ireland of today and tomorrow, an inspiration to his own generation and the founder of the greatest single organisation in modern Ireland ... the greater honour is that Douglas Hyde should be elected unanimously to be the First occupant of the Presidential office ... we suggest that no more fitting choice could be made, that no more worthy name could be found in Ireland today, and that the unanimous election of Dr Douglas Hyde would give pleasure to everyone in the country.

His inauguration ceremony took place on Saturday, 25 June 1938 in Dublin Castle. It began with a fanfare of trumpets to announce the arrival of the president-elect. Hyde then took his seat with the Taoiseach on his left, the chief justice on his right. On a table before Hyde lay the declaration set forth in the constitution. He leaned forward and signed the document, then rose as the chief justice administered the oath of office in Irish. Another fanfare of trumpets echoed through the hall as the chief justice presented Dr Hyde with the great seal. De Valera, speaking for the government and the nation, addressed Hyde formally:[141]

Mr President, on behalf of the Irish nation, on behalf of the living, those who dwell at home as well as our kin beyond the sea, on behalf also of the dead generations who longed to see this day but have not seen it, I salute you. You are now our President, our Head freely chosen under our own laws, inheriting the authority and entitled to the respect which the Gaels ever gave to those whom they recognised to be their rightful chief, but which for centuries they denied to those whom a foreign law would enforce upon them. In you we greet the successor of our rightful princes, and in your accession to office we hail the closing of the breach that has existed since the undoing of our nation at Kinsale.[142]

The entire event took only fifteen minutes, with the band doing 'its best to bring down the rafters with the national anthem'. Then the president, the chief justice and Taoiseach, together with presidential aides, moved slowly from the hall for the conclusion of the ceremony. Outside a guard of honour came to attention and presented arms. The presidential salute was played, the troops sloped arms and the first President of Ireland inspected the guard of honour. With this ceremony the provisions of the constitution were addressed. Hyde was no dictator and neither were any of his successors in an office which has grown in democratic importance as the years have progressed. De Valera himself exhibited no duce-like propensities when he served for two terms. Paradoxically, the office of the President has served as a very important instrument in the deepening of Irish democracy. De Valera, during the arms crisis in 1970, played a very important stabilising role. His successor, Erskine Childers, continued that role during his brief time in that office between 1973 and 1974. Cearbhall Ó

Dálaigh, President from 19 December, 1974 until his resignation on 22 October 1976, protected the integrity of his office by stepping down. Dr Patrick Hillery played an important role, particularly in the early 1980s, in the reinforcement of democratic institutions. Mary Robinson developed and expanded the role of the President. Mary MacAleese, serving two terms, has shown the value of the office of President as a means of healing divisions between the peoples on the island of Ireland. Opposition fears of dictatorship in 1930s have never been realised despite the fact that only one President to date has not been a Fianna Fáil candidate for that office.

In conclusion, the Irish constitution has endured into the 21st century, defying many critics and confounding those who felt that it ought to have been junked and replaced. It has been called de Valera's constitution. In a way, that still holds true. He sought and succeeded in replacing the 1922 constitution. But in doing so, he exercised his judgment in the selection of his team of drafters. He might have chosen otherwise. But the civil servants who were selected to carry out the task were representative of a very broad political culture. Most, if not all, had been formally educated before the foundation of the Irish state as had Éamon de Valera himself. The constitution that they produced was not a step back from the 1922 constitution as has often been suggested. Without the guiding hand of the former colonial power, some historians continue to feel that Irishmen and women could not be trusted to adhere to universal democratic principles. Or, that an article was intrinsically defective if it were Catholic in inspiration and expression.

It may now be of more historical relevance to ask: how did a document so protective of citizens' rights emerge from a decade so heavily influenced by anti-democratic ideas rooted in Catholic authoritarianism, vocationalism, corporatism, fascism and Nazism. Perhaps, or indeed, de Valera was far more complex a political thinker and constitutionalist than may have yet been realised. *Bunreacht na hÉireann* revealed the richness of the constitutional learning of those virtually forgotten civil servants and politicians who rose so discretely and professionally to the challenge set them by de Valera. Suffused in political and constitutional ideals, the work of the drafters has been for far-too-long underappreciated and undervalued – and in some cases - trivialised.

Appendix to Chapter 7

Results from the 1937 Plebiscite on the Draft Constitution and the General Election.

The following table and analysis of the results was prepared by Dr Robert MacNamara.

Constitu-ency	Elector-ate	Total Poll Pleb.	Votes Yes %	Votes No %	Spoilt %	% Non RC	FF FP %	FG FP %	Lab FP	IND. FP %
Cork Bor-ough	53,019	38,850	20,765 (53.45)	15,392 (39.62)	2,693 (6.93)	5.0	14,892 (38.94)	11,516 (30.11)	6,893 (18.02)	4,946 (12.93)
Dublin N-E	50,323	36,579	18,651 (50.99)	16,496 (45.09)	1,432 (3.91)	9.7	12,978 (35.85)	5,192 (14.34)	——	18,033 (49.81)
Dublin N-W	69,174	47,638	26,095 (54.78)	19,210 (40.32)	2,333 (4.9)	5.2	20,451 (43.39)	9,771 (20.73)	6,287 (13.34)	10,623 (22.54)
Dublin South	82,659	57,560	32,669 (56.76)	21,504 (37.36)	3,387 (5.88)	8.6	26,702 (46.83)	17,536 (30.76)	5,395 (9.46)	7,380 (12.94)
Dublin Townships	52,664	37,690	14,810 (39.29)	21,336 (56.60)	1,544 (8.986)	23.0	13,711 (37.08)	16,731 (45.25)	-------	6,535 (17.67)
Athlone/ Longford	38,295	29,849	15,648 (52.42)	11,367 (38.08)	2,834 (9.49)	4.0	10,505 (35.67)	11,143 (37.84)	3,018 (10.25)	4,781 (16.24)
Carlow/ Kildare	48,536	36,793	18,745 (50.95)	14,407 (39.16)	3,641 (9.89)	6.2	14,699 (40.61)	12,071 (33.35)	9,427 (26.04)	-------
Cavan	47,008	37,824	17,412 (46.03)	16,508 (43.64)	3,904 (10.32)	14.5	15,828 (43.20)	10,938 (28.38)	------	10,413 (28.42)
Clare	62,551	49,731	29,279 (58.87)	16,454 (33.09)	3,998 (8.04)	0.7	22,741 (46.37)	11,881 (24.23)	5,262 (10.73)	9,154 (18.67)
Cork North	47,822	39,372	17,458 (44.34)	16,350 (41.52)	5,564 (14.13)	1.7	15,527 (39.72)	13,976 (35.75)	5,824 (14.90)	3,762 (9.62)
Cork South-East	41,669	32,061	13,764 (42.93)	12,733 (39.71)	5,564 (17.35)	6.3	10,882 (35.09)	13,412 (43.24)	6,270 (21.67)	------
Cork West	67,017	53,866	19,741 (36.65)	24,668 (45.79)	9,457 (17.56)	6.4	13,292 (24.81)	25,894 (48.33)	12,179 (22.73)	2,207 (4.12)
Donegal East	48,975	36,908	18,680 (50.61)	13,041 (35.33)	5,187 (14.05)	21.4	18,752 (51.98)	9,234 (25.60)	------	8,090 (22.42)
Donegal West	38,532	27,639	14,160 (51.23)	11,086 (41.11)	2,393 (8.66)	10.0	14,144 (52.18)	12,962 (47.82)		
Dublin County	83,457	58,855	26,901 (45.71)	28,840 (49.00)	3,114 (5.29)	14.6	23,348 (40.28)	21,454 (37.01)	6,412 (11.06)	6,752 (11.65)
Galway East	49,476	34,642	21,273 (61.41)	10,049 (29.01)	3,320 (9.58)	1.1	20,078 (59.24)	10,142 (29.92)	3,672 (10.83)	
Galway West	42,796	26,141	17,836 (68.23)	6,234 (23.85)	2,071 (7.92)	1.1	18,562 (71.92)	7,246 (28.08)		

Kerry North	48,621	35,533	21,292 (60.26)	10,857 (30.73)	3,384 (9.58)	1.4	19,905 (56.83)	10,340 (29.52)	4,783 (13.65)	
Kerry South	35,390	26,325	13,658 (51.88)	9,573 (36.36)	3,094 (11.75)	1.3	14,040 (54.64)	8,125 (31.62)		3,532 (13.74)
Kilkenny	40,900	33,589	16,926 (50.39)	13,746 (40.92)	2,917 (8.68)	3.3	13,548 (41.38)	11,580 (35.37)	7,616 (23.26)	
Leitrim	36,368	27,551	12,583 (45.67)	8,429 (30.59)	6,539 (23.73)	5.5	13,884 (51.00)	9,423 (34.61)		3,919 (14.39)
Leix/Offaly	60,945	48,344	25,654 (53.06)	17,717 (36.65)	4,973 (10.16)	7.4	21,530 (45.24)	15,223 (31.99)	10,834 (22.77)	
Limerick	81,397	66,078	35,187 (53.25)	21,954 (33.22)	8,937 (13.52)	2.2	29,966 (45.73)	23,202 (35.41)	11,011 (16.81)	1,343 (2.05)
Louth	38,570	30,311	16,326 (53.86)	11,688 (38.56)	2,297 (7.58)	4.4	15,983 (53.84)	13,705 (46.16)		
Mayo North	38,170	25,934	15,900 (61.31)	8,247 (45.07)	1,787 (6.89)	1.9	15,935 (62.80)	9,440 (37.22)		
Mayo South	59,999	42,205	22,225 (52.66)	15,734 (37.28)	4,246 (10.06)	0.9	21,538 (53.37)	17,679 (42.99)		1,907 (4.64)
Meath/ W'Meath	61,654	49,094	27,586 (56.19)	18,704 (38.10)	2,804 (5.71)	4.3	25,895 (53.82)	17,910 (37.22)	3,827 (7.95)	486 (1.01)
Monaghan	36,469	31,511	16,189 (51.37)	12,107 (38.42)	3,215 (10.21)	18.9	6,032 (26.94)	8,435 (51.21)		6,838 (21.84)
Roscommon	42,103	32,170	15,481 (48.12)	12,910 (40.12)	3,779 (11.75)	1.5	14,699 (46.81)	13,101 (41.72)		3,599 (11.46)
Sligo	36,516	28,475	10,780 (37.86)	11,916 (41.85)	5,779 (20.29)	6.9	8,282 (29.41)	14,941 (53.06)		4,936 (17.53)
Tipperary	82,727	67,656	34,776 (51.40)	28,041 (41.45)	4,839 (7.15)	2.7	30,104 (44.58)	26,969 (39.94)	6,380 (9.45)	4,072 (6.03)
Waterford	51,596	41,192	22,118 (53.69)	16,578 (40.25)	2,496 (6.059)	2.8	19,353 (47.91)	17,273 (42.76)	3,179 (7.87)	592 (1.47)
Wexford	61,486	48,366	23,129 (47.82)	20,391 (42.16)	4,846 (10.02)	5.4	21,835 (46.72)	16,495 (35.29)	8,410 (17.99)	
Wicklow	38,171	29,875	11,408 (38.19)	12,678 (42.44)	5,789 (19.37)	15.3	9,419 (32.04)	6,771 (23.03)	8,629 (29.35)	4,580 (15.58)
Dublin	333,277	238,322	119,126 (49.99)	107,386 (45.06)	11,810 (4.95)		97,190 (41.31)	70,684 (30.04)	18,094 (7.69)	49,323 (20.96)
Rest of Leinster	388,557	306,221	155,422 (50.76)	120,698 (39.41)	30,101 (9.83)		133,414 (44.48)	104,898 (34.98)	51,761 (17.26)	9,847 (3.28)
Munster	571,809	450,664	228,038 (50.60)	172,600 (38.30)	50,026 (11.10)		190,702 (42.84)	162,588 (36.53)	62,231 (13.98)	29,608 (6.65)
Connacht/ Ulster	476,232	351,100	182,519 (51.98)	126,261 (35.96)	42,220 (12.02)		177,734 (51.65)	123,001 (35.74)	3,672 (1.07)	39,702 (11.54)
Ireland	1,775,055	1,346,207	685,105 (50.89)	526,945 (39.14)	134,157 (9.97)		599,040 (45.23)	461,171 (34.82)	135,758 (10.25)	128,480 (9.70)

Sources: The referendum results by constituency are taken from the Department of the Environment publication, *The Referendum in Ireland* (1999), p. 9. The election results are from the tables in Gallagher, Michael (ed.), *Irish Elections 1922–44* (PSAI Press, Dublin, 1993), pp. 207f. The percentage of non-Catholics is from the Department of Industry and Commerce, *Census 1936: Birthplace and Religion*, Volume V, p. 20

Certain points can be ascertained relatively easily from the above data. The constitution was passed by the majority of the voting electorate but by a very narrow majority. There was a very large number of spoiled votes but not enough to change the referendum. A greater number of people voted for the constitution than for Fianna Fáil but there was very poor cross-party support which must be mainly attributed to the legacy of the Civil War. There was a substantial overlap between support for Fianna Fáil and support for the constitution. It should be noted that in the five constituencies where the constitution was rejected Fianna Fáil was in a minority in the 1937 general election.

It should be borne in mind that while the constitution received more than 85,000 extra votes than Fianna Fáil received in first preferences this would still suggest, as Joe Lee points out, that 50,000 Labour voters withheld their endorsement from the constitution.[143] Interestingly, the total of 'Yes' votes for the constitution are very close to the first preference vote for Fianna Fáil in the January 1933 snap election, which might have some significance when one considers that the period 1933–1936 had by Irish standards relatively low net emigration. However, a constituency by constituency assessment is not possible due to the redistribution of the constituencies.

The 'No' exceeded the 'Yes' vote in just five of thirty-four constituencies. In only one constituency did it exceed 50 per cent of the total poll – Dublin Townships. Dublin Townships, significantly, was the constituency with the largest non-Catholic minority in the state. The Protestant vote would appear to have made a difference in two other 'No' constituencies – Dublin County and Wicklow. However, in Sligo and Cork West, where the 'No' vote won, it was clearly the strength of Fine Gael support in the constituency that won the vote. There were only small non-Catholic populations in both constituencies. Interestingly, there were massive abstentions in both constituencies – 20.29 per cent and 17.56 per cent respectively – and the 'No' vote was significantly behind the Fine Gael first preference vote. This might suggest that the Catholic clauses of the constitution might have had an effect. While Fine Gael voters may have remained reluctant to vote for anything to do with de Valera, they perhaps did not want to vote against a constitution so clearly influenced by Catholic social teaching.

Generally, the more rural a constituency was the higher the level of spoiled votes. In Dublin, less than 5 per cent spoiled their vote. Of the other urban centres,

Waterford and Cork Borough both had a similar low rate of spoils. Limerick was the exception with some 13.52 per cent spoiling. Of course, much of the Limerick constituency was rural. The rural Cork constituencies, Donegal East, Leitrim (where nearly a quarter of the plebiscite votes were spoiled), Sligo and Wicklow all had an above average number of spoiled votes. However, the rural constituencies of Tipperary, Meath/Westmeath and Mayo North all had 2–3 per cent less spoils than the country-wide average of 9.97 per cent. With the exclusion of the spoils the popular endorsement for the constitution looks much more impressive. In Connacht/Ulster the margin was 59.11 per cent to 40.89 per cent, in Munster 56.92 per cent to 43.08 per cent, and in the Rest of Leinster it was 56.29 per cent to 43.71 per cent. Only in Dublin was the result close, with 52.59 per cent to 47.41 per cent in favour and that was mainly because of the lower level of abstentions in Dublin than the rest of the country. The pattern in Dublin might suggest that the spoilers were perhaps those who leaned towards the 'No' camp.

The results and the number of spoilt votes seemed to cause a certain degree of bemusement within the government. Michael McDunphy, the assistant secretary at the Department of the Taoiseach, wondered why there was a discrepancy of over 100,000 valid ballots between the constitution and the general election poll. 'I was under the impression that the figures should be identical, or nearly so, inasmuch as each voter was entitled to get both a ballot paper and a plebiscite paper, and as every copy of both papers whether used properly, not used at all, or misused, should have been taken into account. The figures quoted above, however, indicate a discrepancy of 110,756.' Willard Brown of Local Government replied on 11 August. While just over 6,000 fewer papers were issued for the constitution the big discrepancy between the figures, he said, was altogether due to the '100,426 plebiscite papers rejected as invalid being unmarked or void for uncertainty'.

NOTES

PREFACE

1 Denis Gwynn, , *De Valera* (Jarrolds, London, 1933); Seán O'Faoláin, *Life Study of Éamon de Valera* (Talbot Press, Dublin 1933); Seán O'Faoláin, *De Valera: A New Biography* (Penguin, Harmondsworth, Middlesex, 1939); Desmond Ryan, *Unique Dictator: A Study of Éamon de Valera* (London, 1936); M. J. MacManus, Éamon de Valera (Talbot Press, Dublin, 1944); Mary Bromage, *De Valera and the march of a nation* (Hutchinson, London, 1956); Earl of Longford and Thomas P. O'Neill, *Éamon de Valera* (Hutchinson, London, 1970); John P. O'Carroll and John A. Murphy, (eds) *De Valera and his times* (Cork University Press, Cork 1986); J. J. Lee, and G. Ó Tuathaigh, (eds), *The age of de Valera* (Ward River Press in association with Radio Telefís Éireann, Dublin, 1982); Tim Pat Coogan, *De Valera : Long Fellow, Long Shadow* (Hutchinson, London, 1993); T. Ryle Dwyer, *De Valera : the man and the myths* (Poolbeg, Dublin, 1991). (Only one volume of the 'official' biography covering the period up to 1921, has appeared in Irish. See Tomás O'Neill agus Pádraig Ó Fiannachta, *De Valera* (Clómorainn, Baile Átha Cliath, 1968)

2 Earl of Longford and Thomas P. O'Neill, *Éamon de Valera* (Hutchinson, London, 1970).

3 Dermot Keogh, 'The Irish Constitutional revolution: an analysis of the making of the Constitution', *Administration*, Vol. 35, No. 4, (1988), pp. 4–84; see also Dermot Keogh, 'The Jesuits and the 1937 Constitution', *Studies*, Vol. 78, No. 309 (Spring 1989), pp. 82–95; and Dermot Keogh, *The Vatican, the Bishops and Irish Politics, 1919–1939* (Cambridge University Press, Cambridge, 1986).

4 This introduction has been adapted from a recent article of mine, 'De Valera, the Constitution and the Historians', *The Irish Jurist*, (2005) XL, 291, pp. 293–320.

5 Ibid, p. 294.

6 Ibid., p. 293.

7 See John Coakley, and Michael Gallagher, (eds.), *Politics in the Republic of Ireland*, (Routledge, London; New York, fourth edition, 2005).

8 Gerard Hogan, 'De Valera, the Constitution and the Historians', p. 293.

9 Ronan Fanning, *The Irish Department of Finance, 1922–58* (IPA, Dublin, 1978).

10 See Michael Kennedy, et al., *Documents on Irish Foreign Policy*, Vols. 1–5 (Royal Irish Academy, Dublin, 1998-2006)

11 Deirdre McMahon, *The Moynihan Brothers in Peace and War, 1909–1918: Their New Ireland* (Irish Academic Press, Dublin, 2004).

12 Deirdre McMahon, 'Maurice Moynihan (1902–1999): Irish Civil Servant: an Appreciation', *Studies*, Vol. 89, No. 353 (Spring 2000), p. 71.

13 Dermot Keogh, 'Profile of Joseph Walshe; Secretary of the Department of Foreign

Affairs 1922–46', *Irish Studies in International Affairs*, Vol. 3, No. 2, (Autumn, 1990), pp. 59–80.

14 Dermot Keogh, *The Vatican, the Bishops and Irish Politics* (Cambridge University Press, Cambridge, 1986), p. 316; Keogh, *Ireland and Europe, 1919–1948* (Gill & Macmillan, Dublin, 1988), p. 256; Keogh, *Ireland and Europe 1919–1989* (Hibernian University Press, Cork and Dublin, 1989) p. 340; Keogh, *Twentieth Century Ireland: Nation and State* (Gill and Macmillan, Dublin, 1994), p. 504; Keogh, *Ireland and the Vatican: The Politics and Diplomacy of Church and State, 1922–1960* (Cork University Press, Cork, 1995) p. 410; Keogh, *Jews in Twentieth Century Ireland: Refugees, anti-Semitism and the Holocaust* (Cork University Press, Cork, 1998), p. 336.

15 Dermot Keogh, 'The Irish Constitutional revolution', see also Keogh, 'The Jesuits and the 1937 Constitution',.

16 See Don O'Leary, *Vocationalism and Social Catholicism in twentieth-century Ireland: the search for a Christian social order* (Dublin: Irish academic Press, 2000), Maurice Craig, 'Catholic action as an organised campaign in Ireland, 1921-1947' (PhD Thesis, UCD, 2000), Finín O'Driscoll, *The search for the Christian state : an analysis of Irish social catholicism, 1913-1939* (MA Thesis, UCC, 1994).

17 Dermot Keogh and Gabriel Doherty, (eds), *De Valera's Irelands* (Mercier Press, Cork, 2003); Dermot Keogh, Finbarr O'Shea and Carmel Quinlan, (eds), *The Lost Decade: Ireland in the 1950s* (Mercier Press, Cork, 2004); Dermot Keogh and Mervyn O'Driscoll, (eds), *Ireland in World War Two: Neutrality and Survival* (Mercier Press, Cork, August 2004); Dermot Keogh and Andrew McCarthy, (eds), *Limerick Boycott 1904: Anti-Semitism in Ireland* (Mercier Press, Cork, 2005); Hiram Morgan, (ed.), *Information, Media and Power through the Ages* (University College Dublin Press, Dublin, 2001); Hiram Morgan, (ed.), *The Battle of Kinsale* (Wordwell Books, Bray, 2004); David Edwards, *The Ormond Lordship in County Kilkenny, 1515–1642: The Rise and fall of Butler feudal power* (Four Courts Press, Dublin, 2003); David Edwards, Patrick Duffy and Elizabeth FitzPatrick) (eds.), *Gaelic Ireland, c.1250–c.1650: Land, lordship and settlement* (Four Courts Press, Dublin, 2001); David Edwards, (ed.), *Regions & Rulers in Ireland, c.1100–c.1650: Essays for Kenneth Nicholls* (Four Courts Press, Dublin, 2004); Clodagh Tait, *Death, Burial and Commemoration in Ireland, 1550–1650* (Palgrave MacMillan, Basingstoke, 2002).

18 Dermot Keogh, 'Introduction: The Vanishing Irish', in Dermot Keogh, Finbarr O'Shea and Carmel Quinlan, (eds), *The Lost Decade: Ireland in the 1950s* (Mercier Press, Cork, 2004); Dermot Keogh, 'Leaving the Blaskets 1953: Willing or Enforced Departures?', in Dermot Keogh, Finbarr O'Shea and Carmel Quinlan, (eds), *The Lost Decade: Ireland in the 1950s* (Mercier Press, Cork, 2004); Dermot Keogh, '"Making Aliya": Irish Jews, the Irish State and Israel', in Dermot Keogh, Finbarr O'Shea, and Carmel Quinlan, (eds), *The Lost Decade: Ireland in the 1950s* (Mercier Press, Cork, 2004); David Edwards, 'The Poisoned Chalice: The Ormond inheritance, sectarian division and the emergence of James Butler, 1614–42', in Toby Barnard and Jane Fenlon, (eds), *The Dukes of Ormonde, 1610–1745* (Boydell & Brewer, London, 2000); 'Salvaging History: Hogan and the Irish Manuscripts Commission', in Donnchadh Ó Corráin, (ed.), *James Hogan: Revolutionary, Historian and Political Scientist* (Four Courts Press, Dublin, 2001); 'Recovering Gaelic Ireland, c.1250–c.1650', co-authored with Patrick Duffy and Elizabeth FitzPatrick, in

Duffy, Edwards & FitzPatrick (eds), *Gaelic Ireland, c.1250–c.1650: Land, lordship and settlement* (Four Courts Press, Dublin, 2001); 'Collaboration without Anglicisation: The MacGiolla Padraig lordship and Tudor reform', in Duffy, Edwards, and FitzPatrick, (eds), *Gaelic Ireland, c.1250–c.1650: Land, lordship and settlement* (Four Courts Press, Dublin, 2001); 'Roscrea Castle, the Butlers, & the O'Carrolls, c.1450–1630', in Conleth Manning, (ed.), *Excavations at Roscrea Castle* (Dúchas: The Heritage Service, Dublin, 2003); 'Legacy of Defeat: The destruction of the Gaelic order after Kinsale', in H. Morgan (ed.), *The Battle of Kinsale* (Wordwell books, Dublin, 2004); 'Tipperary liberty ordinances of the "Black" Earl of Ormond', Dermot Keogh, co-authored with Adrian Empey, in D. Edwards, (ed.) *Regions & Rulers in Old Ireland, c.1100–c.1650* (Four Courts Press, Dublin, 2004), pp. 122–47; 'Tipperary liberty ordinances of the "Black" Earl of Ormond', co-authored with Adrian Empey, in D. Edwards, (ed.), *Regions & Rulers in Old Ireland, c.1100–c.1650* (Four Courts Press, Dublin, 2004), pp. 122–47. See also: Hiram Morgan, 'Spanish Armadas and Ireland', in L. François, and A.K. Isaacs, (eds), *The Sea in European history* (Pisa: Edizioni PLUS, 2001), pp. 219–28; 'The island defenders: humanist patriots in early modern Iceland and Ireland', in G. Halfdánarson, & A.K. Isaacs, (eds), *Nations and nationalities in historical perspective* (Pisa: Edizioni PLUS, 2002), pp. 223–43; 'The real Red Hugh', in Pádraig Ó Riain, (ed.), *Beatha Aodh Ruadh: The life of Red Hugh O'Donnell historical and literary contexts*, Subsidiary series, No.12 (Irish Texts Society, London, 2002), pp. 1–35.

19 Dermot Keogh, 'The Jesuits and the 1937 Constitution', *Studies*, Vol. 78, No. 309 (Spring 1989), pp. 82–95.

FOREWORD

1 This has been a long-standing trend and it could be said of the almost ninety separate instances of declarations of unconstitutionality since 1937 that in the majority of these cases the judicial branch has forced the Oireachtas to come up with a fairer and better law than that which was invalidated. There are also instances of where a judicial decision which did not actually invalidate the law under challenge has effected important changes. *Murphy v. Minister for Environment* [2007] IEHC 185 is a contemporary example of this latter phenomenon. In this case J. Clarke construed the obligations imposed on the Oireachtas by Article 16 in such a fashion as will mean that, henceforth, revision of the constituencies in the wake of a census will have to be immediate and that the latitude for deviations of population ratios as between the constituencies will be far more limited than was previously the case.

2 J.M. Kelly, *The Irish Constitution*, Preface to the first edition (1980).

3 'The ECHR and the Irish Constitutional Scheme of Rights: Complementary or Divergent?' Paper delivered to the 'The Constitution at 70', Conference, Law School, Trinity College, 8 June 2007.

4 This Introduction has been adapted from a recent article of mine, 'De Valera, the Constitution and the Historians' (2005), 41 *Irish Jurist*

5 The classic account is, of course, Keogh, 'The Irish Constitutional Revolution: An Analy-

sis of the Making of the Constitution' in Litton, ed., *The Constitution of Ireland 1937–1987* (IPA, 1988). For an excellent and balanced contemporary account, see, Gallagher, 'The Constitution and the Judiciary' in Coakley and Gallagher, eds, *Politics in the Republic of Ireland* (fourth edition, 2005).

6 Gerard Hogan, 'The Constitution, Property Rights and Proportionality' (1997), 32 *Irish Jurist*, pp. 373, 396.

7 This view is still expressed by some commentators: see, e.g., the somewhat tendentious comments of David Fitzpatrick, *The Two Irelands 1912-1939*, (Oxford, 1998), p. 230: 'De Valera's moral apotheosis coincided with the application in 1937 of his new constitution, much of which had been drafted by Jesuits and other clerical advisers.'

Likewise, in his classic and pioneering work, J.H. Whyte, *Church and State in Modern Ireland 1923–1979* (second edition, 1980) had described (p. 51) the Constitution 'as clearly very much Mr de Valera's own creation.' Writing over a decade later, Nicholas Mansergh, *Nationalism and Independence and Selected Irish Papers* (Cork, 1996), still echoed that view, p. 299: '[de Valera] had drafted the Constitution without conference or committee for discussion or debate, but – and it is remarkable – without enquiry of individuals on occasion, as with John Hearne and also the Archbishop of Dublin on the position of the Church. But any such exchange was on a bilateral basis; save to that limited extent all remained in President de Valera's hands.'

Even some lawyers take this view. Thus, Ivana Bacik, *Kicking and Screaming: Dragging Ireland into the 21st Century* (Dublin, 2004), states that the original text of the Constitution 'was written primarily by Éamon de Valera ... with considerable input from John Charles McQuaid [later] Roman Catholic Archbishop of Ireland.'

8 Cf. the comments of O'Sullivan, *The Irish Free State and its Senate* (London, 1940), p. 496: 'The new Constitution was not the result of the labours of jurists and other experts. So far as known, its author is Mr de Valera himself, aided, no doubt, by Civil Servants and others whose duty it is to advise him and his Government.'

F. S. L. Lyons, *Ireland since the Famine* (London, 1971) described (p. 538) the Constitution as 'remarkable' because 'it was very largely the work of one man, Mr de Valera himself.'

But see Keogh, *Irish Constitution Revolution*, p. 8–11 for a full account of Hearne's involvement.

9 O'Brien, Conor Cruise, *States of Ireland* (London, 1972), p. 120.

10 *Ibid.*, p. 122.

11 Whyte, *op.cit.*, p. 51.

12 Humphreys, Review of Kelly, *The Irish Constitution* (1994) 16 *Dublin University Law Journal*, pp. 222, 223.

13 Lee, *Ireland 1912-1985*, especially pp. 201–211.

14 *Ibid.*, p. 203.

15 Professor Lee does, of course, refer to the *McGee* case at a much later stage in the book.

16 [1974] IR 287. Another example of such an omission may be found in Foster, *op.cit.*, p. 562 where he instanced the Trade Union Act 1941 as 'potentially oppressive' because it curtailed the rights of affiliation to particular unions. But he does not mention the fact

that no sooner than an attempt was made to implement the legislation than it was found unconstitutional by the Supreme Court as contrary to the right of freedom of association in Article 40.6.1: see *National Union of Railwaymen v. Sullivan* [1947] IR 77.

17 Gallagher, 'The Constitution and the Judiciary' in Coakley and Gallagher eds., *Politics in the Republic of Ireland* (4th. Edition, 2005) p. 94.

18 *Ibid.*, pp. 77-78.

19 Foster, *Modern Ireland 1600–1972* p. 544.

20 Keogh, 'The Irish Constitutional Revolution', p.30, described the recognition of the Jewish Congregation as 'a deliberate challenge to the anti-Semitism of the vociferous supporters of right-wing Catholic thought.'

21 See Kelly, *The Irish Constitution*, pp. 2037-2041. In one of the (very) few cases where these deleted provisions might be said to have had some legal impact, *Bank of Ireland Trustee Co. Ltd. v. Attorney General* [1957] IR 257, p. 275, Dixon J., said that: 'it was implicit in the terms of [the deleted provisions] that adherence to and practice of any of the religions there recognised may be presumed to be of public benefit.'

But note the comments of Geoghegan, J. in *O Beolain v. Fahy* [2001] 2 IR 279, p. 365 'Long before [Article 44.1.2] was abolished by referendum the provision as to the special position of the Roman Catholic Church was not considered by constitutional lawyers to have any legal implications. It was merely reflecting what was perceived to be a fact on the ground at the time of the enactment of the Constitution.'

Note also the comments of Barrington, J. in *Campaign to Separate Church and State Ltd. v. Minister for Education* [1998] 3 IR 321, p. 355: 'The better opinion appeared to be that the recognition of the 'special position' of the Roman Catholic Church was merely a recognition of a fact and implied no privileged position at law. Nevertheless the term 'special position' was a source of misunderstanding. As long as it remained there was a latent suspicion that while all citizens were equal, Roman Catholics might, in some sense, be more equal than others.'

22 This was no mere historical anachronism, as King George VI took such an oath upon his coronation of 12 May 1937 just as the Constitution was being debated in the Dáil. Mr de Valera had drawn earlier drawn attention to the religiously discriminatory character of the oath as justifying an attitude of 'detachment and protest' towards the whole coronation ceremony: see 65 *Dail Debates,* p. 869 (24 February 1937).

23 This bracketed provision of Article 2 – which was extant in 1937 – caused the Norwegians no little embarrassment during the diplomatic conference leading up to the signing of the European Convention of Human Rights in 1950. Following some controversy, the Norwegian Government originally proposed a reservation under Article 64 ECHR on the basis that Article 2 of the Constitution merely precluded the propagation of religious doctrine by the Jesuits and did not extend to precluding the admission of Jesuits on to Norwegian soil. Following a parliamentary debate in the Storting in November 1956, the words in brackets in Article 2 were deleted and the reservation withdrawn: see Mose, 'Norway' in Blackburn & Polakiewicz, *Fundamental Rights in Europe, the ECHR and its Member States 1950–2000* (OUP, 2001), pp. 625-626.

24 It may be noted that a slightly modified version of this may be found in Article 25 of the 1997 Polish Constitution:

1. Churches and other religious organisations shall have equal rights.
2. Public authorities in the Republic of Poland shall be impartial in matters of personal conviction, whether religious or philosophical, or in relation to outlooks on life, and shall ensure their freedom of expression within public life.
3. The relationship between the State and churches and other religious organisations shall be based on the principle of respect for their autonomy and the mutual independence of each in its own sphere, as well as on the principle of cooperation for the individual and the common good.
4. The relations between the Republic of Poland and the Roman Catholic Church shall be determined by international treaty concluded with the Holy See, and by statute.
5. The relations between the Republic of Poland and other churches and religious organisations shall be determined by statutes adopted pursuant to agreements concluded between their appropriate representatives and the Council of Ministers.

25 See, e.g., Article 16(3) of the 1991 Bulgarian Constitution: 'Eastern Orthodox Christianity is considered the traditional religion in the Republic of Bulgaria.'

26 Section 2 of the Constitution of Irish Free State Act 1922 not only provided that the Treaty had the force of law, but that insofar as the Constitution was in conflict with the terms of the Treaty, it was void.

27 As Fanning has argued in 'Mr de Valera drafts a Constitution' in Farrell, ed., *De Valera's Constitution and Ours* (Dublin, 1988), p. 42: 'Neither should those who damn the Catholic triumphalism they so readily identify in the 1937 Constitution ignore the residual impact of ingrained anti-Catholicism that had characterised British dealings with Ireland since the sixteenth century. Nor should they forget that an especially vicious form of anti-Catholic prejudice and discrimination was an outstanding feature of that part of Ireland still within the United Kingdom.'

28 See generally, Keogh, *Irish Constitutional Revolution.* A good example of the distaste felt in certain (more extreme) clerical circles may be found in the letter from Fr Edward Cahill, SJ, to de Valera on 23 May 1937 (De Valera Papers 1095/2D): 'I presume you know that the term 'Church of Ireland' which occurs in Art. 44.1.3 has aroused no end of criticism and surprise; for it really seems to be an authoritative approval of a piece of lying propaganda. I hope it will be changed.'

29 Article 44.1 excepted.

30 Article 44.2.1 of the Constitution.

31 Article 44.2.2 of the Constitution.

32 [1998] 3 IR 321.

33 [1998] 3 IR 321, p. 361, per Keane J. In his separate judgment Barrington J. noted that while section 5 of the Government of Ireland Act 1920 had contained a ban on the establishment of any religion, this was not reflected in Article 16 of the Treaty nor Article 8 of the 1922 Constitution. He added ([1998] 3 IR 321, p. 352): 'Why the express prohibition on the establishment of any religion was dropped is not quite clear. But presumably it was because the combined effect of the ban on the endowment of any religion and the prohibition of the granting of any preference on the grounds of religious belief or status was to make an express ban on establishment unnecessary.'

34 [1951] IR 1.

35 See generally Hogan, 'A Fresh Look at *Tilson's* Case' (1998) 32 *Irish Jurist,* p. 311.

36 See the comments of Archbishop Neill, *The Irish Times*, 10 January 2006.

37 Some blame should also attach to the Supreme Court itself because the majority judgment did not sufficiently stress the fact that the Court was *not* relying on the 'special position' clause in Article 44.1.2 in arriving at its conclusion, *especially* in view of the incautious and ambiguous comments of Gavan Duffy P. in the High Court on this particular issue. Murnaghan J. was thus altogether too timid when he observed ([1951] IR 1 at 35): 'If the Court is able to arrive at a decision in the case upon the construction of Article 42 and Article 42 alone and without reference to Article 41 and Article 44, nothing is to be gained by discussing these last mentioned Articles in the present case. It is right, however, to say that the Court in arriving at its decision, is not now holding that these last-mentioned Articles confer any privileged position before the law upon members of the Roman Catholic Church and during the argument counsel for the respondents expressly disclaimed any such privileged position.'

38 In passing, it seems curious that Professor Foster should refer to 'rights' in inverted commas, suggesting, perhaps, that these provisions were of little value. This gives no sense at all of the vast case-law which these provisions have subsequently generated. Thus, for example, the 2004 edition of Kelly, *The Irish Constitution* devotes over 800 pages to a discussion of Articles 40 to Article 45.

39 Costello, 'The Natural Law and the Irish Constitution' (1956), *Studies*, pp. 403, 414.

40 Lyons, *Ireland since the Famine,* p. 544.

41 'Property Rights in the Irish Constitution', Paper delivered at the 'The Constitution at '70 Conference', Law School, Trinity College, Dublin, 7–8 June 2007. Professor Wheare was an English comparative constitutional lawyer who had famously compared the guarantees in Article 43 with the corresponding provisions of the Constitution of former Yugoslavia.

42 It is true that, in the one case where case-law based on Article 6 of the German Basic Law was relied on, *Murphy v. Attorney Genera*l [1982] IR 241, the Supreme Court rather tersely (and quite unconvincingly) said that this case-law did not assist the plaintiffs' contentions. In *Murphy* the plaintiffs had challenged the constitutionality of provisions of the Income Tax Act 1967 which had aggregated the incomes of husbands and wives for tax purposes. Reliance was placed on a decision of the German Constitutional Court in 1957 which had held similar German legislation to be unconstitutional on the ground that it infringed Article 6(1), since it inferred with the right of married persons to make personal decisions, including the right of the wife to decide whether she would devote herself to the home or work outside the home. As the legislature could not directly interfere with that rights, the Court held that it could not do so indirectly by means of tax measures designed to penalise working wives. But it is not easy to see why the Supreme Court so fleetingly dismissed this (very convincingly) reasoned German authority, especially as that Court has in other key decisions recognised that the autonomy of family decision-making from State interference is at the heart of Article 41: see, e.g., *McGee v. Attorney General* [1974] IR 284; *Re Article 26 and the Matrimonial Homes Bill* 1993 [1994] 1 IR 305 and *North Western Health Board v. HW* [2001] 3 IR 622.

43 See, e.g., the extremely close overlap between the provisions of Article 12 and Article 13 dealing with the powers and tenure of office of the President and Article 41 to Article 49 of the Weimar Constitution dealing with the powers of the German President: see Kelly, *The Irish Constitution* (Dublin, 2004), pp. 224-225. Note also the discussion in *Howlin v. Morris* [2004] 2 ILRM 53, pp. 75–76 as to the extent to which the parliamentary privilege provisions in Article 15.10 and Article 15.12 were derived from the corresponding Weimar provisions.

44 [2001] 3 IR 622.

45 [2001] 3 IR 622, p. 757. In *N v. Health Service Executive ('Baby Ann')* [2006] IESC 60 Hardiman J. further observed a propos of this point: 'There is, of course, no doubt that the form and content of our constitutional dispensation in regard to the family and children was significantly influenced by Christian, and specifically Catholic, teaching on those subjects. But that is not to say that the preference for the natural parents as carers for a child is exclusively referable to those sources. In my judgment in *North Western Health Board v. H.W.* I expressed the view that this preference for the parents as the natural and primary guardians was equally consistent with quite different strands of thought, even a Benthamite one. I reiterate that view here, without repeating what was said in the judgment referred to.'

46 But cf. the comments of Aughey, 'Obstacles to Reconciliation in the South' in *Building Trust in Ireland (Studies Commissioned by the Forum For Peace and Reconciliation)* (Belfast 1996), p. 30: 'The source of Catholic social teaching *is* sufficient grounds for unionists to reject the Constitution and the content of the Constitution does *not* matter … because the common goods it seeks may be admirable in itself but it is estranged from unionists.'

47 *North Western Health Board v. HW* [2001] 3 IR 622.

48 *McK v. Information Commissioner* [2004] 1 IR 12 (HC); [2006] 1 LRM 504 (SC).

49 *Fajujono v. Minister for Justice* [1990] 2 IR 152; *Lobe v. Minister for Justice, Equality and Law Reform* [2003] 1 IR 1; *Cirpaci v. Minister for Justice, Equality and Law Reform* [2005] 2 ILRM 547; *AA v. Minister for Justice, Equality and Law Reform* [2005] 4 IR 564.

50 *O'Shea v. Ireland* [2007] 1 ILRM 460.

51 *N v. Health Service Executive* [2006] IESC 60.

52 [2006] IESC 60.

53 [2006] 4 All ER 241.

54 Hogan, 'The Constitution, Property Rights and Proportionality' (1997), 32 *Irish Jurist* pp.373-97.

55 *Report of the Constitution Review Group* (May 1996), p. 2632.

56 Coogan, Tim Pat, *De Valera: Long Fellow, Long Shadow* (Arrow Books, 1993), pp. 493–495.

57 Coogan, *op.cit.*, p. 495, sets out Article 3 (incompletely) as follows: 'Every person without distinction of sex, domiciled in the area of the Irish Free State shall within the jurisdiction of the Irish Free State enjoy the privileges and be subject to the obligations of such citizenship.'

58 As does Article 9.1.3 of the (1937) Constitution. Of course, if Article 3 of the 1922 Constitution was, in fact, some form of free standing equality guarantee as between men and women, the references to domicile and ordinary residence would have been surplusage and entirely unnecessary.

59 Which was subsequently found to be unconstitutional by the Supreme Court in *de Burca v. Attorney General* [1976] IR 38 as being contrary to Article 38.5 (right to jury trial) and Article 40.1 (equality before the law).

60 De Valera made this very point in the Report Stage debate on Article 40.1, 68 *Dáil Debates,* pp. 173–174, 9 June 1937: 'It is extraordinary that it is now Deputies on the other benches are discovering all these prohibitions that were [in Article 3] in the old Constitution. I take it that they accepted in 1924 and, particularly in 1926, when the matter was raised, this question of the discrimination between men and women in the public service, for example. They had the old Constitution and, nevertheless, they went ahead and made that difference.'

The same point was also made by an opposition Deputy, Deputy Frank McDermott, 68 *Dáil Debates,* Col. 171, 9 June 1937: 'Article 3 of the old Constitution, so far as women are concerned, does no more than to assure them the rights of citizenship on the same basis as men. It does nothing whatever to protect them against the kind of legislation which Deputy McGilligan now says he is afraid of.'

61 Kohn, *The Constitution of the Irish Free State* (London, 1932) summarised the position thus: 'These privileges comprise the civic and national rights generally inherent in modern citizenship: the franchise, both parliamentary and municipal, eligibility to the legislative, administrative and judicial bodies, a claim to political protection abroad and the right of immunity from deportation.'

While Kohn devotes seven pages to a discussion of Article 3 (pp. 116–123), it is, perhaps, noteworthy that there is no suggestion at all in this discussion that this provision might constitute a free-standing equality guarantee as between men and women.

62 It was agreed (prior to its ultimate deletion) that these words would then be contained in a separate stand-alone Article 3A (subsequently re-numbered as Article 4 before deletion): see 1 *Dáil Debates,* Cols 662–677 (25 September 1922).

63 1 *Dail Debates,* Cols 1667–1685 (18 October 1922). Note, however, that the doctrine of marital coercion – one of the examples given by the minister as to why there should *not* be a free standing equality guarantee – was subsequently held by the Supreme Court to contravene the equality guarantee in Article 40.1 in *The State (Director of Public Prosecutions) v. Walsh* [1981] IR 412.

64 UCD P. 1029. Note, however, the comments of Oran Doyle, *Constitutional Equality Law* (Dublin, 2004), p. 52: 'From the earliest drafts of the new Constitution, it is clear that Hearne and de Valera intended there to be an equality guarantee, formulated in terms of 'equality before the law'. Although this marked a departure from the 1922 Constitution, which ... contained no equality guarantee, it conformed to the European constitutional trend ... Nevertheless, the drafters of the 1922 Constitution had also been aware of that constitutional trend in continental Europe and had chosen not to include an equality guarantee. For this reason, one cannot conclude that the drafters of the 1937 Constitution were merely following a constitutional trend: one is entitled to assume that they

were, albeit to an unascertainable extent, motivated by an egalitarian ideal. That said, their model for Article 40.1 was almost certainly that popular in continental Europe at the time.'

Doyle goes on to reject the argument that the drafters borrowed from the 14th Amendment, partly because they would not have been happy with a judicial interpretation of that clause (*Plessy v. Ferguson* 163 US 537 (1896)) which 'held that racial segregation was fully consonant with equality.' He may well be correct in this assessment, but for our purposes it suffices to note that he fully agrees from a detailed analysis of the drafting of Article 40.1 that this clause was motivated – at least to some degree – by an egalitarian ideal from contemporary constitutional sources, whether continental or American. This is further underscored by the timing of the first draft of the new equality clause (May 1935) and author of the draft (Hearne), i.e., well before the stage in the early months of 1937 when the drafting committee was being required to consult papal encyclicals at the behest of Fr McQuaid.

65 UCD, P. 1079. For a fuller account of this, see Doyle, Oran, *Constitutional Equality Law*, pp. 51–66.

66 68 *Dáil Debates*, Col. 165–166 (9 June 1937).

67 68 *Dáil Debates*, Col. 169–170 (9 June 1937).

68 [1976] IR 38, p. 68.

69 For which see Kelly, pp. 1323–1386 and Doyle, *Constitutional Equality Law* (Dublin, 2004).

70 *Re Article 26 and the Employment Equality Bill 1996* [1997] 2 IR 321, p. 347, per Hamilton CJ.

71 See, e.g., *Somjee v. Minister for Justice* [1981] ILRM 324 (differing arrangements for citizenship of foreign spouses depending on whether they married an Irish man or an Irish woman not unconstitutional); *Norris v. Attorney General* [1984] IR 36 (where a majority of the Supreme Court held that legislation criminalising male (but not female) homosexual conduct was not contrary to Article 40.1).

72 *De Burca v. Attorney General* [1976] IR 38. The decision was also partly based on the nature of the right to jury trial in Article 38.5.

73 *CM v. TM (No.2)* [1990] 2 IR 56; *W v. W* [1993] 2 IR 476.

74 *The State (Director of Public Prosecutions) v. Walsh* [1981] IR 412.

75 *O'G v. An Bord Uchtala* [1985] ILRM 61.

76 *SM v. Ireland (No.2)* [2007] IEHC 000 (19th century legislation providing for a significantly higher penalty where the victim was male held to be contrary to Article 40.1).

77 *Blascaod Mor Teo. v. Commissioners of Public Works in Ireland (No. 3)* [2000] 1 IR 6.

78 *Redmond v. Minister for Environment* [2001] 4 IR 61 (electoral deposits held unconstitutional).

79 *Kelly v. Minister for Environment* [2002] 4 IR 191.

80 Scannell, Yvonne, 'The Constitution and the Role of Women' in Farrell, Brian (ed), *De Valera's Constitution and Ours* (Dublin, 1988), pp. 124–125. Note, however, the comments of Murray J. in *DT v. CT* [2002] 3 IR 334, p. 407: 'The Constitution … is to be inter-

preted as a contemporary document. The duties and obligations of spouses are mutual and, without elaborating further since nothing turns on the point in this case, it seems to me that [the Constitution] implicitly recognises the value of a man's contribution in the home as a parent.'

81 Indeed, as Lee, *op.cit.*, p. 207 observes: 'De Valera's image of woman was widely cherished in Ireland, not least by women themselves.'

82 68 *Dáil Debates*, Col. 242–248 (9 June 1937); Cols. 258–259 (10 June 1937). For the earlier discussion of the merits of Rowlette amendment, see 67 *Dáil Debates*, Cols 1896–1897 (4 June 1937).

83 Ferriter, Diarmuid, *The Transformation of Ireland 1900–2000,* (Profile Books, London, 20004) pp. 421—22 notes that the Joint Committee of Women's Societies and Social Workers wrote to the Government on 24 May 1937 (National Archives S 9880) objecting to the use of the phrase 'the inadequate strength of women' in the original version of Article 45.2.i on the grounds that: 'the question of the adequacy or inadequacy of strength for any particular work is one which arises in the case of men, as much as in the case of women … much of the heaviest work done by women is in the home, or on the farm.'

Ferriter does not, however, mention the fact that these words were ultimately omitted from Article 45.2.i.

84 68 *Debates* at Col. 298 (10 June 1937).

85 Jackson, Alvin, *Ireland 1798–1998* (Blackwell, 1999), p. 297. By contrast, Beaumont, 'Women, Citizenship and Catholicism in the Irish Free State 1922–1948' (1997) 6 *Women's History Review*, p. 563 considered (p. 576) that 'these amendments marked an important victory in the fight for women's rights to equal citizenship in the Irish Free State'.

86 [1972] IR 330.

87 [1972] IR 300 at 336.

88 68 *Dáil Debates* at Col. 120 (9 June 1937).

89 68 *Dáil Debates* at Col. 153 (10 June 1937). De Valera explained his thinking thus (at Cols 153–154: 'This is to make explicit what I think was already implied in the draft which we had – the fact that there should be no law placing any citizen under disability or incapacity on the grounds of sex, or disqualifying any citizen from voting on that ground. It is simply to meet a point raised by one of the Deputies on the opposite benches in connection with Article 16. There was a general right that they would have irrespective of sex, and then there was a clause dealing with disqualifications to be made by law. It was thought important that those disqualifications could not be made on the grounds of sex.'

90 Mulcahy, Siobhán, 'Women, the Constitution and the Law', *Village*, 26 August 2005.

91 Comments of Dr John Regan, at Dr Douglas Hyde Conference, *The Irish Times*, 24 July 2000.

92 Cf. the comments of Ryan, 'Information, Justice and Politics' in Murphy, Tim & Twomey, Patrick (ed.), *Ireland's Evolving Constitution, 1937–1997: Collected Essays* (Oxford, 1998) pp. 237–8: 'For many in Ireland, an economic and cultural conservatism was identified as overlaying, and, indeed, flowing from, the sectarian character of the Constitution. Of course, the association of the Constitution with Éamon de Valera and with the 1930s is readily interpreted as further confirmation, if such be needed, of anachronism and sectarianism. As a result, a large section of liberal Ireland now appears to subscribe to the view that we need a 'new' or 'modern' or 'simplified' Constitution. By this method, the embarrassment of sectarianism and the overtones of the 1930s' corporatism which some identify could be expunged.'

93 For some other (necessarily incomplete) accounts of the drafting process, see also, Faughnan, 'The Jesuits and the Irish Constitution' (1988), 26 *Irish Historical Studies,* 7, p. 9; Kennedy, 'John Hearne and the Irish Constitution' (1989), 24 *Eire–Ireland,* p. 121; Hogan 'The Constitution Review Committee of 1934' in Ó Muircheartaigh, ed., *Ireland in the Coming Times: Essays to Celebrate TK Whitaker's 80 Years* (IPA, 1997); Hogan, 'Directive Principles, Socio-Economic Rights and the Constitution' (2001), *36 Irish Jurist,* p. 174.

94 Whyte, *Church & State in Modern Ireland,* p. 409.

95 Hogan, 'The Constitution Review Committee of 1934' in O Muircheartaigh, ed., *Ireland in the Coming Times: Essays to Celebrate TK Whitaker's 80 Years* (IPA, 1997), p. 360.

96 Note the comments of rapporteurs to the *Fifth International Congress of the International Secretariat of Lawyers of Pax Romana* (1966), quoted in Golding, *George Gavan Duffy 1882–1951* (Dublin, 1982), p. 134): '… depending on the glasses through which ones reads them, [Articles 41 and 42 of] the Constitution may appear as a set of liberal republican principles or as a solid mass of Catholic Doctrine.'

97 Hogan, 'The Constitution, Property Rights and Proportionality' (1997) 32 *Irish Jurist* 373, p. 376.

98 Coogan, *Long Fellow, Long Shadow,* p. 494.

99 [1990] 2 IR 52.

100 [1990] 2 IR 52 at 63, per Barr J.

101 Whyte, *Church & State in Modern Ireland,* p. 409.

102 Other historians had, however, been more perceptive. Lyons had earlier noted (*Ireland since the Famine,* p. 545) that the Constitution had attempted 'to combine the liberal, democratic mode in which such declarations were commonly expressed with a very specific Catholic content.' Brown, *Ireland: A Social and Cultural History 1922–2002* (London, 2004), describes (p. 152) the fundamental rights provisions of the Constitution as a: 'curious amalgam of ideas … Enshrined in its various clauses are ideas familiar from the liberal tradition together with ideas drawn directly from Catholic social thought …'

Even lawyers who are critical of Mr de Valera fully acknowledge the liberal democratic influence of the fundamental rights provisions of the Constitution. Thus, Bacik, *Kicking and Screaming* (p. 25), notes that these provisions 'are strongly influenced by liberal-democratic values, emphasising the autonomy of the individual and ensuring the protection of classic civil and political freedoms.' See also the comments of Flynn, 'From Individual Protection to Recognition of Relationships? Same-Sex Couples and the Irish Experience of Sexual Orientation Law Reform' in Wintemute and Andenaes, eds, *Legal Recognition of Same-Sex Partnerships: A Study of National; European and International*

Law (Hart Publishing, 2002), p. 592: 'The 1937 Constitution … was in many ways a progressive document for its time. Almost alone among the European States revising their basic laws in the 1930s, it enshrined a separation of powers, instituted judicial review of legislation's constitutionality, and entrenched a bill of personal rights.'

103 Gallagher, 'The Constitution and the Judiciary', p. 97.

104 Keogh, *Irish Constitutional Revolution,* p. 65.

105 Cf. the comments of O'Dowd, 'Equality in Irish Constitutional and Administrative Law' (1999) *European Review of Public Law,* pp. 769, 799: 'Overall, a fair assessment of the debates [on the Constitution] would seem to be that de Valera often showed a better grasp of the fundamental issues of constitution-making that his critics at the time or since have been disposed to give him credit for.'

106 Hogan, 'The Constitution Review Committee of 1934' in Ó Muircheartaigh, ed., *Ireland in the Coming Times: Essays to Celebrate TK Whitaker's 80 Years* (IPA, 1987), p. 361.

CHAPTER 1

1 For useful background reading and analysis of the circumstances of this election, see Fanning, Ronan, *The Four Leafed Shamrock: Electoral Politics and the National Imagination in Independent Ireland* (NUI, Dublin, 1983), p. 10; see also Lee, Joseph, *Ireland 1912–1985: Politics and Society* (Cambridge University Press, Cambridge, 1989), pp. 168ff.

2 McMahon, Deirdre, *Republicans and Imperialists: Anglo-Irish relations in the 1930s* (Yale University Press, New Haven and London, 1984), p. 4.

3 *Ibid.*, p. 30. 'Lunatic', 'crank', 'dreamer' and 'visionary' were some of the terms used to describe de Valera in British papers.

4 Cited in Mansergh, Nicholas, *The Unresolved Question: The Anglo Irish Settlement and its Undoing* (Yale University Press, New Haven and London, 1991), p. 282.

5 Fanning, Ronan, '"The Rule of Order": Éamon de Valera and the IRA 1923–1940', in John P. O'Carroll and John A. Murphy (eds), *De Valera and his Times* (Cork University Press, Cork, 1983), p. 161

6 The fullest account of the drafting of the 1922 constitution and its political effects is in Farrell, Brian, 'The Drafting of the Irish Free State Constitution,' *Irish Jurist*, Vols V, VI, Nos 1–2 (Summer–Winter 1970–1971).

7 Kohn, Leo, *The Constitution of the Irish Free State* (George Allen and Irwin, London, 1932), p. 50.

8 *Ibid.*, p. 80.

9 Cited in Moynihan, Maurice (ed.), *Speeches and Statements by Éamon de Valera* (Gill & Macmillan, Dublin, 1980), p. 162.

10 *Ibid.*, p. 163.

11 Mansergh, Nicholas, *The Commonwealth Experience* (Weidenfeld and Nicolson, London, 1969), p. 203.

12 See Harkness, David, *The Restless Dominion: The Irish Free State and the British Commonwealth of Nations, 1921–31* (New York University Press, New York, 1970). This study gives a detailed account of Irish input into constitutional commonwealth developments in this period.

13 Harkness, *Restless Dominion*, p. 13.

14 Sexton, Brendan, *Ireland and the Crown, 1922–1936: The Governo-Generalship of The Irish Free State* (Irish Academic Press, Dublin, 1989), p. 174.

15 Cited in Ward, Alan J., *The Irish Constitutional Tradition: Responsible Government and Modern Ireland, 1782–1992* (Irish Academic Press, Dublin, 1994), p. 225.

16 Mansergh, *The Unresolved Question*, p. 289, points out: 'If the first wave of the Irish struggle had been memorable for its violence, the next was unprecedented in its exploitation of constitutional devices which almost fortuitously laid ready to hand. In de Valera the moment had its man'.

17 External association meant that Ireland would be associated with, but not a member of, the states of the commonwealth for certain purposes, and for these purposes 'Ireland shall recognise His Britannic Majesty as Head of the Association'.

18 For a reproduction of the election manifesto, see Moynihan, *Speeches*, pp. 188–91.

19 *Ibid.*

20 The money was collected by the Irish Land Commission from the tenant farmers and transferred to the British government. Fianna Fáil argued that these payments were neither morally or legally due and that any inter-governmental agreement was made without requisite parliamentary approval and therefore was not binding. The view of Cosgrave's government was that the annuities were collected from the farmers for the purpose of repaying with interest to the holders of land bonds the money, which had been raised to finance the transfer of holdings from landlords to tenants. According to the latter view, neither the British nor the Irish governments was more than an intermediary in the process of payment by the tenant purchasers to their ultimate creditors, the bondholders. The payments had been the subject of two financial agreements: one in 1923, the other in 1926. Neither agreement had been ratified by the Dáil as both should have been.

21 *Round Table*, (June 1932), p. 496. *Round Table*, Britain's oldest international affairs journal, was founded in 1910 to provide analysis and commentary on all aspects of international affairs. Its subtitle was 'The Commonwealth Journal of International Affairs'. Its Irish correspondent was John J. Horgan, (1881–1967), a solicitor, writer and public figure in his native Cork, who was born into a Parnellite tradition. He combined a busy legal practice with public service as the county coroner for Cork and was also a member of the harbour commissioners. His writings, which ranged from Catholic apologetics through local government (particularly in *Studies* in the 1920s and 1930s) to commentaries on national politics, are now regarded as an invaluable source because they were highly accurate and, to a considerable extent, objective accounts of the political and economic history of his period. He is the author of *From Parnell to Pearse* (1948) and was the Irish correspondent to *Round Table* for many years where his numerous anonymous contributions displayed perspicacity sometimes combined with an acerbic wit. He also wrote for the *Belfast Telegraph*.

22 On 14 October 1931 Article 2A was debated in the Dáil. De Valera rejected as inappropriate the introduction of this measure since it ignored the fundamental cause of the trouble: 'The right way of proceeding is to end the necessity for such organisations ... all the laws in the world are not going to prevent it unless you remedy the causes.' Cited in Moynihan, *Speeches*, pp. 186–7.

23 *Round Table*, (June 1932), p. 496.

24 *Ibid.*, (March 1932), pp. 369–70.

25 Keogh, Dermot, *Twentieth-Century Ireland, Nation and State* (Gill and Macmillan, Dublin, 1994), p. 38.

26 *Ibid.*, p. 62.

27 Lee, *Ireland 1912–1985*, p. 169.

28 See Manning, Maurice, *The Blueshirts* (Gill and Macmillan, Dublin, 1971 [1987 edn]), p. 17.

29 McMahon, *Republicans and Imperialists*, pp. 16–22; Manning, *The Blueshirts*, pp. 18–19.

30 Radio broadcast, 4 March 1932, cited in Moynihan, *Speeches*, p. 190.

31 *Round Table*, (June 1932), p. 510.

32 *Times*, 22 February 1932.

33 Ronan Fanning wrote: 'The amputation of Partition compounded the savage and bloody injuries inflicted on the body politic by the Civil War. Together they created not only a divided nation but a state so bitterly split that a large proportion of its citizens paid it no more than a grudging allegiance, while a smaller number continued to claim the right to bear arms against it.' See Fanning, Ronan, 'Mr. De Valera Drafts a Constitution', in Brian Farrell (ed.), *De Valera's Constitution and Ours* (Gill and Macmillan, Dublin, 1988), p. 42.

34 Fanning, Ronan *The Four Leafed Shamrock*, pp. 3–8.

35 Quoted in Ward, *The Irish Constitutional Tradition*, p. 170.

36 Lyons, F. S. L., *Ireland Since the Famine* (Fontana, London (Revised), 1973), p. 521. See also Keogh, *Twentieth Century Ireland*, p. 67.

37 Harkness, David, 'Mr. De Valera's Dominion: Ireland's relations with Britain and the Commonwealth, 1932–1938', *Journal of Commonwealth Political Studies*, Vol. VIII. No. 3 (November 1970), pp. 206–8.

38 *Round Table*, (February 1932), pp. 374-75.

39 *Ibid.*, (August 1932), p. 761.

40 Bowyer Bell, J., *The Secret Army: The IRA, 1916–1979* (Poolbeg Press, Dublin, 1989), gives a detailed account of the IRA.

41 *Round Table*, (May 1932), p. 510.

42 McMahon, *Republicans and Imperialists*, pp. 50–2.

43 *Round Table*, (September 1932), p. 748.

44 *Ibid.*, (June 1932), p. 490.

45 Mansergh, *The Unresolved Question*, p. 284.

46 *Round Table*, (May 1932), p. 501.

47 *Ibid.*, (August 1932), p. 759.

48 *Ibid.*, (November 1932), pp. 139-40.

49 *Ibid.*, (February 1933), p. 29.

50 *Ibid.*

51 Bowyer Bell, J., *The Secret Army*, p. 104.

52 *Irish Press*, 12 January 1933.

53 *Round Table*, (June 1933), p. 638.

54 *Irish Press*, 21 January 1933.

55 *Dáil debates*, Vol. 1, Col. 1,404.

56 See Ward, *The Irish Constitutional Tradition*, p. 233.

57 Sexton, *Ireland and the Crown*, p. 122.

58 Memorandum by Thomas for British cabinet, November 1933, cited in McMahon, *Republicans and Imperialists*, p. 130.

59 Cited in McMahon, *Republicans and Imperialists*, p. 129.

60 These developments are discussed in further detail in Chapter 2.

61 See McMahon, *Republicans and Imperialists*, p. 129f for a detailed account of these events.

62 *Ibid.* De Valera claimed that the communications to be published were state papers and in vain attempted to prevent the press publishing them.

63 Sexton, *Ireland and the Crown*, pp. 135–8.

64 *Round Table*, (June 1933), pp. 646–8.

65 *Ibid.*, (February 1932), p. 298.

66 Bowyer Bell, *The Secret Army*, p. 99.

67 Manning, *The Blueshirts*, p. 182.

68 *Round Table*, (February 1935), p. 381.

69 Coogan, Tim Pat, *The IRA* (Fontana, London, 1987), p. 153.

70 McMahon, *Republicans and Imperialists*, p. 156.

71 Bowyer Bell, *The Secret Army*, p. 118.

72 Manning, *The Blueshirts*, p. 33.

73 *Round Table*, (November 1932), p. 126.

74 The organisation was founded on 1 February 1932 and its first president was Colonel Austin Brennan. Its objective was to uphold the state and to honour Volunteers who had died in the Anglo-Irish war. Initially it was no more than a club for ex-officers and men of the Free State army. But in August the body opened its ranks to the public and the new body was claiming membership of 30,000.

75 Manning, *The Blueshirts*, p. 27.

76 *Irish Times*, 21 July 1933.

77 See Manning, *The Blueshirts*, Chapter 4 for a detailed account of the circumstances of dismissal and transition to ACA leadership role.

78 *Irish Times*, 12 August 1933.

79 Cited in Manning, *The Blueshirts*, p. 77.

80 Cited in *Round Table*, (November 1933), p. 167.

81 Keogh, *Twentieth Century Ireland*, p. 81.

82 *Irish Times*, 23 August 1933.

83 *Round Table*, (November 1933), p. 172.

84 Bowyer Bell, *The Secret Army*, p. 108.

85 Manning, *The Blueshirts*, p. 110.

86 See O'Leary, Don, *Vocationalism and Social Catholicism in Twentieth- Century Ireland: The Search for a Christian Social Order* (Irish Academic Press, Dublin, 2000), for comprehensive treatment of this topic.

87 Cited in Manning, *The Blueshirts*, p. 130.

88 Bowyer Bell, *The Secret Army*, p. 108.

89 *Round Table*, (February 1934), p. 368.

90 Regan, John M., *The Irish Counter-Revolution 1921–1936: Treatyite Politics and Settlement in Independent Ireland* (Gill & Macmillan, Dublin, 1999), p. 352.

91 Manning, *The Blueshirts*, p. 227.

92 See Manning, *The Blueshirts*, Chapters 8 and 9 for in-depth coverage of the background to these events.

93 *Round Table*, (November 1934), pp. 155-160.

94 Manning, *The Blueshirts*, p. 195.

95 *Round Table*, (November 1934), p. 160.

96 Maurice Manning notes that the Blueshirts never conformed to the European fascist model; they were an organisation derived from the particular circumstances of the civil war. Joseph Lee, in *Ireland 1912-1985*, p. 181, supports this view, adding: 'The Blueshirts deviated widely from the standard fascist model. The shirt and the salute marked the summit of their ideological achievement.'

97 O'Leary, *Vocationalism and Social Catholicism*, p. 40.

98 *Ibid.*, p. 38.

99 *Ibid.*, p. 41.

100 Cited in O' Leary, *Vocationalism and Social Catholicism*, p. 48.

101 Lyons, *Ireland Since the Famine*, p. 517.

102 McMahon, *Republicans and Imperialists*, p. 288.

103 Keogh, *Twentieth Century Ireland*, pp. 71–2.

104 Contrary to popular perception the governor general was not removed in this act. This did not happen until the Consequential Provision Act of June 1937. The delay can be attributed to the death of the chief justice, Hugh Kennedy, who died just as the act was

going through the Dáil and the royal instructions accompanying the governors general letters of patent stipulated that Kennedy's successor had to take the prescribed oath of office before the governor general.

105 Cited in Mansergh, *The Unresolved Question*, p. 297.

106 Longford, Earl of and O'Neill, Thomas P., *Éamon de Valera*, Vol. 2 (Houghton Mifflin, Boston, 1971), p. 289.

107 *Ibid.*, p. 290.

108 *Dáil debates*, Vol. 62, Col. 1, 99, 28 May 1936.

109 *Ibid.*, Col. 1,343.

110 *Seanad debates*, Vol. 20, Cols. 2,433–6, 19 May 1936.

111 See Brian Farrell, 'From First Dáil through Irish Free State', in B. Farrell (ed.), *De Valera's Constitution*, p. 30.

CHAPTER 2

1 This bill, designed to remove the Senate from the constitution, did not become law until 29 May 1936.

2 *Dáil debates*, Vol. 52, Col. 1,169, 17 May 1934.

3 *Ibid.* Article 50 read: 'Amendments of this Constitution within the terms of the Scheduled Treaty may be made by the Oireachtas, but no such amendment passed by both Houses of the Oireachtas after the expiration of a period of [eight] sixteen years [Amendment no. 16 Act] from the date of the coming into operation of this Constitution, shall become law, unless the same shall, after it has passed or deemed to have been passed by the said two Houses of the Oireachtas, have been submitted to a Referendum of the people ...'.

4 *Dáil debates*, Vol. 52, Cols. 1,192–3, 17 May 1934.

5 *Ibid.*, Vol. 52, Col. 1,249, 17 May 1934.

6 Moynihan, Maurice (ed.), *Speeches and Statements by Éamon de Valera 1917–73* (Gill and Macmillan, Dublin, 1980) p. 237.

7 Andrews, C. S., *Man of No Property* (Mercier Press, Dublin, 1982) p. 253.

8 Cited in Kennedy, Brian P., 'Appreciation: John Hearne and the Irish Constitution', in *Éire-Ireland*, Vol. XXIV, No. 2. 1990, p. 122.

9 Mansergh, Diana (ed.), *Nationalism and Independence: Selected Papers of Nicholas Mansergh* (Cork University Press, Cork, 1997), p. 122.

10 *Irish Times*, 25 February 1987.

11 *Ibid.*

12 See *Irish Independent*, *Irish Press* and *Irish Times* for 17 August 1954 and *Irish Times*, 2 September 1954. The three accounts of his career published on 17 August were obviously derived from a press release announcing his impending retirement as the wording in each was almost identical. He was described as 'closely associated with the framing of the Constitution'.

13 The information on Roche was obtained mainly from *Irish Times*, 24 January 1949 and letter to Dermot Keogh from the Department of Justice, 18 April 2002.

14 The following biography was provided by Irene Lynch who describes her relationship to him as follows: 'Paddy Lynch, KC was the uncle of my grandfather, John Bernard (JB) Lynch. His brother, Thomas Alfred Lynch was my great grandfather. My grandfather was born at 5 Bindon Street, Ennis in 1884. When his own father, Thomas Lynch died in October 1903, John Bernard was in the middle of his studies and was financially helped by his uncle, Paddy Lynch, KC to continue his studies. John Bernard Lynch married Helen (Ellen) Glynn and they had eight children, my father Ignatius (Kevin) Lynch, being the youngest.'

15 Family records held by Irene Lynch's father, Ignatius Kevin Lynch, illustrate that Paddy Lynch's nephew, JB Lynch (Irene's grandfather), who was then qualified and practising as a solicitor in Ennis, had advised against opposing de Valera in the East Clare by-election of 1917. JB Lynch had expressed worries that given the new political mood of the time Paddy Lynch's opposition to Éamon de Valera would be detrimental to her grandfather's own practice and work.

16 [1921] 2 IR 241.

17 Kelly, J. M., *The Irish Constitution* (Hogan and Whyte, 3rd Ed, Butterworths, Dublin, 1994), p. 2,175. One of the most historically significant developments must be the enactment of the First Amendment of the Constitution Act, 1939. It was presented as a bill and passed by both houses of the oireachtas, and signed by the President on 2 September 1939, the day after Germany invaded Poland and the day before France and Britain declared war. The same day, immediately after the passing of the first amendment, both houses of the oireachtas passed the resolutions contemplated in the article: that a national emergency existed. The Emergency Powers Act, 1939 was passed the following day. Further acts of the same title were passed between 1940 and 1945 and the original legislation remained in force until it expired in 1946. The resolutions of the houses, that a national emergency existed, remained in force until 1976, when both houses made new resolutions in response to the conflict in Northern Ireland.

18 Initialled memorandum, 24 May 1934, D/T S2679.

19 Dáil Éireann, *Parliamentary Debates Official Report,* Vol. 51, Col. 2,480, 26 April 1934.

20 Constitution Committee 1934, Report on Part 1 of Terms of Reference, 3 July 1934, D/T S1979.

21 Constitution (Amendment No. 17) Act, 1931 inserted Article 2A into the constitution.

22 *Ibid.*

23 NAI D/T S2979. The minutes, memoranda and the report of the constitution committee 1934. There is one study of the work of the committee by Hogan, Gerard, 'The Constitution Review Committee of 1934', in Ó Muirheartaigh, Fionan, *Ireland in the Coming Times: Essays to Celebrate TK Whitaker's 80 Years* (Dublin, IPA, 1997).

24 NAI D/T S2979. Minutes of second meeting of constitution committee, 29 May 1934.

25 McDunphy noted on the file relating to the 1934 committee that no action had been taken on 'Part II of the Committee's terms of reference. The matter gradually became

Government policy and was dealt with on that basis.' Cited in Hogan, 'The Constitution Review Committee', p. 351.

26 NAI D/T S2979. Report of Committee on Part 1 of its terms of Reference Appendix A.

27 NAI D/T S2979. Interdepartmental Committee on the Constitution Note with Special Reference to Article 2A by Mr Roche, 14 June 1934.

28 NAI D/T S2979. Report of Committee on Part 1 of its terms of Reference Appendix B Emergency Powers.

29 NAI D/T S2979. Report of the Committee on Part 1 of its terms of Reference, 3 July 1934.

30 See the explanatory note drawn up on 28 December 1957 by the Department of the Taoiseach in UCDA De Valera papers P150/1090.

31 UCDA P150 De Valera papers 1029/6 Explanatory Memorandum – Draft of Heads of the Constitution, 18 May 1935.

32 *Ibid.*

33 De Valera Annotation on UCDA P150 De Valera papers 1029/6. Draft of Heads of the Constitution, 18 May 1935.

34 *Ibid.*

35 DDE Vol. 56, Col. 2,088, 29 May 1935.

36 *Ibid*, Col. 2,089–91, 29 May 1935.

37 Mansergh, Nicholas, *The Commonwealth Experience* (Weidenfeld and Nicolson, London, 1969), p. 241.

38 *Round Table*, (December 1935), p. 138.

39 Longford, Earl of and O'Neill, Thomas P., *Éamon De Valera* (Hutchinson, London, 1970), p. 422.

40 UCDA P150 De Valera papers 1046. Memorandum sent to His Majesty the King on 8 June.

41 UCDA P150 De Valera papers 1029/1. Department of the Taoiseach T54/1. Constitution of Éire – early Drafts (English).

42 UCDA P150 De Valera papers 1029/1.

43 The origins of some of these phrases can be found in a 1923 document in which de Valera, as the head of the self styled 'Government of the Republic' put forward his principles for a negotiated end to the civil war. See Moynihan, *Speeches and Statements*, p. 113. In that document, as in the constitution, the emphasis was on sovereignty and the fact that the people were the ultimate court of appeal for all questions of national policy. It is worth noting that the claim to Northern Ireland is not contained in these rough notes. This appears to have emerged later, sometime in October 1936.

44 UCDA P150 De Valera papers 1060. 'First Draft'. No date.

45 O'Rahilly would appear to have had an influence on the social provisions. Article 64 of the O'Rahilly constitution stated that: '(1) Ownership, inheritance, distribution and use of land are superintended by the State, so as to ensure to every citizen a healthy residence,

and to secure an efficient exploitation of the soil and in the interests of the community. (2) The land holder is bound, in duty to the community, to secure a reasonably efficient working or utilisation of the land. (3) Increase in the value of the land arising without expenditure of labour or capital thereon shall accrue to the community.'

46 UCDA P150 De Valera papers 1060. 'First Draft'.

47 UCDA P150 De Valera papers 1029/3/1, August 1936.

48 UCDA P150 De Valera papers 1060. 'First Draft'.

49 UCDA P150 De Valera papers 1976/2.

50 UCDA P150 De Valera papers 1050/2, 5 November 1936.

51 *Ibid.*

52 Fr Paddy O'Donoghue, CM, son of Philip O'Donoghue, in conversation with Dermot Keogh. Letter from Fr O'Donoghue to Dermot Keogh, 18 October 2001.

53 UCDA P176/444 Meeting of Fianna Fáil parliamentary party, 12 March 1936.

54 Second house of the oireachtas commission 1936.

55 Report of the commission, 6-12.

56 Additional report from chairman, 18–25.

57 Report by D.A. Binchy, Sir John Keane, E. Lynch, F. MacDermott, J. Moynihan, A. O'Rahilly, M. Tierney, R. Wilson, 26–33.

58 This is the scheme outlined in the UCDA P150 De Valera papers 1029/8/1. There is a handwritten mark 18/11 on the file which very likely refers to the date it was completed or circulated.

59 MacEntee papers. P67/185. MacEntee to De Valera 13 November 1936.

60 Lee, *Ireland, 1912–85*, pp.272–3.

61 *Dáil debates*, 11 December 1936 Vol. 64, Col. 1,230.

62 *Ibid.*, Col. 1,281.

63 Constitution (Amendment No. 27) Act, 1936.

64 During his speech on the second reading of the bills, President de Valera informed the house that the purpose of the two bills was not to administer a 'slap in the face to anybody' but to assert 'our right; and so we are doing this positive act of our own, and doing it under certain conditions, clearly setting down what those conditions are, so that there can be no misinterpretation. That is the purpose of the two bills. That is why they are linked together. I certainly – and this Government – would not take responsibility for one without the other.' As quoted in Moynihan, *Speeches and Statements*, p. 293.

65 *Dáil debates*, 11 December 1936, Vol. 64, Col. 1,280.

66 *Ibid.*, 12 December 1936, Vol. 64, Cols. 1,385–6.

67 *Ibid.*, Col. 1,469.

68 *Ibid.*, Cols. 1,471–2.

69 Note by Michael McDunphy, 22 December 1936, NAI D/T S 8946.

70 John Hearne to Seán Moynihan, 6 August 1936, UCDAD, P150/029. Hearne forwarded a copy of the draft bill entitled 'An Act to make provision in accordance with the

constitution for the exercise and performance of certain of the constitutional rights and functions of Éire in the domain of foreign relations.'

71 *Ibid.*

72 *Ibid.*

73 *Ibid.*

74 Mansergh, Nicholas, 'External Relations 1926–1939', in Diana Mansergh (ed.), *Nationalism and Independence* (Cork University Press, Cork, 1997), p. 114.

75 DVP 1049, 2 January 1937.

CHAPTER 3

1 This chapter was worked on by Dr Carmel Quinlan based substantially on archives collected by Dermot Keogh and copied from the Cahill papers, Jesuit Archives, 35 Lower Leeson Street, Dublin. Dr Quinlan compiled the profiles of the individual Jesuits who worked on the committee set up by the order. See Keogh, Dermot, 'The Jesuits and the 1937 Constitution', *Studies*, (Spring 1989); Keogh, Dermot, 'The Irish Constitutional Revolution', *Administration*, 1987, vol. 35; and Faughnan, Seán, 'The Jesuits and the Irish Constitution', *Irish Historical Studies*, 25, 1987. An Rioghacht was formed on 31 October 1926 in Dublin. It was modelled on the *Volksverein* and other Catholic Action associations in Germany and Italy. Its objects were to make Catholic social principles better known among the Irish; to strive to make those principles effective in Irish public life and, finally, to promote Catholic social action. The organisation never won mass support in Ireland. The minutes of the Jesuit Committee were located by Fr Fergal McGrath following an inquiry from Dermot Keogh. The material was not in the archive and had to be located from elsewhere - probably the Provincial Archive. For many years, the relevant material was left in the archive with the name Dermot Keogh attached.

2 Fitzpatrick, D., *The Two Irelands, 1912–1939* (Oxford University Press, Oxford:, 1998), p. 230.

3 Edward Cahill to de Valera, 22 March 1932. Edward Cahill papers, Jesuit Archives, 35 Lower Leeson Street, Dublin.

4 Edward Cahill to de Valera, 4 February 1933. *Ibid.*

5 Translation: 'It is worth reading and rereading and in my opinion one could return to it often for advice and guidance.' De Valera to Edward Cahill, 2 August 1932. *Ibid.*

6 Keogh, Dermot, 'The Irish Constitutional Revolution: An Analysis of the Making of the Constitution', *Administration*, Vol. 35, No. 4 (1987), pp. 4–84 at pp. 11–19.

7 Edward Cahill to de Valera, 7 July 1934. Edward Cahill papers, Jesuit Archives, 35 Lower Leeson Street, Dublin.

8 De Valera to Edward Cahill, 11 July 1934. *Ibid.*

9 De Valera to Edward Cahill, 19 September 1936. *Ibid.*

10 Edward Cahill to de Valera, 21 September 1936. *Ibid.*

11 Patrick Bartley to Fr Provincial, 11 October 1936. *Ibid.*

12 Report of the Jesuit committee. *Ibid.*

13 Obituary in *Irish Province News*, IV:4, (October 1941), p. 574.

14 See Cahill, Edward, *Ireland's Peril* (An Rioghacht pamphlet, Dublin, 1930); *Freemasonry and the anti-Christian Movement* (An Rioghacht pamphlet, Dublin, 1929); *The Truth about Freemasonry* (CTS Australia, n.d.); and *The Framework of the Christian State* (Gill, Dublin, 1932).

15 Cahill, *The Framework of the Christian State*, pp. 229, 233.

16 Cahill, Edward, 'The Irish National Tradition', *Irish Ecclesiastical Record*, 5th series, 46 (July–Dec 1935), p. 4.

17 Cahill, Edward, 'The Irish in the Early Middle Ages', *Irish Ecclesiastical Record*, 5th series, 46 (July–Dec 1935), p. 363.

18 Cahill, Edward, 'The Influence of Ireland on Medieval Europe', *Irish Ecclesiastical Record*, 5th series, 46 (July–Dec 1935), p. 473.

19 Obituary of Fr Cahill, *Irish Province News*, IV:4, (October 1941), p. 574.

20 *Ibid.*, p. 575.

21 Biographical information on Fr Canavan compiled from information in Jesuit Archives, 35 Lower Leeson Street, Dublin.

22 For an account of the 1936 summer school, see *The Clongownian*, Vol. XIV, No.3 (June 1937).

23 See Longford and O'Neill, *Éamon de Valera*, p. 295.

24 A succinct summary of these two papers is available in *The Clongownian* (1937), pp. 10–11.

25 The Jesuit constitution committee, 24 September–18 October 1936: Minutes, session 1, 24 Sept. 1936. Edward Cahill papers, Jesuit Archives, 35 Lower Leeson Street, Dublin.

26 Bartley to provincial, Lawrence Kieran, 11 October 1936. Edward Cahill papers, Jesuit Archives, 35 Lower Leeson Street, Dublin

27 *Ibid.*

28 *Ibid.*

29 Bartley to provincial, 15 October 1936. *Ibid.*

30 Provincial to Edward Cahill, 16 October 1936. *Ibid.*

31 The submission, as it was finally made to de Valera by Cahill, was changed somewhat from the wording agreed to by the committee. Cahill had included the wording: 'We, the people of Ireland, being the parent nation of the Irish race mindful of the long centuries of persecution we have had to endure ...' That phrase was – in amended form – to remain in the early draft of the preamble. The phrase which ultimately appeared in the preamble, 'who sustained our fathers through centuries of trial', is not in meaning unlike the phrase quoted above. The first line of the Jesuit preamble was based on the Austrian constitution of 1934, and the preamble and Article 54 in the Polish constitution of 1921.

32 Edward Cahill to de Valera, 21 October 1936. Edward Cahill papers, Jesuit Archives, 35 Lower Leeson Street, Dublin.

33 Jesuit submission. *Ibid.*

34 Cahill to de Valera, 13 November 1936, De Valera papers, UCDA P150/2393.

CHAPTER 4

1 The following biography is based on the Blackrock College annual of 1973 and *The Irish Times*, 9 April 1973.

2 Farragher, Seán, 'Dr McQuaid, Éamon de Valera and the Constitution', *Blackrock College Annual* 1987.

3 The envelope is in the DDA McQuaid papers.

4 UCDA P150/2395, McQuaid to de Valera, 16 February 1937.

5 *Ibid.* P150/2406, March 1937.

6 *Ibid.* P150/2411, 'Directive Principles'.

7 *Ibid.* P150/2395, McQuaid to de Valera, 10 March 1936 [this appears to have been incorrectly dated to 1936 by McQuaid; his involvement in the drafting of the constitution did not begin until late 1936 so this letter was most likely written on 10 March 1937].

8 An incomplete draft which is identical to the Nov/Dec draft stops at Part VIII. It has the following written of the last page: 'Part IX etc. given to Dr McQuaid', *Ibid.* P150/2371.

9 *Ibid.* P150/2395, McQuaid to de Valera.

10 Horgan, John, *Seán Lemass, The Enigmatic Patriot* (Gill and Macmillan, Dublin, 1997), p. 151.

11 UCDA P150/2395, McQuaid to de Valera, 16 February 1937.

12 *Ibid.*, McQuaid to de Valera, 8 March 1937.

13 *Ibid.*

14 *Ibid.*, McQuaid to de Valera, 16 March 1937.

15 *Ibid.* P150/2407, McQuaid to de Valera, 25 March 1937. By 'auspicious days' McQuaid was referring to the fact that it was Holy Thursday and also the Feast of the Annunciation.

16 *Ibid.* P150/2411, McQuaid's extract from *Humanun Genus* and *Rerum Novarum.*

17 *Ibid.* P150/2411, undated from McQuaid to de Valera.

18 *Ibid.*, McQuaid extract from *Rerum Novarum.*

19 *Ibid.* P150/2387, marked 'X, Part IX'. Most likely from draft of 5 February 1937.

20 Judicial activism since the 1960s enabled the discovery of a broad tranche of personal rights under Article 40.3 which were not specified in that article or elsewhere in the constitution. These have become known as 'unenumerated rights'.

21 O'Rahilly/Murnaghan, Draft 'C', quoted in Farrell, B., 'The Drafting of the Irish Free State Constitution: III', *The Irish Jurist* , Vol. 6 (New Series), Part I (Summer 1971), p. 133.

22 UCDA P150/2373, October draft. The parts marked in italics didn't survive future drafting.

23 Jesuit submission on the constitution, Article II Marriage, Edward Cahill papers, Jesuit Archives, 35 Lower Leeson Street, Dublin.

24 The wording in italics is changed in the 1937 constitution; it becomes 'to engage in labour to the neglect of their duties in the home'.

25 UCDA P150/2387, 'X Formula', Part IX.

26 *Ibid.* P150/2411, McQuaid extract from *Rerum Novarum.*

27 *Ibid.* P150/2408.

28 *Ibid.*

29 *Ibid.* P150/2411, typed document entitled 'Rights of Women', offers a strong defence of Article 40.

30 *Ibid.* P150/2411.

31 *Dáil debates*, Vol. 67, Col. 67, 11 May 1937.

32 *Ibid.*, Vol. 67, Col. 1,866, 4 June 1937.

33 *Ibid.*, Col. 1,868.

34 UCDA P150/2409. McQuaid's dossier on education contains a series of quotations from papal encyclicals, especially *Divini Illius Magistri.*

35 *Divini Illius Magistri*, 48.

36 UCDA P150/2409.

37 Jesuit submission on the constitution, Education, Article IV(e), Edward Cahill papers, Jesuit Archives, 35 Lower Leeson Street, Dublin.

38 *Ibid.*, Education, Article IV(a).

39 UCDA P150/2395, McQuaid to de Valera, 16 February 1937.

40 *Ibid.*, 17 February 1937.

41 *Ibid.*, 8 March 1937.

42 *Ibid.*

43 UCDA P150/2395, McQuaid to de Valera, no date.

44 McDonagh, Enda, 'Church and State in the Constitution of Ireland', *Irish Theological Quarterly*, Vol. 28, No. 2 (1961), p. 131.

CHAPTER 5

1 Cabinet minutes. Cab 7/599, 12.3.37. Item 3. D/T S9711.

2 Department of Taoiseach memorandum undated: 'Constitution, 1937: Drafting, Enactment and Operation', D/T, S9748.

3 *Ibid.*

4 Roinn an Taoisigh, fax to Dermot Keogh, 10 October 2002.

5 Roinn an Taoisigh, fax to Dermot Keogh, 10 October 2002.

6 Cited in O'Halloran, Marie, 'Central Bank ex-Governor, Maurice Moynihan, dies', *Irish Times*, 23 August 1999.

7 Patrick Lynch, 'Draft Moynihan Obituary', personal communication to J. P. McCarthy, February 2000.

8 He was the recipient of many honours, including an honorary doctorate in economic science from the National University of Ireland (1955) and the papal title of Knight Commander of the Order of St Gregory the Great (1959). 'Obituaries – Dr Maurice Moynihan', *Irish Times*, 28 August 1999.

9 Response of the Department of Finance to the first printed draft of the construction, 23 March 1937. D/T S9715B.

10 Anon. 'Silhouette: J. J. MacElligott', *Administration*, Vol. 1, No. 1 (1953), p. 67.

11 *Ibid.*, p. 68.

12 Department of Finance's response to the first draft of the constitution, 23 March 1937. D/T S9715B.

13 Department of Finance's response to the first draft of the constitution, 23 March 1937. D/T S9715B, Par. 4. Finance's remarks on Articles 1–3 in its commentary on individual articles of the constitution also draw attention to the implications of the doctrine of repugnance for the state. Finance provided extensive and vehement criticism of Articles 38–41 in its commentary on individual articles. Note that individual paragraph numbers mark text here as pagination ceases.

14 *Ibid.* Finance returned to this subject in its commentary on individual articles of the constitution. Commenting on Article 24.12, it states: 'If all the machinery set up by the Ministers and Secretaries Acts is to be dismantled and the organisation and distribution of business among Departments of State to be re-considered, great waste of time and energy will be involved, with corresponding detriment to other more useful activities of Government.'

15 *Ibid.*, Par.5.

16 Cf. Finance's commentary on Article 25 concerning international relations. See below.

17 Article 38.1,2 states: 'The State shall, in particular, in its laws have due regard to individual differences of capacity, physical and moral, and of social function.' Article 39.1,3 states: 'In particular, the State recognises that by her life within the home, woman gives to the State a support without which the common good cannot be achieved. The State shall, therefore, endeavour to secure that women, especially mothers and young girls, shall not be obliged to enter avocations unsuited to their sex and strength.'

18 Article 38.2.2 states: 'The State, shall, however, protect, as best it may, from unjust attack, and, in case of injustice done, vindicate the person, life, good name and property rights of every citizen.' Mr Gerald More O'Ferral was the agent for the Sanderson estate, which was in conflict with the Town Tenants' Association of Edgeworthstown, County Longford in 1934–5. On 9 February 1935, an IRA squad attacked the More O'Ferral residence and one of its members shot the agent's son Richard; he died of his injuries on 21 February. See Bowyer Bell, J., *The Secret Army: The IRA* (Blond, London, 1970; 3rd rev. ed., Poolbeg, Dublin, 1997), pp. 119–20.

19 Article 41.9 states: 'The State shall favour and where necessary supplement private economic initiative.'

20 Article 41.8 states: 'The State shall have regard for such distribution of the centres of industry that, while an opportunity is given for necessary development, the traditional preference of our people for rural life may be duly fostered and maintained.'

21 The observations of the Attorney General to the first printed draft. D/T S9725B, 25 March 1937.

22 Letter from Patrick Lynch, A-G, accompanying his observations. D/T S9725B, 25 March 1937.

23 Observations of the Department of Local Government and Public Health on the first draft of the constitution. D/T S9715B, 22 March 1937.

24 Observations of the Department of Defence on the first draft of the constitution, March 1937. D/T S9715B, 22 March 1937.

25 Observations of the Department of Agriculture on the first draft of the constitution, 18 March 1937. D/T S9715B, 22 March 1937.

26 Observations on the first draft of the constitution by the parliamentary draftsman, Mr Arthur V. Matheson, 22 March 1937. D/T S9715B, 22 March 1937.

27 Observations on the first draft of the constitution by the ceann comhairle. D/T S9715B, 22 March 1937.

28 Observations on the first draft of the constitution by the Department of Lands. D/T S9715B, 22 March 1937.

29 Observations of the Department of the President on the first draft of the constitution, 23 March 1937. D/T S9715B, 22 March 1937.

30 Observations of the Department of Justice, NAI D/T S9715B, 22 March 1937.

31 S Roche to M McDunphy, enclosing Observations of Department of Justice on Second Revise, NAI D/T S10159, 13 April 1937.

32 *Ibid.*

33 We are grateful to Dr Gerard Hogan for making available a copy of his paper to the *Irish Legal History Discourse* on 9 March 2007, entitled '"Headlines to the Legislature"? What did the Drafters really intend?'.

34 *Dáil debates*, Vol. 67, Col. 941, 25 May 1937.

35 *Ibid.*, Col. 942.

36 'Preparation of the Irish Text', 24 August 1937, note by Maurice Moynihan, NAI, D/T S9965.

37 The background to the Irish version of the constitution is the subject of a comprehensive article by Breandán Mac Giolla Choille in the Irish magazine, *Feasta* (October 1988). See Micheál O Cearúil, *Bunreacht na hÉireann: A Study of the Irish text*, The All-Party Oireachtas Committee on the Constitution (Stationery Office, Dublin, 1999), p. 3 for the above quotation from Mac Giolla Choille.

38 'Preparation of the Irish Text'. Undated note by McDunphy, NAI D/T S9965.

39 Letter from Runai Roinn Airgid, 2 Deireadh Fomhair, 1937, D/T S9965.

40 *Ibid.*

41 *Ibid.*

CHAPTER 6

1 This account of the drafting of Article 44 is based substantially on the version of Dermot Keogh's 'The Irish Constitutional Revolution: An Analysis of the Making of the Constitution', *Administration*, Vol. 35, No. 4 (1987) pp. 4–84.

2 Memorandum of Paddy Kennedy, assistant secretary to the government, dated 30 December 1938. NAI D/T S9748.

3 *Ibid.*, Stephen Roche to Michael McDunphy, 13 April 1934.

4 *Ibid.*, Stephen Roche to Michael McDunphy 12 April 1934.

5 *Ibid.*, Stephen Roche to Michael McDunphy, 13 April 1934.

6 This document is annotated presumably by McDunphy. Roche would hardly have circulated an internal departmental memo with minister's comments. From the context it would appear to be McDunphy.

7 T. Ó Deirg to President de Valera, 12 April 1937. NAI D/T S9748.

8 *Ibid.*

9 Department of Finance to president, 22 April 1937, NAI D/T S9748.

10 *Ibid.*

11 Preliminary draft, with the name [Joseph] Walshe written on it., NAI, D/T S9715A.

12 UCDA P150/2395, McQuaid to de Valera, 10 March 1937, McQuaid commented on Articles 11, 12, 13, 14, 16, 18 and 21.

13 'Authoritative Translation', NAI D/T S9715.

14 See also Keogh, Dermot, *The Vatican, The Bishops and Irish Politics 1919–1939*, (Cambridge University Press, Cambridge, 1986), p. 212.

15 UCDA P150/2395, McQuaid to de Valera, 16 March 1937.

16 *Ibid.*, McQuaid to de Valera, 22 March 1937.

17 UCDA P150/2395, 2408, 2409, 2410, 2411.

18 Table of negotiations with the Churches, located in Éamon de Valera papers, UCDA P150/2419.

19 *Ibid.* P150/2419.

20 *Ibid.*

21 *Ibid.* On the original draft article on religion (A), heavily annotated by de Valera and marked twice 'free exercise', is written: 'Copy shown nuncio – Apr. 3rd. Did not leave a copy'. It is not clear from the source whether de Valera let Robinson see the actual copy that he had so heavily minuted and changed or whether he had given him a clear copy to look at.

22 *Ibid.*

23 De Valera knew MacRory from their time on the staff of Maynooth. There had been a difference of opinion between the two men in 1932 around the Patrician celebrations.

24 The following brief biography is taken from Canning, Bernard J., *Bishops of Ireland 1870–1987* (Donegal Democrat, Ballyshannon, 1987). Joseph MacRory was born in March 1861 in Ballygawley, County Tyrone. He attended St Patrick's College, Armagh, and St Patrick's College, Maynooth and was ordained a priest there. He was then appointed to the chair of Moral Theology at SS Oscott, Birmingham, and he was president of St Patrick's College, Maynooth 1889–1915. He was appointed bishop of Down and Connor 1915–1928 and archbishop of Armagh and primate of All Ireland on 22 June 1928.

In June 1930 he deplored the treatment of the Catholic community in the six counties in the sphere of Catholic education. He was papal legate on two occasions; he represented Pius XI at the laying of the foundation stone of Liverpool cathedral of Christ the King in 1933, and again at the International Eucharistic Congress in 1934. He was foremost in promoting the beatification of Oliver Plunkett and was also devoted to the work of the foreign missions. He helped to establish the *Irish Theological Quarterly* in 1906 and was a frequent contributor to the *Irish Ecclesiastical Record.*

25 MacRory draft on nunciature notepaper (MacRory papers).

26 MacRory papers, Armagh Archdiocesan Archives, Armagh.

27 UCDA P150/2419, de Valera memorandum, 'Negotiations with the Churches'.

28 See Canning, *Bishops of Ireland* for biography of Edward J. Byrne. He was born 10 May 1872 in Dublin and attended Belvedere College and Clonliffe College. He was ordained a priest on 8 June 1895 and acted as curate in various Dublin parishes: Rush, Howth, and Blackrock. Appointed vice rector ICR 1901–1904, and CC Pro Cathedral 1904–1920. He was appointed auxiliary bishop of Dublin 19 August 1920 and archbishop 29 August 1921. He died on 9 February 1940.

He became archbishop of Dublin at a particularly sensitive time in Irish history. In the early stages of the conflict he endeavoured to bring about peace, calling a conference of the leaders, but no agreement materialised. Two of the major events of his episcopate were the celebrations in 1929 marking the centenary of Catholic Emancipation and the Eucharistic Congress in Dublin 1932. He did not take a prominent role in public life. In the words of the panegyric delivered by Bishop Patrick Collier of Ossory: '(He) had written his own panegyric himself in his life and works … Dr Byrne was a Godly man. He was intensely religious and prayerful. He viewed everything from the spiritual angle. He was a man of high courage and firmness of purpose … as a churchman he was a wise and prudent ruler. His judgement was calm and sound. He was patient and he had wide understanding and tolerance for the failings and shortcomings of others …'

29 UCDA P150/2419.

30 *Ibid.*

31 See Chapter 3 for a comparison.

32 UCDA P150/2421, 11 April 1937.

33 Mr Roy Irwin, the son of Dr Irwin, provided the following information: James Alexander Hamilton Irwin was born on 3 July 1876 in Ferny, County Down. He was educated at Magee College, Derry and Alexander College, Belfast. He received an MA from the Royal University of Ireland in 1902; BD Presbyterian Theological Faculty of Ireland in 1907; PhD Royal University of Ireland 1910; D Litt, National University of Ireland 1950. He was ordained at Killead, County Antrim in 1903 and spent time in Edinburgh

and Leith, returning to Ireland in 1935 where he served in Lucan and Naas. He married Alexandria and had two sons, Ronald and Roy. Alexandria died in 1911 the day Roy was born. He remarried in 1916. There were no further children. He was a member of the Fianna Fáil executive from 1945 to his death in 1954. The *Presbyterian Herald*, September 1954 also provides brief biographical details.

34 MacRory to Paschal Robinson, 9 April 1937, Nunziatura Apostolica Dublino, Busta 16 fasc. 8, Archives of the Holy See.

35 *Ibid.*

36 *Ibid.*

37 *Ibid.*, Seán T. O'Kelly to Robinson, 11 April 1937.

38 The Church of Ireland diocesan office, Cove Street, Cork provided the following brief biography of Archbishop Gregg: John Allen Fitzgerald Gregg was born on 4 July 1873. Educated at Bedford grammar school. He obtained First Classical Scholarship at Christ's Church College, Cambridge, first Stewart of Kaunock Scholarship and First Classical Tripos 1894 Part 1/Part 2. He also received the Hulsean Prize in 1896. Ordained deacon at St Luke's, Belfast in 1896 and priest at Carraigfergus in 1897. He also served in Ballymena and was residentary preacher of St Finbarre's cathedral, Cork in 1899. He married Anna Alicia Jennings, a native of Cork, in 1902. He had many publications to his name.

39 Seaver, George, *George Allen Fitzgerald Gregg, Archbishop*, (The Faith Press, London, 1963).

40 UCDA P150/2419.

41 *Ibid.*

42 The following information is taken from the *Irish Christian Advocate*, (2 July 1937), pp. 7–10. 'H.H. Massey, President of the Methodist Church, Mr Massey was born in Dublin in 1877 in Booterstown near Blackrock, County Dublin. When he was eighteen years old he went to Portaferry, County Down as an evangelist and entered the Irish Methodist Ministry in 1896. He took the place of Dr McKeag, following the latter's ill health, on the St Stephen's Green circuit. Though born in Dublin it was in the country circuits north and south that his sphere of influence was mainly felt. A year before he died he was unanimously elected to the Presidency of the Church.'

43 UCDA P150/2419, the Methodist Church in Ireland to De Valera, 15 April 1937.

44 *Ibid.* P150/2419. Draft religious article which de Valera has noted 'received from Presbyterian Mod Elect'.

45 NAI D/T S9852, Rabbi Herzog to de Valera, 29 December 1937.

46 Farragher, Seán P., *Dev and His Alma Mater – Eamonn De Valera's life long Association with Blackrock College, 1898–1975* (Paraclete Press, Dublin, 1984), pp. 164–6.

47 UCDA P150/2395.

48 *Ibid.*

49 *Ibid.*

50 Robinson to Pacelli, 17 April 1937, Archevio della Sacra Congregazione degli Affari Ecclesiastici Straordinari, Inghilterra, pos. 275, fasc. 122, Irlanda 1937–1946.

51 *Ibid.*.

52 *Ibid.*

53 Keogh, *The Vatican, The Bishops and Irish Politics*, Chapter 4.

54 *Ibid.*

55 Walshe was no stranger to Rome. In 1923, he had visited the city with the then Minister for External Affairs, Desmond FitzGerald. He was there again in 1929 in an official capacity, negotiating the establishment of diplomatic relations for the Free State. He visited the city in 1933 with de Valera. It is probable that Walshe, who became the first Irish diplomat to be given the rank of ambassador when he went to the Vatican in 1946, was a frequent private visitor to Italy over the years.

56 UCDA P150/2419, Instructions for Mr Walshe, 16 April 1937.

57 UCDA P150/2419.

58 There were two drafts of this document. One was taken by Walshe to Rome on 16 April. Written on the corner in de Valera's hand is 'Copy given J. W. as a reminder 16.IV.37' – UCDA P150/2419. But there is a second version of the document with 'Re-draft from that given J. P. W.' in de Valera's hand – UCDA P150/2419. It is unclear whether the re-draft was sent to Rome to Walshe, but as it did not differ in substance from the first document it is probable that it was not. There is no reference on file as to who drafted the document. It is probable that it was either John Hearne or Maurice Moynihan – or possibly both. De Valera almost certainly took an active part in the drafting of the document.

59 Observations on Walshe's submissions and draft answers of Pope Pius XI. It is probable that Pacelli wrote the drafts, his hand-writing is on the file, Archevio della Sacra Congregazione degli Affari Ecclesiastici Straordinari, Inghilterra, pos. 275, fasc. 122, Irlanda 1937–1946, Archives of the Holy See.

60 UCDA P150/2419.

61 Professor Geoffrey Hand to D. Keogh, February 1978; there is no date for this meeting between Macaulay and MacRory. It has not been possible to locate any reference to such a meeting in diplomatic reports from the Irish envoy to the Vatican. However, sensitive high diplomacy of that nature may not have been committed to paper either in the form of a report or a telegram. It seems unlikely that there was any need for the cardinal to intervene to soften the Vatican's position after the Walshe visit, which implies that MacRory visited Rome before 16 April 1937.

62 Pacelli to Robinson, 10 May 1937, Archevio della Sacra Congregazione degli Affari Ecclesiastici Straordinari, Inghilterra, pos. 275, fasc. 122, Irlanda 1937–1946. Translation of the original Italian text courtesy of Aoife Keogh.

63 *Ibid.*

64 UCDA P150/2421.

65 *Ibid.*

66 *Ibid.*

67 P. J. Ganon to Cardinal MacRory, 9 June 1937, MacRory papers.

68 UCDA P150/2393, Edward Cahill to de Valera, 23 May 1937.

69 *Ibid.* P150/2419, F. W. S. O'Neill, moderator of the Presbyterian assembly, to de Valera, 1 May 1937.

70 *Irish Times*, 11 October 1968. See Keogh, 'The Irish Constitutional Revolution,'p. 25, who states that Boland's account is 'a particularly weak source'.

71 Overheard by Maurice Moynihan; told by latter to Dermot Keogh.

72 Dermot Keogh interview with Seán MacEntee, Dublin, 22 March 1979.

73 *Dáil debates*, Vol. 67, Col. 82, 11 May 1937.

74 *Ibid.*, Vol. 67, Cols 1,890–1, 4 June 1937.

75 Vatican Radio, Christmas 1938.

CHAPTER 7

1 See *Dáil debates*, Vol 67, Col. 29f, 11 May 1937.

2 *Ibid.*, Vol. 67, Col. 1,050, 25 May 1937.

3 *Ibid.*, Vol. 67, Col. 421, 13 May 1937. Aiken earlier made the same point; see *Ibid.*, Col. 238.

4 *Ibid.*, Vol. 67, Col. 421, 13 May 1937.

5 *Ibid.*, Vol. 67, Col. 296, 12 May 1937.

6 *Ibid.*, Vol. 67, Col. 149, 11 May 1937.

7 *Irish Press*, 30 June 1937.

8 *Ibid.*, 17 June 1937. De Valera emphasised this point again the following day in Leitrim; see *Ibid.*, 18 June 1937.

9 *Ibid.*, 23 June 1937.

10 *Ibid.*, 26 June 1937.

11 *Ibid.*, 26 June 1937.

12 *Ibid.*, 22 June 1937.

13 UCDA P150/2454, Copy of Statement by British government, 30 December 1937.

14 *Irish Press*, 1 May 1937. See also same date, *Irish Independent* and *Irish Times*.

15 *Ibid.* This point was further stressed in the Dáil debate by various Fianna Fáil members, especially Seán MacEntee and Frank Aiken.

16 *Ibid.*

17 *Ibid.*

18 Dáil Éireann, Vol. 67, Cols. 30ff, 11 May 1937

19 NAI DFA 2003/17/18/345-423, McDunphy to High Commissioner, London (Dulanty), 1 April 1937.

20 *Dáil debates*, Vol 67, Cols 146–7, 11 May 1937

21 *Ibid.*, Vol. 67, Col. 1,008, 25 May 1937.

22 *Ibid.*, Vol. 67, Cols 268–9, 12 May 1937.

23 *Ibid.*, Vol. 67, Col. 304, 12 May 1937.

24 *Ibid.*, Vol. 67, Cols 275–6, 12 May 1937.

25 *Ibid.*, Vol. 67, Cols 337–8, 13 May 1937.

26 *Ibid.*, Vol. 67, Col. 315, 12 May 193.

27 *Ibid.*, Vol. 67, Cols 1,177–8, 26 May 1937.

28 *Ibid.*, Vol. 67, Col. 1,187, 26 May 1937.

29 *Ibid*, Col. 1,188.

30 *Ibid.*, Vol. 67, Cols 1,923–4, 4 June 1937.

31 *Ibid.*, Vol. 67, Col. 79, 11 May 1937.

32 *Ibid.*, Vol. 67, Col. 1,890, 4 June 1937.

33 *Ibid.*

34 *Ibid.*

35 *Ibid.*, Col. 1891.

36 *Irish Independent*, 5 May 1937.

37 *Ibid.*, 8 May 1937.

38 *Ibid.*, 10 May 1937.

39 Letter from Alasdair MaCaba, *Irish Independent*, 26 May 1937.

40 *Dáil debates*, Vol 67, Col. 269, 12 May 1937.

41 *Ibid.*, Col. 263

42 *Ibid.*, Cols 300, 303.

43 *Ibid.*, Col. 226.

44 *Ibid.*, Cols 381–2.

45 *Ibid.*, Col. 153, 11 May 1937.

46 *Ibid.*, Col 73.

47 *Ibid.*, Col. 194, 12 May 1937.

48 *Irish Independent*, 6 May 1937.

49 *Ibid.*, 7 May 1937.

50 *Ibid.*, 11 May 1937.

51 *Irish Times*, 10 May 1937.

52 *Irish Press*, 11 May 1937. Mrs Kettle's letter was published also in the *Irish Times* and *Irish Independent*.

53 *Ibid.*, 11 May 1937. The reader should refer also to Kettle's published letter in the *Irish Press* of 14 May and rejoinder from the editor for an elaboration of this public debate.

54 *Irish Times*, 11 May 1937.

55 *Irish Press*, 14 May 1937.

56 *Irish Independent*, 11 May 1937. Speakers at the meeting included Professor Agnes O'Farrelly, president of the Irish Federation of Women, Professor Mary Macken, Mary Kettle and Hanna Sheehy Skeffington.

57 *Ibid.*, 12 May 1937.

58 *Irish Press*, 12 May 1937. In a letter to the *Irish Press* on 18 May, Dorothy Macardle declared herself 'strongly' in 'agreement with all she says'.

59 *Ibid.*, 15 May 1937.

60 *Ibid.*, 15 May 1937.

61 *Irish Independent*, 15 May 1937.

62 *Ibid.*, 15 May 1937.

63 *Ibid.*, 20 May 1937. *Irish Press*, 20 May 1937.

64 *Irish Press*, 20 May 1937.

65 *Dáil debates*, Vol 67, Col. 67, 11 May 1937.

66 *Ibid.*, Col. 313, 12 May 1937.

67 *Ibid.*, Col. 242, 12 May 1937.

68 *Ibid.*

69 *Ibid.*, Col. 98, 11 May 1937.

70 *Ibid.*, Col. 247, 12 May 1937.

71 *Ibid.*, Col. 248, 12 May 1937.

72 *Ibid.*, Col 333, 13 May 1937

73 *Ibid.*, Col. 244, 12 May 1937.

74 Kennedy, F., *Cottage to Créche: Family change in Ireland* (IPA, Dublin, 2001), p. 82.

75 *Irish Times*, 22 February 1937, as cited in Kennedy, *Cottage to Créche* p. 82.

76 *Irish Press*, 1 May 1937.

77 *Irish Independent*, 29 May 1937.

78 *Ibid.*, 29 May 1937.

79 *Ibid.*, 18 June 1937.

80 *Ibid.*, 23 May 1937.

81 *Ibid.*, 29 May 1937.

82 *Ibid.*, 9 June 1937.

83 *Irish Times*, 9 June 1937.

84 *Ibid.*, 10 June 1937.

85 *Irish Independent*, 15 May 1937.

86 *Ibid.*, 6 May 1937.

87 *Ibid.*, 15 May 1937.

88 *Ibid.*

89 *Ibid.*, 15 May 1937.

90 *Irish Times*, 15 May 1937.

91 *Ibid.*

92 *Ibid.*, 2 June 1937.

93 *Ibid.*, 15 June 1937.

94 *Ibid.*, 9 June 1937.

95 *Ibid.*, 1 May 1937.

96 *Ibid.*, 8 May 1937.

97 *Irish Independent*, 10 May 1937.

98 *Ibid.*, 4 May 1937.

99 *Irish Catholic*, 1 May 1937.

100 *Ibid.*, 6 May 1937.

101 *Ibid.*

102 *Ibid.*

103 *Irish Independent*, 3 May 1937.

104 *Ibid.*, 6 May 1937.

105 *Irish Times*, 8 July 1937.

106 *Irish Independent*, 8 July 1936.

107 *Irish Press*, 7 July 1937.

108 *Daily Telegraph*, 1 May 1937.

109 *Ibid.*

110 *Ibid.*

111 *Ibid.*

112 *Ibid.*

113 *Morning Post*, 1 May 1937.

114 *Ibid.*

115 *Observer*, 2 May 1937.

116 *Sunday Times*, 2 May 1937.

117 *Manchester Guardian*, 3 May 1937.

118 The following section was compiled by Dr Robert MacNamara.

119 There is a good and growing literature on aspects of the south and Northern Ireland but the constitution, particularly its immediate effect, is a relatively neglected subject. Much of the material is seen through a southern prism, most notably Bowman, John, *De Valera and the Ulster Question* (Oxford, 1982) and O'Halloran, Clare, *Partition and the Limits of Irish Nationalism* (Gill and Macmillan, Dublin, 1987). Thanks to a more open archival policy in the south, a book like Michael Kennedy's *Division and Consensus* (Dublin: IPA, 2000) was possible, giving previously hidden views from north and south. It must be said that a considerable amount of relevant material remains closed in PRONI. The study that this owes the greatest debt to is Kennedy, Denis, *The Widening Gulf: Northern Attitudes to the Independent Irish State, 1919–49* (Blackstaff, Belfast, 1988). Northern nationalist reaction to the constitution is still relatively under-researched, receiving only passing treatment in the otherwise path-breaking study by Phoenix, Eamon, *Northern Nationalism* (Belfast: Ulster Historical Association, 1994). A more indepth study is the

work of Staunton, Enda, *The Nationalists of Northern Ireland, 1918–1973* (Columba, Dublin, 2001).

120 For the political positions of the unionist papers, see the excellent outline provided by Kennedy, Denis, *The Widening Gulf*, pp. 11–18. Kennedy's book also provides a more wide-ranging treatment of, particularly, newspaper coverage of the south from independence to the declaration of the republic.

121 Phoenix, Eamon, 'A century of change', in Eamon Phoenix (ed.), *A Century of Northern Life* (Ulster Historical Foundation, Belfast, 1995)

122 *Irish News*, 3 May 1937.

123 *Belfast Newsletter*, 11 May 1937.

124 *Belfast Telegraph*, 1 May 1937.

125 *Northern Whig*, 1 May 1937.

126 *Belfast Newsletter*, 1 May 1937.

127 *Ibid.*

128 *Northern Whig*, 7 May 1937.

129 All reported in the *Belfast Newsletter*, 3 May 1937.

130 *Belfast Newsletter*, 6 May 1937.

131 *Irish News*, 6 May 1937 – The *Irish News* was passionately pro-Franco.

132 *Belfast Newsletter*, 6 May 1937.

133 *Ibid.*, 22 May 1937.

134 *Derry Journal*, 3 May 1937.

135 *Ibid.*

136 *Ibid.*

137 *Belfast Newsletter*, 8 June 1937.

138 The details can be followed in just some of the papers. See, for example, the *Belfast Telegraph*, 8, 10, 12, 17, 18 June 1937; *Irish News*, 9 June 1937; *Derry Journal*, 9 June 1937; *Northern Whig*, 18 June and 13 July 1937; *Belfast Newsletter*, 13 July 1937; see also Denis Kennedy, *The Widening Gulf*, pp. 172–3.

139 Presidential Election Act No. 32 of 1937.

140 *Irish Times*, 22, April 1938.

141 *Ibid.*, 1–2 July 1980.

142 *Irish Press*, 27 June 1938. Address in St Patrick's Hall, Dublin Castle, at the inauguration ceremony of Douglas Hyde, first President of Ireland.

143 Lee, *Ireland 1912–1985*, p.210

BIBLIOGRAPHY

PRIMARY SOURCES

Archive Material

Armagh Diocesan Archive – Cardinal MacRory Papers
Dublin Diocesan Archive – Archbishop McQuaid Papers
Fransiscan Order, Killiney, Dublin – De Valera Papers
Jesuit Archives, Dublin – Constitution Committee and Father Cahill Papers
National Archive of Ireland – Department of An Taoiseach Files (S Series)
Pontifical Irish College, Rome – Monsignor Hagan Papers
University College Dublin Archives – De Valera Papers (P150 Series)
Vatican Archives, Rome

Newspapers

Belfast Newsletter
Belfast Telegraph
Cork Examiner
Daily Telegraph
Derry Journal
Irish Independent
Irish News
Irish Press
Irish Times
The Guardian
Morning Post
Northern Whig
Observer
Sunday Times
Times (London)

Interviews

Dermot Keogh with Seán MacEntee, March 1979

SECONDARY SOURCES

Journals

Administration
Capuchin Annual
Éire-Ireland
Irish Historical Studies
Irish Jurist
Irish Studies in International Affairs
Round Table
Studia Hibernia
Studies

Select Publications

Akenson, Donald and Fallin, J.F., 'The Irish Civil War and the Drafting of the Irish Free State Constitution', in *Éire-Ireland*, 2, (Summer 1970)

Barrington, Donal, 'The North and the Constitution', in Brian Farrell (ed) *De Valera's Constitution and Ours* (Gill and Macmillan, Dublin, 1988)

Barrington, Donal, 'The Irish Constitution – I-XII', *Irish Monthly*, February 1952–March 1953

Beth, Loren P., *The Development of Judicial Review in Ireland 1937-1966* (Institute of Public Administration, Dublin, 1967)

Beytagh, Francis.X., 'Individual Rights, Judicial Review and Written Constitutions', in James O'Reilly (ed) *Human Rights and Constitutional Law: Essays in honour of Brian Walsh* (Round Hall Press, Dublin, 1992)

Beytagh, Francis X., 'Equality under the Irish and American Constitutions', *Irish Jurist*, New Series, Vol XVIII, 1983

Binchy, D.A., 'Proposals for a New Senate' *Studies* (25) March 1936

Bowyer Bell J., *The Secret Army 1916-1979* (Poolbeg Press, Dublin, 1986)

Bowman, John, *De Valera and the Ulster Question 1917-1973* (Clarendon, Oxford, 1982)

Brown, Terence, *Ireland: A Social and Cultural History 1922 – 2002* (HarperCollins, Canada, 2004)

Browne, Michael, 'The Source and Purpose of Political Authority', *Studies* (25) September 1936

Cahill, Edward, *The Framework of a Christian State* (Gill and Macmillan, Dublin, 1932)

Canning, Paul, *British Policy Towards Ireland: 1921-1941* (Clarendon, Oxford, 1985)

Canny, Nicholas, 'The Birth of the Modern Constitution', in Brian Farrell (ed) *De Valera's Constitution and Ours* (Gill and Macmillan, Dublin, 1988)

Casey, James, *Constitutional Law in Ireland* (Sweet and Maxwell, London, 1992)

Casey, James, 'Changing the Constitution: Amendment and Judicial Review', in Brian Farrell (ed) *De Valera's Constitution and Ours* (Gill and Macmillan, Dublin, 1988)

Casey, James, *The Office of the Attorney General in Ireland* (Institute of Public Administration, Dublin, 1980)

Casey, James, 'The Constitution and the Legal System', *Irish Jurist*, New Series, Vol XIV, 1979

Casey, James, 'The Development of Constitutional Law under Chief Justice O'Higgins' *Irish Jurist*, New Series, Vol XXI, 1986

Chubb, Basil, 'Government and Dáil: Constitutional Myth and Political Practice', in Brian Farrell (ed) *De Valera's Constitution and Ours* (Gill and Macmillan, Dublin, 1988)

Chubb, Basil, *The Government and Politics of Ireland* (Longman, London, 1982)

Chubb, Basil, *The Constitution and Constitutional Change in Ireland* (Institute of Public Administration, Dublin, 1978)

Clarke, D.M., 'The Role of Natural Law in Irish Constitutional Law,' *Irish Jurist*, New Series, Vol XVII, 1982

Clarke, D.M., 'Emergency Legislation, Fundamental Rights and Article 28.3.3 of the Irish Constitution,' *Irish Jurist*, New Series, Vol XII, 1977

Clifford, Angela, *The Constitutional History of Ireland* (Athol Press, Belfast, 1985)

Coogan, Tim Pat, *Ireland Since the Rising* (Pall Mall Press, London, 1966)

Coogan, Tim Pat, *The IRA* (Pall Mall Press, London, 1970)

Cooney, John, *John Charles McQuaid: Ruler of Catholic Ireland* (O'Brien Press, Dublin, 1999)

Costello, Declan, 'Limiting Rights Constitutionally', in James O'Reilly (ed) *Human Rights and Constitutional Law: Essays in honour of Brian Walsh* (Round Hall Press, Dublin, 1992)

Costello, Declan, 'The Natural Law and the Irish Constitution', *Studies* (45) 1956

Cronin, Mike, *The Blueshirts and Irish Politics* (Four Courts, Dublin, 1997)

Cronin, Mike and Regan, John M. (eds) *Ireland: The Politics of Independence, 1922–49* (Macmillan, London, 2000)

Dudley Edwards, Owen, *Éamon De Valera* (GPC, Cardiff, 1987)

Dudley Edwards, Owen, *Conor Cruise O'Brien Introduces Ireland* (Andre Deutsch, London, 1969)

Dunphy, Richard, *The Making of Fianna Fáil Power in Ireland 1926–48* (Oxford University Press, Oxford, 1995)

English, Richard, *Radicals and the Republic: Socialist Republicans in the Irish Free State* (Oxford University Press, Oxford, 1994)

Fanning, Ronan, 'Mr de Valera Drafts a Constitution', in Brian Farrell (ed) *De Valera's Constitution and Ours* (Gill and Macmillan, Dublin, 1988)

Fanning, Ronan, *The Irish Department of Finance 1922–58* (Institute of Public Administration, Dublin, 1978)

Farragher, Seán, *Dev and his Alma Mater: Eamon de Valera's Lifelong Association with Blackrock College, 1898–1975* (Paraclete Press, Dublin, 1984)

Farrell, Brian, 'From First Dáil through Free State', in Brian Farrell (ed) *De Valera's Constitution and Ours* (Gill and Macmillan, Dublin, 1988)

Farrell, Brian (ed) *De Valera's Constitution and Ours* (Gill and Macmillan, Dublin, 1988)

Farrell, Brian, 'The Drafting of the Irish Free State Constitution', *Irish Jurist*, New Series, Vol V, 1970

Farrell, Brian, *Chairman or Chief: The Role of the Taoiseach in Irish Government* (Gill and Macmillan, Dublin, 1971)

Farry, Michael, *Education and the Constitution* (Round Hall Sweet & Maxwell, Dublin, 1996)

Faughnan, Seán, 'The Jesuits and the Irish Constitution', *Irish Historical Studies*, 25, 1987

FitzGerald, Garret, 'The Irish Constitution in its Historical Context', in Tim Murphy and Patrick Twomey (eds) *Ireland's Evolving Constitution, 19937–97: Collected Essays* (Hart Publishing, Oxford, 1998)

Fitzpatrick, David, *The Two Irelands 1912–39* (Oxford University Press, Oxford, 1998)

Foley, J.A. and Lalor, S., *Gill and Macmillan Annotated Constitution of Ireland* (Gill and Macmillan, Dublin, 1995)

Foster, Robert F., *Modern Ireland 1600–1972* (Allen Lane, London, 1988)

Gallagher, Michael, 'The President, the People and the Constitution' in Brian Farrell (ed) *De Valera's Constitution and Ours* (Gill and Macmillan, Dublin, 1988)

Grogan, Vincent, 'Constitution of Ireland – its development, 1921-50', *Studies* (40) 1951

Gwynn Morgan, David, *The Separation of Powers in the Irish Constitution* (Round Hall, Sweet and Maxwell, Dublin, 1997)

Gwynn Morgan, David, *Constitutional Law of Ireland: The Law of the Executive, Legislature and Judicature* (Round Hall, Dublin, 1990)

Gwynn Morgan, David, 'The Emergency Powers Bill Reference – I', *Irish Jurist*, New Series, Vol XIII, 1978

Gwynn Morgan, David, 'The Emergency Powers Bill Reference – II', *Irish Jurist*, New Series, Vol XIV, 1979

Harkness, David, *The Restless Dominion: the Irish Free State and the British Commonwealth of Nations 1921–1931* (Macmillan, London, 1971)

Hogan, G.P.S, 'The Constitutional Basis of Financial Control', *Administration*, Summer 1959

Hogan, Gerard, 'A fresh look at Tilson's Case', *Irish Jurist*, New Series, Vol XXXIII, 1998

Hogan, Gerard, 'The Constitution, Property Rights and Proportionality,' *Irish Jurist*, New Series, Vol XXXII, 1997

Hogan, Gerard, 'The Constitution Review Committee of 1934' in Fionan O'Muircheartaigh (ed), *Ireland in the Coming Times: Essays to Celebrate TK Whitaker's 80 Years* (Institute of Public Administration, Dublin, 1997)

Hogan, Gerard, 'The Early Judgements of Mr Justice Brian Walsh', in James O'Reilly (ed) *Human Rights and Constitutional Law: Essays in honour of Brian Walsh* (Round Hall Press, Dublin, 1992)

Hogan, Gerard, 'Law and Religion: Church-state Relations in Ireland from Independence to the Present Day', *American Journal of Comparative Law*, Vol. 35, 1987

Hogan, Gerard, 'Irish Nationalism as a Legal Ideology', *Studies*, Vol. 75, 1986

Keane, Ronan, 'Fundamental Rights in Irish Law: A Note on the Historical Background', in James O'Reilly (ed) *Human Rights and Constitutional Law: Essays in honour of Brian Walsh* (Round Hall Press, Dublin, 1992)

Keane, Ronan, 'Property in the Constitution and in the Courts', in Brian Farrell (ed) *De Valera's Constitution and Ours* (Gill and Macmillan, Dublin, 1988)

Kelly, John, Gerard Hogan and Gerry Whyte, *The Irish Constitution* (3rd Edition) (Butterworths, Dublin, 1994)

Kennedy, Brian P., 'John Hearne and the Irish Constitution (1937)' *Éire-Ireland*, 2, 1989

Keogh, Dermot, *Twentieth Century Ireland* (Gill and Macmillan, Dublin, Revised Edition 2005)

Keogh, Dermot, 'The Jesuits and the 1937 Constitution', *Studies*, (Spring 1989)

Keogh, Dermot, 'The Constitutional Revolution: An Analysis of the Making of the Constitution', in *Administration*, Vol. 35, 1987

Keogh, Dermot, 'Church, State and Society', in Brian Farrell (ed) *De Valera's Constitution and Ours* (Gill and Macmillan, Dublin, 1988)

Keogh, Dermot, *The Vatican, the Bishops and Irish Politics, 1919-1939* (Cambridge University Press, Cambridge, 1986)

Kohn, Leo, *The Constitution of the Irish Free State* (George Allen and Unwin, London, 1932)

Lee, J.J., *Ireland 1912-85: Politics and Society* (Cambridge University Press, Cambridge, 1989)

Litton, Frank, (ed) *The Constitution of Ireland 1937-1987* (Institute of Public Administration Dublin, 1987)

Longford, Earl of and Thomas P. O'Neill, *Éamon de Valera* (Gill and Macmillan, London, 1970)

Lucey, Cornelius, 'The principles of constitution making', *Irish Ecclesiatical Record*, January 1937

Lyons, F.S.L, *Ireland Since the Famine* (Fontana, London, 1974)

Mahony, T.P, *Report of the Committee on the Constitution* (Stationery Office, Dublin, 1968)

Manning, Maurice, *The Blueshirts* (Gill and Macmillan, Dublin, 1970)

Mansergh, Nicholas, *The Unresolved Question: The Anglo-Irish Settlement and its Undoing 1912-72* (Yale University Press, New Haven and London, 1991)

Mansergh, Nicholas, *The Irish Free State: Its Government and Politics* (Allen and Unwin, London, 1934)

McMahon, Deirdre, *Republicans and Imperialists: Anglo-Irish Relations in the 1930s* (Yale University Press, New Haven, 1984)

McDunphy, Michael, *The President of Ireland* (Brown and Nolan, Dublin, 1945)

Moynihan, Maurice (ed), *Speeches and Statements by Eamon de Valera, 1917-73* (Gill and Macmillan, Dublin, 1980)

Murphy, John A., 'The 1937 Constitution – Some Historical Reflections', in Tim Murphy and Patrick Twomey (editors) *Ireland's Evolving Constitution, 1993–97: Collected Essays* (Hart Publishing, Oxford, 1998)

Murphy, John A., *Ireland in the Twentieth Century* (Gill and Macmillan, Dublin, 1975)

Murphy, Tim and Patrick Twomey (editors) *Ireland's Evolving Constitution, 1993–97: Collected Essays* (Hart Publishing, Oxford, 1998)

O'Carroll, J. P. and Murphy John A., (editors), *De Valera and His Times* (Cork University Press, Cork, 1983)

Ó Cearúil, Micheál, *Bunreacht na hÉireann: Two Texts or Two Constitutions?* (Ireland Institute, Dublin, 2002)

O'Sullivan, Donal, *The Irish Free State and its Senate* (Faber and Faber, 1940, London)

Parliamentary Debates Dáil Éireann (Dáil Debates) (Stationery Office, Dublin, 1919 et seq)

Regan, John, *The Irish Counter Revolution 1921–1936* (Gill and Macmillan Dublin 1999)

Scannell, Yvonne, 'The Constitution and the Role Of Women', in Brian Farrell (ed) *De Valera's Constitution and Ours* (Gill and Macmillan, Dublin, 1988)

Sexton, Brendan, *Ireland and the Crown 1922–1936* (Irish Academic Press, 1989 Dublin)

Ward Alan J., *The Irish Constitutional Tradition: Responsible Government and Modern Ireland 1782-1992* (Irish Academic Press, Dublin, 1994)

Whyte J.H., *Church and State in Modern Ireland* (Gill and Macmillan, Dublin, 1971)

APPENDIX 1

The Constitution Committee, 1934
[Source NAI D/T S2979]

CONSTITUTION COMMITTEE 1934

PRESIDENT:

1. In accordance with your verbal direction of the 24th May, we have examined the Constitution from the point of view of

I. ascertaining which of its Articles should be regarded as fundamental in the sense that they safeguard democratic rights;

and

II. submitting a recommendation as to how these Articles might be specially protected from change.

2. We have now completed our task as regards part I of our terms of reference and accordingly submit this our report thereon.

3. After careful examination we have come to the conclusion that the following twenty-two Articles, or portions thereof, should be regarded as fundamental, and should, to the extent and with such modifications as are recommended in this report, be rendered immune from easy alteration, viz :

6, 7, 8, 9, 18, 19, 24, 28, 41, 43, 46, 49, 50, 61, 62, 63, 64, 65, 66, 68, 69, 70.

4. In dealing with these Articles we have taken their text in the form which will obtain when the following Bills, which are either held up by the Seanad, or are in the course of passage through the Oireachtas, have become law, viz :

- CONSTITUTION

CONSTITUTION (AMENDMENT NO.24) BILL, 1934.

(Abolition of Seanad Eireann as a constituent House of the Oireachtas)

(Rejected by Seanad Eireann on 1st June, 1934),

and

CONSTITUTION (AMENDMENT NO.23) BILL, 1934

(Abolition of University representation in the Oireachtas)

(At present with Dáil Eireann).

5. For convenient reference we have set out in Appendix A. the text of each of the Articles in question as so modified, together with a note as to our views in respect of each.

6. In those cases where we have proposed amendments, we have confined ourselves to indicating the nature of the changes suggested and our reasons therefor. We have assumed that it is not our function to submit drafts of articles as so revised.

7. We have given special consideration to Article 2A, and in doing so we have borne in mind the statement made by you in the Dáil on Committee Stage of the Constitution (Amendment No.24) Bill on 26th April last, column 2480, viz :

> "that it is necessary to ensure, in cases of real urgency and real public emergency, that an Executive would not be prevented from taking the action that might be considered necessary to safeguard public interests"

8. We are of opinion that Article 2A in its present form is not a proper one for retention in the Constitution. We

- suggest

suggest that it should be replaced by a simple Article which would enable the Oireachtas, by ordinary legislation, to empower an Executive to take any measures necessary to deal effectively with a state of public emergency not amounting to armed rebellion or state of war, including, when necessary, the temporary suspension of many Articles of the Constitution which under normal conditions are rightly regarded as fundamental.

9. We realise the great importance of providing safeguards to prevent such drastic powers being resorted to except in the abnormal circumstances for which they are designed, and at the same time to secure that an Executive which has real occasion to use them will not be in danger of finding its efforts to cope with a serious situation hampered or defeated by appeals to the Courts based on normal constitutional rights.

10. A suggested scheme which might meet the position is briefly outlined in Appendix B.

11. In addition to the Articles referred to in paragraphs 3 and 7 above we have given special consideration to the following :

Article 4 - THE NATIONAL AND OFFICIAL LANGUAGES.
Article 10 - EDUCATION.
Article 72 - TRIAL BY JURY.

We have not, however, included these among the fundamental Articles, and we set out in Appendix C annexed, our reasons for their omission.

12. As bearing on the suggestion made by you in the course

- of

of the Debate in the Dáil on 17th May, 1934, (Column 1193) on Report Stage of Constitution (Amendment No.24) Bill that agreement might be obtained between both sides of the House as to what Articles are fundamental, it will be observed that the Articles selected by us, after independent examination, as falling within that category, include all of those proposed for special treatment by Deputies William T. Cosgrave (former President of the Executive Council), John A. Costello (former Attorney General) and Patrick McGilligan (former Minister for Industry & Commerce and Minister for External Affairs), viz :

6, 7, 8, 9, 18, 24, 28, 43, 46, 49, 50,
61, 62, 63, 64, 65, 66, 68, 69, 70,

the only difference between our respective selections being that we have included Article 41 which compels the Executive Council to present, without delay, for the last formal stage of enactment, bills which have been duly passed by Parliament through all other legislative stages.

(Signed) S.A. Roche
M. McDunphy
John J. Hearne
P.P. O'Donoghue

3rd July, 1934.

REPORT OF CONSTITUTION COMMITTEE

1934.

APPENDIX A.

Articles 6, 7, 8, 9, 18, 19, 24, 28,
41, 43, 46, 49, 50, 61, 62, 63,
64, 65, 66, 68, 69, 70.

For explanation see paragraphs 3, 4, 5 and 6 of the report.

APPENDIX A.

Page 1.

Article 6.

The liberty of the person is inviolable, and no person shall be deprived of his liberty except in accordance with law. Upon complaint made by or on behalf of any person that he is being unlawfully detained, the High Court and any and every judge thereof shall forthwith enquire into the same and may make an order requiring the person in whose custody such person shall be detained to produce the body of the person so detained before such Court or judge without delay and to certify in writing as to the cause of the detention and such Court or judge shall thereupon order the release of such person unless satisfied that he is being detained in accordance with the law :

Provided, however, that nothing in this Article contained shall be invoked to prohibit control or interfere with any act of the military forces of the Irish Free State (Saorstát Eireann) during the existence of a state of war or armed rebellion.

OBSERVATIONS OF THE COMMITTEE:

In our opinion this Article should be regarded as fundamental.

We do not suggest that any alteration should be made in the text.

APPENDIX A.

Page 2.

Article 7.

The dwelling of each citizen is inviolable and shall not be forcibly entered except in accordance with law.

OBSERVATIONS OF THE COMMITTEE:

In our opinion this Article should be regarded as fundamental.

We do not suggest that any alteration should be made in the text.

Article 8.

Freedom of conscience and the free profession and practice of religion are, subject to public order and morality, guaranteed to every citizen, and no law may be made either directly or indirectly to endow any religion, or prohibit or restrict the free exercise thereof or give any preference, or impose any disability on account of religious belief or religious status, or affect prejudicially the right of any child to attend a school receiving public money without attending the religious instruction at the school or make any discrimination as respects State aid between schools under the management of different religious denominations, or divert from any religious denomination or any educational institution any of its property except for the purpose of roads, railways, lighting, water or drainage works, or other works of public utility, and on payment of compensation.

OBSERVATIONS OF THE COMMITTEE.

In our opinion this Article should be regarded as fundamental.

We do not suggest that any alteration should be made in the text.

Article 9.

The right of free expression of opinion as well as the right to assemble peaceably and without arms, and to form associations or unions is guaranteed for purposes not opposed to public morality. Laws regulating the manner in which the right of forming associations and the right of free assembly may be exercised shall contain no political, religious or class distinction.

OBSERVATIONS OF THE COMMITTEE.

Subject to the observations which follow, we are of opinion that this Article should be regarded as fundamental.

We recommend that it be amended so as to make it clear that laws may be passed, and police action taken, to prevent or control open-air meetings which might interfere with normal traffic or which otherwise become a nuisance or danger to the general public.

We understand that legislation on these lines has been delayed by reason of doubts as to whether such legislation could be validly enacted in view

- of

APPENDIX A.

Page 5.

Article 9 (Contd.)

of the present wording of the Article.

Copies of Articles in other Constitutions which bear on this matter are annexed (See Appendix D.).

APPENDIX A.

Page 5.

Article 18.

Every member of the Oireachtas shall, except in case of treason, felony or breach of the peace, be privileged from arrest in going to and returning from, and while within the precincts of Dáil Eireann, and shall not, in respect of any utterance in Dáil Eireann, be amenable to any action or proceeding in any Court other than Dáil Eireann itself.

OBSERVATIONS OF THE COMMITTEE.

In our opinion this Article should be regarded as fundamental.

We do not suggest that any alteration should be made in the text.

APPENDIX A.

Page 7.

Article 19.

All official reports and publications of the Oireachtas or of Dáil Eireann shall be privileged and utterances made in Dáil Eireann wherever published shall be privileged.

OBSERVATIONS OF THE COMMITTEE.

In our opinion this Article should be regarded as fundamental.

We do not suggest that any alteration should be made in the text.

APPENDIX A.

Page 8.

Article 24.

The Oireachtas shall hold at least one session each year. The Oireachtas shall be summoned and dissolved by the Representative of the Crown in the name of the King and subject as aforesaid Dáil Eireann shall fix the date of re-assembly of the Oireachtas.

OBSERVATIONS OF THE COMMITTEE.

This Article provides for three distinct matters, viz :

(a) THE HOLDING OF AT LEAST ONE SESSION OF THE OIREACHTAS EACH YEAR.

(b) THE SUMMONING AND DISSOLVING OF THE OIREACHTAS BY THE REPRESENTATIVE OF THE CROWN IN THE NAME OF THE KING.

(c) THE RIGHT OF DAIL EIREANN SUBJECT TO (b) TO FIX THE DATE OF RE-ASSEMBLY.

In our opinion, the principles embodied in portions (a) and (c) are fundamental.

Subject to the observations which follow, we recommend that they should be separated from (b) and made the subject of a distinct Article or Articles.

With regard to (a), the obvious intention of this provision, which is contained in the first sentence of the Article, is to ensure that democratic control through Parliament will not be defeated by

- unduly

Article 24 (Contd.).

unduly prolonged non-assembly of that body, but as no specific machinery is prescribed and no individual or institution is charged with the responsibility of putting it into effect, the provision might in practice prove to be of little real value.

We realise that the necessity for invoking it is not likely to arise, as long as the present practice continues of requiring the Oireachtas to assemble annually for the purpose of granting the Executive the necessary monies for the carrying on of the administration of the State.

It is not inconceivable, however, that a situation might arise in which the Oireachtas might be induced to forego this practice and to empower an Executive to obtain the necessary moneys without having to resort annually to Parliament.

The apparently strict requirements of Article 36, a copy of which is annexed (see Appendix H), might in such circumstances prove to be no safeguard.

In other Constitutions (see Appendix E) the desired result is secured by providing

(i) that Parliament shall meet on a specified date in each year, if not previously convoked, and/or

(ii) that if a certain proportion of the total number of its members so requires, Parliament must be convened within a prescribed time.

We recommend that an effective provision on the

Article 24 (Contd.).

lines of (i) be substituted for the first sentence of Article 24.

We suggest also for favourable consideration the insertion of an additional provision on the lines of (ii).

APPENDIX A.

Page 11.

Article 28.

At a General Election for Dáil Eireann the polls shall be held on the same day throughout the country, and that day shall be a day not later than thirty days after the date of dissolution. Dáil Eireann shall meet within one month of such day, and shall unless earlier dissolved continue for six years or such shorter period as may be fixed by legislation from the date of its first meeting, and not longer. Dáil Eireann may not at any time be dissolved except on the advice of the Executive Council.

OBSERVATIONS OF THE COMMITTEE:

The provisions of this Article deal with five distinct matters :

(a) THE HOLDING OF THE POLLS FOR A GENERAL ELECTION ON THE SAME DAY THROUGHOUT THE COUNTRY.

(b) THE PERIOD AFTER A DISSOLUTION WITHIN WHICH A GENERAL ELECTION MUST BE HELD.

(c) THE DATE OF ASSEMBLY OF DAIL EIREANN AFTER A GENERAL ELECTION.

(d) THE MAXIMUM DURATION OF DAIL EIREANN.

(e) A PROVISION THAT DAIL EIREANN MAY NOT BE DISSOLVED EXCEPT ON THE ADVICE OF THE EXECUTIVE COUNCIL.

We are of opinion that the principles underlying (b) (c) (d) and (e) are fundamental.

The trend of policy, however, indicates that it is not desirable to make permanent the present form of the portion dealing with heading (e) which is based on the procedure laid down in the present form of Article 24 whereby the Oireachtas is summoned and dissolved by the Representative of the Crown in the name of the King.

APPENDIX A.

Page 11A.

Article 28 (Contd.).

We suggest that this aspect of the Article should be separated from the other aspects and left open for the present to amendment by ordinary legislation.

With regard to (a) we do not consider this provision to be fundamental.

APPENDIX A.

Page 12

Article 41.

So soon as any Bill shall have been passed by Dáil Eireann, the Executive Council shall present the same to the Representative of the Crown for the signification by him, in the King's name, of the King's assent.

OBSERVATIONS OF THE COMMITTEE.

In our opinion the principle that an Executive should have no power to delay the last formal stage of enactment of Bills which have been duly passed by Parliament through all other legislative stages is fundamental.

The trend of policy, however, indicates that it is not desirable to make permanent the present machinery of assent.

If the two aspects of the Article, viz. the principle which we have referred to, and the machinery which has to be utilised in its application, can be separated, we suggest that they be made the subject of two distinct Articles, that relating to the machinery of assent or promulgation being left open to amendment by ordinary legislation.

APPENDIX A.

Page 13.

Article 43.

The Oireachtas shall have no power to declare acts to be infringements of the law which were not so at the date of their commission.

OBSERVATIONS OF THE COMMITTEE.

In our opinion this Article should be regarded as fundamental.

We do not suggest that any alteration should be made in the text.

APPENDIX A.

Page 14.

Article 46.

The Oireachtas has the exclusive right to regulate the raising and maintaining of such armed forces as are mentioned in the Scheduled Treaty in the territory of the Irish Free State (Saorstát Eireann) and every such force shall be subject to the control of the Oireachtas.

OBSERVATIONS OF THE COMMITTEE:

We are of opinion that the principle underlying this Article is fundamental.

We suggest, however, that

(a) the reference to the Treaty, and

(b) the limitation to the territory of the Irish Free State

should be eliminated.

The suggested amendment in regard to (b) is a corollary to recent constitutional developments whereby the right of Saorstát Eireann to raise and maintain armed forces outside its own territory has been recognised.

APPENDIX A.

Page 15.

Article 49.

Save in the case of actual invasion, the Irish Free State (Saorstát Eireann) shall not be committed to active participation in any war without the assent of the Oireachtas.

OBSERVATIONS OF THE COMMITTEE.

We are of opinion that the principle underlying this Article is fundamental.

We suggest, however, that the Article should be re-drafted in the light of the following considerations :

(i) The restriction imposed by the word "active" in reference to participation of the Saorstát in war should be removed.

This word was not in the draft of the Treaty submitted by the Provisional Government to the British Government in 1922. It was inserted at the instance of the latter Government in conformity with the theory that once the King has declared war, even though in making such declaration he acts on the advice of British Ministers only, the declaration automatically involves the Dominions also in the State of war created.

This theory is contrary to the principle now accepted that the King in respect of matters affecting the Saorstát can act only on the advice of the Executive Council of the Saorstát, and a provision based on this theory should not, therefore, be permitted to remain in the Constitution.

(ii) It is clear that an Executive should have power to take immediate steps to deal with an invasion, but we are of opinion that it should not be possible for an Executive to take advantage of such an occasion to commit the State, without the specific approval of

- the

APPENDIX A

Page 16.

Article 49 (Contd.).

the Oireachtas, to participation in a war which might conceiveably involve the country to an extent far beyond that necessary to deal with the invasion.

We think that the principle that the country shall not be committed ~~permitted~~ to participation in any war without the prior assent of the Oireachtas should be made absolute, but that subject thereto, powers should be conferred on the Executive to take such measures as are necessary to deal with an invasion.

Copies of Articles from other Constitutions bearing on this matter are attached (See Appendix F.).

APPENDIX A.

Page 17.

Article 50.

Amendments of this Constitution may be made by the Oireachtas, but no such amendment, passed by Dáil Eireann after the expiration of a period of sixteen years from the date of the coming into operation of this Constitution, shall become law, unless the same shall, after it has been passed by Dáil Eireann have been submitted to a Referendum of the people, and unless a majority of the voters on the register shall have recorded their votes on such Referendum, and either the votes of a majority of the voters on the register, or two-thirds of the votes recorded, shall have been cast in favour of such amendment. Any such amendment may be made within the said period of sixteen years by way of ordinary legislation.

OBSERVATIONS OF THE COMMITTEE:

The subject matter of this Article, which has a direct bearing on Part II of our terms of reference, will be dealt with in a separate report.

APPENDIX A.

Page 18.

Article 61.

All revenues of the Irish Free State (Saorstát Eireann) from whatever source arising, shall, subject to such exception as may be provided by law, form one fund, and shall be appropriated for the purposes of the Irish Free State (Saorstát Eireann) in the manner and subject to the charges and liabilities imposed by law.

OBSERVATIONS OF THE COMMITTEE.

We understand from informal conversations that the Department of Finance regard this Article as fundamental. A formal expression of their views on the financial provisions of the Constitution generally, has been promised.

APPENDIX A.

Page 19.

Article 62.

Dáil Eireann shall appoint a Comptroller and Auditor-General to act on behalf of the Irish Free State (Saorstát Eireann). He shall control all disbursements and shall audit all accounts of moneys administered by or under the authority of the Oireachtas and shall report to Dáil Eireann at stated periods to be determined by law.

OBSERVATIONS OF THE COMMITTEE.

We are of opinion that this Article should be regarded as fundamental.

We do not suggest that any alteration should be made in the text.

APPENDIX A.

Page 20.

Article 63.

The Comptroller and Auditor-General shall not be removed except for stated misbehaviour or incapacity on a resolution of Dáil Eireann for the passing of which not less than four-sevenths (exclusive of the Chairman or presiding member) of the full membership of Dáil Eireann shall have voted. Subject to this provision the terms and conditions of his tenure of office shall be fixed by law. He shall not be a member of the Oireachtas nor shall he hold any other office or position of emolument.

Notwithstanding anything contained in any other Article of this Constitution a bill for legislation to amend this Article in relation to the passing of the said resolution shall not be introduced in Dáil Eireann unless or until the amendment proposed by such Bill has been approved by a resolution of Dáil Eireann for the passing of which not less than four-sevenths (exclusive of the Chairman or presiding member) of the full membership of Dáil Eireann shall have voted.

OBSERVATIONS OF THE COMMITTEE.

In our opinion this Article should be regarded as fundamental.

The provision contained in the second paragraph, however, will naturally arise for consideration in connection with Part II of our terms of reference.

APPENDIX A.

Page 21.

Article 64.

The judicial power of the Irish Free State (Saorstat Eireann) shall be exercised and justice administered in the public courts established by the Oireachtas, by judges appointed in manner hereinafter provided. These Courts shall comprise Courts of First Instance and a Court of Final Appeal to be called the Supreme Court. The Courts of First Instance shall include a High Court, invested with full original jurisdiction in and powers to determine all matters and questions whether of law or fact, civil or criminal, and also Courts of local and limited jurisdiction with a right of appeal as determined by law.

OBSERVATIONS OF THE COMMITTEE:

We are of opinion that this Article should be regarded as fundamental.

We suggest, however, that it should be carefully re-drafted so as to meet the present position in which judicial or quasi-judicial functions are necessarily performed by persons who are not judges within the strict terms of the Constitution, e.g. Revenue Commissioners, Land Commissioners, Court Registrars, etc.

APPENDIX A.

Page 22.

Article 65.

The judicial power of the High Court shall extend to the question of the validity of any law having regard to the provisions of the Constitution. In all cases in which such matters/shall come into question, the High Court alone shall exercise original jurisdiction.

OBSERVATIONS OF THE COMMITTEE.

The principle that some court should have power to decide on the validity of laws having regard to the provisions of the Constitution is in our opinion fundamental.

In the course of our consideration of this Article the following points were discussed, viz:

I. Whether the power of deciding the validity of laws, having regard to the provisions of the Constitution, should be vested

(a) in the Supreme Court alone, or

(b) in a special "Constitution" Court appointed or designated for that purpose, e.g. a combination of the Supreme and High Courts, or

(c) in the High Court with right of appeal to the Supreme Court as at present,

and

II. Whether a time limit, commencing from the date of enactment in each case should be fixed within which the question of the validity

- of

APPENDIX A.

Page 22A

Article 65 (Contd.)

of any law could be submitted to or decided on by the Courts.

We have been unable to reach unanimity on either of these questions and, therefore, make no recommendation regarding them.

We think it well, however, to place on regord that they have arisen.

APPENDIX A.

Page 23.

Article 66.

The Supreme Court of the Irish Free State (Saorstat Eireann) shall, with such exceptions (not including cases which involve questions as to the validity of any law) and subject to such regulations as may be prescribed by law, have appellate jurisdiction from all decisions of the High Court. The decision of the Supreme Court shall in all cases be final and conclusive, and shall not be reviewed or capable of being reviewed by any other Court, Tribunal or Authority whatsoever and no appeal shall lie from a decision of the Supreme Court or of any other Court in Saorstát Eireann to His Majesty in Council, and it shall not be lawful for any person to petition His Majesty for leave to bring any such appeal.

OBSERVATIONS OF THE COMMITTEE.

We are of opinion that this Article should be regarded as fundamental, subject, however, to the observations which follow.

The reference to Appeals to His Majesty in Council should, if possible, be now repealed.

The purpose for which this portion of the Article was inserted has been effected, and we understand that its repeal if enacted in appropriate terms would not result in the restoration of the position which its enactment brought to an end.

If this amendment is not regarded as feasible, at present, the Article should be left open to change by ordinary legislation.

APPENDIX A.

Page 24.

Article 68.

The Judges of the Supreme Court and of the High Court and of all other Courts established in pursuance of this Constitution shall be appointed by the Representative of the Crown on the advice of the Executive Council. The Judges of the Supreme Court and of the High Court shall not be removed except for stated misbehaviour or incapacity, and then only by a resolution of Dáil Eireann for the passing of which not less than four-sevenths (exclusive of the Chairman or presiding member) of the full membership of Dail Eireann shall have voted. The age of retirement, the remuneration and the pension of such judges on retirement and the declarations to be taken by them on appointment shall be prescribed by law. Such remuneration may not be diminished during their continuance in office. The terms of appointment of the judges of such other courts as may be created shall be prescribed by law.

Notwithstanding anything contained in any other Article of this Constitution, a bill for legislation to amend this Article in relation to the passing of the said resolution shall not be introduced in Dáil Eireann unless or until the amendment proposed by such Bill has been approved by a resolution of Dail Eireann for the passing of which not less than four-sevenths (exclusive of the Chairman or presiding member) of the full membership of Dail Eireann shal have voted.

OBSERVATIONS OF THE COMMITTEE.

We are of opinion that this Article should in the main be regarded as fundamental.

It deals with two separate matters, viz :

(a) the method of appointment of Judges, and

(b) their tenure of office and other relevant matters.

The trend of policy makes it clear that it is not desirable to make permanent the present machinery of appointment, and for that reason the Article might be divided into two separate Articles dealing respectively with (a) and (b).

APPENDIX A.

Page 25.

Article 68 (Contd.)

We suggest that the provisions relating to (b) should be amended so as to make it clear that the age of retirement of all Judges, whether of the Supreme, High, Circuit or District Courts, their remuneration, their pension on retirement and the declarations to be made by them on appointment, shall be prescribed by law. The present wording is ambiguous.

Having regard to the possibility of wide variations in the purchasing power of money, over long periods, and the undesirability of the Oireachtas being debarred from adjusting, within reasonable limits the salaries of any class of State functionary, we further suggest that powers be taken in the Article to regulate the salaries of Judges by law, safeguards being provided to prevent the possibility of individuals or particular classes of Judges being victimised or subjected to undue influence by this means.

The provision contained in the second paragraph of the Article will naturally arise for consideration in connection with part II of our terms of reference.

APPENDIX A.

Page 26.

Article 69.

All judges shall be independent in the exercise of their functions, and subject only to the Constitution and the law. A judge shall not be eligible to sit in the Oireachtas, and shall not hold any other office or position of emolument.

OBSERVATIONS OF THE COMMITTEE.

We are of opinion that this Article should be regarded as fundamental.

We do not suggest that any alteration should be made in the text.

APPENDIX A.

Page 27.

Article 70.

No one shall be tried save in due course of law and extraordinary courts shall not be established, save only such Military Tribunals as may be authorised by law for dealing with military offenders against military law. The jurisdiction of Military Tribunals shall not be extended to or exercised over the civil population save in time of war or armed rebellion, and for acts committed in time of war or armed rebellion, and in accordance with the regulations to be prescribed by law. Such jurisdiction shall not be exercised in any area in which all civil courts are open or capable of being held, and no person shall be removed from one area to another, for the purpose of creating such jurisdiction.

OBSERVATIONS OF THE COMMITTEE.

We are of opinion that this Article should be regarded as fundamental.

Subject to the appended note we do not suggest that any alteration should be made in the text.

Note: The suggestions submitted by us under the heading "Emergency Provisions" - see paragraphs 7, 8, 9 and 10 of the Report in conjunction with Appendix B - might, if adopted, necessitate a revision of the text of Article 70, but this question would naturally receive attention in connection with the drafting of the new provisions.

APPENDIX B.

Page 1.

EMERGENCY POWERS.

SUGGESTIONS OF THE COMMITTEE:

1. What may be regarded as the first serious phase in the development of a grave state of disorder throughout the country is the failure of the ordinary Courts, either through intimidation of jurors and/or witnesses, or lack of civic spirit on the part of either or both, to secure the conviction of offenders, particularly in the case of offences of a semi-political nature.

2. The resultant immunity of offenders from punishment leads inevitably to the spread of offences of this character, resulting sometimes in a serious situation with which the ordinary processes of law are unable to cope.

3. We are of opinion that the development of a situation of this nature could in most cases be arrested by the application of suitable measures in the early stages, and we think that, to this end, the Constitution should contain a permanent provision to supplement the operation of the ordinary Courts.

- 4

APPENDIX B.

Page 2.

EMERGENCY POWERS.

4. Our suggestion, which for convenient reference we call Scheme A. is as follows :-

SCHEME A.

(a) Power should be provided in the Constitution for the enactment of legislation to provide, as part of the permanent judicial machinery of the State, for the trial by special Courts of persons accused of crime, in respect of whom the appropriate ordinary Judge or Justice certifies, at any stage of the proceedings, either on his own initiative, or on the application of the Attorney General, that it is desirable, in the interests of justice, that the trial should be removed to a special court set up under this scheme.

(b) The exact constitution and powers of these special courts would remain to be settled by legislation, but what we have in contemplation is something in the nature of the Constitution (Special Powers) Tribunal, with such changes as experience has shown to be desirable.

5. In addition to the Scheme A, outlined above, which may be regarded as a preventive measure, aimed at stopping, where possible, the development of a state of public emergency, we consider it essential that the State should be in a position to deal effectively with such an emergency in the event of its occurring, and for that purpose, we suggest Scheme B. which is outlined hereunder.

Scheme B.

APPENDIX B.

Page 3.

EMERGENCY POWERS.

SCHEME B.

(a) In substitution for the present Article 2A, a new Article should be inserted in the Constitution which would authorise the Oireachtas to provide by ordinary legislation such powers as the Oireachtas might consider necessary, (including power to suspend temporarily any Article of the Constitution), to meet the requirements of any period during which the ordinary laws are not adequate for the preservation of public order, such legislation to come into effect at the times and in the manner set out hereunder.

noted

(b) The Article should provide that nothing in the Constitution or in any Act should be capable of being invoked or cited as invalidating anything in the Article or in any legislation enacted or any other action taken under it.

(c) All such legislation should, by way of title or preamble state expressly that its object is to carry out the provisions of the said Article.

(d) The Article should provide that, if and whenever the Executive Council is of opinion that it is desirable so to do, they may request the President, or the senior available Judge, of the High Court (hereinafter called the summoning officer) to summon all Judges or Justices exercising criminal jurisdiction, but not including Judges of the Supreme or High Court nor any person acting only as a temporary Judge or Justice, to meet at a stated place and

time -

APPENDIX B.

Page 4.

EMERGENCY POWERS.

SCHEME B. (contd.)

time, (not being sooner than three days or later than seven days after the issue of such summons) for the purpose of advising the Executive Council as to whether the state of the country is such that the ordinary laws are not adequate for the preservation of public order.

(e) The said Judges shall meet accordingly under the Chairmanship of the summoning officer, and shall, after such discussion as they shall think fit, decide, by way of majority vote, on a secret ballot, on the question referred to them by the Executive Council, and the summoning officer shall report to the Executive Council in writing (attested by the signatures of all present at the meeting) as to the result of the vote, without specifing the names or numbers of persons voting for or against.

(f) To provide against wilful abstention from the meeting of judges and justices, severe penalties, amounting if necessary to automatic removal from office, should be provided. In case of unavoidable absence, a certificate from the summoning officer setting out the reason for such absence would be essential.

(g) If and whenever the Executive Council receives from the summoning officer a report in the affirmative, they may by Order declare that the provisions of all such legislation as is mentioned in paragraph (a) above shall come into operation on a day which shall be appointed in such Order and the said provisions shall come into operation on such day.

(h) The Order of the Executive Council should,

inter alia, -

APPENDIX B.

Page 5

EMERGENCY POWERS.

SCHEME B. (Contd.)

inter alia

(1) cite that the report referred to in the preceding paragraph has been duly received;

(2) be so worded and operate as to summon the Dáil forthwith if not already in session.

(3) be published in Iris Oifigiuil not later than the day preceding the appointed day;

(4) be laid before the Dáil forthwith, and unless and until a resolution annulling such Order is passed by the Dáil within the next subsequent twenty-one days on which the Dáil has sat after such Order is laid before it, such Order shall have full force and effect, but no such resolution shall operate to prejudice the validity of anything previously done under such Order.

(i) The effect of the Order and the operation of all legislation brought into effect under it shall cease, without prejudice to anything done under it:

(a) six months after the appointed day, or

(b) on an earlier date named in an ad hoc Order, by the Executive Council, or

(c) on an earlier date named in an express resolution passed by Dáil Eireann for that purpose.

(j) If the Executive Council consider it is desirable that the period of six months should be extended, they may at any time, either during the operation of the Order, or after its termination, take steps as provided in paragraph (d) et seq. above with a view to the making of a new Order to bring the scheme into operation for a further period.

/6.

APPENDIX C.

Page 1.

Article 4.

The National language of the Irish Free State (Saorstat Eireann) is the Irish language, but the English language shall be equally recognised as an official language. Nothing in this Article shall prevent special provisions being made by the Parliament of the Irish Free State (otherwise called and herein generally referred to as the "Oireachtas") for districts or areas in which only one language is in general use.

OBSERVATIONS OF THE COMMITTEE.

While in our opinion this Article is not fundamental in the sense that it safeguards democratic rights, we recognise that from the National point of view it is important because of the status which it gives to the Irish language.

We realise, however, that in course of time it may be found desirable to modify the recognition which it accords to English as an equally official language throughout the State, and for that reason we are of opinion that the Article should be left open to change by ordinary legislation.

APPENDIX C.

Page 2.

Article 10.

All citizens of the Irish Free State (Saorstát Eireann) have the right to free elementary education.

OBSERVATIONS OF THE COMMITTEE.

The views of the Department of Education on this Article were sought and were duly furnished in a letter from the Secretary dated 2nd July, 1934.

A relevant extract is quoted in Appendix G (4) annexed.

Having regard to these views we recommend that Article 10 be not included in the category of fundamental Articles.

APPENDIX C.

Article 72.

No person shall be tried on any criminal charge without a jury save in the case of charges in respect of minor offences triable by law before a Court of Summary Jurisdiction and in the case of charges for offences against military law triable by Court Martial or other Military Tribunal.

OBSERVATIONS OF THE COMMITTEE.

We have decided not to recommend this Article for inclusion in the category of fundamental Articles.

The relations between the Executive, the judiciary, and the ordinary citizen, are very different in a modern democratic State, such as ours, from those which prevailed in England at the time when the establishment of the right to trial by jury was regarded as a matter of the first importance.

Both in England and in America the jury system has been subjected in recent years to considerable criticism and in our State it cannot even claim to be a spontaneous national growth.

With an Executive dependent on, and responsible to, a Parliament elected on full adult suffrage, and with Judges whose independence is guaranteed by the Constitution, which also forbids the setting up of "extraordinary Courts" the right to trial by jury has lost its original importance.

This change in conditions is reflected in the modern tendency to give more and more criminal

Article 72 (Contd.)

jurisdiction to magistrates, sitting without a jury.

We are inclined to think that the question of how far this tendency should be allowed to develop in this State is one which might safely be left to the discretion of the Oireachtas, and we observe, in this connection that the Article in question was not included by the leaders of the Opposition in the list of fundamental articles referred to in paragraph 11 of our report.

It may be useful to observe that if we had decided to include the Article in our list we would have recommended amendments designed to make it clear :

(a) that the Article does not bind us to the present English system of requiring a jury of twelve and an unanimous verdict,

and

(b) that when the Oireachtas has designated any particular offense as a "minor" offence, fit to be tried summarily, it shall not be open to a defendant to raise the point that the offence is so serious that it cannot reasonably be called a "minor" offence and that the law declaring it to be triable summarily is therefore ultra vires Article 72 and invalid.

APPENDIX 2

Draft Heads of a Constitution, May 1935 [Source UCDA P150/2370]

1029/6

4

leaṫán miontuairisce. m.a.b.

Tagairt________

Draft Heads of a Constitution.

Secretary,

I now submit the draft of Heads of a Constitution which I have prepared on the verbal instructions of the President. I attach a short explanatory memorandum stating the scope of the President's instructions and giving the reasons for the preliminary method adopted in the preparation of the present draft.

The next stage of the work would appear to be to recast those Articles of the Constitution of 1922 which it is intended to retain but which have been found defective in one way or another during the past twelve years.

The draft Heads now submitted would, it is thought, form a suitable basis for a general discussion with the President at this stage on the scope of the project as a whole.

John J. Hearne

18th May 1935.

EXPLANATORY MEMORANDUM.

The Preliminary Draft of Heads of a Constitution which accompanies this memorandum is based upon verbal instructions given by the President on Wednesday, the 30th April, and on Friday, the 2nd May. In general, the instructions of the President were to prepare a draft of the Heads of a new Constitution for Saorstát Eireann. In particular, the draft was

A. to contain certain basic Articles guaranteeing fundamental human rights;

B. to place the said Articles in a specially protected position, i.e., to render them unalterable save by the people themselves or by an elaborate constitutional process;

C. to provide for the suspension of the said Articles during a state of public emergency only;

D. to contain machinery for effectively preserving public order during any such emergency;

E. to provide for the establishment of the office of President of Saorstát Eireann, the holder of which would fulfil all the functions now exercised by the King and the Governor General in internal affairs; and

F. to contain provision for the retention of the King as a constitutional officer of Saorstát Eireann in the domain of international relations.

The draft Heads are an attempt to write down the President's instructions and insert them into the text of the existing Constitution rather than an effort to construct - at this stage - a completely new Constitution. This preliminary method has been adopted for the following reasons:- (1) The task to be undertaken appears to be to effect a far-reaching constitutional reform within the framework, as far as possible, of the existing State rather than to establish a new State with a constitutional system fundamentally different from that now obtaining. (2) The method adopted has, it is thought, the advantage of showing the precise extent to which the changes contemplated will modify the Constitution of 1922.

The President's proposals raise ~~three~~ two major questions, namely:-

(1) whether the new Constitution should (or could) be enacted by the existing Oireachtas, and, if not, whether a Constituent Assembly should be called and, if so, how?

(2) whether a new Constitution on the lines indicated in the President's instructions would be in accord with the constitutional provisions of the Treaty of 1921 or would involve a breach of that instrument.

Each of these questions will be examined in separate memoranda. The specially difficult problem of fitting the King as a constitutional officer for the purposes of international relations only into the framework of a State internally organised on a Presidential basis will fall to be discussed in the second of the separate memoranda referred to. The several alternative drafts of Articles 7 and 53 of the draft Heads will illustrate the complexity of the matter. But a formula may be devised which would obviate the necessity of inserting any specific provision in the written Constitution in relation to those functions of the King which it is intended to retain.

17th May, 1935.

2r

Preliminary Draft

- of -

HEADS OF A CONSTITUTION

- for -

SAORSTÁT ÉIREANN.

(6)

P R E A M B L E .

In the Name of Almighty God, We, the Sovereign Irish People through our elected representatives assembled in this Dáil Eireann sitting as a Constituent Assembly, in order to declare and confirm our constitutional rights and liberties, consolidate our national life, establish and maintain domestic peace on a basis of freedom, equality and justice, ensure harmonious relations with neighbouring peoples, and promote the ultimate unity of Ireland do hereby, as of undoubted right, ordain and enact this Constitution.

(2)

The name of the State shall be Eire

Introductory.

Article 1.

Eire

Saorstát Eireann is an independent sovereign State.

All powers of government and all authority, legislative, executive and judicial, ~~are~~ derived from God through the people ~~and~~ shall be exercised in Saorstát Eireann through the organizations continued or established by, or established under, and in accord with this Constitution.

Citizenship.

Article 2.

The citizens of Saorstát Eireann shall be all persons who are citizens of Saorstát Eireann by or under the law in force at the date of the coming into operation of this Constitution or who hereafter become citizens by or under the said law or any future law.

Put general clause born etc or who are

The National Language.

Article 3.

The Irish language is the National language of Saorstát Eireann. The English language shall be equally recognised as an official language. Special provisions may be made by law for districts in which only one of the said languages is in general use.

The President.

Article 4.

The President of Saorstát Eireann (hereinafter referred

/to

Uachtarán

to as "the President") shall be elected by the people of Saorstát Eireann.

Every citizen of Saorstát Eireann who has completed his thirty-fifth year is eligible for the office of President.

The President shall hold office for seven years and shall be eligible for re-election. He shall remain in office until his successor is elected.

The President shall not be a member of the Chamber of Deputies established by this Constitution (hereinafter referred to as "Dáil Eireann").

The first President shall be elected at an election at which the area of jurisdiction for the time being of Saorstát Eireann shall form one electoral area and the election shall be conducted in accordance with a law to be passed by the existing Legislature. The second and every subsequent President shall be elected in accordance with the said law or any future law passed by the Parliament of Saorstát Eireann created by this Constitution (hereinafter referred to as "the Oireachtas").

Should the President die or resign during his term of office the election of a new President shall be held not later than two months from the date of such death or resignation and such election shall be conducted in accordance with the law for the time being in force relating to the election of President and the President so elected shall hold office for seven years and shall be eligible for re-election.

In the event of the President becoming ill or incapacitated for more than six months the Council of Ministers established by this Constitution (hereinafter referred to as "the Council of Ministers") may, by a majority decision taken with three fourths of its members present, call upon Dáil Eireann

/to

to appoint a Deputy President who shall act until the President is able to resume his functions. The appointment of a Deputy President by Dáil Eireann under this Article shall be made by a Resolution of Dáil Eireann passed by a simple majority of the total membership thereof.

Article 5.

The President when entering upon his office shall take the following oath before Dáil Eireann:-

> "I swear by Almighty God that I will maintain
> "the Constitution of Saorstát Eireann and uphold
> "its laws and that I will dedicate my powers to
> "the service and welfare of the people of Saorstát
> "Eireann and defend the State against all its
> "enemies whomsoever domestic and external and
> "fulfil my duties faithfully and conscientiously
> "in accordance with the Constitution and the law.
> "So help me God."

Article 6.

The supreme command of the defence forces of Saorstát Eireann is hereby vested in the President, who shall exercise the same in accordance with the law. All commissioned officers of the defence forces shall hold their commissions from him.

Article 7.

The President shall, as hereinafter mentioned, represent Saorstát Eireann in international relations:

(1) He shall appoint the diplomatic representatives and consuls of Saorstát Eireann in other States and receive the diplomatic representatives of other States accredited to Saorstát Eireann,

(2) He shall negotiate and conclude treaties and conventions,

(3) He shall sign

(a) the Letters of Credence and Recall of the diplomatic representatives of Saorstát Eireann accredited to other States,

(b) the Commissions of consuls appointed for Saorstát Eireann in other States,

(c) the full powers of plenipotentiaries empowered to conclude international treaties and conventions in the Heads of States form,

(d) the instruments of ratification of such treaties and conventions, and

(e) the exequaturs of consular representatives appointed in Saorstát Eireann.

Article 8.

The right of pardon, and power to remit or commute sentences imposed, and to remit the legal consequences of verdicts given, by any courts exercising criminal jurisdiction are hereby vested in the President.

Article 9.

The President (a) shall appoint the Prime Minister on the nomination of Dáil Eireann and (b) shall, on the nomination of the Prime Minister assented to by Dáil Eireann, appoint the other members of the Council of Ministers.

He shall appoint the judges of the Supreme Court, the High Court and all other Courts continued by or established under this Constitution.

Article 10.

The Oireachtas shall be summoned and dissolved by the President.

Article 11.

The President shall in accordance with this Constitution assent to and sign Bills passed by Dáil Eireann and presented to him for his assent and signature hereunder.

Article 12.

The existing statutory powers and duties of the Governor-General shall cease to be exercisable and performable by the Governor-General and shall be exercised and performed by the President in accordance with this Constitution.

/Article 13.

Article 13.

The salary of the President shall be determined by law.

Article 14.

The powers and duties conferred and imposed on the President by this Constitution or by any Act of the Oireachtas shall not be exercisable and performable by him save only upon the advice of the Council of Ministers.

The Oireachtas.

Article 15.

A Parliament is hereby created otherwise called and herein generally referred to as the Oireachtas. The Oireachtas shall consist of the President and Dáil Eireann. The sole and exclusive power of making laws for Saorstát Eireann is hereby vested in the Oireachtas.

Article 16.

The Oireachtas shall hold at least one session each year.

Article 17.

The Oireachtas shall be summoned and dissolved by the President on the advice of the Council of Ministers. Provided, however, that the power of dissolution shall not be exercisable on the advice of a Council of Ministers which has ceased to retain the support of a majority in Dáil Eireann.

Article 18.

The sole and exclusive right to raise and maintain armed forces is hereby vested in the Oireachtas.

Article 19.

The Oireachtas shall have no power to declare acts to be infringements of the law which were not so at the date of their commission.

/Dáil

Dáil Eireann.

Article 20.

There shall be a Chamber of Deputies (to be known and called and herein generally referred to as "Dáil Eireann"). Every citizen who has reached the age of twenty-one years and who is not placed under disability or incapacity by this Constitution or by law shall be eligible to become a member of Dáil Eireann.

Article 21.

All citizens of Saorstát Eireann without distinction of sex who have reached the age of twenty-one years and who comply with the provisions of the electoral laws from time to time in force shall have the right to vote for members of Dáil Eireann. It shall be composed of members who represent constituencies determined by law. The first Dáil Eireann to be elected after the coming into operation of this Constitution shall be composed of members representing the existing constituencies, and the election of the members of the said first Dáil Eireann shall be conducted in accordance with the provisions of the existing electoral law.

Article 22.

Every member of Dáil Eireann shall, except in case of treason, felony, or breach of the peace, be privileged from arrest in going to and returning from, and while within the precincts of Dáil Eireann, and shall not, in respect of any utterance therein, be amenable to any action or proceeding in any Court other than Dáil Eireann itself.

Article 23.

All official reports and publications of Dáil Eireann and of the Oireachtas shall be privileged, and utterances made therein wherever published shall be privileged.

Article 24.

Dáil Eireann shall make its own Rules and Standing Orders, with power to attach penalties for their infringement and shall have power to ensure freedom of debate, to protect its official documents and the private papers of its members, and to protect itself and its members against any person or persons interfering with, molesting or attempting to corrupt its members in the exercise of their duties.

how to have courts? [illegible]? Law Courts-?

Article 25.

Dáil Eireann shall elect its own Ceann Comhairle and Leas Ceann Comhairle and shall prescribe their powers, duties, remuneration, and terms of office. The member of Dáil Eireann who is the Ceann Comhairle immediately before a dissolution of the Oireachtas shall, unless before such dissolution he announces to Dáil Eireann that he does not desire to continue to be a member thereof, be deemed without any actual election to be elected in accordance with this Constitution at the ensuing general election as a member of Dáil Eireann for the constituency for which he was a member immediately before such dissolution or, in the event of a revision of constituencies having taken place, for the revised constituency declared on such revision to correspond to such first-mentioned constituency. Whenever a former Ceann Comhairle is so deemed to have been elected at a general election as a member for a constituency the number of members actually to be elected for such constituency at such general election shall be one less than would otherwise be required to be elected therefor.

Article 26.

Subject to the right of the President to dissolve the Oireachtas in accordance with this Constitution Dáil Eireann shall fix the date of reassembly of the Oireachtas, and the date of the conclusion of the session of Dáil Eireann.

Article 27.

At a General Election for Dáil Eireann the polls shall be held on the same day throughout the country, and that day shall be a day not later than thirty days after the date of the dissolution of the Oireachtas. Dáil Eireann shall meet within one month of such day, and shall unless earlier dissolved continue for six years or such shorter period as may be fixed by legislation from the date of its first meeting, and not longer.

Article 28.

In case of death, resignation or disqualification of a member of Dáil Eireann, the vacancy shall be filled by election in manner to be determined by law.

Article 29.

Dáil Eireann shall as soon as possible after the commencement of each financial year consider the Estimates of receipts and expenditure of Saorstát Eireann for that year, and, save in so far as may be provided by specific enactment in each case, the legislation required to give effect to the Financial Resolutions of each year shall be enacted within that year.

Article 30.

Money shall not be appropriated by vote, resolution or law, unless the purpose of the appropriation has in the same session been recommended by a message from the President acting on the advice of the Council of Ministers.

/The

The Council of Ministers.

Article 31.

There shall be a Council otherwise called and herein generally referred to as the Council of Ministers to advise the President in the government of Saorstát Eireann. The Council of Ministers shall be responsible to Dáil Eireann. Every Minister shall be a member of the Council of Ministers.

The number of Ministers and their respective powers, duties and functions shall be determined by law. Pending the enactment of laws determining their number, the Council of Ministers shall be composed of the same number of members as is the Executive Council in existence at the date of the coming into operation of this Constitution.

The existing Departments of State are hereby continued.

The President of the Council of Ministers shall be called and known as "the Prime Minister", and the Vice-President of the Council of Ministers shall be called and known as "the Deputy Prime Minister".

Every member of the Council of Ministers shall be a member of Dáil Eireann.

The Prime Minister and the other members of the Council of Ministers shall be appointed by the President in accordance with the provisions of this Constitution.

General transition art.

Subject as aforesaid, the laws in force at the date aforesaid in relation to the Executive Council, the existing Departments of State and the rights, powers, duties and functions of the respective heads of the said Departments shall continue in force pending the enactment of further laws. References in the laws hereby continued in force to the Executive Council, the President and Vice-President of the Executive Council, and to any Minister, head of a Department of State, shall be

(construed

construed and have effect as references respectively to the Council of Ministers, the Prime Minister and Deputy Prime Minister, and to the member of the Council of Ministers administering such Department as aforesaid.

The existing Department of External Affairs shall be called and known as the Department of Foreign Affairs and the Minister who is head of the said Department at any time after the enactment of this Constitution shall be called and known as "the Minister for Foreign Affairs".

Article 32.

The Council of Ministers shall meet and act as a collective authority and shall be collectively responsible for all matters concerning the Departments of State administered by the members thereof. The Council of Ministers shall prepare estimates of receipts and expenditure of Saorstát Eireann for each financial year and shall present them to Dáil Eireann before the close of the previous financial year.

co-ordinate [illegible]

Article 33.

The appointment of a member of Dáil Eireann to be a member of the Council of Ministers shall not entail upon him any obligation to resign his seat as a member of Dáil Eireann.

The Judicial Power.

Article 34.

The judicial power of Saorstát Eireann shall, subject as hereinafter mentioned, be exercised and justice administered by the public Courts at present existing. Every judge or justice being a member of any such Court, holding office at the date on which this Constitution comes into operation, shall continue to be a member thereof and hold office by the like tenure and

/upon

upon the like terms as, heretofore unless he signifies to the President his desire to resign. Future appointments of judges and justices of the existing Courts and appointments of judges and justices of any Courts hereafter established under this Constitution shall be made by the President.

Subject as hereinafter provided, the existing Courts shall for the time being continue to exercise the same jurisdiction as heretofore.

The exclusive original jurisdiction heretofore vested in the High Court to determine the validity of any law having regard to the provisions of the Constitution hereby repealed is hereby terminated. The said Court shall have exclusive original jurisdiction to determine the validity of any law having regard to the provisions of this Constitution. Every decision of the High Court on the question of the validity of any law shall be subject to the like appeal as that to which, at the date of the coming into operation of this Constitution, a decision of the said Court on the question of the validity of any law having regard to the provisions of the Constitution hereby repealed was subject.

The Oireachtas may at any time reconstitute or reogranize the existing Courts or redistribute the jurisdiction of the said Courts or of the judges thereof or terminate the said Courts and establish other public Courts in lieu thereof. The Oireachtas may reconstitute or reoganize or redistribute the jurisdiction of any public Courts (or of the judges thereof) established hereunder. The public Courts of Saorstát Eireann shall always comprise Courts of First Instance and a Court of Final Appeal. The Courts of First Instance shall always include a High Court invested with full original jurisdiction in and power to determine all matters and questions whether of law or fact, civil or criminal, and also Courts of local and

/limited

limited jurisdiction with a right of appeal as determined by law.

The Court of Final Appeal shall with such exceptions (not including cases which involve questions as to the validity of any law having regard to the provisions of this Constitution) and subject to such regulations as may be prescribed by law, have appellate jurisdiction from all decisions of the High Court.

Article 35.

The judges and justices of the existing Courts and all judges and justices hereafter appointed to the said Courts or to any Courts established under this Constitution shall be independent in the exercise of their functions and subject only to the Constitution and the law. A judge or justice shall not be a member of Dáil Eireann and shall not hold any other office or position of emolument.

The Comptroller and Auditor-General.

Article 36.

Dáil Eireann shall from time to time appoint a Comptroller and Auditor-General to act on behalf of Saorstát Eireann. He shall control all disbursements and shall audit all accounts of moneys administered by or under the authority of the Oireachtas and shall report to Dáil Eireann at stated periods to be determined by law.

Article 37.

The Comptroller and Auditor-General shall not be removed from office except for stated misbehaviour or incapacity on a resolution passed by Dáil Eireann. He shall not be a member of Dáil Eireann.

/Subject

Subject as aforesaid, the existing Comptroller and Auditor-General shall continue to hold office by the like tenure and upon the like terms as heretofore.

Fundamental Rights.

Article 38.

All citizens of Saorstát Eireann are equal before the law.

Article 39.

Freedom of conscience and the free expression and practice of religion are, subject to public order and morality, guaranteed to every citizen, and no law may be made either directly or indirectly to endow any religion, or prohibit or restrict the free exercise thereof or give any preference, or impose any disability on account of religious belief or religious status, or affect prejudicially the right of any child to attend a school receiving public money without attending the religious instruction at the school, or make any discrimination as respects State aid between schools under the management of different religious denominations, or divert from any religious denomination or any educational institution any of its property except for the purpose of roads, railways, lighting, water or drainage works or other works of public utility, and on payment of compensation.

Article 40.

The right of free expression of opinion as well as the right to assemble peaceably and without arms, and to form associations or unions is guaranteed for purposes not opposed to public morality. Laws regulating the manner in which the right of forming associations and the right of free assembly may be exercised shall contain no political, religious or class distinction.

Article 41.

The liberty of the person is inviolable, and no person shall be deprived of his liberty except in accordance with law. Upon complaint made by or on behalf of any person that he is being unlawfully detained, the High Court and any and every judge thereof shall forthwith enquire into the same and may make an order requiring the person in whose custody such person shall be detained to produce the body of the person so detained before such Court or judge without delay and to certify in writing as to the cause of the detention and such Court or judge shall thereupon order the release of such person unless satisfied that he is being detained in accordance with the law.

Article 42.

The dwelling of each citizen is inviolable and shall not be forcibly entered except in accordance with law.

Trial of Criminal Offences.

Article 43.

No one shall be tried save in due course of law and extraordinary courts shall not be established, save only

(a) such Military Tribunals as may be authorised by law for dealing with military offenders against military law, and

(b) such other extraordinary tribunals as may be established under this Constitution to deal with a state of public emergency proclaimed under this Constitution.

The jurisdiction of military tribunals shall not be extended to or exercised over the civil population save in time of war or armed rebellion or during a period of public emergency proclaimed under this Constitution, and for acts done during such time or period, and in accordance with law.

Article 44.

A member of the defence forces of Saorstát Eireann not on

/active

active service shall not be tried by any Court Martial or other Military Tribunal for an offence cognisable by the Civil Courts, unless such offence shall have been brought expressly within the jurisdiction of Courts Martial or other Military Tribunal by any existing code of laws or regulations for the enforcement of military discipline or any such code which may be hereafter approved by the Oireachtas.

Article 45.

No person shall be tried on any criminal charge without a jury save in the case of charges in respect of minor offences triable by law before a Court of Summary Jurisdiction, charges for offences against military law triable by Court Martial or other Military Tribunal, and charges for offences triable before a Military Tribunal or other extraordinary court in time of war or armed rebellion, or during a state of public emergency proclaimed under this Constitution.

Emergency Powers.

Article 46.

If and whenever Dáil Eireann or, if Dáil Eireann is not sitting, the Council of Ministers is satisfied that a grave state of public disorder exists throughout Saorstát Eireann or in any specified area thereof and that the ordinary laws and the civil courts are not adequate for the preservation of public order Dáil Eireann or the Council of Ministers (as the case may require) may, by proclamation, declare a state of public emergency in respect of the area to which such proclamation relates.

/Whenever

Whenever the Council of Ministers declares a state of public emergency under this Article the President shall forthwith summon the Oireachtas. Upon the reassembly of the Oireachtas the proclamation of the Council of Ministers declaring a state of public emergency shall forthwith be laid before Dáil Eireann and if within seven days after such proclamation is laid before it Dáil Eireann passes a resolution annulling such proclamation such proclamation shall be annulled accordingly but without prejudice to the validity of anything previously done in pursuance thereof. A proclamation issued by Dáil Eireann or by the Council of Ministers under this Article declaring a state of public emergency may be expressed, and, if so expressed, shall operate to suspend temporarily the operation of such and so many of the Articles of this Constitution as may be specified in such proclamation.

The Oireachtas may enact such legislation establishing such extraordinary courts and investing such courts with such jurisdiction as may in the opinion of Dáil Eireann be necessary to deal with any such state of public emergency as aforesaid; but such legislation shall not come into operation unless and until a proclamation is issued under this Article declaring a state of public emergency, and then only for the period of such emergency.

Nothing in this Constitution or in any law continued thereby or passed thereunder shall be invoked to nullify any provision of this Article or of any legislation passed under this Article or to oust the jurisdiction of any Court established hereunder or to invalidate any act or thing done in pursuance of this Article or of any legislation enacted for the purposes thereof.

/The

The decisions of any Court established under this Article shall not be subject to appeal to or review by any other court.

War and Defence.

Article 47.

Saorstát Eireann shall not be committed to a war with any other State save only with the consent of Dáil Eireann.

In the event, however, of an invasion of the territory of Saorstát Eireann the President and the Council of Ministers shall take immediate measures for the defence of the State pending the enactment by the Oireachtas of such legislation as may be necessary for that purpose.

Exercise of Treaty-Making Power.

Article 48.

A treaty of alliance shall not be concluded with any other State save with the approval of Dáil Eireann signified by a resolution of Dáil Eireann passed before the ratification of such treaty.

Article 49.

International agreements affecting the revenue shall not be binding unless and until approved by a resolution of Dáil Eireann.

Amendment of the Constitution.

Article 50.

The Oireachtas may amend any Article of this Constitution with the exception of the Articles relating to fundamental rights (namely, Article 38, Article 39, Article 40, Article 41 and Article 42) and this Article by way of ordinary legislation expressed to be an amendment of the Constitution.

/The

(24)

The Articles relating to fundamental rights (hereinbefore expressly mentioned) and this Article shall not be amended by the Oireachtas unless and until the Bill containing the proposed amendment or amendments of any such Article, after it has been passed by Dáil Eireann and before being presented to the President for his assent, shall have been submitted to a Referendum of the people, and unless a majority of the voters on the register shall have recorded their votes on such Referendum and either the votes of a majority of the voters on the register or two thirds of the votes recorded shall have been cast in favour of such amendment or amendments.

Every Referendum shall be conducted in accordance with laws enacted by the Oireachtas for that purpose and for the time being in force.

State Seals.

Article 51.

The present Great Seal of Saorstát Eireann and any Great Seal of Saorstát Eireann hereafter established shall be in the custody of the President. Neither the present nor any future Great Seal of Saorstát Eireann shall be affixed to any instrument save upon the advice of the Council of Ministers. Every such Seal shall be authenticated on every document to which it is affixed by the countersignature of the Minister for Foreign Affairs.

The present Signet Seal and any or other similar Seal hereafter established in lieu thereof shall be in the custody of the Minister for Foreign Affairs, and shall not be affixed on any document save on the advice of that Minister.

/Repeal

Repeal of Constitution of 1922
and
Continuance of Laws.

Article 52.

The Constitution enacted and given the force of law by the Constitution of the Irish Free State (Saorstát Eireann) Act, 1922 is hereby repealed save in so far and so long as any provision or provisions thereof is or are continued in force by any Article of this Constitution. Every such provision so continued in force by this Constitution shall remain in force unless and until amended or repealed by the Oireachtas

All other laws in force at the date of the coming into operation of this Constitution, save in so far as they are in conflict with this Constitution or any provision thereof, are hereby continued in force and shall remain in force unless and until amended or repealed by the Oireachtas.

Transitory Provisions.

Article 53.

So long as Saorstát Eireann remains associated as a Member of the British Commonwealth of Nations the following documents shall before being issued be countersigned by the Minister for Foreign Affairs of Saorstát Eireann, that is to say:-

(a) the Letters of Credence and Recall of the diplomatic representatives of Saorstát Eireann accredited to other States,

(b) the Commissions of consuls appointed for Saorstát Eireann in other States,

(c) the full powers of plenipotentiaries empowered to conclude international treaties and conventions,

(d) the instruments of ratification of such treaties and conventions, and

(e) the exequaturs of consular representatives appointed in Saorstát Eireann.

(26)

ALTERNATIVE DRAFT A OF
ARTICLES 7 AND 53.

Article 7.

The President shall receive the diplomatic representatives accredited by other States to Saorstát Eireann.

He shall sign

(a) the Letters of Credence and Recall of the diplomatic representatives of Saorstát Eireann accredited to other States,

(b) the Commissions of consuls appointed by Saorstát Eireann in other States,

(c) the full powers of plenipotentiaries empowered to conclude international treaties and conventions,

(d) instruments of ratification of treaties and conventions,

(e) the exequaturs of consuls appointed in Saorstát Eireann.

Transitory Provisions.

Article 53.

So long as Saorstát Eireann remains associated as a Member of the British Commonwealth of Nations the Minister for Foreign Affairs shall countersign

(a) the Letters of Credence and Recall of the diplomatic representatives of Saorstát Eireann accredited to other States,

(b) the Commissions of consuls appointed by Saorstát Eireann in other States,

(c) the full powers of plenipotentiaries empowered to conclude international treaties and conventions,

(d) instruments of ratification of treaties and conventions,

(e) the exequaturs of consuls appointed in Saorstát Eireann.

ALTERNATIVE DRAFT B OF

ARTICLES 7 AND 53 (JOINTLY).

Article 7.

The President shall receive the diplomatic representatives accredited by other States to Saorstát Eireann.

The following documents, namely,

(a) the Letters of Credence and Recall of the diplomatic representatives of Saorstát Eireann accredited to other States,

(b) the Commissions of consuls appointed by Saorstát Eireann in other States,

(c) the full powers of plenipotentiaries empowered to conclude international treaties and conventions,

(d) instruments of ratification of treaties and conventions,

(e) the exequaturs of consuls appointed in Saorstát Eireann,

shall be countersigned by the Minister for Foreign Affairs.

(Note: This Article would not be accompanied by any Transitory Provision; but should Saorstát Eireann become a Republic and should it be then decided that the President's functions in international relations be inserted in the written Constitution the Constitution would have to be amended by the insertion of appropriate additional Articles. This would, in my view, be necessary, as the President would have no constitutional functions at all in international relations unless they were expressly given to him by the Constitution itself).

ALTERNATIVE DRAFT C OF

ARTICLES 7 AND 53 (JOINTLY).

Transitory Provisions.

Article 53.

So long as Saorstát Eireann remains associated as a Member of the British Commonwealth of Nations the King shall represent Saorstát Eireann in international relations. No act shall be performed or performable by the King in that capacity save upon the advice of the Council of Ministers communicated through the Minister for Foreign Affairs. In particular the following documents, namely,

(a) the Letters of Credence and Recall of the diplomatic representatives of Saorstát Eireann accredited to other States,

(b) the Commissions of consuls appointed by Saorstát Eireann in other States,

(c) the full powers of plenipotentiaries empowered to conclude international treaties and conventions,

(d) instruments of ratification of treaties and conventions,

(e) the exequaturs of consuls appointed in Saorstát Eireann,

shall be countersigned by the Minister for Foreign Affairs.

ALTERNATIVE DRAFT D OF

ARTICLES 7 AND 53.

Article 7.

In the event of the withdrawal of Saorstát Eireann from membership of the British Commonwealth of Nations the President shall represent Saorstát Eireann in international relations. Pending such withdrawal all executive acts in relation to international affairs shall be performed as heretofore but no such act shall be performable save upon the advice of the Council of Ministers communicated through the Minister for Foreign Affairs.

(Note: This draft would not be accompanied by any Transitory Provisions).

APPENDIX 3

THE 'SQUARED PAPER DRAFT'
[SOURCE UCDA P150/2370]

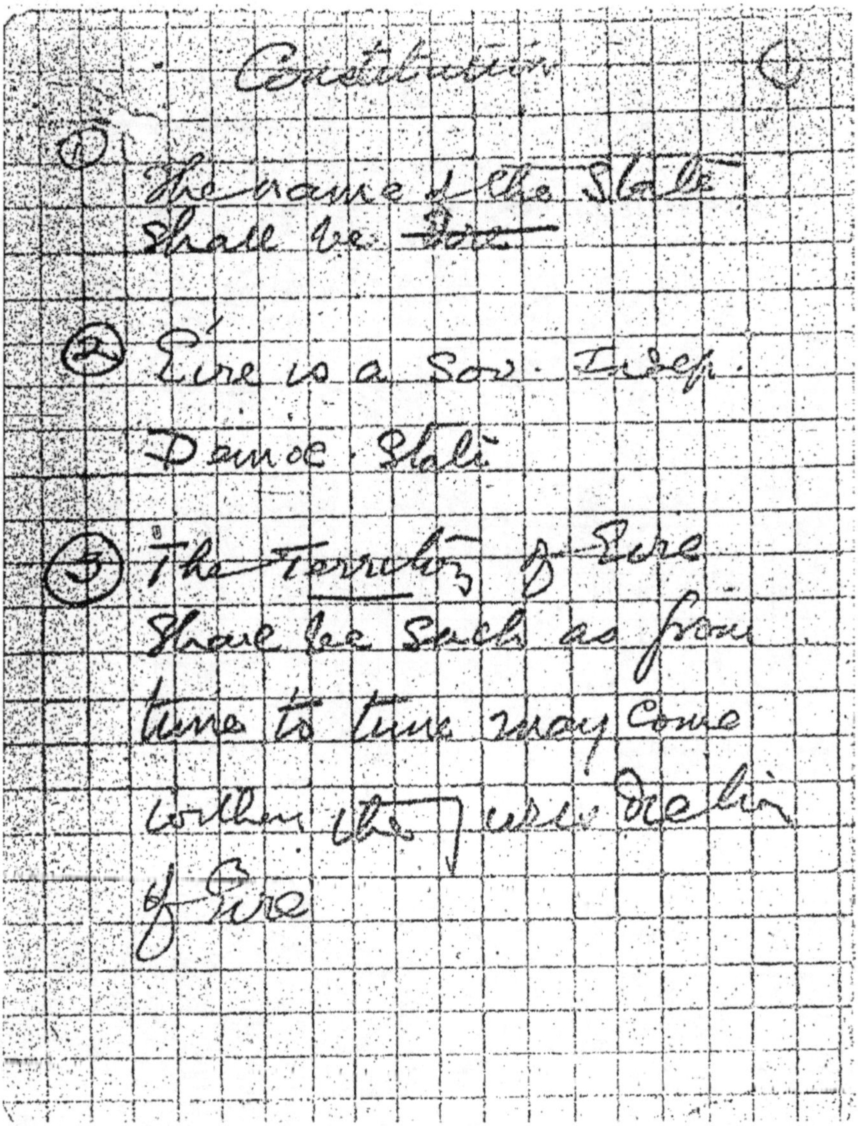
Constitution

(1) The name of the State shall be ~~Eire~~

(2) Eire is a Sov. Indep. Democ. State

(3) The Territory of Eire shall be such as from time to time may come within the jurisdiction of Eire

(2)

(4) In Eire the ultimate Sov power shall rest with the people who shall be the ultimate Court for deciding all national and political questions

(5) From the people under God all Governmental authority, legal, Exe & Judicial shall be derived. These powers

5 Con'd (3)

Shall be Exercised by
the organs of Gov.
Set forth in this Constn

6. This Constitution shall be
changed or amended
only by a referendum
– Vote of the people – citizens
over 21 years of age

6º The Body of Citizens shall be

7º The Legislature shall

consist of Dail Eireann

selected – proportional Represen

and Seanad (?) Eireann

Immunities

(4)

Notes on Constitn (5)

1 Flag, Language, Religion
Coat of arms.

Regency: Constitutional Ct.

[Council of State

✗ Regional & Subordinate Parlts

Page 187 - German Pres T.F.A.

By a 2/3 vote of Diet the P. may be invited to assume office
— a further min. without Portfolio to assist [may have extra ...

If old. Pres. die — new takes up office immed. — otherwise two months

Deputies etc to abide by
Constitn Declaration

(6)

Whilst Eire is assoc. with any League or Group of States it shall be lawful to make the necessary

Every year of such association shall be reviewed – or at any time

Organ. Laws cover (9)

(1) - Election of Presidt

(2) - Election of Dail + constituencies

(3) - Election of Senate Composition

(4) Plebiscite - accept Rules

(5) Law setting up Judiciary

(6) - Length of Office of Parlt

(7) - Secretary + Min Acts

(8) Citizenship Law

(9) Treason

(1) Preamble — The I people
acknowg their dependence
Almighty God, thanks him
for the preservation of their
nation & dedicating thems
to his Service accepting
the ten comdts as fund
law give themselves
this Constitn ^fundamental So ces(?) to
to (1)
(2)
(3)
(8)
See Proc 1916, Decl of In 1919 & Dem Progm

Transitional (9)

1 The next parlt shall be at liberty to pass Organic laws to have immed. effect — but must be ratified by referendum at time of next general electn.

(2) Existing laws carried over —
(1) Electoral Boundary
(2) Dail Elect.
(3) Judiciary
(4) Ministers + Secs

(10)

Eire may associate
itself with any other
State or group of States
or become a member
of any league of States
or Nations. Organic
Laws may specify
the

Bor.

(N)

1 ~~That~~ S.W.F. note altogether disappts & shows no real apprec. of ~~how I . . .~~ the fundamentals in the problem.

2. ~~In~~ def. as many times pts out the I. people have no imperl. interests or aspirations – They want to keep out of war.

(1) The only right they concede is that I. shd not be used as basis of attack on Britain

(2) When common threat invasion of the two islands – co-operation wd. come.

The State guarantees to all its citizens

To the family it guarantees etc

(1) Secret Voting —

(12)

(2) — Powers + duties in addition to those prescribed in Constn by law

(3) Number present when law -organic- is being discussed

(4) Re residence within State + V.P

(5) Laws of Treason —

Constn. Court determines such not to be taken into account p.53 SMcN

(13)

Referendum — (1) amendmt of Constn
(2) organic laws at discretion of P.
(3) major legislatn at request of maj of 2nd H.

Recall

Tribunal

Amendt. — [may summon constit. assembly with notice of the referendum]

Phrasing, order, Tribunal, K. Send me draft

Transitional — at end and to disappear.

APPENDIX 4

Draft Constitution Considered at Cabinet, October 1936 [Source UCDA P150/2373]

PART 1. : THE STATE.

ARTICLE ONE. The name of the State is E.

ARTICLE TWO. E. is a sovereign, [independent], democratic State.

ARTICLE THREE. All powers of government, legislative, executive and judicial in E. emanate from the people, and are exercisable only through the Organs established by this Constitution or established or recognised by Organic Laws made thereunder.

ARTICLE FOUR. The national flag of E. is a tricolour in green, white and orange.

ARTICLE FIVE. The Irish language is the official language of E. The English language is recognised as a second official language. [Special provision may be made by law for the recognition of only one of the said languages as the official language in districts or areas in which that language only is in general use.]

ARTICLE SIX. The following are of Irish nationality and are citizens of E. , namely:-

1. All persons born in Ireland.
2. All persons born outside Ireland of Irish parentage or descent as defined or limited by law.
3. All other persons on whom Irish nationality is conferred by naturalization in accordance with law.
4. Irish nationality shall not be conferred

by naturalization upon any person who disbelieves in or is opposed to organized government or is a member of or affiliated with any society or organisation entertaining or teaching disbelief in or opposition to organized government.

5. The conditions governing the acquis loss of Irish nationality shall be regulated by law.

1076/3 File no 10.

PART II.: THE PRESIDENT OF E.

ARTICLE SEVEN. CREATION AND TENURE OF OFFICE.

1. The office of President of E. is hereby created. The President of E. (hereinafter called "the President") shall exercise and perform the powers and functions conferred on the President by this Constitution or by Organic Laws made thereunder.

2. The President shall be elected by direct vote of the people,

3. The President shall hold office for seven years from the date upon which he enters upon his office (unless he previously dies, resigns, becomes permanently incapacitated, or is removed from office) and shall be eligible for re-election.

4. Every person of Irish nationality who has completed his thirty-fifth year of age, who has ordinarily resided in Ireland during the ten years immediately preceding his nomination and who is nominated by not less than twenty members of the Oireachtas shall be eligible for the office of President. A member of the Oireachtas shall not be entitled to participate in the nomination of more than one candidate for the office of President in respect of the same election.

5. Elections to the office of President by direct vote of the people shall, subject to the provisions of Section 4 of this Article, be regulated by Organic Laws.

6. The President shall not be a member of either House of the Oireachtas and shall not, save as provided by this Constitution, hold any other office.

/7.

7. The President shall enter upon his office on a date not later than two calendar months from the date of his election.

8. The President shall enter upon his office by taking and subscribing publicly the following oath before the Chief Justice of E.:

"I swear by Almighty God that I will
"maintain the Constitution of E.
"and uphold its laws, ~~that I will defend~~
"the State against ~~all its~~ enemies
"whomsoever domestic and external,
"that I will fulfil my duties faith-
"fully and conscientiously in accord-
"ance with the Constitution and the law,
"and that I will dedicate my powers to
"the service and welfare of the People
"of E. So help me God."

9. The President shall not leave E. during his term of office save with the consent of the Council of Ministers. (hereinafter).

10. In the event of the temporary incapacity or absence from E. of the President, the functions of the office of President shall be discharged by a Commission which shall consist of such ~~two~~ three or ~~more~~ members of the Council of State as, after consultation with the said Council, the President shall appoint for that purpose.

11. The President shall be removed from office on impeachment ~~by~~ before Dáil Eireann for violation of the Constitution treason, bribery, or other high crimes or misdemeanours and on conviction thereof by two-thirds of the total membership of both Houses of the Oireachtas at a joint session thereof.

/12.

to be fixed

in the presence of both Houses

before the members of both Houses

[Govt.?]

[who is to judge? Suppose he was unconscious]

(originate Dáil)

[cease to be Presdt]

Presdt. Dying in interval

Office Vacant

12. In the event of the removal from office of the President or of his death, resignation or permanent incapacity to discharge the functions of the office an election to fill the office shall be held within two calendar months after such event as aforesaid. Pending the entry upon his office of the President so to be elected the functions of the office of President shall devolve upon an Acting President who shall be elected for that purpose by Dáil Eireann. An Acting President shall enter upon his office by taking and subscribing the oath required by Section 8 of this Article to be taken by the President and he shall hold office for a period not exceeding four months from the date upon which he enters upon his office as Acting President.

13. The President shall take precedence over all other persons in the State.

14. The President shall have an official residence, an official staff and secretariat and shall receive such emoluments and allowances as may be determined by law. The emoluments and allowances of the President shall not be diminished during his term of office.

ARTICLE ~~EIGHT~~ Seven. POWERS AND FUNCTIONS OF THE PRESIDENT.

1. The President shall summon and dissolve the Oireachtas on the advice of the Prime Minister: Provided, however, that the Oireachtas shall not be dissolved on the advice of a Prime Minister who has ceased to retain the support of a majority in Dáil Eireann.

12.

2. The President shall promulgate laws in the manner provided by Article ___ of this Constitution.

3. The President shall exercise the functions in relation to the Referendum conferred on him by the provisions of Article ___of this Constitution.

4. The President shall exercise the functions in relation to the suspension of the provisions of Article___of this Constitution conferred on him by Article___hereof.

5. The supreme command of the Defence Forces of E. is hereby vested in the President. The manner in which the President shall exercise this command shall be regulated by Organic Laws.

6. All commissioned officers of the Defence Forces of E. shall hold their commissions from the President.

7. The President shall, on the nomination of Dáil Eireann, appoint the Prime Minister, and shall, on the nomination of the Prime Minister, and with the previous approval of Dáil Eireann, appoint the other members of the Council of Ministers. A member of the Council of Ministers may be removed from office by the President acting on the advice of the Prime Minister.

en bloc.

wording

[Shall relinquish office.

8. The judges of the Supreme Court, the High Court and all other the Courts of E. shall be appointed by the President.

A judge of the Supreme Court, or the High Court, or the Circuit Court shall be removed from office by the President upon his being notified in the manner hereinafter provided that resolutions calling for the removal of such judge on the ground of stated misbehaviour or incapacity have been passed /by

Should there be a veto on appt of judges

All Courts?

Question of appointing an

by both Houses of the Oireachtas. The Chairman of Dáil Eireann shall notify the President of any such resolution as aforesaid passed by Dáil Eireann by sending a copy of such resolution signed by him to the President. The Chairman of the Second House shall similarly notify the President of any such resolution passed by the Second House.

9. The right of pardon, and power to remit or commute sentences imposed, and to remit the legal consequences of verdicts given by any courts exercising criminal jurisdiction are hereby vested in the President.

~~10. The President may, at the request of the Council of Ministers and with the concurrence of Dáil Eireann, become Chairman of a national Government during a period of national crisis or emergency whether internal or international.~~

11. Upon the re-assembly of the Oireachtas after a dissolution thereof and on such other occasions as he may consider it right so to do the President may communicate with the Houses of the Oireachtas by message or address on such matters of national or public importance as, after consultation with the Council of State, to him shall seem meet.

12. Additional powers and functions may be conferred on the President by Organic Laws, and such powers and functions shall be exercised by him in accordance with such Laws.

13. The President shall not be held answerable in any court of law or equity for the exercise of the functions of his office or for any act done or purporting to be done by him in pursuance thereof. No action at law or in equity or other legal proceeding shall lie against the President in his

/private

private capacity during his tenure of office. [Criticism in Dáil Senate]

14. Save where otherwise provided by this Constitution, the functions conferred on the President by this Constitution shall be exercisable by him only on the advice of the Council of Ministers.

Presdt shall be ~~apprised~~ notified immed. of all dec. of the Council of Ministers and shall be apprised in advance of all important matters on which a gov. decision is to be taken.

Oct. 22. 1936

Put aside

1076/5

File no 4

PART I. : THE STATE

ARTICLE ONE:

The name of the State is E.

ARTICLE TWO:

E. is a sovereign, independent, democratic State.

ARTICLE THREE:

All powers of government, legislative, executive and judicial in E. are ~~vested~~ resides in the people. These powers are exercisable only through the Organs established by this Constitution or established or recognised by Organic Laws made under this Constitution.

4 Flag ?

ARTICLE ~~FOUR~~: 5

The Irish language is the official language of E. The English language is recognised as a second official language.

Special provision may be made by law for the recognition of only one of the said languages as the official language in districts or areas in which that language only is in general use.

ARTICLE ~~FIVE~~: 6

The following are of Irish nationality and have the rights of citizens of E.

1. All persons born in Ireland.
2. All persons born outside Ireland of Irish parentage or descent as defined or limited by law.
3. All other persons on whom Irish nationality is conferred by naturalization.

in accordance with law ?

The conditions governing the acquisition and the loss of Irish national shall be regulated by law.

PART II.: THE PRESIDENT OF E.

ARTICLE ~~SIX~~ 7: OFFICE OF PRESIDENT

who shall take precedence etc

1. There shall be a President of E. (hereinafter called the President), and who shall exercise and perform the powers and functions conferred on the President by this Constitution or by Organic Laws made under this Constitution

2. The President shall be elected by direct vote of the people. The voting shall be by secret ballot and in accordance with the system of proportional representation known as the single transferrable vote.

3. The President shall hold office for seven years from the date upon which he enters upon his office (unless he previously dies, resigns, becomes permanently incapacitated, or is removed from office) and shall be eligible for re-election.

4. Every person of Irish nationality who has completed his thirty-fifth year of age, who has ordinarily resided in Ireland during the ten years immediately preceding his nomination is eligible for election to the office of President. Every candidate for election (not a former ~~President~~ or retiring Pres.) must be nominated by not less than twenty persons, each of whom is at the time a member of one of the Houses of the Oireachtas. No person shall be entitled to participate in the nomination of more than one candidate in respect of the same election.

Former or retiring Presidents may become candidates on their own nomination.

5. Subject to the provisions of Section 4 of this Article, elections to the office of President may be regulated by Organic Law.

ARTICLE SIX.: (con.)

6. The President shall not be a member of either House of the Oireachtas, and shall not, save as provided by this Constitution, hold an other office.

7. The President shall enter upon his offic on a date to be fixed by law not later than two calendar months from the date of his election.

8. The President shall enter upon his offic by taking and subscribing publicly, in the presence of members of both Houses of the Oireachtas, ~~the Judiciary~~ of the Supreme and High Courts, and other public personages, the following oath:

> "I swear by Almighty God that I will
> "maintain the Constitution of E. and
> "uphold its laws, that I will fulfil
> "my duties faithfully and conscientiously
> "(in accordance with the Constitution
> "and the law), and that I will dedicate
> "my powers to the service and welfare
> "of the people of E. God is witness of
> "this."

To be inserted in Irish

9. Immediately upon entering upon office the President shall nominate three members of the Council of State, (Article)to act as a Commission to discharge the function of the office of President in the case of resignation, death, temporary incapacity or absence of the President from the territory of E. or his removal from office, and pending the ~~appmk~~ election of his successor.

(In case of failure to nominate such Commission, the Commssion should be brought into being by the Council of State nominating three of their members to act.) Shall take oath.

Oath ? ?

ARTICLE SIX: (con.)

10. The President shall not leave the territory of E. during his term of office save with the consent of the Council of Ministers (Article). The

11. The President may be impeached by Dail Eireann for violation of the Constitution, for treason, bribery, or other high crimes or misdemeanours. The charges shall be preferred before the Supreme Court, who shall investigate and report upon the facts to the two Houses of the Oireachtas. On receipt of the report the two Houses shall meet and consider it in joint session, and if a resolution of condemnation be passed, supported by two-thirds of the total membership of both Houses of the Oireachtas, the President shall thereupon ~~cease to be President,~~ vacate his office and an election for (his successor) [President] ? shall be ordered.

Provided that he may go forward for election.

12. The mental [unsound mind(?)] incapacity of the President shall be certified by the Council of State after having received the report of not less than three competent medical experts. ?

In the event of the removal from office of the President or of his death, resignation or permanent incapacity to discharge the functions of the office, an election to fill the office shall be held within two calendar months after such event as aforesaid.

Pending the entry upon his office of the President so to be elected, the functions of the office of President shall devolve upon the Commission provided for in Article ______ insert earlier

13. The President shall take precedence over all other persons in the State.

14. The President shall have an official residence, an official staff and secretariat and shall receive such emoluments and allowances as may be determined by law. The emoluments and allowances of the President shall not be ~~xxxxx~~ diminished during his term of office.

ARTICLE SEVEN: (Powers and Functions of the President).

1. The President on the advice of the Prime Minister, (Article) shall summon and dissolve the Oireachtas: provided, however, that the President shall not be obliged to ~~xxxxxxxxxx~~ dissolve the Oireachtas on the advice of the Prime Minister whose Government had ceased to ~~retain~~ the support of the majority in Dail Eireann.

2. The President shall promulgate laws in the manner provided ~~xxx~~ by Article ___ of this Constitution.

3. The President shall exercise the functions in relation to the Referendum conferred on him by the provisions of Article ______ of this Constitution.

4. The President shall exercise the functions in relation to the suspension of the provisions of Article ______ of this Constitution conferred on him by Article ____ hereof.

5. The supreme command of the Defence Forces of E. is hereby vested in the President. The manner in which the President shall exercise this command shall be regulated by Organic Laws.

ARTICLE SEVEN (con.):

6. All commissioned officers of the Defence Forces of E. shall hold their commissions from the President.

7. The President shall, on the nomination of Dail Eireann, appoint the Prime Minister, and shall, on the nomination of the Prime Minister, and with the previous approval of Dail Eireann, appoint the other members of the Council of Ministers. The President shall, on the advice of the Prime Minister, accept the resignation of, or remove from office any member of the Council of Ministers.

8. The President shall appoint the Judges of the Supreme Court, ~~and~~ the High Court and all other (the) Courts of E.

Veto ? after consulting C. of S. All Judges?

The President shall remove from office any Judge of the Supreme or the High Court, or the Circuit Court upon his being notified in the manner hereinafter provided that resolutions calling for the removal of such judge on the ground of stated misbehaviour or incapacity have been passed by both Houses of the Oireachtas. The Prime Minister shall duly notify the President of any such resolutions as aforesaid, passed by either House of the Oireachtas ~~xxxxxxxxxxxxxxx~~ and send him copies of such resolutions certified by the Chairman (Clerks ?) of the respective Houses.

9. The right of pardon, and power to remit or commute sentences imposed, and to remit the legal consequences of verdicts given by any courts exercising criminal jurisdiction are hereby vested in the President.

ARTICLE SEVEN (con.):

10. The President may, upon the re-assembly og the Oireachtas after the dissolution and on such other occasions as he may consider it proper, communicate with the Houses of the Oireachtas by message or address on ~~xxxxh~~ matters of national or public importance in such terms as, after consultation with the Council of State and with the consent of the Council of Ministers to him shall seem meet.

Presdt need not read speech to which he objects not puppet of exec!

11. Additional powers and functions may be conferred on the President by Organic Laws. All such powers and functions shall be exercised by him in accordance with such Laws.

12. The President shall not be held answerable in any court of law or equity for the exercise of the functions of his office or for any act done or purporting to be done by him in pursuance thereof. No action at law or in equity or other legal proceeding shall lie against the President in his private capacity during his tenure of office.

(7)

13. The President shall not be criticised in either House of the Oireachtas, save on a motion for his impeachment.

14. Except where otherwise provided by this Constitution, the functions conferred on the President by this Constitution shall be exercisable by him only on the advice of the Council of Ministers.

15. President shall be notified immediately of all decisions of the Council of Ministers, and shall be apprised in advance of impending Government decisions on all matters of importance.

APPENDIX 5

FIRST DRAFT, UNDATED LATE 1936, [SOURCE UCDA P150/2385]

First Draft

DVP 1060

Irish & English – compared copies

DeV. Papers and one uncompared extra Irish copy

– the latter taken by P. Ó [illegible]

ARTICLE I.

The Irish Nation.

Definition of membership of the political community of the Nation in terms of persons who possess Irish nationality by virtue of this Constitution or of laws made thereunder.

ARTICLE II.

The National Territory.

Declarations

(a) that the national territory consists of the whole of Ireland and its territorial seas.

(b) that the right of the Nation to the whole of the national territory is absolute and indefeasible.

(c) that without prejudice to the right referred to provision may be made for the application of the laws of E___ to such portion of the national territory as is for the time being under the jurisdiction of the Parliament and Government of E___.

ARTICLE III.

The National Language.

The national language of Ireland is the Irish language.

ARTICLE IV.

The Form of the State.

Declaration of right of the Sovereign Irish People to determine the Form of the State and of the constitutional

/organs

organs of the State.

Declaration that such right is vested in the Sovereign Irish People to the exclusion of every other power or authority whatsoever.

ARTICLE V.

Relations with other States

Declaration that

(a) the relations of the State with other States and

(b) the extent of its co-operation with any other State or any league or group of States

are matters of vital concern to the Irish Nation and within the exclusive competence of the Sovereign Irish People to decide as they think right in the national interest and in the interests of harmonious and pacific international relationships.

PART 1. : THE STATE.

ARTICLE ONE. The name of the State is E.

ARTICLE TWO. E. is a sovereign, independent, democratic State.

ARTICLE THREE. All powers of government, legislative, executive and judicial in E. emenate from the people and are exercisable only through the Organs established by this Constitution or established or recognised by Organic Laws made thereunder.

ARTICLE FOUR. The national flag of E. is a tricolour in green, white and orange.

ARTICLE FIVE. The Irish language is the official language of E. The English language is recognised as a second official language. Special provision may be made by law for the recognition of only one of the said languages as the official language in districts or areas in which that language only is in general use.

ARTICLE SIX. The following are of Irish nationality and are citizens of E. , namely:-

1. All persons born in Ireland.
2. All persons born outside Ireland of Irish parentage or descent as defined or limited by law.
3. All other persons on whom Irish nationality is conferred by naturalization in accordance with law.
4. Irish nationality shall not be conferred

by naturalization upon any person who disbelieves in or is opposed to organized government or is a member of or affiliated with any society or organisation entertaining or teaching disbelief in or opposition to organized government.

5. The conditions governing the loss of Irish nationality shall be regulated by law.

ask for a meeting with [illegible] of the Cab...

(D)

ARTICLE SEVEN. CREATION AND TENURE OF OFFICE.

1. The office of President of E. is hereby created. The President of E. (hereinafter called "the President") shall exercise and perform the powers and functions conferred on the President by this Constitution or by Organic Laws made thereunder.

2. The President shall be elected by direct vote of the people.

3. The President shall hold office for seven years from the date upon which he enters upon his office (unless he previously dies, resigns, becomes permanently incapacitated, or is removed from office) and shall be eligible for re-election.

4. Every person of Irish nationality who has completed his thirty-fifth year of age, who has ordinarily resided in Ireland during the ten years immediately preceding his nomination and who is nominated by not less than twenty members of the Oireachtas shall be eligible for the office of President. A member of the Oireachtas shall not be entitled to participate in the nomination of more than one candidate for the office of President in respect of the same election.

5. Elections to the office of President by direct vote of the people shall, subject to the provisions of Section 4 of this Article, be regulated by Organic Laws.

6. The President shall not be a member of either House of the Oireachtas and shall not, save as provided by this Constitution, hold any other

7. The President shall enter upon his office on a date not later than two calendar months from the date of his election.

8. The President shall enter upon his office by taking and subscribing publicly the following oath before the Chief Justice of E.:

"I swear by Almighty God that I will
"maintain the Constitution of E.
"and uphold its laws, that I will defend
"the State against all its enemies
"whomsoever domestic and external,
"that I will fulfil my duties faith-
"fully and conscientiously in accord-
"ance with the Constitution and the law,
"and that I will dedicate my powers to
"the service and welfare of the People
"of E. So help me God,"

9. The President shall not leave E. during his term of office save with the consent of the Council of Ministers.

10. In the event of the ~~temporary incapacity or~~ absence from E. of the President, the functions of the office of President shall be discharged by a Commission which shall consist of such two or more members of the Council of State as, after consultation with the said Council, the President shall appoint for that purpose.

11. The President shall be removed from office on impeachment by Dáil Eireann for treason, bribery, or other high crimes or misdemeanours and on conviction thereof by two-thirds of the total membership of both Houses of the Oireachtas at a joint session thereof.

/12.

12. In the event of the removal from office of the President or of his death, resignation or permanent incapacity to discharge the functions of the office an election to fill the office shall be held within two calendar months after such event as aforesaid. Pending the entry upon his office of the President so to be elected the functions of the office of President shall devolve upon an Acting President who shall be elected for that purpose by Dáil Eireann. An Acting President shall enter upon his office by taking and subscribing the oath required by Section 7 of this Article to be taken by the President and he shall hold office for a period not exceeding four months from the date upon which he enters upon his office as Acting President.

13. The President shall take precedence over all other persons in the State.

14. The President shall have an official residence an official staff and secretariat and shall receive such emoluments and allowances as may be determined by law. The emoluments and allowances of the President shall not be diminished during his term of office.

ARTICLE EIGHT. POWERS AND FUNCTIONS OF THE PRESIDENT.

1. The President shall summon and dissolve the Oireachtas on the advice of the Prime Minister: Provided, however, that the Oireachtas shall not be dissolved on the advice of a Prime Minister who has ceased to retain the support of a majority in Dáil Eireann.

/2.

2. The President shall promulgate laws in the manner provided by Article ___ of this Constitution

3. The President shall exercise the functions in relation to the Referendum conferred on him by the provisions of Article ___of this Constitution.

4. The President shall exercise the functions in relation to the suspension of the provisions of Article___of this Constitution conferred on him by Article___hereof.

5. The supreme command of the Defence Forces of E. is hereby vested in the President. The manne in which the President shall exercise this command shall be regulated by Organic Laws.

6. All commissioned officers of the Defence Forces of E. shall hold their commissions from the President.

7. The President shall, on the nomination of Dáil Eireann, appoint the Prime Minister, and shall, on the nomination of the Prime Minister, and with the previous approval of Dáil Eireann, appoint the other members of the Council of Ministers. A member of the Council of Ministers may be removed from office by the President acting on the advice of the Prime Minister.

8. The judges of the Supreme Court, the High Court and all other the Courts of E. shall be appointed by the President.

A judge of the Supreme Court, or the High Court, or the Circuit Court shall be removed from office by the President upon his being notified in the manner hereinafter provided that resolutions calling for the removal of such judge on the ground of stated misbehaviour or incapacity have been passe

/by

by both Houses of the Oireachtas. The Chairman of Dáil Eireann shall notify the President of any such resolution as aforesaid passed by Dáil Eireann by sending a copy of such resolution signed by him to the President. The Chairman of the Second House shall similarly notify the President of any such resolution passed by the Second House.

9. The right of pardon, and power to remit or commute sentences imposed, and to remit the legal consequences of verdicts given by any courts exercising criminal jurisdiction are hereby vested in the President.

10. The President may, at the request of the Council of Ministers and with the concurrence of Dáil Eireann, become Chairman of a national Government during a period of national crisis or emergency whether internal or international.

11. Upon the re-assembly of the Oireachtas after a dissolution thereof and on such other occasions as he may consider it right so to do the President may communicate with the Houses of the Oireachtas by message or address on such matters of national or public importance as, after consultation with the Council of State, to him shall seem meet.

12. Additional powers and functions may be conferred on the President by Organic Laws, and such powers and functions shall be exercised by him in accordance with such Laws.

13. The President shall not be held answerable in any court of law or equity for the exercise of the functions of his office or for any act done or purporting to be done by him in pursuance thereof. No action at law or in equity or other legal proceeding shall lie against the President in his
/private

private capacity during his tenure of office.

14. Save where otherwise provided by this Constitution, the functions conferred on the President by this Constitution shall be exercisable by him only on the advice of the Council of Ministers.

PART III.

THE NATIONAL PARLIAMENT.

ARTICLE NINE.

1. The National Parliament of E. shall be called and known (and is herein generally referred to) as the Oireachtas. The Oireachtas shall consist of the President and two Houses; the Primary House or Chamber of Deputies (otherwise called and herein generally referred to as "Dáil Eireann") and the Second House (otherwise called and herein generally referred to as "S".).

2. The Oireachtas is the supreme legislative authority of E. No other legislative authority whatsoever has power to make laws for E.

3. The Oireachtas shall hold at least one session each year.

4. The right to raise and maintain armed forces is vested exclusively in the Oireachtas.

No armed force (other than armed forces raised and maintained by the Oireachtas) shall be raised or maintained in E. for any purpose whatsoever.

5. The State shall not declare or participate in any war without the assent of the Oireachtas, provided, however, that in the case of actual invasion the Council of Ministers may take such steps as they may consider necessary for the protection of the State.

6. The Oireachtas shall have no power to declare acts to be infringements of the law which are not so at the date of their commission.

7. Organic Laws may provide for the creation of

subordinate legislatures and for the powers and functions thereof.

8. Each House of the Oireachtas shall elect its own Chairman and Deputy Chairman and shall prescribe their powers, duties, remuneration, and terms of office.

9. Each House shall make its own Rules and Standing Orders, with power to attach penalties for their infringement and shall have power to ensure freedom of debate, to protect its official documents and the private papers of its members, and to protect itself and its members against any person or persons interfering with, molesting or attempting to corrupt its members in the exercise of their duties.

10. Sittings of each House of the Oireachtas shall be public. In cases of special emergency either House may hold a private sitting with the assent of two-thirds of the members present.

11. All matters in each House shall, save as otherwise provided by this Constitution, be determined by a majority of the votes of the members present other than the Chairman or presiding member, who shall have and exercise a casting vote in the case of an equality of votes. The number of members necessary to constitute a meeting of either House for the exercise of its powers shall be determined by its Standing Orders.

12. All official reports and publications of the Oireachtas or of either House thereof shall be privileged and utterances made in either House wherever published shall be privileged.

13. Every member of the Oireachtas shall, except

in case of treason as defined in this Constitution, felony, or breach of the peace, be privileged from arrest in going to and returning from, and while within the precincts of either House, and shall not, in respect of any utterance in either House, be amenable to any action or proceeding in any Court other than the House itself.

14. No person may be at the same time a member of both Houses of the Oireachtas, and, if any person who is already a member of either House is elected to be a member of the other House, he shall forthwith be deemed to have vacated his first seat.

15. The Oireachtas shall make provision for the payment of its members and may in addition provide them with free travelling facilities in any part of E. and such free postal facilities as the Oireachtas may determine.

DÁIL ÉIREANN.

ARTICLE TEN.

1. Every person of Irish nationality who has reached the age of twenty-one years and who is not placed under disability or incapacity by law shall be eligible for membership of Dáil Eireann. Every person of Irish nationality who has reached the age of twenty-one years and who complies with the provisions of the Organic Laws relating to the election of members of Dáil Eireann shall have the right to vote for members of Dáil Eireann.

2. Dáil Eireann shall be composed of members who represent constituencies determined by Organic Laws. The number of members shall be fixed from time to time by such Laws, but the total number of

members of Dáil Eireann shall not be fixed at less than one member for each thirty thousand of the population, or at more than one member for each twenty thousand of the population: Provided that the proportion between the number of members to be elected at any time for each constituency and the population of each constituency, as ascertained at the last preceding census, shall, so far as possible, be identical throughout the country. The members shall be elected upon principles of Proportional Representation, the election to be by means of the Single Transferable Vote. No Organic Law shall be enacted whereby the number of members to be returned for any constituency shall be less than three. The Oireachtas shall revise the constituencies at least once in every ten years, with due regard to changes in distribution of the population, but any alterations in the constituencies shall not take effect during the life of Dáil Eireann sitting when such revision is made.

3. A general election for members of Dáil Eireann shall take place not later than thirty days after a dissolution of the Oireachtas.

4. Polling at every such election shall take place on the same day throughout E.

5. The member of Dáil Eireann who is the Chairman of Dáil Eireann immediately before a dissolution of the Oireachtas shall, unless before such dissolution he announces to Dáil Eireann that he does not desire to continue to be a member thereof, be deemed without any actual election to be elected in accordance with this Constitution at the ensuing general election as a member of Dáil Eireann for the constituency for

which he was a member immediately before such dissolution or, in the event of a revision of constituencies having taken place, for the revised constituency declared on such revision to correspond to such first-mentioned constituency. Whenever a former Chairman of Dáil Eireann is so deemed to have been elected at a general election as a member for a constituency the number of members actually to be elected for such constituency at such general election shall be one less than would otherwise be required to be elected therefor,

6. Subject to the foregoing, provision shall be made by Organic Laws for the following matters that is to say:-

(a) The number of members of Dáil Eireann,

(b) the creation and revision of constituencies, and

(c) the election of members of Dáil Eireann, including provision for the filling of casual vacancies, and

(d) the payment of members of Dáil Eireann and the provision of travelling facilities for such members.

7. Dáil Eireann shall have legislative authority exclusive of S. in relation to Money Bills as hereinafter defined.

A Money Bill means a Bill which contains only provisions dealing with all or any of the following subjects, namely, the imposition, repeal, remission, alteration or regulation of taxation; the

imposition/

imposition for the payment of debt or other financial purposes of charges on public moneys or the variation or repeal of any such charges; supply, the appropriation, receipt, custody, issue or audit of accounts of public money; the raising or guarantee of any loan or the repayment thereof; subordinate matters incidental to those subjects or any of them. In this definition the expressions "taxation", "public money" and "loan" respectively do not include any taxation, money or loan raised by local authorities or bodies for local purposes.

8. (Insert provision for certification of Money Bill as heretofore).

9. As soon as possible after the commencement of each financial year Dáil Eireann shall consider the Estimates of receipts and expenditure of the State for that year, and, save in so far as may be provided by specific enactment in each case, the legislation required to give effect to the Financial Resolutions of each year shall be enacted within that year.

10. Money shall not be appropriated by vote, resolution, or law, unless the purpose of the appropriatio has in the same session been recommended by a message in writing from the Council of Ministers signed by the Prime Minister.

Changed'

THE SECOND HOUSE ("S").

ARTICLE ELEVEN.

1. The number of members of S. shall be forty-five.

2. Every person of Irish nationality who has /reached

reached the age of thirty-five years and who is not placed under disability or incapacity by law shall be eligible for membership of S.

3. Provision as to term of office of members of S. (Decision to be taken).

4. Provision as to method or methods of selection of members of S. (Decision to be taken).

5. Every Bill initiated in Dáil Eireann shall (whether before or after its passage by Dáil Eireann) be sent to S. and shall be considered by S.

6. S. may amend any Bill (other than a Money Bill) sent to it by Dáil Eireann. Every such amendment shall be considered by Dáil Eireann

7. S. shall return a Bill sent to it by Dáil Eireann with its amendments (if any) not later than ninety days after the date on which the Bill was sent to S. , or such longer period as may be agreed to in respect of such Bill by both Houses.

8. In the event of the failure of S. to pass a Bill (other than a Money Bill) sent to it by Dáil Eireann within the said ninety days (or any such longer period as aforesaid) or its failure to pass such Bill within the said ninety days (or such longer period) with amendments to which Dáil Eireann agrees such Bill may, at the expiration of the said ninety days (or such longer period), be sent to S. a second time. Should S. fail to pass such Bill within a period of ninety days from the date on which such Bill is so sent to it a second time or fail within the

/said

said period to pass such Bill with amendments to which Dáil Eireann agrees such Bill shall if Dáil Eireann by a resolution passed at the expiration of the said period so declares be deemed to have been passed by both Houses.

9. If and whenever the Prime Minister on the introduction of a Bill certifies by message in writing addressed to both Houses that such Bill is urgent and immediately necessary for the preservation of the public peace and security, or is rendered necessary by the existence of a national emergency, whether internal or international, the time for consideration of such Bil by S. may by resolution of Dáil Eireann be abridged to such period as shall be specified in that behalf in such resolution.

10. S. shall have no power to reject or amend a Money Bill, but shall have power to make recommendations to Dáil Eireann with regard to every such Bill. Every such recommendation shal be made not later than twenty-one days after the date on which the Money Bill to which they relat is sent to S. by Dáil Eireann.

11. A Bill (other than a Money Bill) may be initiated in S. by a member of the Council of Ministers or a member of S.

PART IV.

THE GOVERNMENT.

ARTICLE TWELVE.

1. The Government of E. shall consist of a Council (herein generally referred to as "the

/Council

Council of Ministers"). The Council of Ministers shall exercise and perform the powers and functions conferred on the Council of Ministers by this Constitution or by Organic Laws made thereunder.

2. The President of the Council of Ministers shall be called and known as "the Prime Minister", and the Vice-President of the Council of Ministers shall be called and known as "the Deputy Prime Minister".

and shall have prec. next to the Uachtarán.

3. The Council of Ministers shall be composed of not less than nine [and not more than fifteen] members.

The Prime Minister, the Deputy Prime Minister and the members of the Council of Ministers who ~~is~~ are the Minister in charge of the Department of Finance, shall be members of Dáil Eireann. Not more than two of the other members of the Council of Ministers may be a member of S. Every member of the Council of Ministers who is not a member of S. shall be a member of Dáil Eireann.

and of External affairs and of Defence

4. The Prime Minister, the Deputy Prime Minister and the other members of the Council of Ministers shall be appointed respectively in the manner provided by section 7 of Article Eight of this Constitution.

The Deputy Prime Minister shall act for all purposes in the place of the Prime Minister should the Prime Minister die, resign, or become permanently incapacitated until a new Prime Minister shall have been appointed. The Deputy

/Prime

Prime Minister shall also act in the place of the Prime Minister during his temporary absence.

5. The Council of Ministers shall meet and act as a collective authority and shall be collectively responsible to Dáil Eireann concerning any Departments of State administered by the members of the Council of Ministers.

6. The Council of Ministers shall prepare Estimates of the receipts and expenditure of E. for each financial year, and shall present them to Dáil Eireann before the end of the previous financial year.

7. Every member of the Council of Ministers shall have the right to attend and be heard in each House of the Oireachtas.

8. A member of the Council of Ministers may resign from office by placing his resignation in the hands of the Prime Minister.

The Prime Minister may at any time, for reasons which to him seem sufficient, request a member of the Council of Ministers so to resign, and, in the event of the failure of such member to comply with such request, the appointment of such member may be terminated by the President on the advice of the Prime Minister.

9. In the event of the Prime Minister ceasing to retain the support of a majority in Dáil Eireann, the Prime Minister and the other members of the Council of Ministers shall retire from office but shall continue to carry on their duties until [illegible]

2

appointed.

10. The members of the Council of Ministers shall receive such remuneration as may from time to time be determined by law, but the remuneration of any Minister shall not be diminished during his term of office.

PART V.

THE COUNCIL OF STATE.

ARTICLE THIRTEEN.

1. There shall be a Council (herein generally referred as "the Council of State") to aid and counsel the President on all matters on which the President may consult the said Council in relation to the exercise and performance by him of such of his powers and functions as are by this Constitution declared to be exercisable and performable after consultation with the Council of State.

2. The Council of State shall consist of the ex-officio members hereinafter mentioned and the members appointed by the President under this Article.

3. The following shall be ex-officio members of the Council of State, namely,

The Prime Minister
The Deputy Prime Minister
The Chief Justice of E.
The Chairman of Dáil Eireann
The Chairman of S.
The President of the High Court
The Attorney General, and
Every person who shall have held the office of President.

4. Three members of the Council of State shall be appointed by the President as soon as may be after the date on which he enters upon his office, and every member then appointed shall, unless he previously dies, resigns or becomes permanently incapacitated, hold office for so long ad the President by whom he is appointed holds office as President.

/5.

Title Councillor of State

5. The President may, from time to time, appoint such and so many other members of the Council of State as in his absolute discretion he may consider it advisable to appoint from amongst persons who shall have held any of the following offices, that is to say, the office of President of the Executive Council of Saorstát Eireann, the office of Prime Minister, the ~~office of Chief Justice of Saorstát Eireann,~~ and the office of ~~Chief~~ Justice of E.

of S.E. or Provisional

6. Every appointment to membership of the Council of State under sections 4 and 5 of this Article shall be made by warrant issued under the hand and Seal of the President. A member of the Council of State appointed under section 5 of this Article shall hold office by such tenure as shall be specified in the warrant of his appointment.

unpaid?

7. The President may by warrant under his hand and Seal appoint members of the Council of State to fill casual vacancies in the membership thereof caused by the death, resignation or permanent incapacity of members appointed by him.

8. Meetings of the Council of State may be convened by the President at such times and places as he may determine either generally or with regard to any particular meeting thereof.

9. The Council of State in existence at the date on which the President ceases to hold office shall continue to exercise its functions until a new President takes office.

ARTICLE FOURTEEN.

1. As soon as may be after the appointments required by section 4 of ARTICLE THIRTEEN hereof to be made by the President shall have been made by him (and whether before or after he shall have made any other appointments to the Council of State) the President shall nominate three members of the Council of State to exercise and perform the powers and functions of the President under this Constitution during his temporary absence from E. or during his temporary incapacity.

2. In the event of the death, resignation from the Council of State or incapacity of any of the members nominated as aforesaid, the President shall nominate another member of the Council of State to take the place of such member.

3. Any two of the members of the Council of State nominated under this Article may exercise and perform the powers and functions of the President during his temporary absence from E. or during his temporary incapacity.

ARTICLE FIFTEEN.

In the event of the failure of the President to make the appointments and nominations required by the preceding Articles of this Part of this Constitution to be made by him, the same shall be made by a majority of the ex-officio members of the Council of State then available.

ARTICLE SIXTEEN.

1. The President shall not exercise or perform any of the powers or functions which are by this Constitution declared to be exercisable and performable by him after consultation with the Council of State unless, before so doing, the President shall have convened a meeting of the Council of State and the members of the Council of State present at such meeting shall have been heard by him in the matter.

2. The provisions of the foregoing section of this Article shall apply in relation to the exercise and performance of the powers and functions of the President by the members of the Council of State nominated for that purpose under Article Fourteen hereof, with the following modifications, that is to say, meetings of the Council of State shall be convened by the said nominated members thereof or by any two of their number, and the consultation referred to in the said foregoing section shall be consultation by the said nominated members with the other members of the Council of State present at a meeting so convened.

ARTICLE SEVENTEEN/

PART VI.

THE COURTS.

ARTICLE SEVENTEEN.

1. Justice shall be administered in public courts established by Organic Laws by judges appointed in the manner provided By this Constitution.

2. The Courts shall comprise Courts of First Instance and a Court of Final Appeal.

ARTICLE EIGHTEEN.

1. The Courts of First Instance shall include a High Court invested with full origina jurisdiction in and power to determine all matters and questions whether of law or fact, civil or criminal.

2. The High Court shall have original jurisdiction to entertain and determine the question of the validity of any law having regard to the provisions of this Constitution.

3. The Courts of First Instance shall also include Courts of local and limited jurisdiction with a right of appeal as determined by law.

ARTICLE NINETEEN.

1. The Court of Final Appeal shall be calle the Supreme Court. The President of the Supreme Court shall be called "The Chief Justi of E."

2. The Supreme Court shall, with such excep tions (not including cases which involve questions as to the validity of any law) and subject to such regulations as may be

prescribed by Organic Laws, have appellate jurisdiction from all decisions of the High Court. The decision of the Supreme Court shall in all cases be final and conclusive.

ARTICLE TWENTY.

All judges shall be independent in the exercise of their judicial functions and subject only to this Constitution and the law.

No judge shall be eligible to sit in the Oireachtas or to hold any other office or position of emolument.

ARTICLE TWENTY-ONE.

The judges of the High Court and the Supreme Court shall not be removed from office save only for either or both of the reasons and in the manner mentioned in section 8 of Article Eight of this Constitution.

ARTICLE TWENTY-TWO.

The remuneration of any of the judges referred to in the preceding Section of this Article shall not be reduced during his continuance in office.

ARTICLE TWENTY-THREE.

Subject to the foregoing provisions of this PART of this Constitution, the following matters and things may be regulated by Organic Laws and Rules of Court made thereunder, that is to say:-

(a) the number of judges of the Supreme Court, the High Court, and all other Courts established under this Constitution, the declarations to be taken by /them

them on appointment, the remuneration, age of retirement and pensions of such judges, and

(b) the constitution and organization of the said Courts, the distribution of business and jurisdiction among the said Courts and judges, and the procedure of such Courts.

PART VII.

The Comptroller and Auditor General.

ARTICLE TWENTY-FOUR.

1. There shall be a Comptroller and Auditor General to control on behalf of E. all disbursements and to audit all accounts of moneys administered by or under the authority of the Oireachtas.

2. The Comptroller and Auditor General shall be appointed by the President on the nomination of Dáil Eireann. He shall not be a member of either House of the Oireachtas and shall not hold any other office or position of emolument. The terms and conditions of his tenure of office shall be determined by Organic Laws.

3. The Comptroller and Auditor General shall report to Dáil Eireann at stated periods to be determined by Organic Laws.

4. He shall not be removed from office save only for either or both of the reasons and in the manner mentioned in section of Article Eight of this Constitution.

/PART VIII.

PART VIII.

Amendment of the Constitution:

THE REFERENDUM.

ARTICLE TWENTY-FIVE.

1. This Constitution shall not be amended save in the manner provided by this Article.

2. Every Bill containing a proposal for the amendment of this Constitution or of any provision thereof (including this Article or any provision thereof) shall, upon having been passed or deemed to have been passed by both Houses of the Oireachtas, be submitted by Referendum to the decision of the people in accordance with the Organic Law for the time being in force relating to the Referendum.

3. Every such Bill as aforesaid shall in the long title thereof be entitled "an Act to amend the Constitution".

4. A Bill containing a proposal or proposals for the amendment of this Constitution shall not contain any other proposal.

ARTICLE TWENTY-SIX.

1. Any Bill to which this Article applies may be submitted by Referendum to the decision of the people, subject to and in accordance with the provisions of this Article.

2. This Article applies to any Bill passed or deemed to have been passed by both Houses of the Oireachtas, other than a Money Bill or a Bill in respect of which a resolution shall have been passed by Dáil Eireann under section 9 of Article Eleven of this Constitution.

/3.

3. A majority of the members of S. may, on any mne or more of the grounds hereinafter specified, request the President, by a petition addressed to him for that purpose in the manner hereinafter mentioned, that any Bill to which this Article applies (the subject of such petition) be submitted by Referendum to the decision of the people.

4. Every petition addressed to the President under this Article shall be based on any one or more of the following grounds, namely, that the Bill or any provision thereof to which the petition relates

(a) is in conflict with any Article of this Constitution, or

(b) embodies a principle which has not already been pronounced upon by the electorate, or

(c) is contrary to settled national policy, or

(d) affects the credit or prestige of the State to its detriment.

5. Every such petition as aforesaid shall be in writing signed by the members of S. who are parties thereto, shall contain a statement of the ground or grounds on which such request is based, and shall be presented to the President together with a copy of the Bill to which it relates not later than four days after the date on which such Bill shall have been passed or deemed to have been passed by both Houses of the Oireachtas.

6. Upon receipt of a petition addressed to him under this Article, the President shall

after consultation with the Council of State, pronounce his decision thereon not later than six days after the date on which the Bill to which such petition relates shall have been passed or deemed to have been passed by both Houses of the Oireachtas.

7. In every case in which the President decides that a Bill the subject of a petition under this Article shall be submitted by Referendum to the decision of the people, he shall inform the Chairman of S. and the Prime Minister accordingly in writing under his hand and Seal, and shall, at the same time and in the same manner, direct the Prime Minister to make arrangements for the submission of such Bill to the decision of the people not later than three months from the date of such direction and in accordance with the Organic Law for the time being in force relating to the Referendum.

8. In every case in which the President decides that a Bill the subject of a petition under this Article shall not be submitted by Referendum to the decision of the people, he shall inform the Chairman of S. and the Prime Minister accordingly, and such Bill shall thereupon be presented to the President for signature and promulgation by him in the manne provided and within the time specified by Article   of this Constitution.

9. In this Article and the subsequent Articles of this Part of this Constitution the word "Bill" includes any provision of a Bill.

/ARTICLE TWENTY-SEVEN.

33

ARTICLE TWENTY-SEVEN.

1. A majority of the members of S. may by a petition addressed to the President for that purpose request the President that any Bill the subject of such petition containing proposals for an Organic Law (as defined in this Constitution) which shall have been passed or deemed to have been passed by both Houses of the Oireachtas, may be submitted by Referendum to the decision of the people.

2. Every such petition shall contain a statement of the ground or grounds on which such request is based and the provisions of sections 5, 6, 7 and 8 of Article Twenty-five hereof shall apply to such petition and to the Bill the subject thereof in like manner in all respects as those provisions apply to a petition presented to the President under the said Article Twenty-five and to a Bill the subject of such petition.

ARTICLE TWENTY-EIGHT.

Every Bill which, in pursuance of this Part of this Constitution, is submitted by Referendum to the decision of the people, shall be presented to the President for signature and promulgation as law by him under Article   hereof if, upon having been so submitted, a majority of the voters on the Register shall have recorded their votes on such Referendum and either

(a) the votes of the majority of voters on the Register, or

(b) two-thirds of the votes recorded,

shall have been cast in favour of such Bill.

ARTICLE TWENTY-NINE.

In the event of a dissolution and re-assembly of the Oireachtas after the date on which the President shall have directed that a Bill the subject of a petition to him under Article Twenty-five or Article Twenty-six hereof be submitted by Referendum to the decision of the people and before the date on which the Referendum on such Bill shall have taken place, such Bill, if again passed by both Houses of the Oireachtas after such re-assembly and before the date on which the Referendum thereon shall have taken place, shall be presented to the President for signature and promulgation by him under Article   of this Constitution.

ARTICLE THIRTY.

1. The Council of Ministers may, of their own motion, by an Order made under this Article direct that any Bill which shall have been passed or deemed to have been passed by both Houses of the Oireachtas be submitted by Referendum to the decision of the people in accordance with the Organic Law for the time being in force relating to the Referendum.

2. No Order made by the Council of Ministers under this Article shall have any effect unless it shall have been made not later than four days after the date on which the Bill to which it relates shall have been passed or deemed to have been passed by both Houses of the Oireachtas.

ARTICLE THIRTY-ONE.

1. Every person of Irish nationality who has

reached the age of twenty-one years shall be entitled to vote at a Referendum held under this Part of this Constitution.

2. Subject as aforesaid the Referendum shall be regulated by Organic Laws.

(3¼)

PART IX.

CONSTITUTIONAL GUARANTEES.

ARTICLE THIRTY-TWO. 1. All citizens are equal before the law. No titles of nobility shall be conferred, but Orders of Merit may be created. Only citizens are eligible for civil or military offices save in special cases provided for by law.

2. A decision of the Courts in any action or other proceeding shall not be nullified as regards the parties to such proceeding by retrospective legislation.

3. Freedom of conscience and the free expression and practice of religion are, subject to public order and morality, guaranteed to every person.

No disability shall be imposed or preference given by law on the ground of religious belief or religious status.

4. The following rights are guaranteed to all citizens, subject to public order and morality:-

(1) the right of free expression of opinion,

(2) the right to assemble peaceably and without arms, and

(3) the right to form associations and unions.

Laws may be passed to prevent or control meetings which are calculated to cause a breach of the peace or to be a danger or nuisance to the general public. Open air /meetings

(37)

meetings shall be subject to police regulations and control so as not to interfere with public convenience or normal traffic.

Laws regulating the manner in which the right of forming associations and unions and the right of free assembly may be exercised shall contain no political, religious or class distinction.

5. (1) The liberty of the person is inviolable, and no person shall be deprived of his liberty except in accordance with law.

(2) Upon complaint made by or on behalf of any person that he is being unlawfully detained, the High Court and any and every judge thereof shall forthwith enquire into the same and may make an order requiring the person in whose custody such person shall be detained to produce the body of the person so detained before such Court or judge without delay and to certify in writing as to the cause of the detention and such Court or judge shall thereupon order the release of such person unless satisfied that he is being detained in accordance with the law.

(3) Nothing in this Article shall be invoked to prohibit control or interfere with any act of the defence forces of E. during the existence of a state of war or armed rebellion.

6. The dwelling of each citizen is inviolable and shall not be forcibly entered except in accordance with law.

/ARTICLE THIRTY-THREE.

ARTICLE THIRTY-THREE.

1. Every religious association has the right of assembly for the conduct of religious services in private and in public, subject to public order and morality. No law shall be passed to prohibit or restrict the free exercise of such right.

2. Every religious association has the right to manage its own affairs, own or acquire movable and immovable property, administer and dispose of the same, possess and enjoy its revenues and endowments and maintain institutions for religious and charitable purposes.

3. No religion shall be endowed directly or indirectly by law.

4. Legislation providing for State aid for schools shall contain no discrimination against schools under the management of a particular religious denomination.

5. The property of any religious denomination shall not be diverted save for the purpose of works of public utility and upon payment of compensation.

ARTICLE THIRTY-FOUR.

1. The State guarantees the constitution and protection of the family as the basis of moral education and social discipline and harmony, and the sure foundation of ordered society.

2. (1) The constitution of the family depends upon valid marriage.

(2) Marriage, as the basis of family life, is under the special protection of the State; attacks on the sanctity of marriage or of family life are prohibited

- -

(3) Contraception and advocacy of the practice of contraception are prohibited and the possession, use, sale, and distribution of contraceptives shall be punishable by law.

(4) No law shall be enacted authorising the dissolution of a valid consummated marriage of baptized persons. No law shall be enacted authorising the annulment of marriage save on the following grounds, namely, that either or both of the parties did not agree to enter into the marriage contract, or was or were not free to enter, or did not freely enter into the marriage contract, or that the marriage was under the law for the time being in force invalid in form. Subject to the foregoing, the contract of marriage shall be regulated by law.

(5) The State shall encourage early marriage and foster the production of large families by appropriate grants of remission of taxation in respect of children, by the promotion of saving and thrift schemes and by facilitating the provision of housing accommodation on reasonable terms.

(6) Maternity is under the special protection of the State. Provision may be made by law for the supervision and inspection of lying-in hospitals and maternity nursing homes.

/ARTICLE THIRTY-FIVE.

ARTICLE THIRTY-FIVE. 1. The right to private ownership of property is hereby affirmed to be a natural human right and a basic principle of ordered human society.

2. The State guarantees protection of their private property to all citizens and all bodies corporate and unincorporate within the State, and no such property shall be limited or acquired by the State save for general utility purposes and upon payment of compensation. Nothing in this Article shall operate to prevent the seizure or forfeiture of property under an order of a court in accordance with law.

ARTICLE THIRTY-SIX. 1. The right of parents to the custody of their minor children, subject to the law, and, subject as aforesaid, the duty of parents to exercise authority and control over their minor children, are hereby affirmed.

2. Parents shall not be deprived of the custody of a minor child save by the due exercise of its jurisdiction by a court having jurisdiction in the matter.

3. Children deprived of parental care have the right to the special protection of the State within the limits determined by law.

/4.

4. Parents or other persons having the legal custody of children are obliged to provide education for such children in their homes or to require them to attend national or other suitable schools.

5. Wage-earning by children of less than fifteen years of age shall be prohibited.

ARTICLE THIRTY-SEVEN. 1. The State undertakes to take measures to prevent the corruption of public morals.

2. The State will in particular maintain, duly administer, and, as the Oireachtas may determine, improve laws regulating the following matters, that is to say,

(a) the protection of young girls, the suppression of brothels and prostitution and the punishment of sexual crimes,

(b) the conditions of employment of women and young persons in industrial works,

(c) a censorship of publications,

(d) a censorship of cinematograph performances, stage plays and other entertainments,

(e) the sale of noxious drugs and intoxicating liquors, and

(f) the licensing and supervision of clubs and public dance-halls.

/ARTICLE THIRTY-EIGHT.

ARTICLE THIRTY-EIGHT. 1. All citizens have the right to free elementary education.

2. Primary instruction is obligatory and may be given in the home or private schools or in official schools established or recognised by the State. All such instruction shall have for its aim the formation of character, the cult of moral and civic virtue, as well as the development of the physical and intellectual faculties.

3. The State shall maintain primary and secondary schools as well as institutes of higher education.

4. Professional degrees or diplomas shall not be granted except by institutions established or recognised for that purpose by the State.

5. Private schools may be established subject to inspection by authorised officers of the State.

6. In all schools and educational establishments for the instruction of young persons who have not reached the age of eighteen years, the teaching of religion is compulsory for all pupils. The direction and control of such teaching is the province of the particular Church or religious communion to which the pupils concerned belong, without prejudice to the supreme right of control reserved to the State educational authorities.

PART X.

ECONOMIC LIFE.

ARTICLE THIRTY-NINE. 1. All the lands, waters, mines, minerals, and other natural resources, and also all royalties and franchises heretofore vested in Saorstát Eireann shall, as from the date of the coming into operation of this Constitution, belong to E. subject to any trusts, grants, leases or concessions then existing in respect thereof or any valid private interest therein.

2. The said natural resources, and the said royalties and franchises shall be controlled and administered by the Oireachtas, and the same or any part thereof shall not be alienated, but may from time to time in the public interest be granted by way of lease or licence to be worked or enjoyed under the authority and subject to the control of the Oireachtas. No such lease or licence may be made for a term exceeding ninety-nine years beginning from the date thereof, and no such lease or licence may be renewable by the terms thereof.

3. The natural resources of E. (including the air and all forms of potential energy) are dedicated to the maintenance of the people of E. and are under the special control and supervision of the State. Rights of private

/property

property in any of the said natural resources shall be exercised and the use and exploitation thereof by private owners shall be conducted with a view to the conservation and development of the said resources for the benefit of the community.

4. All natural resources which have not yet been effectively appropriated by private individuals or associations are hereby declared to be vested in E. as from the date of the coming into operation of this Constitution.

ARTICLE FORTY.

1. The ownership, distribution and use of land are under the special control and supervision of the State, and such control and supervision shall be exercised so as to promote the creation and development of the maximum number of economic holdings privately owned, the relief of congestion, and the establishment of working farmers on the land.

2. It is hereby declared to be the duty of landowners to work their holdings in accordance with proper methods of husbandry so as to maintain and develop the productivity of the soil to their own advantage and for the benefit of the community.

ARTICLE FORTY-ONE.

The State undertakes to protect the sea fisheries and to develop the sea fishing industry for the benefit of the community.

/ARTICLE FORTY-TWO.

ARTICLE FORTY-TWO.

The transport services of E. (including railways, waterways and airways) shall be under the control and supervision of the State and shall be administered, operated, co-ordinated and developed with a view to facilitating agricultural development and industrial and commercial progress in time of peace and the defence of the country in time of war.

ARTICLE FORTY-THREE.

It shall be the aim of social legislation to promote the association of employers and employed in the management and control of industry, to favour the diffusion of property, to encourage co-operative ownership and organization, and to facilitate the formation and functioning of professional and occupational guilds.

(116)

PART XI.

POWER TO SUSPEND CERTAIN CONSTITUTIONAL GUARANTEES.

ARTICLE FORTY-FOUR. 1. If and whenever Dáil Eireann or, if Dáil Eireann is not sitting, the Council of Ministers is satisfied that a grave state of public disorder exists or is threatened throughout E. or in any specified district or districts thereof, and that the ordinary laws and the civil courts are not adequate for the preservation of public order, Dáil Eireann or the Council of Ministers (as the case may require) may, by proclamation, declare the existence of a state of public emergency in respect of the area to which such proclamation relates.

2. Whenever the Council of Ministers declares a state of public emergency under this Article, the President shall forthwith summon Dáil Eireann.

3. Upon the reassembly of Dáil Eireann, the proclamation of the Council of Ministers declaring a state of public emergency shall forthwith be laid before Dáil Eireann and, unless Dáil Eireann, within a period of seven days after such re-assembly, shall have passed a resolution confirming such proclamation, such proclamation shall, at the expiration of the said seven days, cease to have effect.

4. Upon a proclamation being made by Dáil Eireann under this Article, or upon a proclamation made by the Council of Ministers being confirmed by Dáil Eireann under this

(7)

Article (as the case may be), the President shall issue an order under his hand and seal directing that the provisions section 4, section 5 and section 6 of ARTICLE THIRTY-ONE of this Constitution be suspended in respect of the area to which such proclamation relates (which shall be defined in such order), and for the period specified in such order, and, upon such order being made, the provisions of the sections herein before mentioned of the said ARTICLE THIRTY-ONE shall be suspended accordingly.

5. The Oireachtas may enact such legislation establishing such extraordinary courts and investing such courts with such jurisdiction as the Oireachtas may consider to be necessary and adequate to deal with any such state of publi emergency as aforesaid; but such legislation shall not come into operation unless and until an order shall have been made by the President under this Article, and then only in respect of the area mentioned in such order and for the period specified therein.

6. Nothing in this Constitution or in any law continued thereby or made thereunder shall be invoked to nullify any provision of this Article or of any legislation passed under this Article or to oust the jurisdiction of any Court established hereunder or to invalidate any act or thing done in pursuance of this Article or of any legislation enacted for the purposes thereof.

7. The decisions of any court established under this Article shall not be subject to appeal or to review by any other court.

(48)

PART XII.

GENERAL.

ARTICLE FORTY-FIVE. 1. All crimes and offences prosecuted on indictment in any court shall be prosecuted in the name of the People and at the suit of the Attorney General of E.

2. The trial of all crimes shall be by jury, except in the case of treason (as defined in this Constitution), crimes triable by impeachment, minor offences triable by a court of summary jurisdiction, charges for offences against military law by persons subject to military law, and charges for offences triable by extraordinary courts during a state of war or armed rebellion or during a state of public emergency proclaimed under this Constitution.

ARTICLE FORTY-SIX. 1. Treason against E. shall consist only in (a) levying war against E. or assisting any state or person or inciting or conspiring with any person to levy war against E. or in (b) attempting by force of arms or other violent means to overthrow the organs of government established by this Constitution or taking part or being concerned in or inciting or conspiracy with any person to make or to take part or be concerned in any such attempt.

2. All charges of treason shall be triable on indictment and, subject as aforesaid, provision shall be made by law for the trial and punishment of treason.

/ARTICLE FORTY-SEVEN.

ARTICLE FORTY-SEVEN. 1. Organic Laws may be enacted by the Oireachtas to regulate any matter or thing relating to the exercise of the powers of government of E., legislative, executive and judicial, the regulation of which by Organic Laws is required or authorised by this Constitution.

2. Every Organic Law Bill shall be entitled "An Organic Law" in the long and short titles thereof.

ARTICLE FORTY-EIGHT. 1. The Constitution given the force of law by the Constitution of the Irish Free State (Saorstát Eireann) Act, 1922, as amended by any Act of Oireachtas of Saorstát Eireann, is hereby repealed.

ARTICLE FORTY-NINE. 1. This Constitution shall be submitted to a plebiscite in accordance with a law to be passed by the Oireachtas of Saorstát Eireann for that purpose.

To be recast

2. A general election for Dáil Eireann shall take place at the same time as the said plebiscite. Polling for the purpose of the said election and polling for the purpose of the said plebiscite shall take place on the same day.

3. Every person who is registered in the register of electors for the purpose of election for Dáil Eireann shall be entitled to vote at such plebiscite.

4. If, upon the submission of this Constitution to such plebiscite, a majority of the voters on the Register shall have recorded /their

(50)

their votes at such plebiscite and either

(a) the votes of the majority of voters on the register, or

(b) two-thirds of the votes recorded

shall have been cast in favour of this Constitution, this Constitution shall come into operation on a date to be fixed by a resolution passed for that purpose by a majority of the members of Dáil Eireann elected at the general election to be held as aforesaid: Provided that the date so fixed shall not be later than six months after the date of the first meeting of Dáil Eireann to be held after such general election as aforesaid.

PART XIII.

TRANSITORY PROVISIONS.

APPENDIX 6

KING EDWARD CRISIS : SUMMARY OF EVENTS [SOURCE NAI DFA S57]

KING EDWARD CRISIS.

Summary of events in so far as Saorstát Eireann is concerned up to Sunday night, 6th December.

On Sunday, 29th November, Sir Harry Batterbee, Assistant Secretary of the Dominions Office, visited the President in Government Buildings and gave him, on behalf of Mr. Baldwin, in a "purely friendly personal and secret way", the following information.

Mr. Baldwin had felt it his duty "recently" to broach to the King the subject of his relations with Mrs. Simpson , and to warn him of the grave consequences which might flow from the existing state of affairs, especially if the pending divorce suit was proceeded with. The King summoned Mr. Baldwin for an interview on November 16th after the granting of the decree nisi. He informed the Prime Minister that it was his fixed intention to marry Mrs. Simpson. He appreciated, however, that it would be out of the question that she should become Queen and that her children should succeed to the Throne (as would be the position unless otherwise provided ~~for~~ by legislation). He therefore contemplated abdicating, leaving the Duke of York to succeed. The Prime Minister was surprised at this suggestion, and asked for a few days to think it over. The King later informed the Queen and his brothers of this intended course of action. Mr. Baldwin did not think the King could be dissuaded from marrying Mrs. Simpson once the decree was made absolute, and it did not seem to him to be a practical alternative to try to dissuade him. The Dominions were, of course, as much concerned with this question touching the Crown as the United Kingdom. A declaration by the King renouncing the Throne would have to be made simultaneously to all

/the

the peoples in the British Commonwealth of Nations, would have to be followed by legislation amending the Act of Settlement, and the constitutional principles contained in the Statute of Westminster would apply.

Mr. Baldwin saw the King again on November 25th, and the King outlined to him a new proposal which "had been put to him from some outside quarter" and on which he asked Mr. Baldwin's view. Mrs. Simpson according to this proposal would not be Queen, but the marriage should not necessitate abdication. An undertaking would be given by the King that while his wife would be resident in Buckingham Palace with him she would not be treated as Queen, would not appear on State occasions, and legislation could be introduced to fix her position as the King' wife and to amend the Act of Settlement so as to bar any issue of the marriage from succession. It would be a necessary part of the suggested arrangement that the Governments on their side would undertake to acquiesce in the marriage on these conditions and would be responsible for any legislation necessary to put it into effect. Mr. Baldwin replied that he did not think there was any chanc of such a suggestion receiving the approval of Parliament in the United Kingdom, and he further reminded the King that the position had to be considered in relation to the Dominions, "whose assent would be equally essential".

Sir Harry Batterbee went on to say that Mr. Baldwin felt convinced that neither the Parliament nor the great majority of the public in all parties in Great Britain would accept such a plan any more than they would accept the proposal that Mrs. Simpson should become Queen. Moreover, it was very probable that pressure would be brought to bear later with a view to Mrs. Simpson becomin Queen. Mr. Baldwin asked for the President's personal

/view

view regarding the three following possibilities:-

(1) The King's marriage to Mrs. Simpson, she becoming Queen.

(2) The King's marriage to Mrs. Simpson without abdication, Mrs. Simpson not becoming Queen, and the necessary legislation.

(3) A voluntary abdication of the King in favour of the Duke of York.

The President informed Sir Harry Batterbee that he would incline to favour Course 2, but that if it was clear, having regard to all the circumstances of the case, that public opinion would not stand for anything in the nature of Course 2, he supposed there was no alternative to Course 3. The Bresident added that if we had the same interest that the British have we should certainly consider the person in that position should be above reproach The President's opinion expressed on Course 2 was on the assumption that divorce was a recognised institution in England. This opinion was later confirmed by the President in a telegram to the Prime Minister (3rd Decembe

<u>Views of Prime Ministers of Canada, Australia, South Africa and New Zealand.</u>

These were communicated to the President in a letter from Mr. Baldwin dated the 2nd December.

<u>Canada</u>.

Generally accepts British view, but is opposed to abdication imposed by Ministers and not voluntarily proposed by King.

/<u>Australia</u>.

Australia.

Accepts completely British position. Goes so far a to say that even if the King now dropped the proposal of marriage he should abdicate. There was no possibility c compromise.

New Zealand.

Favours Course 2, but submits to judgment of United Kingdom Government inspired by "deeper knowledge" and th wish to achieve the best result for Empire unity.

South Africa.

Accepts British view completely.

Message from Mr. Baldwin sent to all Members of the Commonwealth, received by the President on Friday, 4th December, proposes that, if the King voluntarily abdicate the necessary steps to regularise the position and to establish the Duke of York as King should be taken promptly, accurately synchronised, and of course after consultation and agreement between the various Government Everything should be arranged in detail in advance. The King's abdication would be his own act not taken on the advice of any of his Ministers. It would thus be plain that it was his personal act addressed to all his peoples simultaneously. The "contents" would be communicated by the King himself to the Governors-General so as to ensure that they reached the other Commonwealth Governments at the same time as the United Kingdom Government.

In Great Britain the procedure would be as follows:-

Prime Minister would at once communicate the declaration of abdication to the House of Commons, and the Leader

/of

of the House of Lords would make a similar communication to the Upper House. Prime Minister would announce to Parliament that legislation was necessary to carry into effect the abdication of the King, and that this legislation would be introduced immédiately. Mr. Baldwin did no think that any controversy would arise on the Bill. The Bill would be so framed that the Throne would pass to the Duke of York as soon as the King had given his Assent. A modification in the Act of Settlement was necessary to secure the title of the Duke of York and his children to the Throne. With regard to the Preamble and Section 4 of the Statute of Westminster, he asked for comments on the British tentative appreciation of the position. They recognised that the question of action by the other Governments was a matter for themselves, but as the situation was unprecedented the less legislation and the less opportunity for public discussion the better, and accordingly it would be better to confine legislation to the United Kingdom Act. Section 4 of the Statute of Westminster made it possible for the Dominions to request and consent to the anactment of the proposed United Kingdom Act, and though Australia and New Zealand had not adopted Section 4 they could be associated in the consequent recital to the Act. The British Government hoped the Dominions would be associated with the Act. They suggested as a way out that the meaning of the word "King" in the South Africa Act of 1909, the Status of the Union Act 1934 and the Commonwealth of Australia Act (where the expression "the King, his heirs and successors in the sovereignty of the United Kingdom of Great Britain and Ireland" could be interpreted as an acceptance of any King set up by the United Kingdom Government) should be

/held

held to be implicit in the Constitutions of the other States of the Commonwealth. They suggested furthermore t a resolution in Parliament would be the appropriate metho for complying with the constitutional doctrine enunciated in the Preamble to the Statute of Westminster. If, however, the other Governments considered that the request and consent of their Parliaments was necessary to make th United Kingdom Act fully effective, notice of their reque and consent prior to the initiation of the Bill would be required. At this point Mr. Baldwin states that in his informal talk with the King he got the impression that the King might make his declaration of abdication on Monday, the 7th, and that legislation would have to be introduced on Tuesday. The urgency of receiving the views of the other Governments was therefore apparent.

A draft of the proposed British Bill was received on the same day (Friday, 4th December). On the same evening Mr. Baldwin informed all the other Governments by cable that the King still contemplated the possibility of Course 2, and that a section of the popular Press was canvassing the idea. He felt that the course was not acceptable to the "overwhelming majority" of the people in Great Britain, but that a week-end of Press campaign in favour of it would be extremely undesirable. He felt obliged therefore to make a statement in the House of Commons that evening before it adjourned. The exact terms of the statement were not yet decided, but would be telegraphed as soon as possible, but the general line was that he would make it clear that the British Government regarded Course 2 as "utterly impracticable", and that he would add that generally, from information received by him, Course 2 would be similarly unacceptable to the

/Dominions

Dominions. He felt that this latter was an essential part of the statement. He expressed great regret at not being able to consult the other Governments prior to the statement being made, but felt that they would understand the need for urgent action. The following is the text of the statement made by Mr. Baldwin:-

"In view of widely circulated suggestions as to certain possibilities in the event of the King's marriage, I think it would be advisable for me to make a statement.

"Suggestions have appeared in certain organs of the press yesterday and again to-day that if the King decided to marry his wife need not become Queen. These ideas are without any constitutional foundation. There is no such thing as what is called morganatic marriage known to our law.

"The Royal Marriages Act of 1772 has no application to the sovereign himself. Its only effect is that the marriage of any other member of the Royal Family is null and void unless the sovereign's consent, declared under the Great Seal, is first obtained. This Act therefore has nothing to do with the present case. The King himself requires no consent from any other authority to make his marriage legal.

"But, as I have said, the lady whom he marries, by the fact of her marriage to the King, necessarily becomes Queen. She herself therefore enjoys all the status, rights, and privileges which both by positive law and by custom attach to that position and with which we are familiar in the case of her late Majesty

/Queen

> Queen Alexandra and her Majesty Queen Mary, and her children would be in the direct line of succession to the Throne.
>
> "The only way in which this result could be avoided would be by legislation dealing with a particular case. His Majesty's Government are not prepared to introduce such legislation.
>
> "Moreover, the matters to be dealt with are of common concern to the Commonwealth as a whole, and such a change could not be effected without the assent of all the Dominions. I am satisfied from inquiries I have made that this assent would not be forthcoming.
>
> "I have felt it right to make this statement before the House adjourns to-day in order to remove a widespread misunderstanding. At this moment I have no other statement to make."

We were later informed in another telegram that the Prim Minister's statement was received with cheers in all par of the House. In a message received at 8.30 on the nigh of Friday, the 4th, Mr. Baldwin said that in order to avert danger of further delay the Cabinet had decided tha he should tell the King that afternoon that he must make very early decision, and that the choice before him was to give up Mrs. Simpson or voluntarily abdicate. He agai expressed regret at not having previously consulted with the other Governments, but "situation had become so grave that it brooked no delay, and the British felt in view of helpful telegrams they had received from the Commonwealth Members that the British view would be assured generally by these Governments. He went on to say that it was, of

/course

course, proper that the King should know the view of his other Governments as well as of that of Great Britain, and that in the light of latest developments the other Governments would no doubt wish to communicate their views direct to the King. It would be helpful if their views could be communicated direct to the King within 24 hours. Mr. Baldwin requested a copy of any message sent to the King, for his information.

Late on the same night (Friday, 4th December) the Prime Minister informed the other Governments by cable that the King had suggested to him the previous night that he should "make a personal broadcast to the Empire" on the subject of his marriage. The main burden of the broadcast was that he wanted to be happily married, and that he was firmly resolved to marry the woman he loved when she was free to marry him, and that neither she nor he had ever sought to insist that she should become Queen. The King would also say that he felt it was best to go away to give time for calm reflection on what he had said. The broadcast would end with the words "Nothing is nearer my heart than that I should return, but whatever may befall I shall always have a deep affection for my country and Empire and for you all". Mr. Baldwin consulted his colleagues on Friday morning about the broadcast, and they came to the conclusion that it could not be allowed, as every sentence spoken by the King would involve the responsibility of his advisers. They accordingly decided that Mr. Baldwin should tender to the King on Friday night advice from the Government to that effect, and adding that the King could not in the present circumstances constitutionally make a broadcast on the lines proposed save on the advice of "all his Governments".

/This

This is the first communication we have of a formal advice being given to the King in the crisis. As far as we have been informed, the first formal advice given to the King was given on the afternoon of Friday in the form of an ultimatum that he should make an early decision and that his choice was to give up Mrs. Simpson or voluntarily abdicate. The second formal advice related to the broadcast.

On Saturday morning at 1 a.m. the President sent the following telegram to Mr. Baldwin:-

> "Your telegram containing the news of intended sudden action on Monday next within a week of the receipt of the first information concerning the position gives me serious cause for anxiety. Apart from other reasons legislation in our Parliament would be necessary in order to regularise the situation about public declaration. Such legislation at this moment would cause grave difficulty. Is there no alternative to immediate abdication? Surely delay at least is advisable even if no ultimate solution in sight."

Methods proposed to be used by the other Governments of the Commonwealth in relation to the British legislation.

They have all agreed to assent to the British legislation. Australia intends to call Parliament for the purpose. The British have strongly urged on all of them to proceed by way of resolution, thus avoiding the need for the Assent of the King, whose abdication by that time

/would

would have been completed through his Assent to the British Bill. There are certain variations in the methods by which the Assent is to be formulated, but it may be taken that they have all agreed to accept the British legislation as something done on their behalf.

At 3.30 on Sunday, the 6th December, the President sent the following advice to the King:-

"I have been informed that Your Majesty has under consideration the question of your voluntary abdication within the next few days. I should be glad to learn direct from Your Majesty for the information of my Government what Your Majesty's intentions are in this matter since this step could not be effected, in so far as the Irish Free State is concerned, without the authority of the Parliament of the Irish Free State. I beg to advise Your Majesty accordingly."

At the moment (11 o'clock, Monday the 7th December). the situation still remains doubtful. Mr. Baldwin is to make a statement in the House of Commons this afternoon. Opinion in Great Britain amongst large sections seems to favour the King's remaining on the Throne, and the Government appear to be wavering in the resolution to force a voluntary abdication.

(7th December, 1936).

APPENDIX 7

Jesuit Constitution Committee Minutes, 1936
[Source Jesuit Archive – Cahill Papers]

Constitution Committee

24 Sept. – 18 Oct.

1936

Session I. 1936, 24 Sept.

A Committee having been appointed by Fr Provincial to advise on certain matters connected with the Constitution, the first meeting of the Committee was held on Thursday September 24th 1936 at Milltown Park, 10.0 am

There were present Fr Bartley (President), Fr Cahill, Fr Canavan and Fr E. Coyne

The following points were decided:–

I A preamble is to be drawn up on the model of the preamble to the Polish Constitution

II Articles are to be drafted on the following subjects:–

a) The rights of the family particularly with regard to the education of the children

1930, 24 Sept Session I

b) Religion to be taught in all schools, which are to be ~~as far as possible~~ denominational wherever there is no insuperable difficulty.

✓ c) The state cannot dissolve a valid marriage

✓ d) The relations between the Catholic Church and the State to be defined by a Concordat

e) Freedom of religious worship

f) Ecclesiastical property

g) Private property

h) Freedom of speech and of the press and the limitations of this freedom

Session I 24 Sept. 1936

gi) Any other matters that may be suggested by a study of Concordat and existing Constitutions

The meeting was adjourned to Thursday October 1st.

P. Bartley S.J.
Oct. 1st 1936

Session I   24 Sept. 1936

A Committee having been appointed by the Provincial to advise on certain matters connected with the Constitution, the first meeting of this Committee was held at Milltown Park at 10.0 a.m. on Thursday 24 September 1936

There were present FF. Bartley (president), Cahill, Canavan, and E. Coyne. Fr. MacErlean (Secretary) was absent, being on retreat.

The following points were decided:—

1. A preamble is to be drawn up on the model of the preamble to the Polish Constitution

2. Articles are to be drafted on the following subjects:—

a) The rights of the family, particularly with regard to the education of the children

b) Religion is to be taught in all schools, which are to be denominational whenever there is no insuperable difficulty.

c) The State can not dissolve a valid marriage.

d) The relations between the Catholic Church and the State is to be defined by ~~a~~ Concordat.

e) Freedom of religious worship.

f) Ecclesiastical property.

Session I

24 Sept. 1936

g) Private property.

h) Freedom of speech and of the press, and the limitations of this freedom

i) Any other matters that may be suggested by a study of Concordats and existing Constitutions

The meeting was adjourned to Thursday 1st Oct. 1936

1 Oct. 1936

Session II

The Committee met at Milltown Park, at 10 am, 1 Oct. 1936

Present PP. Bartley, MacErlean, Cahill, Canavan, E. Coyne

Three drafts of the Preamble, differing but little one from the other were submitted by PP. Cahill, Canavan, and Coyne. It was discussed clause by clause, and certain changes were approved. In its new form it will be considered at the next meeting.

The article on relations between the Catholic Church and the State submitted by P. Bartley, was approved with slight modification.

The article declaring that the State cannot dissolve a valid marriage was found hard to draft. Various attempts to find a satisfactory wording that would embrace all possible cases were discussed and further consideration held over till next meeting, when drafts on private property, liberty of conscience, press, and meetings will be examined.

The meeting then adjourned till 10 a.m. 8 Oct 1936

P. Bartley S.J.
Oct 8th 1936

Sessio III 8 Oct. 1936

At Milltown Park, 10 am, 8 Oct. 1936

Present PP. Bartley MacErlean, Cahill, Canavan, E. Coyne

Many draft articles were considered and approved with slight modifications or none viz

1. Relations of Church & State (P. Bartley). – passed, with an addition proposed by P. Canavan.

2. Catholic marriage and State (P. Bartly) – everybody except P. Canavan approved P. Bartley's draft. As P. Canavan objected to this it was decided to add P. Canavan's draft as an alternative.

3. Freedom of worship (P. Bartley) – approved.

4. Freedom of press (P. Bartley) – approved

5. Freedom of cinema &c. An article on this to be added on suggestion of P. Canavan to the effect: The same control shall also be exercised by law over cinemas, radios, theatres and such like

6. Family: P. Coyne's draft §1 was approved

7. Parents and education of children: Coyne-Bartley draft approved

8. Religion in school: article to conform with Poland A. 120, with slight change.

Sessio III 8 Oct. 1936

9. Right to found &c schools (P. Coyne § VI from Poland A ..) was approved

10 Private property (P. Coyne § 1) should run 'The right of individual citizens, of associations of citizens, and autonomous bodies to own private property is one of the fundamental rights &c... of human society, of liberty and social peace and of economic ... is acknowledged and guaranteed by this Constitution.

11. Limits of private property (P Coyne § II) – approved with insertion of 'acquisition' before 'distribution'

12 Family living wage (P. Coyne § III). It was decided to omit this and to insert instead an article by P. Canavan 'The State guarantees to all its inhabitants protection of their property, but may limit or abolish &c as in Poland A. 99 p. 99.

13 Religious property (F. Canavan) as in Poland A 113 approved

Meeting was then adjourned till Thursday 15 Oct. 1936

P. Bartley SJ.
Oct 15th 1936

15 Oct. 1936

Session IV

All the members of the Committee were present at the meeting held at Milltown Park, on 15 Oct. 1936

Fr. Bartley read the articles as amended by previous decisions of the Committee, together with a few additions and modifications handed in by Fr. Cahill. The changes were mostly verbal.

In the article on private property, the right to productive and non-productive property was stated, and also that the State should aim at a wide distribution of private productive property especially in land.

An article on private schools was approved

Typed copies of the whole were to be distributed before Saturday to all the members, who might add any further comments they considered advisable, as well as references to existing foreign Constitutions tending to confirm important clauses.

The meeting then adjourned till Sunday 18th Oct. 1936, at midday

P. Bartley S.J.
Oct 18th 1936

18 Oct. 1936

Session V

All members of the Committee were present at the meeting held at Milltown Park at midday 18 Oct. 1936 viz. PP. Bartley, MacErlean, Cahill, Canavan, E. Coyne.

The Preamble was slightly changed so as to read 'In the Name of the Most Holy Trinity and of our Lord Jesus Christ, the Universal King, we the people of Ireland &c full of gratitude to God who has so mercifully preserved us from innumerable dangers in the past, hereby, as an united independent Christian Nation, establish this Sovereign Society of the Irish people &c. And so in accordance with the principles laid down &c we freely and deliberately to the glory of God and honour of Ireland, sanction this Constitution and decree and enact as follows:—

Art. I Religion: 'may' ~~was~~ substituted for will in 'The relations of the State to other religious bodies will be determined by an agreement' &c

Religion art. II or. ~~the Draft~~ 4(b). In Father Canavan's alternative article the final words 'profess the Catholic Faith' were changed to 'are members of the Catholic Church'

Art. 4 Education (b) Delete 'religious bodies or' & say 'All citizens and all associations of citizens'

Education (d) for 'subsidized wholly or in part' say 'maintained or subsidized'

Session V 18 Oct 1936

Education

Education (e) Read "Schools maintained or subsidized by the State shall be in principle denominational, and except in special circumstances to be defined by law, boys and girls of adolescent age shall be educated separately"

Education (f) Dele "as defined by law" & read "Primary education is compulsory on all Irish citizens"

Article V Private Property

(a) Say "The right of individual citizens and of associations of citizens to own private property in productive as well as in nonproductive goods is acknowledged &c

(d) Say "The state &c may not limit &c except when the law &c

It was resolved unanimously that references to Constitutions and Concordats of Catholic states should be added to the various assertions made above, that those who have the task of drawing up the Constitutions may come to know what the Catholics of of other Catholic European States have already secured.

APPENDIX 8

Jesuit Submission, October 1936 [Source UCDA P150/ 2393]

Milltown Park

Dublin

October 21 1936.

To

the President
Eamonn de Valera

My dear Mr. President

Enclosed herewith I send a typed copy of a draft Preamble, and of draft articles for the prposed Constitution. I have , in drawing them up, cofined myself to the minimum that I would consider necessary to realise a Christian Constitution,as I feared to outstep the limits of what you asked me to do. I should like to send in addition.,should you wish and consider it, useful,some few other draft articles,which I believe would be really necessary, or which would certainly be very useful. In the draft articles which I am sending several essential matters are not touched, on some because they are left to be settled by a Concordat,such as the observance of Sundays and holydays, the juridical personality of religoius Congregations and communities in regard to property. (At present religious houses or Congregations have no juridical standing,andtheir property is held in the names of individuals): others are omitted because there is no need to mention them, seeing that they already fairly well attended to;such as thw obligation of the State to provide for the religious interests of all those undwr its charge,such as soldiers, prisoners &c. Nevertheless,I realise how desireable it would be to have such things embodied in a Constitution,whch is meant to be permanent,

Again,there are some other headings not pertaining directly to the matter of religion,which I should like to see included in the Constitution,as a portion of the general principles and guarantees. These I could send on,should you wish it,without much delay. These articles would refer to the State (its essential functions&c); the Citizens (their rights &c.);associations,industrial and others;and the rural population. Under one of the last two headings would come a suggestion in which I am much interested,viz. the formation of parochial rural Councils or committees to be elected solely by the heads of families in the parish, (as is provided in the Portuguese Constitution of 1933),and which would be the nuclei of the social and cultural and economic life of the parish. If the principle were adopted in the Constitution,the detailed plan could be elaborated in due time by a law. Such parochial councils would,I believe, be of incalculable help to the rural population,and if elected by heads of families, would serve to give a statutory recognition to the Christian family, such as is given in the Portuguese Constitution, marking a definite departure from the Liberal, unchristian ideal and a return to the solid Christian tradition.

I have, in drawing up the drafts which I am sending you, availed myself of the advice and assistance of three or four others, some of whom have made a special study of these matters; others, although not specialists, are pretty well informed on them, and are men on whose judgment I have confidence.

I considered that it may be useful to indicate the sources which are relied on in making the drafts; and so I have had the references to the official ecclesiastical documents on which the particular section is based, written in, under each separate section; and in some references to the parallel articles in some of the Catholic Constitutions of European Catholic States, especially Austria (the Constitution of 1934) and Poland, both of which have non-Catholic minorities about as large as the non-Catholic minorty of the 32 counties of Ireland. The further sections to which I refer above that I would like to send would be modelled largely on the Portuguese Constitution of 1933.

I hope sincerely that you will find all this or some of it helpful and useful in the arduous work you have on hand. If you consider that I can be of any further assistance, I shall be always at your service.

I wish you and yours all blessings, and have the honour to remain

your obedient servant in Christ

Edward Cahill SJ

S U G G E S T I O N S

For a

C A T H O L I C   C O N S T I T U T I O N.

October 1936.

Abbreviated References.

A.Conc. Austrian Concordat, of 1934. (published in French in D.C.(vide infra) vol. 32, col. 1250 ff. 1934).

A.Const. Austrian Constitution of 1934 (published in D.C.(vide infra) vol32. col.78

C.I.C. Codex Juris Canonici

C.S.G. Catholic Social Guild (Oxford) publications, among which is the English translation of Pius XI's Quadragesimo Anno.

C.S.P. Code of Social Principles published by C.S.G. (vide supra). This is a translation of the original French Code Social, which is a summary of Catholic social principles, drawn up by the Malines International Union. This latter includes the leading specialists of Europe in Catholic Social Science.

C.T.S. booklets of the Catholic Truth Society, London, among which are English translations of the chief Papal Encyclicals issued 1928 - 31.

D.C. Documentation Catholique, Paris, especially vol. 32 (1934).

F.C.S. Framework of a Christian State by Rev. E.Cahill, Dublin

Pol. Polish Constitution of 1921, published in S.C.W.(vide infra).

Port. Portuguese Constitution of 1933 (English Translation, typed copy)

~~P.P. The Pope and the People, a selection of Papal Encyclicals, in English,~~ published by the C.T.S.(vide supra), London, 1931.

S.C.W. Select Constitutions of the World. 2nd Edition edited by Shiva Rao. (Madras 1934).

P R E A M B L E

IN THE NAME OF THE MOST HOLY TRINITY AND OF OUR LORD JESUS CHRIST THE UNIVERSAL KING,

we, the people of Ireland, being the parent nation of the Irish race, mindful of the long centuries of persecution we have had to endure, and full of gratitude to God who has so mercifully preserved us from innumerable dangers in the past;

hereby as an independent Christian nation establish this sovereign Civil Society of the Irish people.

Acknowledging that all supreme political and civil authority, legislative, executive and judicial, and all other moral powers of government come to us from God;

and recognising that for the just and efficient exercise of this authority and these powers it is necessary to transfer, separate and distribute them to such persons and bodies as are hereinafter described and set up in and by this Constitution;

we declare that all such authority and powers shall be exercised only in accord with the precepts of ~~the Divine Law,~~ natural and positive, and that any other exercise of them is, and shall be null and void, and of no moral force, and in no way sanctioned by us.

With the sacred purpose and intention of maintaining social unity and order on the eternal principles of Justice, and Liberty and of ensuring the development of all the moral, spiritual and material resources of our citizens and country,

we guarantee to all citizens of this State full equality.

Preamble

before the law as human persons, and full recognition and protection by the State of all their personal and family rights. 4)

And so in accordance with the principles laid down in this Preamble and the following fundamental Law; we freely and deliberately, to the glory of God, and the honour of Ireland, sanction this Constitution, and decree and enact as follows:- 4)

1) Title: A Const. (1934) in DC. (1934) col 77
Pol. preamble in SCW p.85 ; Pol. art. 57 (SCW p.92)

~~2) Pol preamble (SCW p.85~~
2) Pol Preamble in SCW p 85
3) A Const preamble (1934) in DC. (1934 col. 77)

4) Pol. preamble (SCW p.85)

3

Article I (Religion)

(a). Freedom of religious worship (in public and in private) is guaranteed to all within the limits of public order and morality. Pol. art. 111 (SCW. p. 101). A Const. (1934) art. 27 (DC. col 81)

(b). The Catholic Faith, which is the faith of the vast majority of the nation, and which is inseparably bound up with the nation's history, traditions and culture, occupies among religions in our country a unique and preponderant position.
Pol. art. 114 (SCW p. 101)

K

(c). The relations between the Catholic Church and the State, in matters that concern both Church and State, shall be determinedby an agreement to be entered into with the Holy See. This agreement shall be ratified by the Oireachtas, and after such ratificationshall have the force of law.
Pol. art. 114 (SCW p. 101)

(d). The relations to the State of other religious bodieswihin the nation may be determined by an agreement between the State and the official representatives the bodies in question.
Pol. art. 115 (SCW p. 101); A Const. (1934) art. 28 n. 5 (DC. 1934, col. 82)

(e). Every religious association recognised by the State may freely manage its own affairs, own and acquiremovable and immovable property, administer and dispose of the same, possess and enjoy its revenues and endowments, and maintain institutions

Article I (4) Religion 4

forreligious , educational and charitable purposes, Pol. art. 113 (SCW p.101); A. Const. (1934) art. 29 (DC. col. 81)

Article II (Marriage)

(a).The Civil Power cannot dissolve a marriage validly contracted.
CIC. 118; Leo XIII Quod Apostolici Muneris, 1878 (PP. 17-18); Leo XIII Arcanum Divinae, 1880 (PP. pp. 31-33, 36-37)

(b). The conditions required for the civil validity of the bethrothals and marriages of Catholics shall be identical with those laid down in the Code of Canon Law of the Catholic Church. The competent authority of the Catholic Church shall, where a member of that Church is concerned, decide finally all questions as to the existence or non-existence of the marriage bond. All such decisions, when they have been duly communicated to the State, shall be registered by it and given civil effect.
Italian Concordat art. 34 cf. Acta Apostolicae Sedis, 1929, p. 290; Pius XI Casti Connubii 1930 (CTS pp. 64-65) A. Const. (1934) art. 7 (DC. col. 1260) and protocol to art. 7 (DC. col. 1271)

Note. In case it should be found impossible to include paragraph (b) in the Constitution, the following is suggested as an alternative:-

(b). (Alternative). Seeing that the Catholic Church has its own marriage laws, the State shall, after agreement with the Holy See, bring its marriage laws into conformity with the Canon Law, where one or both parties to a marriage are members of the Catholic Church.

Article III.(The Family)

The Family, being a Natural Society, and being the fundamental unit of Civil Society, possesses natural, inalienable, andimprescriptible rights, prior and superior to all positive law. Being moreover indispensable to the continuance, strength, and well-being of the Nation, the Family shall have its essential nature, its just independence, and its rights respected and in a very special way protected by the State and its laws.

Leo XIII Rerum Novarum, 1891 (PP. 130-140); Pius XI Casti Connubii (on Christian Marriage, CTS pp. 62-63; CSP. nn. 10-17 pp. 18-19

Article IV (Education)

(a). It is the natural right as well as the duty of parents to provide, as far as in them lies, for the educationreligious, moral, physical and intellectual of their children. Parents may freely chooseteachers for their children, and freely select the schools to which their children's education is to be entrusted.

Pol. art. 94 (SCW. p. 98), and art. 117 (SCW. p. 107); A. Const. (1934) art. 31 (BC. col. 82)
Belgium art. 17 (SCW. p. 576)
~~CIC. 1113, 1373; Pius XI Divini Illius Magistri~~, 1929 (CTS pp 13-16 on Christian Education)

(b). All citizens and all associations of citizens have the right of founding, owning and administering schools and educational institutions, provided that they fulfil the conditions required by law relative to the welfare physical and moral of the children, and provided that they are well disposed to the State.

Pol. art. 117 (SCW p. 102); A. Const. (1934) art. 31 (BC. col. 82); CIC. 1375.

Article IV Education

(c). The State has the duty and the right to asist in the work of education, and to supplement private effort, as far as the public good requires.

Pius XI Divini Illius (CTS on Christian Education, pp. 18-21); CSP n. 22

(d). The teaching of religion within school hours, and as a part of the curriculum, shall be obligatory in all schools, maintained or susidized by the State. This teaching shall be under the direction of the religious body to which the ~~children~~ pupils belong. *Pol. art. 120 (SCW p. 102); A. Const. (1920) art. 31 (DC. col. 82); A. Conc. art. 6 (DC. col. 1258); CIC 1373.*

(e). Schools, maintained or subsidized by the State shall be in principle denominational; and, except in special circumstances to be defined by law, boys and girls of adolescent age shall be educated separately.

CIC. 1374; Pius XI Divini Illius (CTS. on Christian Education pp. 32-33, 36-40)

(f) Primary education is compulsory on all Irish citizens

Pol. art. 118 (SCW. p. 102); Pius XI Divini Illius (CTS. on Christian Education p. 20)

Article V (Private Property)

(a). The right of individual citizens and of associations of citizens to own private property, in productive ~~as~~ as well as in non-productive goods, is acknowledged and guaranteed by this Constitution.

Pol. art. 99 (SCW. p. 99); Leo XIII Rerum Novarum (FP. pp. 135-140); Pius XI Quadragesimo Anno (CSG p. 17); CTS on the Social Order p. 20)

Article V Private Property

(b). The right of property has, however, a double aspect, individual and social. Hence the State has the right and duty to see that neither the acquisition nor accumulation of private, especially in land, takes place in such a way as to injure the common good. It is also the right and duty of the State to see that the use which owners make of their property, especially goods of a productive nature, is in accord with the common good and with social justice.

Leo XIII Rerum Novarum (PP. pp. 151-153); Pius XI Quadragesimo Anno (CSG. pp 18-20; CTS on the Social Order pp. 20-23); CSP nn. 77-78.

(c). The State shall prevent by suitable laws the natural resources of the country, such as land, mimes, fisheries, waterways &c, from being unduly held up by private individuals or syndicates, and shall so adjust property rights as to secure that those are duly developed and utilized in the interestsof the common good ~~Pol. art. 99 (SCW p. 99)~~ Pius XI Quadragesimo Anno (CSG. pp. 18-20; CTS. on the Social Order pp. 19-20); CSP nn. 77-78

(d). The State shall guarantee the protection of private property, and may not limit or abolish individual or collective private property, except when the law so provides for reasons of public utility and with fair compensation.

Pol. art. 99 (SCW p. 99)

(e). It shal be the aim of the State to promote a wide distribution of private property, especially in land.

Leo XIII Rerum Novarum (PP. pp. 158-159); Pius XI Quadragesimo Anno (CSG pp. 23-25; CTS on the Social Order pp. 27-29)

Article VI. (Liberty of Speech, of the Press &c.)

Liberty of speech and liberty of the Press, which are conceded to all within due limits, shall not extend to the utterance, publication, or circulation of anything that is subversive of the Christian religion, of Christian morality, or of public order in the State. The law, when occasion demands, shall define more clearly the limits of these liberties.

The liberty accorded to the theatre, the cinema, the radio, and such like is confined within the same limits, which shall, when necessary, be defined by law.

A. Const. (1934) art. 26 (DG. col. 80-81); Norway art. 100 (SCW p. 625); Pius VII Post tam diuturnas (1814) in FCS. pp 469-470; Leo XIII Officiorum ac Munerum (1897) in FCS p. 470; Pius XI Casti Connubii (1930) in CTS on Christian Marriage pp. 22-23.

F.7 Cahill

P R E A M B L E

IN THE NAME OF THE MOST HOLY TRINITY AND OF OUR LORD JESUS CHRIST THE UNIVERSAL KING, (1)

we, the people of Ireland, being the parent nation of the Irish race, mindful of the long centuries of persecution we have had to endure, and full of gratitude to God who has so mercifully preserved us from innumerable dangers in the past; hereby, as an independent Christian nation, establish this sovereign Civil Society of the Irish people, (2)

Acknowledging that all supreme political and civil authority, legislative, executive and judicial, and all other moral powers of government come to us from God; (3)

and recognising that for the just and efficient exercise of this authority and these powers it is necessary to transfer, separate and distribute them to such persons and bodies as are hereinafter described and set up in and by this Constitution;

we declare that all such authority and powers shall be exercised only in accord with the precepts of the Divine Law, natural and positive, and that any other exercise of them is, and shall be null and void, and of no moral force, and in no way sanctioned by us.

With the sacred purpose and intention of maintaining social unity and order on the eternal principles of Justice, and Liberty, and of ensuring the development of all the moral, spiritual and material resources of our citizens and country, (4)

we guarantee to all citizens of this State full equality before the law as human persons, and full recognition and protection by the State of all their personal and family rights. (4)

And so in accordance with the principles laid down

Preamble and the following fundamental Law; we freely and deliberately, to the glory of God and the honour of Ireland, sanction this Constitution, and decree and enact as follows:- (4)

(1) Title: A Const. (1934) in D.C.(1934) col. 77
Pol. preamble in S.C.W. p.85; Bol. art. 54 (SCW p.93))

(2) Pol. Preamble in S.C.W. p.85;

(3) A Const. preamble (1934) in D.C. (1934 col.77)

(4) Pol. preamble (S.C.W. p.85)

Article I. (Religion)

(a) Freedom of religious worship (in public and in private) is guaranteed to all within the limits of public order and morality.

Pol. Art.III (S.C.W.p.101) A Const.(1934) Art.27 (D.C.col.81)

(b) The Catholic Faith, which is the faith of the vast majority of the nation, and which is inseparably bound up with the nation's history, traditions and culture, occupies among religions in our country a unique and preponderant position.

Pol. Art.114 (S.C.W. p.101)

(c) The relations between the Catholic Church and the State, in matters that concern both Church and State, shall be determinedly an agreement to be entered into with the Holy See. This agreement shall be ratified by the Oireachtas, and after such ratification shall have the force of law.

Pol. Art.114 (S.C.W.p.101)

(d) The relations to the State of other religious bodies within the nation may be determined by an agreement between the State and the official representatives the bodies in question.

Pol.Art.115 (S.C.W.(p.101);
A Const.(1934)Art.28 n.5 (D.C.1934,Col.8

(e) Every religious association recognised by the State may freely manage its own affairs, own and acquire movable and immovable property, administer and dispose of the same, possess and enjoy its revenues and endowments, and maintain institutions for religious, educational and charitable purposes.

Pol.Art.113 (S.C.W.p.101);
A Const.(1934) Art.29 (D.C.col.81)

ARTICLE II (Marriage)

(a) The Civil Power cannot dissolve a marriage validly contracted.

(CIC.118; Leo XIII Quod Apostolici Muneris, 1878 (PP.17-18); Leo XIII, Arcanum Divine, 1880 (PP.pp.31-33, 36-37)

(b) The conditions required for the civil validity of the bethrothals and marriages of Catholics shall be identical with those laid down in the Code of Canon Law of the Catholic Church. The competent authority of the Catholic Church shall, where a member of that Church is concerned, decide finally all questions as to the existence or non-existence of the marriage bond. All such decision, when they have been duly communicated to the State, shall be registered by it and given civil effect.

(Italian Concordat Art.34 of Acta Apostolicae Sedis,1929, p.290; Pius XI Casti Connubii 1930 (C.T.S.pp.64-65) A Cons.(1934)Art.7 (DC col.1260) and protocol to Art. 7 (DC.col. 1271)

Note: In case it should be found impossible to include paragraph (b) in the Constitution, the following is suggested as an alternative:-

(b). (Alternative). Seeing that the Catholic Church has its own marriage laws, the State shall, after agreement with the Holy See, bring its marriage laws into conformity with the Canon Law, where one or both parties to a marriage are members of the Catholic Church.

ARTICLE III. (The Family)

The family, being a Natural Society, and being the cundamental unit of Civil Society, possesses natural, inalienable, and imprescriptible rights, prior and superior to all positive law. Being moreover indispensable to the continuance, strength, and well-being of the Nation, the Family shall have its essential nature, its just independence, and its rights respected and in a very special way protected by the State and its laws.

Leo.XIII. Rerum Novarum,1891 (PP.130-140);
Pius XI. Casti Connubii (On Christian marriage, C.T.S.pp.62-63;CSP.nm.10-17 pp.18-19

ARTICLE IV. (Education)

(a) It is the natural right as well as the duty of parents to provide, as far as in them lies, for the education religious, moral, physical and intellectual of their children. Parents may freely choose teachers for their children, and freely select the schools to which their children's education is to be entrusted.

Pol.Art.94 (SCW.p.98), and Art.117 (SCW. p.107);
A.Const.(1934)Art.31 (DC.col.82) Belgium Art.17 (SCW.p.576)
CIC.1113, 1373; Pius XI Divini Illius Majistri,1929 (CTS pp.13-16 on Christian Education)

(b). All citizens and all associations of citizens have the right of founding, owning and administering schools and educational institutions, provided that they fulfil the conditions required by law relative to the welfare physical and moral of the children, and provided that they are well disposed to the State.

Pol.Art.117 (SCW p.102); A Const.(1934) Art.31 DC.col.82); CIC. 1375.

ARTICLE IV. Education

(c) The State has the duty and the right to assist in the work of education, and to supplement private effort, as far as the public good requires.

Pius.XI Divini Illius (CTS. pn Christian Education, pp.18-21); CSP. n.22

3 (d) The teaching of religion within school hours, and as a part of the curriculum, shall be obligatory in all schools, maintained or subsidized by the State. This teaching shall be under the direction of the religious body to which the pupils belong.

Pol.Art.120 (SCW p.102); A Const.(1934) Art.31 (D.C.col.82); A.Cobc.Art.6 (D.C.col.1258) CIC 1373.

2 (e). Schools, maintained or subsidized by the State shall be in principle denominational; and, except in special circumstances tp be defined by law, boys and girls of adolescent age shall be educated separately.

CIC.1374; Pius XI Divini Illius (CTS. on Christian Education pp.32-33,36-40).

(f) Primary education is compulsory on all Irish citizens.

Pol.Art.118 (SCW.p.102); Pius XI Divini Illius (C.T.S.on Christian Education, p.20)

ARTICLE V. (Private Prpperty

(a) The right of individual citizens and of associations of citizens to own private property in productive as well as in non-productive goods is acknowledged and guaranteed by this Constitution.

Pol.Art.99 (SCW.p.99); Leo XIII Rerum Novarum (PP.pp.135-140); Pius XI Quadragesimo Arno (CSG p.17; CTS on the Social Order p.20)

ARTICLE V. (Private Property)

(b) The right of property has, however, a double aspect, individual and social. Hence the State has the right and duty to see that neither the acquisition nor accumulation of private, especially in land, takes place in such a way as to injure the common good. It is also the right and duty of the State to see that the use which owners make of their property, especially goods of a productive nature, is in accord with the common good and with social justice.

Leo.XIII Rerum Novarum (PP.pp.151-153); Pius XI Quadrogesimo Anno (CSG.pp.18-20; CTS on the Social Order pp.20-23) CSP nn.77-78.

(C) The State shall prevent by suitable laws the natural resources of the country, such as land, mines, fisheries, waterways, etc. from being unduly held up by private individuals or syndicates, and shall so adjust property rights as to secure that these are duly developed and utilized in the interests of the common good.

Pius XI.Quadragesimo Anno (CSG.pp.18-20;C.T.S.on the Social Order pp.19-20); CSP nn.77-78.

(d) The State shall guarantee the protection of private property, and may not limit or abolish individual or collective private property, except when the law so provides for reasons of public utility and with fair compendation.

Pol. Art.99 (SCW p.99)

(e) It shall be the aim of the State to promote a wide distribution of private property, especially in land.

Leo XIII. Rerum Novarum (PP.pp.158-159); Pius XI Quadragesimo Anno (CSG pp.23-25; CTS on the Social Order pp.27-29).

ARTICLE VI. (Liberty of Speech, of the Press, etc.)

Liberty of speech and liberty of the Press, which are conceded to all within the limits, shall not extend to the utterance, publication, or circulation of anything that is subversive of the Christian religion, of Christian morality, or of public order in the State. The law, when occasion demands, shall define more clearly the limits of these liberties.

The liberty accorded to the theatre, the cinema, the radio, and such like is confined within the same limits, which shall, when necessary. be defined by law.

A.Const. (1934) Art. 26 (DC.col.80-81); Norway art.100 SCW p.625); Pius VII Post tam diuturnas (1814) in FCS.pp.469-470; Leo XIII Officiorum ai Munerum (1897) in FCS p.470; Pius XI Casti Connubii (1930) in CTS on Christian Marriage pp.22-23.

Milltown Park

Dublin.

November 13 1936.

To the President
Eamonn de Valera

My dear President

I am sending herewith the further draft articles which I referred to in my letter of October 21. I have been delayed unavoidably much longer than I foresaw, and I hope that what I send may still be in time for your consideration in connection with the new Constitution.

When I came to draft the proposed articles in reference to the rights of citizens, I found that practically all the points which I had in mind, except those referring to the rights of association were included or implied in the draft articles already sent in. I found further that the whole matter of associations (already touched on in nn. XI, XII and XVIII of my previous letter of August 4) is so complicated and many sided, and would require so many draft articles that I considered it useless to handle it in my present state of ignorance as to how far you would be at present prepared to go in dealing with it, fundamental and important as it undoubtedly is.

I am not without hope that you may at least be able to do something towards realising my suggestion (contained in my letter of October 21) in regard to the setting up of parochial rural committees. I believe that such parochial commitees elected by the heads of families (and of which the principal ministers of any considerable religious body within the parish would be ex-officio members) would little by little open the way towards solving the (at present) almost hopeless problem of rural and agricultural organisation; and, being founded on the natural basis of the family and the parish, would be saved from the corruption and jobbery, which apparently prevailed in the previous rural councils, which were based on an artificial and individualistic basis, and from which the ministers of religion, who in the rural districts are practically the only well educated leaders, were excluded by law. If the proposed councils had each a parish hall, with a playground &c in the neighbourhood of the Church, the end would be substantially secured even though their powers were very limited.

The article concerning the denominational character of the public hospitals would, if adopted, serve to undo a very grave injury to our poor, practically all of whom are Catholics, and who naturally desire to have a proper religious environment when they are ill or dying. It would besides serve to anticipate the danger which has proved so real in Continental countries of an undue ingerence of non-Christian aliens into the medical profession.

Hoping that what I send may be useful, and wishing you and yours all blessing, I have the honour to remain

your obedient servant in Christ

Edward Cahill SJ

Supplementary Suggestions

for the
New Constitution of the

Irish State

November 1936

Suggestions (Supplementary) regarding the New Constitution of the Irish State

Supplementary to Art. I.(Religion)

(f). The State is bound to provide moral ptotection and religious ministration to citizens with whom it is directly concerned in public institutions such as educational institutions, ,barracks,hospitals, houses of detention ~~and~~ mental homes &c. (3)

(3)Pol.art 102. (S.C.W.pp99-102)

(g).Hospitals,mental homes,houses of refuge &c. maintained or subsidized from public funds shall be in principle denominational.

Supplementary to Art. III (The Family)

(b).The rural families as being the most important element of the population ,and the element upon which the strength and welfare/of the nation mainly depends shall be a special object of the care of the State.

(c).The stability of the rural families shall be safeguarded by laws of inheritance, preventing the mortgaging or alienation of the family inheritance within limits to be fixed by law.

(d).The conditions of the employment of women and minors in industry shall be fixed by law, in accordance with the interests of the family and the common good. (3).

(3). Leo XIII.Rerum NOv. 1891 (P.P.p156)
Pius XI.Quad.Anno.1931 (C.S.G.pp27-28,and 51)

Supplementary to Art. V. (Private Property).

(f)The voluntary subdivision of larger farms within the limits of economic proportions shall be encouraged and facilitated by subsidizing the erection of suitable homesteads in newly formed farms.

(g).Special facilities shall be given to agricultural labourers to acquire independent homes with a specified minimum of land of sufficient extent to supply milk and vegetables for the labourer's family.

Supplementary to Art. VI. (Liberty of Speech, of the Press &c.)

(a). Public opinion, being of the highest importance as a social force, must be safeguarded from such factors as may lead it astray from truth, justice and the common good. (3)

(3) Port. art. 20.

(b). Liberty of speech &c (as in Art.VI. above referred to)

(c) The Press ~~as an organ of public opinion~~ exercises a public function, and cannot ~~refuse to~~ publish such notes of reasonable ~~length~~ dimensions as shall be issued to it by the Government. (3)

(3).Port. art.21

(d). The law shall secure to every citizen and recognised corporate body the right to insert free of charge, and without legal process, a vindication of character in any periodical in which such citizen or corporate body may have been injured or defamed. (3)

(3).Port.art 8.sect 2.

The Fundemental duties of the State

The following articles, summarising Catholic teaching regarding the general duties of government are adapted from the Portuguese Constitution of 1933. Whether or not quasi-abstac articles of that kind can be fitted into the proposed Irish Constitution the present does not know. They are put here on the chance that they may be useful or suggestive. They would be useful in the Constitution for educative purposes :-

(a) It is the primary function of the State to take all necessary measures to safeguard the common good in regard to the life, liberty, property, morals, and all the natural or justly acquired rights of all the citizens, and to promote as far as possible their material, intellectual and moral interests

(b). The State shall respect and safeguard the due autonomy of the family, and in due measure, the free and proper functioning of the lesser social units within the nation.

(c). It is the duty of the State, while encouraging the private initiative of individuals and organised bodies, to stimulate, assist and coordinate their activities; and where necessary to supplement and complete them; and to take measures that a just harmony of interests prevail, and that particular interests be subordinated to those of the community.

(d). It is also the duty of the State to protect in a special way the interests of the poor and the less favoured social classes, that they may participate in the advantages of civilisation.

Portuguese Constitution (1933) art 6. Cf. also C.S.P. nn43-50

The following eight articles borrowed with certain adaptations from the Portuguese Constitution of 1933, may be of some use.

1. The territory of the Irish State includes all the land of Ireland and the adjacent islands; the territorial waters; the inland rivers and lakes, and the air above them. (1)

(1) Port. art.1

2. No portion of the national territory shall be acquired by a government or legal entity of another country, save for the setting up of diplomatic representation, when such other country accords reciprocal priveleges th the Irish State. (2)

(2) Port. art.2

~~3. No portion of the national territory shall be acquired by a government of legal entity~~

3. The Irish nation includes all Irish citizens residing within or without its territory and all these shall be regarded as dependents of the State, and subject to its laws save in as far as the provisions of international law shall require otherwise. (3)

(3) Port. art 3.

4. All foreigners in, or residing in the Irish State, whether temporarily or permanently, are likewise subject to the laws of the Irish State, due regard being had to the provisions of international law. (4)

(4). Port. art. 3.

5. The Irish State is organised on the principles of the equality of all its citizens before the law, and the free access of all classes of the community to the bene-

fits of civilisation

6 The State may grant honourable distinctions or recompense to those citizens who shall have become conspicous by personal merit or by their civic or military achievements; and the law may establish orders, decorations medals, or diplomas for this purpose. (a)

(a) Port. art 27

7. No rights or goods of the State that affect either its own prestige or the greater utility of the nation may be alienated. (3)

(3) Port. art. 51.

8. Objects of artistic, historic or national value, officially recognised as such, are under the protection of the State, and may not be injured or alienated in favour of foreigners. (4)

(4). Port. art 51.

Irish is the official language of the Irish state; but English shall also be recognised as an official language, except in those districts (to be delimited by law) where Irish is the usual language of the home.

Every member of the Government, and every servant of the state, shall before entering upon office swear to uphold the Constitution of the State.

APPENDIX 9

First Official Draft of Constitution [Source NAI D/T S9715]

(3086) N. 5323. Wt. 2859. D.56. 5,000. 10-36.—F.P.—G.26.
(3318) N.9546. Wt.4684. D.96. 2,000—2-37—F.P.—G.26.

Misc.
F. 2.

Uimhir: S9715

ROINN AN UACHTARÁIN

Sgeul, Constitution, 1937

Preliminary Draft.

The attached preliminary draft of the Constitution was circulated privately by the President.

The first draft to be circulated generally to Departments was that of the 16th March, 1937.

1st Official Draft 5.3.37.

Confidential. No. 64

TO______________________________

To be returned to Department of The President.

Dréacht-Bhunreacht na hÉireann

Authoritative Translation

PREAMBLE.

THE NATION.

Article 1.

The Irish nation hereby affirms its inalienable, indefeasible, and sovereign right to choose its own form of Government, to determine its relations with other nations, and within the national territory to develop its own life, economic, social and political, free from external interference.

Article 2.

The national territory consists of the whole of Ireland, its islands and the territorial seas.

Article 3.

Pending the re-integration of the national territory, and without prejudice to the right of the Parliament and Government established by this Constitution to exercise jurisdiction over the whole of the national territory, the laws enacted by that Parliament shall have the like area and extent of application as the laws of Saorstát Eireann and the like extra-territorial effect.

THE STATE.

Article 4.

The name of the State is Éire.

Article 5.

Éire is a sovereign, independent, democratic State.

Article 6.

1. All powers of government, legislative, executive and judicial, derive, under God, from the people, whose right it is to designate the rulers of the State and, in final appeal, definitively

Article 6 *(continued)*.

to decide all questions of national policy, according to the requirements of the common good.

2. These powers are exercisable by or on the authority of the Organs of State established by this Constitution.

Article 7.

The national flag of Éire is the tricolour of green, white and orange.

Article 8.

1. The Irish language is the official language of Éire.

2. The English language is recognised as a second official language.

3. Special provision may be made by law for the recognition of only one of these languages as the official language in districts in which only that language is in general use.

Article 9.

1. The following persons are of Irish nationality and citizenship :—

   i. All persons born in Ireland.

   ii. All persons born outside Ireland of Irish parentage or descent as defined or limited by law.

   iii. All other persons on whom Irish nationality and citizenship are conferred in accordance with law.

2. Irish nationality and citizenship may be lost by any citizen : the circumstances shall be defined by law.

3. Love of the Motherland and loyalty to the State are fundamental political duties of all citizens of Éire.

Article 10.

1. All mines, minerals, and other natural resources (including the air and all forms of potential energy) within

Article 10 *(continued).*

the jurisdiction of the Government and Parliament established by this Constitution and all royalties and franchises within that jurisdiction belong to Éire subject to all estates and interests therein lawfully vested in private persons immediately before the coming into operation of this Constitution.

2. All land and all inland waters which belonged to Saorstát Eireann immediately before the coming into operation of this Constitution belong to Éire to the same extent as they then belonged to Saorstát Eireann.

3. Provision shall be made by law for the management of the property vested in Éire by this Article and for the control of the alienation, whether temporary or permanent, of that property.

4. Provision shall also be made by law for the management of land and inland waters acquired by Éire after the coming into operation of this Constitution and for the control of the alienation, whether temporary or permanent, of the land and inland waters so acquired.

THE PRESIDENT.

Article 11.

1. There shall be a President of Éire (*Uachtarán na hEireann*) hereinafter called the President who shall take precedence over all other persons in the State and who shall exercise and perform the powers and functions conferred on the President by this Constitution and by law.

2. 1° The President shall be elected by direct vote of the People.

2° Every citizen who has completed the age of twenty-one years and who complies with the law relating to the election of President shall be entitled to vote at such election.

3° The voting shall be by secret ballot and on the system of proportional representation by means of the single transferable vote.

Article 11 *(continued).*

3. 1° The President shall hold office for seven years from the date upon which he enters upon his office (unless he previously dies, resigns, becomes permanently incapacitated, or is removed from office) and shall be eligible for re-election.

2° His successor shall enter upon his office on the day following the expiration of this period of seven years and elections for the office of President shall be held not more than sixty and not less than thirty days before its expiration.

4. 1° Every citizen who has completed his thirty-fifth year of age, who is not placed under disability or incapacity by this Constitution or by law, and who has ordinarily resided in Ireland during the ten years immediately preceding his nomination, is eligible for election to the office of President.

2° Every candidate for election (not a former or retiring President) must be nominated either by

i. not less than twenty persons, each of whom is at the time a member of one of the Houses of the Oireachtas, or

ii. by the Councils of not less than four Counties, (including County Boroughs) in Éire.

3° No person and no such Council shall be entitled to subscribe to the nomination of more than one candidate in respect of the same election.

4° Former or retiring Presidents may become candidates on their own nomination.

5. Subject to the foregoing conditions, elections for the office of President shall be regulated by law.

6. 1° The President shall not be a member of either House of the Oireachtas.

2° If a member of either House of the Oireachtas be elected President, he shall be deemed to have vacated his seat in that House.

3° The President shall not hold any other office or position of emolument.

7. The President shall enter upon his office by taking and subscribing publicly, in the presence of members of both Houses of the Oireachtas, of Judges of the Supreme Court

Article 11 *(continued)*.

and of the High Court, and other public personages, the following declaration:—

"In the presence of Almighty God I promise that I will maintain the Constitution of Éire and uphold its laws, that I will fulfil my duties faithfully and conscientiously in accordance with the Constitution and the law, and that I will dedicate my abilities to the service and welfare of the people of Éire."

8. The President shall not leave Éire during his term of office save with the consent of the Government.

9. During the temporary absence from Éire of the President, and in the event of his death, resignation, incapacity or removal from office, the powers and functions of the office of President shall be exercised and performed by a Commission as provided in Article 29 of this Constitution.

10. 1° The President may be impeached at the instance of Seanad Eireann for treason as defined in this Constitution or other high crimes or misdemeanours.

2° The charge shall be preferred before Dáil Eireann, which shall investigate the charge.

3° The President shall have the right to be represented at the investigation by Dáil Eireann.

4° If, as a result of the investigation, a resolution be passed supported by not less than three-fourths of the total membership of Dáil Eireann declaring that the charge preferred against the President has been sustained, this resolution shall operate to remove the President from his office.

11. In the event of the removal from office of the President or of his death, resignation or permanent incapacity to discharge the functions of his office, an election to fill the office of President shall be held within sixty days after such event and the President then elected shall enter upon his office as soon as may be after his election.

12. 1° The President shall have an official residence in or near the City of Dublin, and an official staff and secretariat.

2° The President and his official staff and secretariat shall receive such emoluments and allowances as may be determined by law.

Article 11 *(continued).*

3° The emoluments and allowances of the President shall not be diminished during his term of office.

Article 12.

1. 1° The President shall, on the nomination of Dáil Eireann, appoint the Taoiseach, that is, the head of the Government.

2° On the nomination of the Taoiseach, the President, with the previous approval of Dáil Eireann, shall appoint the other members of the Government.

3° The President shall, on the advice of the Taoiseach, accept the resignation of any member of the Government, or remove any member of the Government from office.

2. 1° Dáil Eireann shall be summoned and dissolved by the President on the advice of the Taoiseach.

2° The President may refuse to dissolve Dáil Eireann on the advice of a Taoiseach who has ceased to retain the support of a majority in Dáil Eireann.

3. 1° Every Bill passed or deemed to have been passed by both Houses of the Oireachtas shall require the signature of the President for its enactment into law.

2° The President shall promulgate laws made by the Oireachtas.

4. The President shall exercise the functions conferred on him by this Constitution in relation to

   i. the reference of certain Bills of the Parliament to the Supreme Court,

   ii. the reference of certain Bills of the Parliament to the People, and

   iii. the reference of certain Bills of the Parliament to a Committee of Privileges.

5. The President shally exercise the functions conferred on him by Article 43 hereof with regard to the suspension of certain provisions of this Constitution.

6. The supreme command of the Defence Forces of Éire is hereby vested in the President.

Article 12 *(continued)*.

7. 1° The exercise of the command of the Defence Forces by the President shall be regulated by law.

2° All commissioned officers of the Defence Forces of Éire shall hold their commissions from the President.

8. The President shall appoint the Judges of the Supreme Court, the High Court, and all other Courts and tribunals established by law.

9. The President shall appoint the Attorney-General on the nomination of the Taoiseach.

10. The President shall appoint the Comptroller and Auditor-General on the nomination of Dáil Eireann.

11. The right of pardon, and power to remit or commute sentences imposed, and to remit the legal consequences of verdicts given by any courts exercising criminal jurisdiction, shall be exercised by the President.

12. 1° The President may, after consultation with the Council of State, communicate with the Houses of the Oireachtas by message or address on any matter of national or public importance.

2° The President may, after consultation with the Council of State, address a message to the Nation at any time on any such matter.

3° The terms of every such message or address must, however, have received the prior approval of the Government.

13. 1° Save as provided by section 11 of Article 11 the President shall not be held answerable to either House of the Oireachtas for the exercise and performance of the powers and functions of his office or for any act done or purporting to be done by him in the exercise and performance of these powers and functions.

2° In the event, however, of the impeachment of the President under section 11 of Article 11 hereof his conduct of the office of President may be brought under review in Dáil Eireann in so far only as is, in the opinion of the Chairman of Dáil Eireann, necessary for the proper investigatian of the charge.

Article 12 *(continued)*.

3° No action at law or in equity or other legal proceeding, civil or criminal, shall lie against the President during his tenure of office.

14. Except where otherwise provided by this Constitution, the powers and functions conferred on the President by this Constitution shall be exercisable and performable by him only on the advice of the Government formally conveyed to him by the Taoiseach.

15. 1° Subject to this Constitution, additional powers and functions may be conferred on the President by law.

2° No such power or function shall be exercisable or performable by him save only on the advice of the Government formally conveyed to him by the Taoiseach, or after consultation with the Council of State, as may be determined by such law.

THE NATIONAL PARLIAMENT.

Constitution and Powers.

Article 13.

1. 1° The National Parliament of Éire shall be called and known, and is in this Constitution generally referred to, as the Oireachtas.

2° The Oireachtas shall consist of the President and two Houses, viz.: a Chamber of Deputies to be called " Dáil Eireann " and a Senate to be called " Seanad Eireann ".

3° The Oireachtas shall sit in or near the City of Dublin or in such other place as from time to time it may determine.

2. 1° The Oireachtas is the supreme legislative authority of Éire.

2° No other authority whatsoever has power to make laws for Éire.

3° Provision may be made by law for the creation or recognition of subordinate legislatures and for the powers and functions of these legislatures.

Article 13 *(continued)*.

3. 1° The Oireachtas may provide for the establishment or recognition of functional or vocational councils representing branches of the social and economic life of the State.

2° A law establishing or recognising any such council shall determine its rights, powers and duties, and its relation to the Oireachtas and to the Government of Éire.

4. The Oireachtas shall not declare acts to be infringements of the law which were not so at the date of their commission.

5. 1° The Oireachtas shall not enact any law which is in any respect repugnant to this Constitution or any provision thereof.

2° Every law enacted by the Oireachtas which is in any respect repugnant to this Constitution or to any provision thereof, shall, but to the extent only of such repugnancy, be invalid.

6. 1° The right to raise and maintain military or armed forces is vested exclusively in the Oireachtas.

2° No military or armed force, other than a military or armed force raised and maintained by the Oireachtas, shall be raised or maintained for any purpose whatsoever.

7. 1° War shall not be declared, and Éire shall not participate in any war, without the assent of Dáil Eireann.

2° In the case of actual invasion, however, the Government may take whatever steps they consider necessary for the protection of the State.

8. The Oireachtas shall hold at least one session each year.

9. Each House of the Oireachtas shall elect its own Chairman and Deputy Chairman, and shall prescribe their powers, duties, remuneration, and terms of office.

10. Each House shall make its own Rules and Standing Orders, with power to attach penalties for their infringement, and shall have power to ensure freedom of debate, to protect its official documents and the private papers of its members, and to protect itself and its members against any person or

A[illegible]le 13 *(continued).*

persons interfering with, molesting or attempting to corrupt its members in the exercise of their duties.

11. 1° Sittings of each House of the Oireachtas shall be public.

2° In cases of special emergency, either House may hold a private sitting with the assent of two-thirds of the members present.

12. 1° All questions in each House shall, save as otherwise provided by this Constitution, be determined by a majority of the votes of the members present other than the Chairman or presiding member.

2° The Chairman or presiding member shall have and exercise a casting vote in the case of an equality of votes.

3° The number of members necessary to constitute a meeting of either House for the exercise of its powers shall be determined by its Standing Orders.

13. All official reports and publications of the Oireachtas or of either House thereof and utterances made in either House wherever published shall be privileged.

14. The members of each House of the Oireachtas shall, except in case of treason as defined in this Constitution, felony or breach of the peace, be privileged from arrest in going to and returning from, and while within the precincts of either House, and shall not, in respect of any utterance in either House, be amenable to any Court other than the House itself.

15. No person may be at the same time a member of both Houses of the Oireachtas, and, if any person who is already a member of either House be elected to be a member of the other House, he shall forthwith be deemed to have vacated his first seat.

16. The Oireachtas may make provision by law for the payment of allowances to the members of each House thereof in respect of their duties as public representatives and for the grant to them of free travelling and such other facilities in connection with those duties as the Oireachtas may determine.

Dáil Eireann.

Article 14.

1. 1° Every citizen who has reached the age of twenty-one years, and who is not placed under disability or incapacity by this Constitution or by law, shall be eligible for membership of Dáil Eireann.

2° Every citizen who has reached the age of twenty-one years, and who complies with the provisions of the law relating to the election of members of Dáil Eireann, shall have the right to vote for members of Dáil Eireann.

3° No voter may exercise more than one vote at an election for Dáil Eireann, and the voting shall be by secret ballot.

2. 1° Dáil Eireann shall be composed of members who represent constituencies determined by law.

2° The number of members shall from time to time be fixed by law, but the total number of members of Dáil Eireann shall not be fixed at less than one member for each thirty thousand of the population, or at more than one member for each twenty thousand of the population.

3° The proportion between the number of members to be elected at any time for each constituency and the population of each constituency, as ascertained at the last preceding census, shall, so far as it is practicable, be identical throughout the country.

4° The Oireachtas shall revise the constituencies at least once in every fifteen years, with due regard to changes in distribution of the population, but any alterations in the constituencies shall not take effect during the life of the Dáil Eireann sitting when such revision is made.

5° The members shall be elected on the system of proportional representation by means of the Single Transferable Vote.

6° No law shall be enacted whereby the number of members to be returned for any constituency shall be less than three.

3. 1° Dáil Eireann shall be summoned and dissolved as provided by section 2 of Article 12 of this Constitution.

2° A general election for members of Dáil Eireann shall take place not later than thirty days after a dissolution of the Oireachtas.

Article 16 *(continued)*.

3. The nominated members of Seanad Eireann shall be nominated by the Taoiseach.

4. The elected members of Seanad Eireann shall be elected as follows:—

   i. Three shall be elected by the National University of Ireland.

   ii. Three shall be elected by the University of Dublin.

   iii. Forty-three shall be elected by the electorate hereinafter specified from panels of candidates constituted as hereinafter provided.

5. Every election of the elected members of Seanad Eireann shall be held on the system of proportional representation, by means of the single transferable vote, and by secret postal ballot.

6. The members of Seanad Eireann to be elected by the Universities shall be elected by an electorate and in the manner provided by law.

7. The members of Seanad Eireann to be elected from panels of candidates shall be elected as follows:

1° Before each general election of such members five panels of candidates shall be formed containing respectively the names of persons having practical knowledge and experience of the following public interests and services, namely:—

   i. National Language and Culture, Education and the learned professions (including any other professional interest specified by law);

   ii. Farming (including live-stock breeding) and Fisheries;

   iii. Labour, whether organised or unorganised;

   iv. Industry and Commerce (including banking, finance, accountancy, engineering and architecture);

   v. Public Administration (including local government and social services).

2° The number of members of Seanad Eireann to be elected from each of these panels and the method of nomination to these panels shall be determined by law.

Article 16 *(continued).*

3° The electorate for the purpose of every such election shall consist of every person who shall have been a candidate for membership of Dáil Eireann at the general election for Dáil Eireann last held prior to such election, and who shall have received more than five hundred first preference votes at such general election.

4° Every elector shall be entitled to cast one vote for every one thousand first preference votes received by him.

In calculating the number of votes to which any elector shall be entitled, an incomplete thousand first preference votes if over five hundred shall be reckoned as one thousand first preference votes.

5° At every such election, Éire shall form one electoral area.

Article 17.

1. A general election for Seanad Eireann shall take place not later than ninety days after a dissolution of Dáil Eireann.

2. Every member of Seanad Eireann shall, unless he previously dies, resigns, or becomes disqualified, continue to hold office until the day before the polling day of the general election for Seanad Eireann next held after his election or nomination.

3. Dáil Eireann shall not be dissolved between the date of its re-assembly after a dissolution and the polling day of the general election for Seanad Eireann consequent on such dissolution.

Article 18.

1. Subject to the provisions of the foregoing Articles, elections of the elected members of Seanad Eireann shall be regulated by law.

Article 18 *(continued)*.

2. Casual vacancies in the number of the nominated members of Seanad Eireann shall be filled by nomination by the Taoiseach.

3. Casual vacancies in the number of the elected members of Seanad Eireann shall be filled in the manner provided by law.

Article 19.

In the event of the establishment or recognition under this Constitution of any functional or vocational council, provision may be made by law for the direct election by such council of so many members of Seanad Eireann as may be fixed by such law, in substitution for an equal number of the members to be elected from panels of candidates constituted under Article 16.

Legislation.

Article 20.

1. 1° Every Bill initiated in and passed by Dáil Eireann shall be sent to Seanad Eireann and may, unless it be a Money Bill, be amended in Seanad Eireann and Dáil Eireann shall consider any such amendment.

2° Every Money Bill passed by Dáil Eireann shall be sent to Seanad Eireann for its recommendations.

2. 1° A Bill may be initiated in Seanad Eireann, and if passed by Seanad Eireann, shall be introduced in Dáil Eireann.

2° If amended in Dáil Eireann, a Bill initiated in Seanad Eireann shall be considered as a Bill initiated in Dáil Eireann.

3. A Bill passed by either House and accepted by the other House shall be deemed to have been passed by both Houses.

4. 1° Every Money Bill sent to Seanad Eireann for its recommendations shall at a period not longer than twenty-one days after it shall have been sent to Seanad Eireann be returned to Dáil Eireann which may accept or reject all or any of the recommendations of Seanad Eireann.

Article 20 *(continued).*

2° If such Money Bill is not returned by Seanad Eireann to Dáil Eireann within such twenty-one days or is returned within such twenty-one days with recommendations which Dáil Eireann does not accept, it shall be deemed to have been passed by both Houses.

5. This section applies to every Bill passed by Dáil Eireann and sent to Seanad Eireann other than a Money Bill or a Bill in respect of which a resolution shall have been passed by Dáil Eireann under section 7 of this Article.

1° Whenever a Bill to which this section applies is within the stated period defined in the next following sub-section either rejected by Seanad Eireann or passed by Seanad Eireann with amendments to which Dáil Eireann does not agree or is neither passed (with or without amendment) nor rejected by Seanad Eireann within the stated period, the Bill shall, if Dáil Eireann so resolves within thirty days after the expiration of the stated period be deemed to have been passed by both Houses of the Oireachtas at the expiration of the thirty days.

2° The stated period is the period of ninety days commencing on the day on which the Bill is first sent by Dáil Eireann to Seanad Eireann or any longer period agreed upon in respect of the Bill by both Houses of the Oireachtas.

6. 1° The preceding section of this Article shall apply to a Bill which is initiated in and passed by Seanad Eireann, amended by Dáil Eireann, and accordingly deemed to have been initiated in Dáil Eireann.

2° For the purpose of this application the stated period shall in relation to such a Bill commence on the day on which the Bill is first sent to Seanad Eireann after having been so amended by Dáil Eireann.

7. 1° If and whenever on the introduction of a Bill in Dáil Eireann the Taoiseach certifies by messages in writing addressed to the President and to the Chairman of each House of the Oireachtas that, in the opinion of the Government, the Bill is urgent and immediately necessary for the preservation of the public peace and security, or is urgent and immediately necessary by reason of the existence of a national emergency, whether domestic or international, the time for the consideration

Article 20 *(continued).*

of such Bill by Seanad Eireann shall, if Dáil Eireann so resolves, be abridged to such period as shall be specified in the resolution.

2° Every such Bill shall be deemed to have been passed by both Houses of the Oireachtas at the expiration of the period thus specified.

3° A law the Bill for which shall have been the subject of a resolution passed by Dáil Eireann under this section shall remain in force for a period of three months from the date of its enactment and no longer unless, prior to its passing, both Houses shall have agreed that such law shall remain in force for a longer period and the longer period shall have been expressly specified in the law.

Article 21.

1. As soon as any Bill (other than a Bill expressed to be a Bill containing a proposal for the amendment of this Constitution) shall have been passed or deemed to have been passed by both Houses of the Oireachtas, the Taoiseach shall present the same to the President for his signature and for promulgation by him as a law in accordance with the provisions of this Article.

2. 1° Save as otherwise provided by this Constitution, every Bill so presented to the President for his signature and for promulgation by him as a law shall be signed by the President not earlier than five and not later than seven days after the date on which the Bill shall have been presented to him.

2° At the request of the Government, with the concurrence of Seanad Eireann, the President may sign any Bill the subject of such request on a date which is earlier than five days after such date as aforesaid.

3. Every Bill in respect of which a resolution shall have been passed by Dáil Eireann under section 7 of Article 20 of this Constitution shall be signed by the President on the day on which such Bill is presented to him for signature and promulgation as a law.

4. 1° Every Bill signed by the President under this Constitution shall become and be the law of Éire as on and from the day on which the Bill shall have been so signed.

Article 21 *(continued).*

2° Every Act signed by the President shall come into operation on the date on which it is so signed unless the contrary intention appears.

3° Every Bill so signed shall be promulgated by the President as a law by the publication by his direction of a notice in the *Iris Oifigiúil* stating that such Bill has become law.

4° As soon as may be after the President has signed any Bill and promulgated it as a law, such signed copy shall be returned to the Clerk of Dáil Eireann or such officer as Dáil Eireann may appoint for the purpose who shall cause it to be enrolled for record in the office of the Registrar of the Supreme Court and such signed copy shall be conclusive evidence as to the provisions of such law.

5° The Clerk of Dáil Eireann or such officer as aforesaid shall cause to be issued an authoritative text in the Irish language of every law enacted by the Oireachtas.

Article 22.

This Article applies to any Bill passed or deemed to have been passed by both Houses of the Oireachtas other than a Money Bill, or a Bill expressed to be a Bill containing a proposal to amend the Constitution, or a Bill in respect of which a resolution shall have been passed by Dáil Eireann under section 7 of Article 20 of this Constitution.

1. 1° The President may, after consultation with the Council of State, refer any Bill to which this Article applies to the Supreme Court for an advisory opinion on the question as to whether such Bill or any provision thereof is repugnant to this Constitution or to any provision thereof.

2° Every such reference shall be made not later than four days after the date on which such Bill shall have been passed or deemed to have been passed by both Houses of the Oireachtas.

3° The President shall not sign any Bill the subject of a reference to the Supreme Court under this Article pending the pronouncement of the opinion of the Court.

2. 1° The Supreme Court shall consider every question referred to it by the President under this Article for an

Article 22 *(continued).*

advisory opinion, and, having heard arguments by counsel assigned by the Court, shall pronounce its opinion on such question in open court not later than seven days after the date of such reference.

2° The opinion of the majority of the judges of the Supreme Court shall, for the purposes of this Article, be the opinion of the Court, and dissentient opinions shall not be pronounced.

3. In every case in which the Supreme Court is of the opinion that any Bill or any provision of a Bill the subject of a reference to the Supreme Court under this Article is repugnant to this Constitution or to any provision thereof, the President shall decline to sign such Bill.

4. In every case in which the Supreme Court is of the opinion that none of the provisions of a Bill the subject of a reference to the Supreme Court under this Article is repugnant to this Constitution or to any provision thereof, such Bill shall be signed by the President not later than two days after the date on which the Supreme Court shall have pronounced such opinion as aforesaid and shall be duly promulgated by him as a law.

Article 23.

This Article applies to any Bill (other than a Bill expressed to be a Bill containing a proposal for the amendment of this Constitution) which shall have been deemed, by virtue of section 5 of Article 20 hereof, to have been passed by both Houses of the Oireachtas.

1. A majority of the members of Seanad Eireann and four-ninths of the members of Dáil Eireann may by a joint petition addressed to the President by them under this Article request the President to decline to sign and promulgate as a law any Bill to which this Article applies on the ground that the Bill contains a proposal of fundamental national importance on which the will of the people ought to be ascertained.

2. Every such petition shall be in writing signed by the petitioners, shall contain a statement of the particular ground or grounds on which the request is based, and shall be presented

Article 23 *(continued).*

to the President not later than four days after the date on which the Bill shall have been deemed to have been passed by both Houses of the Oireachtas.

3. Upon receipt of a petition addressed to him under this Article, the President shall forthwith consider such petition and shall, after consultation with the Council of State, pronounce his decision thereon not later than six days after the date on which the Bill to which such petition relates shall have been deemed to have been passed by both Houses of the Oireachtas.

4. 1° In every case in which the President decides that a Bill the subject of a petition under this Article contains a proposal of fundamental national importance on which the will of the people ought to be ascertained, he shall inform the Taoiseach and the Chairman of each House of the Oireachtas accordingly in writing under his hand and Seal and shall decline to sign and promulgate such Bill as a law unless and until the proposal shall have been approved either

   i. by the people at a Referendum in accordance with the provisions of section 2 of Article 46 of this Constitution within a period of eighteen months from the date of the President's decision, or

   ii. by a resolution of Dáil Eireann passed within the said period after a dissolution and re-assembly of Dáil Eireann.

   2° Every such Bill which shall have been approved either by the people or by a resolution of Dáil Eireann in accordance with the foregoing provisions of this section shall as soon as may be after this approval be presented to the President for his signature and promulgation by him as a law and the President shall thereupon sign the Bill and duly promulgate it as a law accordingly.

5. In every case in which the President decides that a Bill the subject of a petition under this Article does not contain a proposal of fundamental national importance on which the will of the people ought to be ascertained, he shall inform the Taoiseach and the Chairman of each House of the Oireachtas accordingly in writing under his hand and Seal, and such Bill shall be signed by the President not later

Article 23 *(continued).*

than seven days after the date on which the Bill shall have been deemed to have been passed by both Houses of the Oireachtas and shall be duly promulgated by him as a law.

THE GOVERNMENT.

Article 24.

1. The Government of Éire, herein generally referred to as the Government, shall consist of not less than seven members who shall be appointed by the President in accordance with the provisions of this Constitution.

2. The executive power of Éire shall, subject to the provisions of this Constitution, be exercised by or on the authority of the Government.

3. 1° The Government shall be responsible to Dáil Eireann.

2° The Government shall meet and act as a collective authority, and shall be collectively responsible for the Departments of State administered by the members of the Government.

3° The Government shall prepare Estimates of the Receipts and Estimates of the Expenditure of Éire for each financial year, and shall present them to Dáil Eireann for consideration.

4. 1° The head of the Government, or Prime Minister, shall be called, and is herein generally referred to as, the Taoiseach.

2° The Taoiseach shall keep the President generally informed on matters of domestic and international policy and of the decisions taken thereon by the Government, and shall duly report to the President on all such matters as and when desired by the President so to do.

5. 1° The Taoiseach shall nominate a deputy who shall be called, and is in this Constitution referred to as, the Tánaiste.

2° The Tánaiste shall act for all purposes in the place of the Taoiseach if the Taoiseach should die, or become permanently incapacitated, until a new Taoiseach shall have been appointed.

3° The Tánaiste shall also act for or in the place of the Taoiseach during the temporary absence of the Taoiseach.

Article 24 *(continued).*

6. 1° The Taoiseach, the Tánaiste and the member of the Government who is in charge of the Department of Finance shall be members of Dáil Eireann.

2° The other members of the Government must be members of Dáil Eireann or Seanad Eireann, but not more than two may be members of Seanad Eireann.

7. Every member of the Government shall have the right to attend and be heard in each House of the Oireachtas.

8. 1° The Taoiseach may resign from office at any time by placing his resignation in the hands of the President.

2° Any other member of the Government may resign from office by placing his resignation in the hands of the Taoiseach for submission to the President.

3° The President shall accept the resignation of a member of the Government, other than the Taoiseach, if so advised by the Taoiseach.

4° The Taoiseach may at any time, for reasons which to him seem sufficient, request a member of the Government to resign; should the member concerned fail to comply with the request, his appointment shall be terminated by the President if the Taoiseach so advises.

9. 1° In the event of the death, resignation or permanent incapacity of a member of the Government, other than the Taoiseach, or the termination of the appointment of any such member while Dáil Eireann is not sitting, the President may, on the advice of the Taoiseach, appoint an existing member of the Government to hold temporarily the office held by such member.

2° The member so appointed shall not hold such office for longer than a period of ten days from the date of the first meeting of Dáil Eireann next held after his appointment.

10. The Taoiseach shall resign from office upon his ceasing to retain the support of a majority in Dáil Eireann unless on his advice the President dissolves the Oireachtas and on the reassembly of Dáil Eireann after the dissolution the Taoiseach secures the support of a majority in Dáil Eireann.

11. If the Taoiseach at any time resigns from office the other members of the Government shall be deemed also to have

Article 24 *(continued)*.

resigned from office, but the Taoiseach and the other members of the Government shall continue to carry on their duties until their successors shall have been appointed.

12. Provision shall be made by law for

i. the establishment of Departments of State,

ii. the organization of and distribution of business amongst the Departments of State,

iii. the designation of members of the Government to be the Ministers in charge of the several Departments,

iv. the discharge of the functions of the office of a member of the Government during his temporary absence or incapacity, and

v. the remuneration of the members of the Government.

INTERNATIONAL RELATIONS.

Article 25.

1. The executive power of Éire in or in connection with the external relations of Éire shall be exercised by or on the authority of the Government.

2. Éire affirms its acceptance of agreed principles of international law as its rule of conduct in its relations with other States.

3. Éire affirms its adherence to the principle of the peaceful settlement of international disputes by international arbitration or judicial decision.

4. The Government may take such measures as they may consider necessary or desirable to foster friendly co-operation between Éire and any group or league of nations with which Éire is or becomes associated for the purpose of international co-operation in matters of common concern.

5. Provision may be made by law for giving effect to any such measures and such law may authorise the Government,

Article 25 *(continued).*

for the purpose of the exercise of any executive function of Éire in connection with its external relations, to avail of or adopt any organ, instrument, or method of procedure used or adopted for the like purpose by the members of any such group or league of nations.

6. Every international agreement to which the State becomes a party shall be laid before Dáil Eireann : this provision shall not, however, apply to international conventions of a purely technical and administrative character.

7. The State shall not be bound by any international agreement involving a charge upon public funds unless the terms of the agreement shall have been approved by Dáil Eireann.

THE ATTORNEY GENERAL.

Article 26.

1. The Attorney General of Éire, herein referred to as the Attorney General, shall represent the State and the Government of Éire in all legal proceedings for the enforcement of law and the assertion or protection of public rights and he shall exercise and perform all powers, functions and duties connected with the same respectively.

2. The Attorney General shall be the adviser of the Government of Éire in matters of law and legal opinion.

3. All crimes and offences prosecuted in any court other than a court of summary jurisdiction shall be prosecuted in the name of the State and at the suit of the Attorney General or some other person appointed in accordance with law to act for that purpose on his behalf.

4. The Attorney General shall exercise and perform all other powers, authorities, duties and functions conferred on him by law.

5. The Attorney General shall not be a member of the Government.

Article 26 *(continued)*.

6. 1° The Attorney General shall be appointed in the manner provided by this Constitution.

2° He may at any time resign from office by placing his resignation in the hands of the Taoiseach for submission to the President.

3° The Taoiseach may, for reasons which to him seem sufficient, request the resignation of the Attorney General.

4° In the event of failure to comply with the request, the appointment of the Attorney General may, on the advice of the Taoiseach, be terminated by the President.

5° The Attorney General shall retire from office upon the resignation of the Taoiseach.

7. Subject to the foregoing provisions of this Article, the office of Attorney General, including the remuneration to be paid to the holder of the office, may be regulated by law.

THE COUNCIL OF STATE.

Article 27.

1. There shall be a Council of State to aid and counsel the President on all matters on which the President may consult the said Council in relation to the exercise and performance by him of such of his powers and functions as are under this Constitution exercisable and performable only after consultation with the Council of State.

2. The Council of State shall consist of the following members:

i. As *ex-officio* members; the Taoiseach, the Tánaiste, the Chief Justice of Éire, the President of the High Court, the Chairman of Dáil Eireann, the Chairman of Seanad Eireann, the Attorney General, and the Comptroller and Auditor General.

ii. Every person able and willing to act as a member of the Council of State who shall have held the office of President, or the office of Taoiseach, or the office of Chief Justice of Éire, or the office of President of the Executive Council of Saorstát Eireann.

Article 27 *(continued).*

iii. Such other persons (if any) as may be appointed by the President under this Article to be members of the Council of State.

3. The President may at any time or from time to time by warrant under his hand and seal appoint such other persons as, in his absolute discretion, he may think fit, to be members of the Council of State, but not more than five persons so appointed shall be members of the Council of State at the same time.

4. Every member of the Council of State shall at the first meeting thereof which he attends as a member take and subscribe a declaration in the following form:—

> "In the presence of Almighty God I promise and declare that I will fulfil my duties as a member of the Council of State faithfully and conscientiously in accordance with the Constitution."

5. Every member of the Council of State appointed by the President, unless he previously dies, resigns, becomes permanently incapacitated, or is removed from office, shall hold office until the successor of the President by whom he was appointed shall have entered upon his office.

6. Any member of the Council of State appointed by the President may resign from office by placing his resignation in the hands of the President.

7. The President may, for reasons which to him seem sufficient, by an order under his hand and Seal, remove from office any member of the Council of State appointed by him.

8. Meetings of the Council of State may be convened by the President at such times and places as he shall determine.

Article 28.

The President shall not exercise or perform any of the powers or functions which are by this Constitution expressed to be exercisable and performable by him after consultation with the Council of State unless, and on every occasion before so doing, the President shall have convened a meeting of the Council of State and the members of the said Council present at such meeting shall have been heard by him.

Article 29.

1. 1° The powers and functions of the President under this Constitution shall be exercised and performed during the temporary absence of the President from Éire by a Commission consisting of three members of the Council of State appointed by the President for that purpose by a warrant under his hand and Seal.

2° The President shall nominate one of the members of every such Commission to be the Chairman.

2. 1° In the event of the death of the President or his resignation, permanent incapacity established to the satisfaction of the Council of State, or his removal from office, or at any other time at which the office of President may be vacant the powers and functions of the President under this Constitution shall be exercised and performed by a Commission consisting of three members of the Council of State appointed by the Council of State for that purpose.

2° The Council of State shall nominate one of the members of every such Commission to be the Chairman.

3. The Council of State may make such provision as to them may seem meet for the exercise and performance of the powers and functions of the President under this Constitution in any contingency in which the President is unable to exercise and perform the said powers and functions or any of them and which is not provided for by the foregoing provisions of this Article.

4. A Commission appointed under this Article may act by any two of their number.

5. 1° The powers and functions of the President under this Constitution which are exercisable and performable by him only on the advice of the Government or the Taoiseach shall not be exercisable or performable by a Commission appointed under this Article save upon the like advice.

2° No such Commission shall exercise or perform any of the powers or functions of the President under this Constitution which are exercisable and performable by him only after consultation with the Council of State unless, and on every occasion before so doing, the Commission shall

Article 29 *(continued).*

have convened a meeting of the Council of State and the members present at such meeting other than the members of the Commission shall have been heard.

THE COMPTROLLER AND AUDITOR GENERAL.

Article 30.

All revenues of Éire from whatever source arising, shall, subject to such exception as may be provided by law, form one fund, and shall be appropriated for the purposes of Éire in the manner and subject to the charges and liabilities imposed by law.

Article 31.

1. There shall be a Comptroller and Auditor General to control on behalf of Éire all disbursements and to audit all accounts of moneys administered by or under the authority of the Oireachtas.

2. 1° The Comptroller and Auditor General shall not be a member of either House of the Oireachtas and shall not hold any other office or position of emolument.

2° The terms and conditions of his tenure of office shall be determined by law.

3. The Comptroller and Auditor General shall report to Dáil Eireann at stated periods as determined by law.

4. 1° The Comptroller and Auditor General shall not be removed from office except on the ground either of misbehaviour or incapacity, and then only upon resolutions passed by Dáil Eireann and by Seanad Eireann calling for his removal.

2° The Taoiseach shall duly notify the President of any such resolutions as aforesaid passed by Dáil Eireann and by Seanad Eireann and shall send him a copy of each such

Article 31 *(continued).*

resolution certified by the Chairman of the House of the Oireachtas by which it shall have been passed.

3° Upon receipt of such notification and of copies of such resolutions, the President shall forthwith, by an order under his hand and Seal, remove the Comptroller and Auditor General from his office.

THE COURTS.

Article 32.

1. Justice shall be administered in public courts established by law by judges appointed in the manner provided by this Constitution.

2. The Courts shall comprise Courts of First Instance and a Court of Final Appeal.

3. 1° The Courts of First Instance shall include a High Court invested with full original jurisdiction in and power to determine all matters and questions whether of law or fact, civil or criminal (not including the question of the validity of any law).

2° The Courts of First Instance shall also include Courts of local and limited jurisdiction with a right of appeal as determined by law.

4. 1° The Court of Final Appeal shall be called the Supreme Court.

2° The President of the Supreme Court shall be called "The Chief Justice of Éire".

3° The Supreme Court shall have full original jurisdiction in and power, exclusive of all other courts, to determine questions as to the validity of any law having regard to the provisions of this Constitution.

The Supreme Court shall not, however, entertain any question as to the validity of any law the Bill for which shall have been referred to the Supreme Court by the President under Article 22 of this Constitution and in respect of which that Court shall have pronounced the opinion that no provision of such Bill is repugnant to this Constitution or to any provision thereof.

Article 32 *(continued).*

4° The Supreme Court shall, with such exceptions and subject to such regulations as may be prescribed by law, have appellate jurisdiction from all decisions of the High Court, and shall also have appellate jurisdiction from such decisions of other courts as may be prescribed by law.

5° The decision of the Supreme Court shall in all cases be final and conclusive.

5. 1° Every person appointed a judge under this Constitution shall make and subscribe the following declaration:

> " In the presence of Almighty God I do solemnly and sincerely promise and declare that I will duly and faithfully and to the best of my knowledge and power execute the office of Chief Justice of Éire (*or* President of the High Court, *or* Judge of the Supreme Court, *or* of the High Curt, *or* of judge or justice of any other court *as the case may be*) of Éire without fear or favour, affection or ill-will towards any man, and that I will uphold the Constitution of Éire."

2° This declaration shall be made and subscribed by the Chief Justice in the presence of the President of Éire, and by each of the other judges of the Supreme Court, the judges of the High Court and the judges of any other Court in the presence of the Chief Justice in open court.

3° Any judge who declines or neglects to make such declaration in the manner aforesaid shall be deemed to have vacated his office.

Article 33.

1. All judges shall be independent in the exercise of their judicial functions and subject only to this Constitution and the law.

2. No judge shall be eligible to be a member of either House of the Oireachtas or to hold any other office or position of emolument.

3. 1° A judge of the Supreme Court or the High Court shall not be removed from office except on the ground either of misbehaviour or incapacity, and then only upon resolutions

Article 33 *(continued)*.

passed by Dáil Eireann and by Seanad Eireann calling for his removal.

2° The Taoiseach shall duly notify the President of any such resolutions passed by Dáil Eireann and by Seanad Eireann, and shall send him a copy of every such resolution certified by the Chairman of the House of the Oireachtas by which it shall have been passed.

3° Upon receipt of such notification and of copies of such resolutions, the President shall forthwith, by an order under his hand and Seal, remove from office the judge to whom they relate.

4. The remuneration of any of the judges of the Supreme Court or the High Court shall not be reduced during his continuance in office.

Article 34.

Subject to the foregoing provisions of this Constitution relating to the Courts, the following matters shall be regulated by law and Rules of Court made thereunder, that is to say:—

i. the number of judges of the Supreme Court, the High Court, and all other Courts of Éire, the declarations to be taken by the judges of the said Courts on appointment, the remuneration, age of retirement and pensions of such judges, and

ii. the constitution and organization of the said Courts, the distribution of jurisdiction and business among the said Courts and judges, and all matters of procedure.

Article 35.

Nothing in this Constitution shall operate to invalidate the exercise of limited functions of a judicial nature, in matters other than criminal matters, by any person or body of persons duly authorised by law to exercise such functions, notwithstanding that such person or such body of persons is not a judge or a court appointed or established as such under this Constitution.

TRIAL OF OFFENCES.

Article 36.

1. 1° No person shall be tried save in due course of law.

2° Extraordinary courts shall not be established save only such extraordinary courts as may be established by law for dealing with a state of war or armed rebellion or a state of public emergency proclaimed under this Constitution and such military tribunals as may be authorised by law for the trial of military offenders against military law.

2. A member of the Defence Forces of Éire not on active service shall not be tried by any court martial or other military tribunal for an offence cognisable by the civil courts unless such offence shall have been brought expressly within the jurisdiction of courts martial or other military tribunal by any law or regulations for the enforcement of military discipline.

3. The trial of all crimes shall be by jury, except in the case of minor offences triable by a court of summary jurisdiction, charges for offences triable by extraordinary courts during a state of war or armed rebellion or during a state of public emergency proclaimed under this Constitution and charges for offences against military law alleged to have been committed by persons while subject to military law.

Article 37.

1. Treason shall consist only in

   i. levying war against Éire, or

   ii. assisting any state or person or inciting or conspiring with any person to levy war against Éire, or

   iii. attempting by force of arms or other violent means to overthrow the organs of government established by this Constitution or

   iv. taking part or being concerned in or inciting or conspiring with any person to make or to take part or be concerned in any such attempt.

PERSONAL RIGHTS AND SOCIAL POLICY.

Personal Rights.

Article 38.

1. 1° The State acknowledges that all citizens are as human persons equal before the law.

2° The State shall, in particular, in its laws have due regard to individual differences of capacity, physical and moral, and of social function.

Titles of nobility shall not be conferred; Orders of Merit may, however, be created.

2. 1° The State guarantees to respect, defend, and vindicate the personal rights of each citizen.

2° The State shall, however, protect, as best it may, from unjust attack, and, in case of injustice done, vindicate the person, life, good name and property rights of every citizen.

3. 1° No citizen shall be deprived of his personal liberty save in accordance with law.

2° Upon complaint being made by or on behalf of any person that he is being unlawfully detained, the High Court and any and every judge thereof shall forthwith enquire into the same and may make an order requiring the person in whose custody such person shall be detained to produce the body of the person so detained before such court or judge without delay and to certify in writing as to the cause of the detention and such Court or judge shall thereupon order the release of such person unless satisfied that he is being detained in accordance with the law.

3° Nothing in this Article, however, shall be invoked to prohibit control or interfere with any act of the defence forces of Éire during the existence of a state of war or armed rebellion.

4. The dwelling of a citizen shall not be forcibly entered save in accordance with law.

5. The State shall permit the exercise by the citizens of the following rights, always provided that the exercise of these rights shall not conflict with true morality or social order.

1° The State shall permit citizens to express freely their convictions and opinions.

Article 38 *(continued).*

The education of public opinion being, however, a matter of such grave import to the common good, the State shall see to it that the organs of public opinion, such as the Radio, Press and Cinema, while preserving their rightful liberty of expression, shall not be used to undermine social order or right morality, or, especially in times of war, the authority of the State.

The publication or utterance of blasphemous, seditious, or indecent matter are offences punishable by law.

2° The State shall permit citizens to assemble peaceably and without arms.

Laws, however, may be passed to prevent or control meetings which are calculated to cause a breach of the peace or to be a danger or nuisance to the general public.

Open air meetings shall be subject to police regulations and control so as not to interfere with public convenience or normal traffic.

3° The State shall permit citizens to form associations and unions.

Laws regulating the manner in which the right of forming associations and unions and the right of free assembly may be exercised shall contain no political, religious or class discrimination.

The Family.

Article 39.

1. 1° The State recognises the Family as the natural primary and fundamental unit of Society, and as a moral and juridical institution possessing inalienable and imprescriptible rights, antecedent and superior to all positive law.

2° The State, therefore, guarantees to protect the Family in its constitution, authority and government, as the necessary basis of social order and as indispensable to the welfare of the Nation.

3° In particular, the State recognises that by her life within the home, woman gives to the State a support without which the common good cannot be achieved. The State shall, therefore, endeavour to secure that women, especially mothers and young girls, shall not be obliged to enter avocations unsuited to their sex and strength.

Article 39 *(continued).*

2. 1° The State pledges itself to guard with special care the institution of Marriage, on which the Family is founded, and to protect it against attack.

2° No law shall be passed which shall impair its essential properties of unity and indissolubility.

3° No person whose marriage has been dissolved under the civil law of any other State shall be capable of contracting a valid marriage in Éire during the lifetime of the other party to the marriage so dissolved.

Education.

Article 40.

1. The State acknowledges the Family as the primary and natural educator of the child, and guarantees to respect the inalienable right and duty of the parents to provide, according to their means, for the religious and moral, intellectual, physical and social education of their children.

2. Parents shall be free to provide this education in their homes or in private schools or in schools established by the State.

3. The State pledges itself not to oblige parents, in violation of their conscience and lawful preference, to send their children to Schools established by the State.

4. The State, however, as guardian of the common good, shall require in view of actual conditions a certain minimum education, intellectual and moral, physical and social.

5. The State shall aid and supplement private and corporate educational initiative, particularly by providing free primary education and, when the public good requires it, other institutions, with due respect, however, for the rights of parents, especially in the matter of religious and moral formation.

6. In exceptional cases, where the parents for physical or moral reasons fail in their duty towards their children, the State as guardian of the common good, by appropriate means shall supply the place of the parents, but always with due respect for the natural and imprescriptible rights of the child.

Private Property.

Article 41.

1. The State acknowledges that man, in virtue of his rational being, has the natural right, antecedent to positive law, to the private ownership of external goods.

2. The State recognises that the exercise of this natural right is not only allowable, but is, for social needs, absolutely necessary, and therefore guarantees to pass no law attempting to abolish the right of private ownership.

3. Since the use by individuals of private property ought, in civil society, be regulated by the principles of social justice, the State may lawfully delimit this use when the need arises with a view to reconciling it with the exigencies of the common good.

4. The State shall use its best endeavour to provide that the material resources of the nation may be so distributed among private individuals and the various classes of the population as adequately to procure the common good of the community as a whole.

5. The State shall strive to promote the economic welfare of the whole people, by securing, protecting and defending, as effectively as it may, an economic order in which social justice and social charity shall imbue all the institutions of public life, and in particular

   i. endeavour to ensure that the adult working man, especially the fathers of families, shall receive a wage sufficient to meet adequately their domestic needs, present and future.

   ii. by providing, as best it can, opportunities for work for those who are willing and able to work.

   iii. by attempting to regulate, according to social justice, with the co-operation of vocational groups and associations, such a scale of wages, as shall offer to the greatest number opportunities of adequate means of livelihood.

   iv. by ensuring that the tender age of children or the adequate strength of women shall not be abused nor mothers forced to engage in labour to the neglect of their own proper duties.

Article 41 *(continued).*

6. 1° The State shall make it a duty so to restrain free competition, within just limits, that no combination shall be formed whereby the undue monopoly of the resources of the State or of a particular class of goods may pass into the ownership and control of one or of a few individuals.

2° In particular, the State shall see to it that the economic domination of the few, in what pertains to the control of credit, shall not endanger the common good of the community as a whole.

7. 1° The State pledges itself to safeguard with special care the economic rights of the less favoured classes of Society, to contribute to the support of the infirm, the widow, the orphan, and the aged poor who are past their labour.

2° In particular, with a view to obtaining a more just balance between wealth and poverty, to securing a more abundant yield of the produce of the earth, and to attaching its citizens more closely to their native country, the State shall endeavour to give to as many families as practicable a share in the land.

8. The State shall have regard for such distribution of the centres of industry, that, while an opportunity is given for necessary development, the traditional preference of our people for rural life may be duly fostered and maintained.

9. The State shall favour and where necessary supplement private economic initiative.

10. With a view to procuring the common good of the Nation as a whole, and to securing a more equitable social balance, the State shall favour the due constitution of vocational groupings, on the basis of the various forms of social activities.

Religion, Church and State.

POWER TO SUSPEND CERTAIN PROVISIONS OF THE CONSTITUTION.

Article 43.

1. If and whenever the Government are satisfied that a grave state of public disorder exists or is threatened throughout Éire, or in any specified district or districts thereof, or that the ordinary laws and the civil courts are not adequate for the preservation of public order, the Government may, by proclamation, declare the existence of a state of public emergency in respect of the area to which such proclamation relates.

2. 1° Upon a proclamation being made by the Government under this Article, the President shall forthwith issue an order under his hand and seal directing that the provisions section , section , and section , of Article of this Constitution be suspended in respect of the area to which the proclamation relates, and for the period specified in the order.

2° Upon such order being made, the provisions of the sections hereinbefore mentioned of the said Article . shall be suspended accordingly.

3. 1° Every proclamation made by the Government and every order made by the President under this Article shall forthwith be laid before Dáil Eireann if sitting, and if Dáil Eireann is not sitting, at the sitting thereof which takes place next after such proclamation and such order shall have been made.

Article 43 *(continued).*

2° If Dáil Eireann is not sitting, but not dissolved, the President shall forthwith summon Dáil Eireann.

3° If Dáil Eireann is dissolved, the President shall summon Dáil Eireann for the earliest practicable date after the polling day for the general election for Dáil Eireann.

4° If, in the opinion of the President, after consultation with the Council of State, the public emergency is such that a meeting of Dáil Eireann is not practicable, the President shall postpone the summoning of Dáil Eireann until the earliest date on which, in his opinion, after consultation with the Council of State, a meeting of Dáil Eireann is practicable.

5° If, within a period of fourteen days on which Dáil Eireann shall have sat next after the proclamation and the order shall have been laid before it, Dáil Eireann shall not have passed a resolution confirming the proclamation and the order, the proclamation and the order shall on the expiration of the said fourteen days cease to have effect but without prejudice to the validity of anything previously done thereunder.

Article 44.

1. 1° The Oireachtas may enact legislation establishing such extraordinary courts and investing such courts with such jurisdiction as the Oireachtas may consider to be necessary and adequate to deal with any such state of public emergency as aforesaid.

2° Legislation enacted under this Article shall not come into operation unless and until an order shall have been made by the President under this Article, and shall then come into operation in respect only of the area mentioned and for the period specified in such order.

2. Nothing in this Constitution or in any law continued thereby or made thereunder shall be invoked to invalidate any provision of this Article or of any legislation passed under this Article or to oust the jurisdiction of any Court established by, or to nullify any act or thing done in pursuance of, any such legislation as aforesaid.

3. The decisions of a court established under this Article shall not be subject to appeal to or to review by any other court

Article 44 *(continued)*.

save only such court of appeal or such reviewing authority, if any, as may be established by legislation enacted under this Article.

Article 45.

1. Any provision of this Constitution may be amended, whether by way of variation, addition, or repeal, in the manner provided by this Article.
2. Every proposal for an amendment of this Constitution shall be introduced in Dáil Eireann as a Bill of the Oireachtas, and shall, upon having been passed or deemed to have been passed by both Houses of the Oireachtas, be submitted by Referendum to the decision of the people in accordance with the law for the time being in force relating to the Referendum.
3. Every such Bill shall be expressed to be " An Act to amend the Constitution ".
4. A Bill containing a proposal or proposals for the amendment of this Constitution shall not contain any other proposal.
5. A Bill containing a proposal for the amendment of this Constitution shall be signed by the President and promulgated by him as a law upon his being satisfied after consultation with the Council of State that the provisions of this Article have been complied with in respect thereof and that such proposal has been duly approved by the people in accordance with the provisions of section 1 of Article 46 of this Constitution.

THE REFERENDUM.

Article 46.

1. Every proposal for an amendment of this Constitution which is submitted by Referendum to the decision of the people shall, for the purpose of Article 45 of this Constitution, be held to have been approved by the people, if, upon having been so submitted, a majority of the votes cast at such Referendum shall have been cast in favour of its enactment into law.

Article 46 *(continued)*.

2\. 1° Every Bill and every proposal (other than a proposal to amend the Constitution) which is submitted by Referendum to the decision of the people shall be held to have been vetoed by the people if a majority of the votes cast at such Referendum shall have been cast against its enactment into law and such majority shall have amounted to not less than thirty-five per cent., of the voters on the Register.

2° Every Bill and every proposal (other than a proposal to amend the Constitution) which is submitted by Referendum to the decision of the people shall for the purposes of Article 23 hereof be held to have been approved by the people unless vetoed by them in accordance with the provisions of the foregoing sub-section of this section.

3\. Every citizen who has reached the age of twenty-one years shall be entitled to vote at a Referendum held under this Constitution.

4\. Subject as aforesaid, the Referendum shall be regulated by law.

REPEAL OF CONSTITUTION OF SAORSTÁT EIREANN AND CONTINUANCE OF LAWS.

Article 47.

The Constitution of Saorstát Eireann in force at the date of the coming into operation of this Constitution shall be and is hereby repealed as on and from that date.

Article 48.

1\. All powers, functions, rights and prerogatives whatsoever exercisable in or in respect of Saorstát Eireann immediately before the 11th day of December, 1936 (whether in virtue of the Constitution then in force or otherwise), by the authority in which the executive power of Saorstát Eireann was then vested are hereby declared to belong to the people of Éire.

2\. It is hereby enacted that, save to the extent to which provision is made by this Constitution or may hereafter be made by law for the exercise of any such power, function, right or prerogative by any of the organs established by

Article 48 *(continued).*

this Constitution, the said powers, functions, rights and prerogatives shall not be exercised or be capable of being exercised in or in respect of Éire save only by or on the authority of the Goverment.

3. The Government of Éire shall be the successors of the Government of Saorstát Eireann as regards all property, assets, rights and liabilities.

Article 49.

Subject to this Constitution and to the extent to which they are not inconsistent therewith, the laws in force in Saorstát Eireann at the date of the coming into operation of this Constitution shall continue to be of full force and effect until the same or any of them shall have been repealed or amended by enactment of the Oireachtas.

TRANSITORY PROVISIONS.

Article 50.

1. Notwithstanding anything contained in Article 45 hereof, any of the provisions of this Constitution (except the provisions of the said Article 45 and this Article) may, subject as hereinafter provided, be amended by the Oireachtas (whether by way of variation, addition or repeal) within a period of three years after the date on which the first President shall have entered upon his office.

2. A proposal for the amendment of this Constitution under this Article shall not be enacted into law if, prior to such enactment, the President, after consultation with the Council of State, shall have signified in a message under his hand and Seal addressed to the Chairman of each of the Houses of the Oireachtas that the proposal is in his opinion a proposal to effect an amendment of such a character and importance that the will of the people thereon ought to be ascertained by Referendum before its enacament into law.

3. The foregoing provisions of this Article shall cease to have the force of law immediately upon the expiration of the period of three years referred to in section 1 hereof.

Article 50 *(continued).*

4. This Article shall be omitted from every official test of this Constitution published after the expiration of the said period.

Article 51.

1. This Article and the subsequent Articles shall be omitted from every official test of this Constitution published after the date on which the first President shall have entered upon his office, but shall, nevertheless, continue to have the force of law.

2. Every provision of this Constitution, other than the provisions of section 1 and section 2 of Article 50, which is hereafter omitted in accordance with the said Article 50 or this Article from the official text of this Constitution shall nevertheless continue to have the force of law.

Article 52.

1. On the coming into operation of this Constitution a general election for Seanad Eireann shall be held in accordance with the relevant Articles of this Constitution as if a dissolution of Dáil Eireann had taken place on the date of the coming into operation of this Constitution.

2. For the purposes of this Article references in the relevant Articles of this Constitution to a dissolution of Dáil Eireann shall be construed as referring to the coming into operation of this Constitution, and in those Articles the expression "Dáil Eireann" shall include the Chamber of Deputies established by the Constitution hereby repealed.

Article 53.

1. After the coming into operation of this Constitution and until the first assembly of Seanad Eireann, the Oireachtas shall consist of one House only.

2. The House forming the Oireachtas under this Article shall be the Chamber of Deputies established by the Constitution hereby repealed, but if a dissolution takes place before the first assembly of Seanad Eireann, the said House shall, after such dissolution, be Dáil Eireann.

Article 53 *(continued).*

3. Until the first President enters upon his office, the Oireachtas shall be complete and capable of functioning notwithstanding that there is no President.

4. Until the first President enters upon his office, bills passed or deemed to have been passed by the House or by both Houses of the Oireachtas shall be signed and promulgated by the Commission hereinafter mentioned instead of by the President.

Article 54.

1. The Chamber of Deputies established by the Constitution hereby repealed and existing immediately before that repeal shall, on the coming into operation of this Constitution, become and be Dáil Eireann for all the purposes of this Constitution.

2. Every person who is a member of the said Chamber of Deputies immediately before the said repeal shall, on the coming into operation of this Constitution, become and be a member of Dáil Eireann as if he had been elected to be such member at an election held under this Constitution.

Article 55.

1. From and after the date of the coming into operation of this Constitution and pending the entry upon his office of the first President the members of any Government for the time being responsible to the Chamber of Deputies hereinbefore referred to shall, without any appointment under Article 12 hereof, be the Government of Éire for the purposes of this Constitution.

2. The members of the Government of Éire in office on the date on which the first President shall enter upon his office shall receive official appointments from the President as soon as may be after the said date.

3. Every existing officer of the Government of Saorstát Eireann at the date of the coming into operation of this Constitution shall on that date become and be an officer of the Government of Éire and shall hold office by a tenure corresponding to his previous tenure.

Article 55 *(continued)*.

4. The Departments of State and the Department of the Attorney General of Saorstát Eireann shall as on and from the date of the coming into operation of this Constitution and until otherwise determined by law become and be the Departments of State and the Department of the Attorney General of Éire.

Article 56.

1. The first President shall enter upon his office and the first assembly of Seanad Eireann shall take place not later than six months after the date of the coming into operation of this Constitution.

2. After the date of the coming into operation of this Constitution and pending the entry of the first President upon his office the powers and functions of the President under sections of Article 12 of this Constitution may be exercised by a Commission consisting of the following persons, namely, the Chief Justice of Éire, the President of the High Court, and the Chairman of the Chamber of Deputies hereinbefore referred to.

3. The said Commission may act by any two of their number, but shall not exercise any of the powers and functions exercisable by them under this Article save only upon the advice on which such power or function is exercisable under this Constitution by the President.

Article 57.

1. On and after the coming into operation of this Constitution and until otherwise determined by law, the Supreme Court of Justice, the High Court of Justice, the Circuit Court of Justice and the District Court of Justice in existence on the said date shall (subject to the provisions of this Constitution relating to the determination of questions as to the validity of any law) continue to exercise the same jurisdiction as heretofore, and any judge or justice being a member of any such Court shall, subject to compliance with the subsequent provisions of this Article, continue to be a member thereof and shall hold office by the like tenure and on the like terms as heretofore unless he signifies to the Taoiseach his desire to resign.

Article 57 *(continued).*

2. Every such judge and justice as aforesaid who shall not have so signified his desire to resign shall make and subscribe the declaration set forth in section 5 of Article 32 of this Constitution.

3. This declaration shall be made and subscribed by the Chief Justice in the presence of the Taoiseach, and by each of the other judges of the said Supreme Court, the judges of the said High Court and the judges of the said Circuit Court in the presence of the Chief Justice in open court.

4. In the case of the justices of the said District Court the declaration shall be made and subscribed in open court.

5. Every such declaration shall be made immediately upon the coming into operation of this Constitution, or, in the event of the temporary incapacity of any such judge or justice as aforesaid, as soon as may be thereafter, and in the case of every such judge or justice before he shall perform any of the functions of his office after the date of the coming into operation of this Constitution.

6. Any such judge or justice who declines or neglects to make such declaration in the manner aforesaid shall be deemed to have vacated his office.

Article 58.

The Comptroller and Auditor General in office at the date of the coming into operation of this Constitution shall on that date become and be the Comptroller and Auditor General of Éire and shall hold office by the like tenure as a Comptroller and Auditor General appointed under Article 12 of this Constitution.

Article 59.

1. The Defence Forces and the Police Forces of Saorstát Eireann in existence at the date of the coming into operation of this Constitution shall as on and from that date become and be the Defence Forces and the Police Forces respectively of Éire.

2. 1° Every commissioned officer of the Defence Forces of Saorstát Eireann at the date of the coming into operation of

Article 59 *(continued)*.

this Constitution shall on that date become and be a commissioned officer of the Defence Forces of Éire and shall hold his commission by a tenure corresponding to his previous tenure.

2° Every officer of the Defence Forces of Éire at the date on which the first President enters upon his office shall receive a commission from the President as soon as may be after that date.

Article 60.

This Constitution shall come into operation

i. on the day following the expiration of a period of six months after its approval by the people signified by a majority of the votes cast at a plebiscite thereon held in accordance with law, or,

ii. on such earlier day as may be fixed by a resolution of the Chamber of Deputies elected at the general election the polling day for which shall have taken place on the same day as the said plebiscite.

Do Chum Glóire Dé
agus
Onóra na hÉireann.

Éamon de Valera (1882 – 1975)
President of the Executive Council of the Irish Free in 1937

James. J. MacElligott (1893 – 1974)
Secretary of the Department of Finance in 1937

John. J. Hearne (1893 – 1969)
Legal Adviser to the Department of External Affairs in 1937

Joseph P. Walshe (1886–1956)
Secretary of the Department of
External Affairs in 1937

Maurice Moynihan (1902 – 1999)
Secretary to the Government
in 1937

Fr Edward Cahill SJ (1868 – 1941)
Professor of Sociology at the Jesuit
Miltown Park Institute, Dublin, in 1937

Fr John C. McQuaid C.S.Sp
(1895- 1973) President of Blackrock
College, Dublin, in 1937

Patrick Lynch
(1866 – 1947)
Attorney General in 1937

Stephen A. Roche
Secretary of the Department of
Justice in 1937

INDEX OF ARTICLES OF THE CONSTITUTION

INDEX